Aboriginal Rights and Self-Gover
The Canadian and Mexican Experience
in North American Perspective

This collection of essays is a timely exploration of the progress of
Aboriginal rights movements in Canada, Mexico, and the United
States. Contributors compare the situations in Canada and Mexico, in
both of which demands by Aboriginal people for political autonomy
and sovereignty are increasing, and explore why there is very little
corresponding activity in the United States. The essays address problems of constructing new political arrangements, practical questions
about the viability of multiple governments within one political system, and epistemological questions about recognizing and understanding the "other."

CURTIS COOK is professor of political science, The Colorado College.
JUAN D. LINDAU is associate professor of political science,
The Colorado College.

McGill Queen's Native and Northern Series
Bruce G. Trigger, Editor

Aboriginal Rights and Self-Government

The Canadian and Mexican Experience in North American Perspective

EDITED BY CURTIS COOK
AND JUAN D. LINDAU

McGill-Queen's University Press
Montreal & Kingston · London · Ithaca

© McGill-Queen's University Press 2000
ISBN 0-7735-1884-3 (cloth)
ISBN 0-7735-1885-1 (paper)

Legal deposit first quarter 2000
Bibliothèque nationale du Québec

Printed in Canada on acid-free paper

This book has been published with the help of a grant
from Colorado College.

Canadä

McGill-Queen's University Press acknowledges the
financial support of the Government of Canada
through the Book Publishing Industry Development
Program (BPIDP) for its activities. We also acknowledge
the support of the Canada Council for the Arts for our
publishing program.

Canadian Cataloguing in Publication Data

Aboriginal rights and self-government: the Canadian and
    Mexican experience in North American perspective
    (McGill-Queen's native and northern series; 21)
    Includes bibliographical references and index.
    ISBN 0-7735-1884-3 (bound)
    ISBN 0-7735-1885-1 (pbk)
    1. Native peoples – Canada – Politics and government.
    2. Native peoples – Canada – Government relations.
    3. Indians of Mexico – Politics and government.
    4. Indians of Mexico – Government relations.
    5. Indians of North America – Politics and
    government. 6. Indians of North America –
    Government relations – 1934–   . I. Cook, Curtis,
    1937–   . II. Lindau, Juan David. III. Series.

E91.A26 2000   323.1'197071   C99-900856-0

Typeset in New Baskerville 10/12
by Caractéra inc., Quebec City

Contents

Preface

Most of the chapters in this work were originally prepared for a colloquium on the subject held at The Colorado College, incident to the college's program on North American studies. Support for the North American Studies program has come from the Hewlett Foundation, the Donner Foundation, and the Canadian government. Support for the colloquium was from the Hewlett Foundation. Further support for preparation of this book was provided by The Colorado College. The authors wish to thank these and the many unnamed others who make scholarly research, writing, and instruction possible.

The editors wish also to thank Philip Cercone and Joan McGilvray at McGill-Queen's University Press, and the contributors to this volume.

Aboriginal Rights and Self-Government

1 One Continent, Contrasting Styles: The Canadian Experience in North American Perspective

JUAN D. LINDAU AND CURTIS COOK

Why compare Aboriginal political demands in Canada with Aboriginal political demands in Mexico?[1] Aboriginal peoples in both countries have pressed for political autonomy and sovereignty. Additionally, the environments in both countries have encouraged the florescence of these demands, albeit to substantially different degrees. Canada's unsettled politics, reflected in prolonged constitutional rounds, and an increasingly fluid and unstable political situation in Mexico have promoted the expansion of political demands in both countries. Most importantly, perhaps, transitional environments, almost by definition, create a context where profound discussions about the legitimacy and efficacy of different structural arrangements become part of political discourse. In North America it is this fact that most powerfully explains why Aboriginal demands for political autonomy and sovereignty have arisen in Canada and Mexico but not in the United States.

Simultaneously, the transitional environments in Canada and Mexico and the political activation of Aboriginal people have encouraged them to seek recognition and accommodation of their cultures and way of life in the midst of profound globalizing forces. The search for governing arrangements capable of operationalizing these demands locates Mexico and Canada in the centre of the most important global issue confronting the contemporary world, namely, the clash between globalizing and localizing forces. If the nation-state faces transformations wrought by the proliferation of supranational arrangements and other globalizing influences, it also confronts infra-national demands from a variety of groups. Canada and Mexico are both experiencing this process and Aboriginal peoples are part of it in both countries (although, especially in the case of Canada, Aboriginal peoples are anything but alone in presenting such demands).

Our observations in this introduction and the works by several Canadian and Mexican authors that follow are directed to the condition of Aboriginal peoples in each country and their quest for self-government. In the case of Canada, the powerful separatist forces at work in Quebec place the national question at the centre of all Canadian political issues. Quebec separatism, the prime drama confronting Canada, may be both cause and effect of the instability in Canadian politics of which the mobilization of Aboriginal peoples partakes. Paradoxically, as we write, the question that Quebec poses for Canada is also overshadowing the Aboriginal agenda. Yet the effort to reform Aboriginal policy is not frozen.

Much the same is true for Mexico. The deterioration of the Mexican regime has created a political situation where demands for change have flourished. Indigenous peoples are part of this broader current. Although they have been important actors in this drama, they are but a part of a much more general movement advocating substantial structural change. As in Canada, this environment has affected both the formulation and the response to indigenous demands.

Contextually, the international environment, especially changing conceptions of human rights since the Second World War, has promoted a somewhat more hospitable milieu in both Canada and Mexico for demands from Aboriginal peoples than had previously existed. More recently, the fall of the Berlin Wall and other instances of the collapse of Marxism have encouraged a shift from class to ethnic awareness. The last few decades have also witnessed growing Aboriginal political organization and activation. These elements, especially fluid domestic political environments joined to multiculturalism and, to the south, the galvanizing effects of the quincentenary of Columbus's voyage, explain the expansion of demands for political autonomy in Canada and Mexico in the early 1990s.

Aboriginal peoples in both countries have been ripe for political activation. Historic patterns of poverty and marginalization, aggravated by depredations of the larger society, including assaults on Aboriginal persons and their cultures and encroachments on Aboriginal lands to extract natural resources, have created environments where such demands could flourish.

In both countries demands for political autonomy and sovereignty have raised profound philosophical questions about rights – although this subject has been treated much more extensively in Canada than in Mexico. Simultaneously, the construction of new political arrangements has created fundamental epistemological questions about the ability to recognize and understand the "other." The shared view in this book is that Aboriginal peoples in North America have a right to self-government that survives from their position as sovereign, self-governing entities before the arrival of European settlers. Thus a reform agenda is implied. Less agreement can be found as to the strategy or content of reform in either Aboriginal or non-Aboriginal society.

CANADA AND MEXICO

In Canada and Mexico the genesis of Aboriginal demands for political autonomy and sovereignty occurs in two countries that differ in almost every other conceivable way. History, culture, ethnicity, the level of economic development, and political organization all distinguish the two countries, influencing the Aboriginal experience in each society and affecting the form and nature of these demands.

Canada's current efforts on behalf of its Aboriginal population may be unique. Some formal measures toward reform adopted just after the Second World War were ineffectual, but they illustrated the receptiveness of Canadians to moral suasion. Since then, other measures and debates have shown this receptiveness even more markedly. Driven not by release from the hold of overbearing government, like the states of the former Soviet bloc, or by intrastate warfare, as is the case elsewhere, or even by the sort of uprising seen in the Mexican state of Chiapas in 1994, Canada, more out of moral choice than social upheaval, launched a project to reformulate its constitutional self to accommodate unassimilated Canadians. The project has not moved forward evenly or, for that matter, even in a coordinated way. But as we write, the project is showing unusual vitality. Mexico's efforts, detailed later in this chapter, have been far less ambitious. At best, Mexico's efforts to reform the relationship between the polity and Aboriginal peoples are still in their infancy.

Mexico and Canada are also ethnically different. Mexico's most distinctive ethnic trait has been extraordinarily widespread miscegenation, which has not taken place in Canada. In Mexico the often violent encounter between overwhelmingly male Spanish colonizers and a large, increasingly female indigenous population – increasingly female since European diseases had an especially devastating effect on the male population – encouraged this miscegenation. Mestizos – the mixture of indigenous peoples and whites – comprise at least 80 percent of Mexico's population, while the Métis, the comparable group among the Aboriginal peoples of Canada, represent only a tiny portion of the

Canadian population. Moreover the Métis, if sympathetically portrayed in Margaret Laurence's stories from Manawaka, were for a long time relegated to the very bottom rung in the Canadian social structure.

Structurally, Canada and Mexico could also not be more distinct. Canada's political structure, belied by the centralizing design adopted at Confederation, has been marked by an extraordinary degree of decentralization, with enormous power vested at the provincial level.[2] Mexico, in contrast, despite a formally federal structure, has had a highly centralized political system. Although the separation of powers also formally exists in Mexico, a disproportionate share of real power is concentrated almost entirely in the hands of the president, who rules for a six-year, nonrenewable term. However, the growing pace of political reform in Mexico in the late 1990s promises to finally permit decentralization and the creation of a real separation of powers. Nonetheless, these different structures in Canada and Mexico have affected the treatment of issues relating to Aboriginal peoples and the options for accommodation.

These structural distinctions are accompanied by even deeper differences in political and legal culture. In Mexico, law has historically been part of the surface rather than the substance of political life, lacking the depth and reach of custom. Constitutions and other legal documents have typically been lodestars, propounding a moral ideal rather than serving as guides to everyday life. For this reason law has not been the primary mechanism used to address indigenous questions in Mexico, although current attempts to reform the relationship between indigenous people and the polity have taken a strongly legalistic form. In contrast, the Canadian faith in law has always led to a preference for legal remedies and opened the way for a significant impact through the courts.

Against the backdrop of these differences the common desire for political autonomy among Aboriginal peoples is especially striking. The pursuit of this goal has led to the establishment of linkages across political boundaries among Aboriginal peoples. It has also elevated the political saliency of Aboriginal rights in both Canada and Mexico.

Who Are the Aboriginal Peoples in Canada and Mexico?

The word "Indian" has denoted both an ethnicity and a category in law in Canada since the Indian Act of 1876. Indians formally recognized as such were "status Indians," while others were "non-status." ("Status" could be, and was, granted to persons who lacked Indian ethnicity or denied to persons not so lacking, in one of the paradoxical twists brought on by legislating ethnicity.) Inuit were traditionally understood to be Aboriginal peoples but were not formally recognized as such in law until a 1939 Supreme Court decision determined them to be Indians for purposes of the Indian Act. Inuit thus do not carry the burden of having been singled out for special and, in reality, invidious treatment, as had been the case for Indians under the act of 1876. The Métis, people of mixed Indian and European heritage, have been grouped with Aboriginal peoples only since 1982, when the patriated constitution provided that designation.

In contrast, in Mexico both the fact and the ideology of *mestizaje* have led to the avoidance of clear ethnic categories. Although indigenous peoples were the subjects of a distinct legal regime during the colonial period, independence brought an end to this practice. Subsequently, the ethnic blurring produced by extraordinarily widespread miscegenation also encouraged cultural rather than ethnic identification. As a consequence, indigenous peoples in Mexico are habitually defined according to both cultural and linguistic criteria. At present, fifty-six distinct indigenous language groups are recognized in Mexico. Even this categorization, however, is subject to some dispute, since often substantial linguistic variations make it possible to construct additional distinctions.

Currently, indigenous peoples comprise between 10 and 15 percent of Mexico's population of 95 million. Including all of Canada's status and non-status Indians (the latter defying exact accounting), Inuit, and Métis would bring the count to less than 5 percent of the population of 29 million.[3] Although most Mexican indigenous peoples live in southwestern Mexico, they are often dispersed and intermingled with the rest of the population. For this reason, it is more accurate to think of indigenous peoples in Mexico as inhabiting thousands of different, often isolated communities, rather than being part of a linguistic group. Correspondingly, loyalties among Mexican indigenous peoples have been tied to the community rather than the group. Canada's Indians are well distributed in the populated areas of Canada, but many live in remote communities and reservations, as well. Inuit are found chiefly in their Arctic and sub-Arctic homelands and not mixed in with the settler Canadians. Métis are concentrated in the Prairies.

Canada's Aboriginal peoples are highly organized politically, the Indians having the Assembly of First Nations (status Indians) and the Aboriginal Congress of Canada, formerly the Native Council of Canada (non-status Indians); the Inuit an Inuit Tapirisat; and the Métis their Métis National Council. Additionally, native women have a national organization, the Native Women's Association of Canada. Not surprisingly, these organizations are not of one mind nor, for that matter, are their component groups.

The 1990s have witnessed an extraordinary expansion of indigenous political organization in Mexico, often building upon the already large number of indigenous organizations established in the 1970s and 1980s. A host of groups have arisen, at both the local and regional level, especially in the southwestern states of Chiapas and Oaxaca, promoting indigenous demands. Over time, these organizations have become increasingly adept at coordinating their efforts through umbrella groups such as the National Indigenous Congress, although political differences also divide these associations.

THE HISTORICAL CONTEXT

Historical experience, in important regards, distinguishes Aboriginal peoples in Canada and Mexico. European colonization, despite a number of common features, was marked by the creation of different economies and polities. These differences were produced by the encounter between distinct European countries and differing local environments.

Canada from European Contact to Confederation

European explorers, entrepreneurs, and settlers brought with them their own particular variations on the European experience when they arrived in North America.[4] Some of those variations would have durable consequences, as one sees in comparing Mexico with Canada. Of importance to Canada, as James Tully points out in chapter 2, was the fact that Europeans treated the Indians of what later would be America and Canada as sovereign nations, equal in law with the European nations who were introducing themselves to North America. Tully endorses Chief Justice (of the U.S. Supreme Court) John Marshall's description of the status of Indians (with the stronger overtones of independent rights in *Worcester v. Georgia, 1832*[5] than in the earlier *Cherokee Nation v. Georgia, 1831*[6]) as "domestic dependent nations."[7] While the settler-native encounters ran the whole range from amicable and cooperative to hostile and combative, the Indians neither were for the most part conquered by European or local governments nor did they surrender. Many Indian groups did enter into treaties with European or local governments that are significant in today's conditions and in reform efforts. Against this backdrop, the governing authority exercised over Aboriginal peoples by settler governments would, according to liberal principles, eventually depend on finding a place for Aboriginals in the social contract. But that inclusion has all along been problematic because European settlers typically did not, in fact, see Aboriginal peoples as suitable for inclusion in the social contract (as Aboriginal peoples). Indians were seen by settlers as serving various economic or military purposes or as people at a primitive stage of history, but not in this early period as candidates for citizenship.[8] Aboriginal peoples were to be protected, but not assimilated or integrated.[9] However, this reading of the history of Aboriginal peoples meant that Aboriginal rights, self-government, and land title would survive, in some form, the Europeanization of North America, at least in principle.

Of special early importance in defining the position of Aboriginal peoples in the Canadian political order were the Royal Proclamation of 1763 and treaties later negotiated between the Crown and particular tribes. With the defeat of France in the Seven Years War of 1756–63, England came to control the former French holdings in North America. The Crown then wished to set a foundation for its added governing responsibilities in North America, especially for relations with the Aboriginal peoples. Hence the Royal Proclamation, essentially a constitution, which set the boundaries of Quebec and the rules regarding treatment of Indians.[10]

As regards Indians, the Royal Proclamation

- claimed Royal sovereignty over Indians ("Nations or Tribes of Indians ... who live under our Protection");
- reserved lands west of the Atlantic drainage, and other lands already reserved to Indians, for Indian use (lands "not having been ceded to or purchased by Us");
- set the terms for cession or purchase of Indian lands west of the Atlantic drainage. Such transactions could be only to the Crown, with other procedural requirements.

The goal of these rules was to preserve Indian lands for Indians and prevent transfer of the lands to non-Indians without Indian and royal consent.[11]

Such transfers did occur, by treaties executed under authority of the Royal Proclamation. The Crown obtained Indian lands amounting to most of Lower Canada and southern Ontario during the pre-Confederation period. Post-Confederation treaties, the "numbered treaties" during the interval 1871–1929, obtained Indian lands adding up to the remainder of Ontario, Manitoba, Saskatchewan, and Alberta and parts of British Columbia, the Yukon, and the Northwest Territories. Boldt tells us that the purposes of the Europeans in pre-Confederation treaties were chiefly strategic, while post-Confederation treaties were for economic development. In both periods, the treaties typically reserved some lands for Indian use and granted some sorts of assistance to the Indians involved in the treaty.[12]

Canada after Confederation

Section 91 of the British North America Act (later renamed the Constitution Act, 1867) enumerates the powers of the *central* government, in the manner of the u.s. Constitution's article I, §8. Section 91(24) gives the federal government legislative authority over "Indians, and Lands reserved for the Indians." This is the authority for the much-maligned Indian Act, the chief legislative basis for Canada's Indian policy. A complication for Aboriginal policy has been §92 of the Constitution Act, 1867, enumerating powers of *provincial* legislative assemblies. Notably, §92A, pertaining to natural resources, licensed concurrent federal-provincial jurisdiction over some Aboriginal lands and thus potentially over Aboriginal policy.

Canada's policy toward Aboriginal peoples from before Confederation up to the 1960s was assimilationist,[13] with four components: conversion to Christianity; removal of land by treaty and confinement to reservations; education of Indian children in residential, Christian schools; and introduction of Western-style self-government to the Indians.[14] Reservations fit an assimilationist mode in that they were seen as temporary locations, pending assimilation. The record throughout this period seems to have been one of the suppression of Indian culture and worsening material and sociological conditions, but with little systematic resistance from Aboriginal peoples or assertion of their rights until the 1960s. Particular leaders or tribes resisted or complained to the government agencies responsible. And the Métis under Louis Riel took to arms.[15] But for the most part the Indians were weakly organized in their tribes and had no pan-Indian organization. During some of this period Indians were by law not allowed to organize beyond the community level, in any case.

Indigenous Peoples in Mexico during the Colonial Period

The Spanish conquerors of present-day Mexico were bearers of a different strand of the European experience. The continuing presence of feudalism, a mercantilist economic system, and the relationship between the Church and the state contributed to the establishment of certain political, social, and economic forms. Simultaneously, certain features of the indigenous civilizations encountered by the Spanish facilitated the implantation of these forms. The most important elective affinity between conquerors and conquered was the preference for highly centralized political and economic arrangements. A large, settled indigenous population provided a source of labour and converts.[16] In addition, the discovery of mineral wealth, especially silver, encouraged mercantilism. By the end of the sixteenth century the conquest of much of present-day Mexico had been completed, and Spanish domination over the indigenous population had been established.

The Conquest produced a long philosophical debate in Spain about the humanity of indigenous peoples, pitting giant figures like Fray Bartolome de las Casas against the former conquistadores and other economic interests.[17] Although the Spanish Crown finally accepted indigenous humanity, it also relegated indigenous peoples to a permanent nonage status requiring the protection and supervision of church and Crown authorities. As a consequence of this conception, indigenous peoples in the Viceroyalty of New Spain were subjected to a different legal regime than Spaniards. Legislation emanating from the Council of the Indies turned indigenous peoples into wards of the Crown. However, a direct relationship with the Crown offered certain effective rights, including the right of petition. At the same time, the Crown, in practice, recognized local customary law, giving indigenous peoples a substantial measure of jurisdiction over local affairs. Phrased differently, New Spain was divided into two republics by the Spanish Crown – the so-called Republic of the Indians and the Republic of the Europeans. These republics occupied the same physical space but were governed by two distinct sets of laws.[18] Despite the presence of two different legal regimes, indigenous sovereignty was not recognized by Spain and treaties were consequently not a central feature of legal discourse. This was one of the fundamental differences distinguishing the legal treatment of indigenous peoples in Canada and Mexico after the arrival of the Europeans.

Although somewhat more benign than the situation after independence from Spain, the paternalistic legal regime established by the Spaniards did not protect indigenous peoples against economic exploitation. This exploitation, joined to the cataclysmic demographic decline produced by exposure to European diseases, defined indigenous life throughout the colonial period. More positively, especially by comparison with later developments, the Crown recognized communal landholdings as a legitimate form of land tenure. This, combined with the relative inefficiency of the hacienda system, provided some additional protection to indigenous communities.

Indigenous Peoples in Mexico after Independence

Indigenous peoples were many of the footsoldiers for both sides in the prolonged war of independence from Spain, although they were otherwise largely excluded from what was an essentially intra-elite struggle pitting *criollos* – people of Spanish descent born in Mexico – against the *peninsulares* – peninsular Spaniards. Life for indigenous peoples in the thirty years after independence in 1821 remained largely unchanged from the colonial period. Continuing strife after the war for independence, the concomitant lack of economic activity, and the persistence of large church landholdings helped to preserve indigenous communal lands. Although confined to a penurious existence and the depredations of different warring factions, indigenous peoples did not face the kind of systematic assault on either their lands or their way of life that they would encounter later in the nineteenth century.

Independence was also accompanied by the abolition of the so-called two republics and of the legal distinctions between indigenous and nonindigenous people. The disappearance of this distinction in the early nineteenth century and the creation of formal juridical equality, ironically, did not improve the situation of indigenous peoples. In fact, the end of this legal division helped to perpetuate a fiction of legal equality and promoted blindness about the actual situation of indigenous peoples. Additionally, ending the protections that had accompanied Spanish rule would facilitate the aggressions experienced by indigenous peoples later in the century.

Though the strife marking the thirty years after independence was fueled, in part, by simple personal ambition and the desire for power, it was also a product of a deeper ideological schism between Liberals and Conservatives.[19] The Liberals advocated free markets, the separation between Church and state, democratic political forms, and federalism, among other things. In contrast, the Conservatives wanted to preserve Church privileges, desired a strong, central, even monarchical, state, and believed in a more managed economy.

The conflict between these two groups finally ended in the 1850s and 1860s when the Liberals decisively defeated the Conservatives on the battlefield, first during the War of the Reform and again during Maximilian's brief rule. The Liberal triumph produced a dramatic deterioration in the situation of Mexico's indigenous peoples. The enshrinement of private property and the disentailment of church lands engendered a speculative land rush that led to the loss of many communal indigenous land holdings.[20] The plight and misery of indigenous peoples deepened even further during the dictatorship of Porfirio Diaz (1880–1910) when economic development, especially the expansion of agribusiness, led to even more massive encroachments against communal lands. Indeed, the period running from the Liberal triumph to the outbreak of the Mexican Revolution in 1910 produced the worst assault on the indigenous way of life since contact with the Spaniards in the sixteenth century. Debt peonage and landlessness both grew enormously during this period, creating unspeakable living conditions for indigenous peoples and other peasants in many areas of the country.

THE RECENT CONTEXT

Canada during the Period of "Megaconstitutional" Politics

Indian self-assertion manifested itself finally with the issuance of the government's white paper of 1969, which called for repeal of the Indian Act, abolition of the Indian Affairs Department, and provision to Indians of the same services as were available to any Canadian. The white paper, that is, would carry out Prime Minister Trudeau's vision of a Canadian community undifferentiated by race or ethnicity or national origin. It would end the collective rights of Indians, substituting the individual rights of all Canadians. Indians, seeing in the white paper both loss of services and destruction of their culture, fought back. From then on, Aboriginal political organizations and Aboriginal elites, many of them well-educated in the Western idiom, have advanced their case for Aboriginal rights and self-government.

Aboriginal self-assertion after 1969 enjoyed sporadic success. Moreover, Aboriginal political strategies became increasingly sophisticated during this period. Early successes had to do chiefly with judicial interpretation of their rights and other benefits stemming from treaties. But Aboriginals also sought and received some legislative remedies and, when it seemed propitious, entered into negotiated settlements with national or provincial governments.[21]

Efforts to reform the constitutional order have been a national preoccupation in Canada since the first round of "megaconstitutional" politics in the 1960s, to use Russell's terminology.[22] That said, the "patriation" process for Canada's constitution was probably the most significant agenda-setting event in this regard. Under the leadership of Prime Minister Pierre Elliot Trudeau, Canada patriated its constitution in 1982 by removing London from its constitutional chain of command and adding to the British North America Act a number of provisions, especially the Charter of Rights and Freedoms and amending procedures. The Charter would, in this design, be the essence of Canadianism. Amending provisions would make the design adaptable within Canada.

Trudeau's plan encountered rough going from the outset, although less from Aboriginal peoples than from other sources. Quebec declined to join the effort, first attempting (with some other provinces) to assert a right to block it, only to find that in the eyes of the Supreme Court of Canada the federal government could legally proceed with patriation without unanimous provincial acquiescence.[23] So then Quebec simply did not participate. Aboriginal peoples fared well in the patriated constitution, but not well enough to keep the principal Aboriginal groups from opposing patriation. Even though Canadian public opinion evidently had come to see the position of Aboriginal peoples in Canada as requiring improvement, some of the Aboriginal leadership concluded for various reasons that the patriated constitution would not be the best way to serve Aboriginal purposes.

Several provisions of the Constitution Act, 1982, and its Charter of Rights and Freedoms bear on Aboriginal issues:

- Nonderogation of Aboriginal rights and treaty rights, according to (Charter) §25
- Gender equality, in (Charter) §28
- Entrenchment of Aboriginal and treaty rights, in §35
- The promise in §37 (since lapsed) of a constitutional conference after patriation to formulate provisions for Aboriginal rights and self-government that would be added to the constitution as amendments

The constitutional conference and three more first ministers conferences were held in fulfillment of this last promise, with Aboriginal peoples represented by a number of their own delegations. These sessions clarified issues, brought Aboriginal rights and self-government to a new stage of recognition, and resulted in three amendments to the Constitution (subsections 35(3) and 35(4) and §35.1). The amendments co-opted into the Constitution, as treaty rights, the Aboriginal rights that come from land claims agreements, both past and future; guaranteed Aboriginal treaty rights equally to women and men; and assured that representatives of Aboriginal peoples would participate in preparing any amendments to parts of the constitution directed to Aboriginal peoples. These amendments, ratified by all provinces except Quebec, fell short of Aboriginal demands, which by now had grown to include demands for rights to self-government and the resources necessary to realize self-government. (Quebec would avoid ratification on grounds that such action might be taken as acceptance of the whole patriated Constitution.)

Canada's "fourth round of megaconstitutional politics" (Russell's terminology again; patriation was round three), the period of the Meech Lake Accord (roughly 1985–90), was addressed chiefly to the

Quebec problem, even though the constitutionally promised (§37) first ministers conferences had failed to assuage Aboriginal demands. This accord did not gain the unanimous provincial approval that had been set as the condition for its adoption. An event dramatizing the discontent of Aboriginal peoples came during Manitoba's consideration of the accord. A Cree who was a member of the Manitoba Legislative Assembly, Elijah Harper, acting according to the will of the Manitoba chiefs, dissented from the unanimous consent that would have been necessary for the assembly to take up its resolution of approval. Harper thus made all of Canada realize that the Meech Lake Accord, whether it met Quebec's reservations about constitutional conditions or not, did not recognize and accommodate Aboriginal wishes.

During the negotiations surrounding the Charlottetown Accord, Canada's fifth round of megaconstitutional politics, much greater effort was applied than during the preceding rounds to designing constitutional arrangements satisfactory to Aboriginal peoples. The accord included the promise, for example, to devise Aboriginal self-government as a "third order" of government in Canada, along with the federal and provincial orders. Moreover, it attempted to reconcile the communitarian approach to rights characteristic of Aboriginal peoples with the more individualistic approach of the Charter. However, in a national referendum on 26 October 1992, the Charlottetown Accord failed 55 percent to 45 percent. A majority of Aboriginal peoples voted against the accord, along with the rest of Canada.

During this period of megaconstitutional politics, the courts in Canada were providing an additional forum for the resolution of Aboriginal rights. Cases tended toward rights relating to title to or occupation and use of land, and to other treaty rights. Since the federal government held the responsibilities of the Crown in treaty and constitutional rights, these cases were primarily about the responsibilities of, or restraints on, the federal government. But often §91 of the constitution (placing the governance of Aboriginal peoples as a federal responsibility) was material, giving some cases the effect of clarifying federal versus provincial responsibility.

Whether the Canadian constitution would be interpreted as making Aboriginal self-government an inherent right or a delegated power would have to be worked out. The effort applied in the Charlottetown Accord to designing the constitutional provisions for Aboriginal self-government suggests that some settler and Aboriginal Canadians had doubts, even though the Accord specified that the proposed constitutional revisions were to "recognize ... the inherent right of [Aboriginal] self government."[24]

Post-Megaconstitutional Politics

Even before the Charlottetown Accord was voted on, Ottawa, moved at least in part by the Mohawk uprising at Oka in 1990, appointed a Royal Commission on Aboriginal Peoples (RCAP) with a sixteen-point agenda for research and proposals.[25] The impact of the RCAP was felt almost from its appointment, in the form of the research and recommendations sponsored by or aimed at the commission, and of the activities of the commission itself. Its final report, released in the fall of 1996, while comprehensive and passionate in its calls for recognition and accommodation of the Aboriginal agenda, seemed to be without effect in public policy. The commission, many thought, had over-reached itself. Yet the Liberal government elected in 1993 promised action, and after its mandate was renewed in the election of June 1997, the minister of indian affairs, Jane Stewart, moved. In January 1998 she announced an Aboriginal action plan of initiatives apparently intended to be limited and specific enough to be achievable.[26] Beginning with a "statement of reconciliation" that apologizes for Canada's treatment of its Aboriginal peoples for more than a century before 1970 – especially its treatment of Indians in residential schools – the plan goes on to make numerous commitments relating to Aboriginal self-governance, fiscal arrangements, and community-building. Announcement of the action plan came in parallel with the Supreme Court's release of the eagerly awaited decision in the *Delgamuukw* case, to be discussed in a moment.[27] And the Assembly of First Nations had selected a new leadership but six months earlier. All these developments resulted in new energy for the cause of Aboriginal rights.

In the long-running *Delgamuukw* case, which was greeted upon the Court's hearing it as a "landmark" (*Ottawa Citizen*, 16 June 1997) and upon decision on 11 December 1997 as a "native win on land rights" (*Globe and Mail*, 12 December 1997), the Supreme Court of Canada rendered a complex judgment. This case gave the Court an opportunity to speak systematically to Aboriginal title, although it came up short as a vehicle for legal analysis of Aboriginal self-government. The immediate result was for the case to be remanded for rehearing, which required the trial court to hear and evaluate native oral histories in deciding native claims.

On the question of Aboriginal self-government, the trial court had found against, arguing that all legislative jurisdiction had been filled up by the provincial and federal governments incident to British Columbia's joining Canada. The British Columbia Court of Appeal agreed, seeing Aboriginal self-government as a matter for legislation. The Supreme Court, in returning the case for retrial, said that the case presented on appeal was so contaminated by the trial court's errors of fact that it could not say if the claim for self-government had been made out. Nor did the Supreme Court lay down any principles on which a claim about self-government might be decided. A trial court must weigh Aboriginal oral histories, but in this case, after having done so, it might make the same decision as it had made before.

But the Supreme Court did air out its views on Aboriginal rights in relation to land and the varieties of forms these rights might take. The decision tells us that §35(1) goes beyond common law in protecting Aboriginal rights, and it restates the proposition that §35(1) is the doorway to a doctrine of Aboriginal rights.[28] In the 1990 case *R. v Sparrow*, the court had posed tests that legislation must meet if it is to infringe upon Aboriginal rights (valid legislative purpose, attention to the government's fiduciary responsibility, minimal infringement on Aboriginal rights).[29] In *Delgamuukw*, the court turned to the tests that Aboriginal claims would be held to: precise identification of the claim; continuous use and occupation of the area claimed (generously interpreted), going back to the assertion of Crown sovereignty; and a showing that the area is part of the traditional way of life for the group. And while a successful Aboriginal claim would be a senior claim, it would not, under *Sparrow*, be immune to proper federal or provincial legislative action. As to this case, the widespread interpretation of the decision as a "native win" was based on the assumption that under the Supreme Court's reasoning the Gitksan and Wet'suwet'en peoples had a good claim and that the requirement on trial courts to hear native oral histories as evidence would help the Aboriginal side in other cases.

Nor had the reform agenda languished otherwise in the 1990s. For example, a program was developed to dismantle the Indian and Northern Affairs infrastructure in Manitoba, and offices and agencies run by Indians were to take over delivery of services. Plans for Nunavut, a new territory created by separating the eastern portion of the Northwest Territories, moved forward toward a spring 1999 launch. Thus these and other reforms in the direction of Aboriginal rights and self-government were advancing below the level of megaconstitutional politics, and they continue to do so.

Indigenous Peoples in Mexico during the Twentieth Century

The increasingly desperate situation of indigenous peoples and the rest of the peasantry in Mexico played a large role in fueling the outbreak of the Mexican Revolution in 1910. Indeed, one of the most important revolutionary factions, led by Emiliano Zapata in the state of Morelos, fought almost entirely for land reform. Although the Zapatistas were not among the factions that emerged triumphant from the revolution, their demands for land reform were nonetheless incorporated in the Constitution of 1917.

However, land reform did not begin in earnest until the 1930s. During that decade, when much of Mexico's land reform took place, a large number of landed estates were seized and their lands granted to peasants in landholdings patterned on pre-Columbian forms called the *ejido*. *Ejido* lands could not be bought or sold, and they were granted to communities rather than to individuals: individual families privately controlled the product of the land but did not have title to the land itself, whose ownership remained vested in the community.

Although the land reform benefited many peasants, including indigenous communities, it failed to alter land tenure patterns in significant portions of the country. After the 1930s the regime remained formally committed to land reform, but largely abandoned the pursuit of this goal, and the redistributive thrust of the Mexican Revolution largely ended, to be replaced by a focus on economic growth. Large landholders were also able to use a variety of legal mechanisms to slow down and prevent the expropriation of land, slowing the pace of reform until it came to a virtual halt.

The impact of the land reform on the economic well-being of indigenous people and other peasants was also reduced by a lack of adequate supports, especially credit. Those who provided credit were often corrupt, compounding the problems engendered by the insufficiency of funds. These problems were further aggravated by demographic growth, which created enormous pressure on communal lands. The consequent subdivision of already small plots led to ever less viable holdings, called *minifundios*, driving people off the land.[30]

For all these reasons the land reform did not end the poverty and marginalization of peasant producers. These problems were especially acute in southwestern Mexico, where most of the country's indigenous population is concentrated. Worse, the land reform was most effectively resisted by local landed and political elites in this portion of the country, helping to perpetuate a virtually feudal society, especially in the state of Chiapas.

The glorification of the country's indigenous past and of land reform, if anything, encouraged complacency and neglect. Indeed, the focus on the past facilitated neglect in the present, since contemporary indigenous peoples were perceived as pallid remnants of their Mesoamerican ancestors. Moreover, the mythic strands of revolutionary nationalism, joined to the modest redistribution carried out by the regime, promoted a kind of collective blindness about the lot of indigenous peoples. Indigenous peoples in southwestern Mexico, especially in the states of Chiapas and Oaxaca, continued to live in conditions not dissimilar to those prevailing on the other side of Mexico's border with Guatemala. However, most Mexicans believed that the situation in Mexico differed fundamentally from that in Guatemala.

In addition to these problems, cultural and educational policy favoured integrationist programs. The primary government agency designed to address indigenous affairs, the National Indigenous Institute, or INI (Instituto Nacional Indigenista), created in the 1940s, often reflected this assimilationist thrust. Insufficient funding and corruption also affected INI's operations.

On top of poverty and marginalization, indigenous peoples in Mexico have experienced the worst features of the Mexican political system to a disproportionate extent. The judicial system, in particular, has treated indigenous peoples in an especially predatory fashion. As has been amply documented by a variety of human rights organizations, including Amnesty International and Americas Watch, indigenous peoples have been subjected to illegal apprehensions, torture, extrajudicial killings and "disappearances" more than any other sector of the population.

Indigenous peoples have also been among the largest victims of Mexican agricultural policy since the Second World War. The focus on import-substituting industrialization systematically decapitalized the agricultural sector of the economy. Agricultural productivity steadily declined, turning Mexico into a net importer of agricultural commodities by the early 1970s. The diversion of resources away from rural Mexico steadily deepened the income gap between urban and rural Mexicans. Rural inhabitants, including most indigenous peoples, became increasingly marginalized.

The difficulties of indigenous peoples were also compounded by the nature of the political regime established after the Mexican Revolution. The central institution of this regime has been a ruling party, now called the PRI (Party of the Institutionalized Revolution), that was originally created in 1929. The organization of the party along corporatist lines permitted the preemptive incorporation and demobilization of workers, peasants, and a variety of middle-class groups. The organization of the party also permitted the regular, predictable transfer of power for the first time in Mexico's history. Each president ruled for a nonrenewable six-year term and then personally selected his successor and used the party to insure victory. For these reasons the party was the cornerstone of the enviable political stability that Mexico enjoyed from the late 1920s until the mid-1990s. Less positively, the party's control was preserved by the extreme concentration and centralization of power in the executive branch, the use of electoral fraud, and an authoritarian ruling style. During his six-year term the president enjoyed enormous, although not unlimited, power, since he had to be sensitive to the powerful vested interests in the regime. Political pragmatism and the dictates of regime preservation encouraged responsiveness to significant supporters and opponents. Indigenous peoples, until very recently, did not fit into either of these categories, and were consequently neglected, except in the most symbolic terms.

Demands for Political Autonomy in Mexico

If poverty, marginalization, and exploitation provided a receptive environment among indigenous peoples for the development of demands for political autonomy, other factors encouraged the emergence of these demands. Broadly, these factors can be grouped into three categories: changes within the particular nation state, developments within the indigenous community, and, finally, international elements. Economic development during the twentieth century not only produced greater encroachments upon indigenous peoples but also enhanced feelings of relative deprivation. In addition, various other factors, discussed by Rodolfo Stavenhagen in chapter 3, below, promoted the activation of indigenous people. These factors include the rise of an indigenous intelligentsia, unhappiness with traditional development policies, disenchantment with the workings of the modern nation state; the galvanizing effect of postwar anticolonial struggles; and the role of outside organizing efforts, including the activities of Protestant and Catholic groups. At the same time, changes in rights discourse around the world encouraged much greater sensitivity to the plight of indigenous peoples and political activation among indigenous peoples. The already strong push toward ethnic and cultural identification was given further impetus by the collapse of Marxism. The concomitant retreat from class consciousness encouraged the further elevation of the importance of ethnicity for understanding politics and society.

Indigenous peoples have long sought recognition of their cultures and ways of life. In partial acknowledgment of these demands the government amended the Constitution in 1992 to recognize indigenous peoples in legal and constitutional discourse for the first time since independence. The amendment (article 4) also obligates the state to protect indigenous customs. Although problems of implementation have always plagued the Mexican Constitution, this amendment does represent an important recognition of indigenous peoples.

After enactment of article 4, indigenous people continued to press for further recognition. By the mid-1990s, especially after the outbreak of the Zapatista uprising in the state of Chiapas, these demands became couched in much more explicitly autonomist terms. The Zapatistas, or EZLN (Ejercito Zapatista de Liberacion Nacional), burst upon the world's attention on 1 January 1994, when several hundred indigenous guerrillas captured several cities in Chiapas. Despite government claims that the Zapatistas had a large foreign involvement, the organization was primarily composed of indigenous people. The government counterattack was marked by extreme barbarity and included hundreds of "disappearances." Finally restrained by a massive international and national outcry, the government began a long round of peace negotiations with the Zapatistas, who had been driven back into the jungle. The first phase of these negotiations, on indigenous rights and culture, seemingly concluded in February 1996 with the signature of the so-called San Andres Accords. This agreement, which will be discussed more fully later in this introduction, has become the blueprint for indigenous demands for autonomy and sovereignty. The demands for autonomy contained in the accords correspond to ancient traditions but have been renewed in contemporary terms. Unfortunately, the signature of the agreement did not bring closure to the issue. Conflicts soon arose over the language of the agreement and implementing legislation, pitting the government against the EZLN and the legislative commission that had participated in the negotiation of the accords, the Commission on Pacification and Agreement (COCOPA). These conflicts have continued throughout the rest of the 1990s.

As has been noted, the mid-1990s were marked by the further political activation of indigenous peoples, especially in the southwestern region of the country. Indigenous nongovernmental organizations (NGOS) were virtually nonexistent before the 1970s and 1980s but have grown dramatically since then. In addition, long-existing community groups have coalesced into larger organizations that have become a vibrant part of Mexico's emerging civil society. These organizations were also increasingly prominent as opponents of the Mexican regime. Indigenous political groups are consequently cited as one of the most important manifestations of the emergence of a civil society in Mexico during the last few years.

In Mexico the expansion of indigenous political activism was part of a much broader groundswell of opposition to the Mexican government. By the early to mid-1990s a confluence of factors had substantially

eroded the regime established after the Mexican Revolution. Even by
the late 1980s this regime had been exhibiting increasing signs of
fragility. Mexican society, after decades of modernization, no longer
fit the simple corporatist scheme informing the organization of the
ruling party. In addition, a prolonged economic crisis that had
plagued the country since the mid-1970s, except during a few brief
growth periods, had fundamentally destroyed much of the government's legitimacy. This crisis deepened disaffection with the regime's
persistent authoritarian institutions and ruling practices. Growing
demands for democratization coincided with, and nurtured, increased
political activism among indigenous peoples. At the same time, however, indigenous peoples themselves contributed to the decline of the
regime. Most importantly, the Zapatista uprising played an enormous
role in undermining the last year in office of the Salinas administration
(1988–94), which at the time was on the verge of successfully implementing a neoliberal experiment in Mexico. The uprising ended the
triumphalist phase of these policies and helped to push Mexico into
yet another economic crisis and a long, inconclusive political situation.

The often common opposition to the regime among different indigenous organizations did not always translate into common political
agendas, tactics, or strategies. In some instances political agendas were
largely confined to the resolution of local issues, including such matters as land and water rights. In other cases indigenous organizations
pressed for larger political goals, including regime change. Tactics also
varied substantially. Some organizations used nonviolent methods,
while others opted for armed revolt. At the extreme in terms of their
political tactics and strategy were the armed Zapatistas. Nonetheless,
as has been noted, indigenous political organizations have been
increasingly effective in coordinating their activities.

Several other factors have also fueled the growth of indigenous
political activism. Most importantly, perhaps, as part of its larger
neoliberal agenda the Salinas government fundamentally altered the
land reform, permitting the buying and selling of *ejido* lands. The
reform of the land tenure regime during the Salinas government
promised the same widespread seizure of indigenous communal lands
that occurred during the Reform and the Porfiriato. The Salinas
administration argued that this change in the land tenure regime was
necessary to improve agricultural productivity and encourage the
expansion of private investment in the rural sector. Although under-
capitalization and excessively small landholdings have clearly had a
devastating effect on agricultural productivity, the Salinas reforms and
the potential reconcentration of land into a limited number of private
hands represent fundamental threats to Mexico's peasantry, and, by
extension, to its indigenous peoples.

Another central part of the Salinas administration's neoliberal agenda was the expansion of trade with the United States and Canada through the North American Free Trade Agreement (NAFTA). The agricultural provisions of NAFTA have serious implications for indigenous peoples in Mexico. Liberalization of trade in certain agricultural commodities, especially corn, promises to have a devastating effect on the indigenous way of life because of the central role of maize in indigenous culture and religion. Even though corn was included among the products that enjoy protection under NAFTA for the longest period of time – fifteen years – indigenous peoples rightly saw the agreement as a fundamental economic and cultural threat. Not entirely coincidentally, the day chosen by the Zapatistas to launch their uprising against the Mexican government was 1 January 1994, the day NAFTA went into effect.

After a high point in 1994, a relative decline occurred in the political visibility of indigenous peoples in Mexico. A confluence of factors during the following years made the resolution of indigenous demands a less salient national political issue. During the latter half of 1994 the country's attention became increasingly riveted on electoral issues, because of presidential elections that year. Additionally, high-level scandals, assassinations, and other problems within the regime shifted the population's and the government's interest away from events in southwestern Mexico. Finally, and even more importantly, the collapse of the Mexican economy in December 1994 virtually swept most other issues aside. This economic collapse, prompted by the government's long-delayed decision to revalue the currency, was characterized by a massive devaluation, a huge spike in interest rates and an immediate outbreak of inflation. Unprecedented high levels of consumer and business debt contracted at floating rates during the Salinas years proved unsustainable against this backdrop. Not surprisingly, 1995 and much of 1996 were characterized by a deep recession, increased unemployment, and a wave of bankruptcies. Indeed, because of the level of consumer debt at the time of the collapse, this economic crisis was arguably the worst in Mexico's post-Revolutionary history.

Macroeconomic indicators soon began to steadily improve, however, especially during 1996, and there were significant declines in inflation and interest rates, a stabilization of the currency, and a booming stock market. But renewed economic problems in 1998, caused in part by the collapse of Asian markets, emphasized the continuing fragility of the country's economy. The depth of the 1994 crisis, compounded by the problems of 1998, have kept most of the population's attention focused on dealing with the personal effects of the crisis. Additionally, and especially in the major cities, the population has had to cope with a deepening wave of violent crime, helping to further distance it from other issues.

On the political front, an extraordinarily contentious, complex, and difficult effort to democratize the polity continued to occupy opponents of the government. Reform efforts have included everything from trying to promote further alterations in the electoral system to trying to create a real separation of powers and substantive federalism. These attempts have met with mixed success, but nonetheless they produced some significant changes during 1995 and 1996, including further electoral reforms and the distribution of increased power to the states. Most significantly, these reforms permitted an opposition victory in the 1997 Congressional elections, giving opposition parties their first majority in the legislature since the Mexican Revolution. This development promised ever greater legislative independence and the eventual construction of a real separation of powers.

The relative decline in the political saliency of indigenous demands after 1994 was also produced by other factors. Most significantly, perhaps, signature of the San Andres Accords in early 1996, despite the spread of isolated guerrilla activity in other portions of southwestern Mexico, temporarily neutralized this most visible embodiment of indigenous grievances.

However, indigenous demands have not faded from the political horizon. Perhaps more than any other event, the massacre of forty-five indigenous people by paramilitary groups linked to the PRI in Acteal, Chiapas, on 22 December 1997 once again thrust the situation in Chiapas into much more public view. The massacre highlighted the continuing prevalence of human rights and other abuses and focused attention on the continuing stalemate marking implementation of the San Andres Accords.

DEMANDS FOR POLITICAL AUTONOMY AND SOVEREIGNTY AND GOVERNMENT RESPONSES

Canada

Self-government would be, in the eyes of the Aboriginal peoples of Canada, the best way for them to determine their own way of life. As reaction to the white paper of 1969 dramatized, the issue for Aboriginal peoples is not common treatment of all Canadians, whether Aboriginal or not, but rather constitutional space for Aboriginals to treat themselves according to their own preferences – self-government, that is. Self-government is, in this view, a collective right that Aboriginal peoples had prior to first contact with Europeans, a right that survived that contact and was never surrendered.[31] It is, for those reasons, protected by §35(1) of the Constitution – it is an "existing right." But the issue now is more about implementation of self-government than about the right to do so. The rights of Aboriginal persons within a structure of self-government is a distinct matter, however.[32]

Self-government, to be fully realized, would have to deal with problems of people, place, resources, and authority. Yet in each of these matters, reconciliation with basic law and the other governing authorities of Canada is required.

People. The Indian Act gave to the government of Canada the authority to decide who is or is not an Aboriginal person, making the decision in part political, as mentioned above. But Aboriginal authorities prefer to decide who is to be a member of their communities. This issue is muddied not only by the Indian Act, which could be overcome by legislative action, as has been done in the past,[33] but also by the Charter of Rights and Freedoms, by corresponding judicial interpretation, by the very real problems in allocating scarce government resources, and by different legal and political rights of status and nonstatus persons.

Of all the problems of self-government, the problem of deciding who is an Aboriginal person may be the least contentious. The government's typical interest in avoiding unwarranted certification may be expected to correspond with the equally typical Indian preference for authenticity. One does hear the argument that being a member of an Aboriginal community is not a matter of genetics but of mutual consent.[34] Yet the issue of who is to be governed by an Aboriginal government does not seem overly challenging.

Place. The famous third order of government envisioned in the Charlottetown Accord might not have been territorial, or at least not wholly territorial. Aboriginal government on reservations does not test political innovation, nor will Inuit government in Nunavut in the eastern Arctic. Moreover, other third-order governing arrangements are being worked out incrementally, such as in the dismantling of Department of Indian Affairs and Northern Development (DIAND) offices in favour of Indian delivery agencies. But in other instances the concurrent reach of (third order) Aboriginal government to Aboriginal persons outside its territorial jurisdiction, such as in the administration of justice, might require especially careful thinking. Correspondingly, non-Aboriginal persons resident in areas that Indians may successfully lay claim to might expect to find unsettled jurisdiction. Additionally, important conditions of life within Aboriginal territorial jurisdiction might be affected by federal or provincial laws of general application and by practices outside the territory, as for example when the practices affect migratory fish or wildlife, in which case the Aboriginal government would claim to have a say.

Resources. One characteristic of most reservations and tribal lands is that they have not been a good source of revenues, the few natural resource-rich Aboriginal lands excepted. Moreover, Canadian governments practise "equalization," partial accumulation of financial resources in Ottawa and redistribution from there, in order to achieve balance among "have" and "have not" provinces. Thus Aboriginal peoples want both revenues from their lands, including subsurface rights (if they choose to exploit natural resources), and a financial allocation (equalization) from the national government. The former raises issues with provincial governments, which under §92A of the Constitution have primary authority regarding certain natural resources and land. The latter raises questions not only about distribution and redistribution but about the matters that Aboriginal governments would be expected to govern. Allocation of governing responsibilities alone would not necessarily resolve the financial issues nor would existing practice with regard to fixing financial responsibilities. Rather, they would be the starting points for fitting Aboriginal self-government into a constitutional scheme.

The allocation of federal-provincial authority over natural resources has been a difficult issue in Canadian politics, interacting with the Aboriginal question to mutual irritation. One can see, in this situation, that Aboriginal peoples may resist local arrangements relating to their cause in favour of national arrangements. That is, resource-rich provinces, in particular, may have an interest in exploiting natural resources in ways that would be at odds with Aboriginal preferences about the use of the land or that would even be directly contrary to Aboriginal land claims.

The Aboriginal Action Plan of January 1998 promised a new fiscal relationship between Ottawa and Aboriginal governments, with an integrated approach to both the distributions from Ottawa and the own-source revenues of those governments. The plan envisioned common accounting, data exchange, and standards of accountability. This plan, along with other matters of Aboriginal self-government, is now emerging.

Authority. While sovereignty would include a right to self-government without resort to any other authority, actual efforts to work out self-government for Canada's Aboriginal peoples are under the Constitution Act, 1982. Canada's Supreme Court, in speaking of §35(1) of the Constitution as a *doctrine* of aboriginal rights, suggests a distinct body of principle applicable to Aboriginal peoples. Section 35(1) is plainly material if applicable treaty or land claims agreements can be found. But under *Delgamuukw*, "existing" rights also include those that are unrecorded. In combination with the several other pertinent constitutional interpretations, discussed by Lajoie and others in chapter 7, below, understanding §35(1) as a doctrine leaves little doubt that Aboriginal peoples have an inherent right that allows for Aboriginal initiative in forming their own governments. It would seem that Aboriginal peoples have a sufficient legal basis for self-government within the Confederation, even if not through sovereignty and not outside the Canadian Constitution.

Moreover, while the Canadian Constitution does not recognize third-order government explicitly, accommodation of Aboriginal preferences may not require constitutional overhaul in the manner of the Charlottetown Accord. Aboriginal governments would prefer to ground their authority on traditional ways, whether by consensus within their communities or otherwise. But this preference is not necessarily a constitutional issue. Ordinary legislation or the simpler constitutional amendment procedure under §43 (by Parliament and the province affected) might do, especially given the umbrella of §35.

In any case, the Canadian preference for treaties as media for fundamental arrangements with Aboriginal peoples may help to resolve the authority problem. Treaties, that is, are a quasi-amendment procedure, a way to set essential constitutional conditions in place for Aboriginal peoples, should Parliament otherwise be amenable.[35] More difficult for Canadians than the procedure for accommodation will be defining the interface between Canadian and Aboriginal law and working out concurrent jurisdiction.

The Aboriginal Action Plan promises to reclaim legislative initiative over judicial initiative, moreover. It contains numerous proposals for legislation, treaty-making and remaking, and reallocation of governing responsibilities between Ottawa, the provinces, and First Nations. Treaties, case law, land claims settlements, and the interpretation of §35 of the Constitution Act, 1982, now offer willing negotiators a sufficient ground for mutual satisfaction. The James Bay settlement (between Cree and Inuit negotiators, on one side, and Quebec and federal government and private sector negotiators, on the other), for example, has provisions for land use, treatment of nonnative persons, wildlife management, local government, and assistance with financial resources.[36] This is but one of several such agreements illustrating that the way is open.[37]

Aboriginal demands in Canada spring from a desire to preserve a traditional way of life and to adapt it to contemporary conditions, as Aboriginal peoples themselves see fit, without interference. These demands are often framed as rights. In the interface between Aboriginal and Canadian governing arrangements, such a framework can raise conceptual difficulties in view of Aboriginal doctrines that locate rights in the community, rather than in the individual. As a corollary, additional conceptual and legal difficulties occur when individual Aboriginal persons lay claim to rights against their communities.[38]

While the right to Aboriginal self-government is robust under §35, the Canadian Charter of Rights and Freedoms is also an important context for response to Aboriginal peoples. If the Charter of Rights and Freedoms were to be the essence of Canadianism, as Prime Minister Trudeau hoped – especially late-twentieth-century Canadianism – it would have to make a number of finely tuned compromises between individual rights and collective rights and between contemporary and older conceptions of rights. Some of these compromises apply to Aboriginal peoples. For example, §25 of the Charter says that Charter rights "shall not be construed so as to abrogate or derogate from any aboriginal, treaty or other rights or freedoms that pertain to the aboriginal peoples of Canada." Yet in §28 we find, "Notwithstanding anything in this Charter, the rights and freedoms referred to in it are guaranteed equally to male and female persons." One can see in these provisions the difficulty of resolving claims relating to the collective rights of Aboriginal peoples – who may want the opportunity to define male-female roles according to tradition, outside the jurisdiction of Canada's courts – and of resolving claims relating to the individual rights of female Aboriginal persons. (See Franks, chapter 4, below, for the argument that the Charter does apply fully to Aboriginal government.) Resolution of such conflicts may well occur case-by-case, but the potential for differing conceptions of rights is a complication as Canadians attempt to reconcile the settler-Aboriginal relationship.

As Franks points out in chapter 4, below, efforts to recover or reestablish Aboriginal rights in some uncontaminated, presettlement form may not be profitable. Some of that presettlement form of Aboriginal society is probably gone forever, in the face of increasingly complex political and economic relations. Aboriginal self-government must be situated within the Canadian Constitution and apply to people whose perspective is inevitably changed by contemporary notions of how persons should relate to themselves, to others, and to the collective. Aboriginal communities will not be isolated from economic relations with non-Aboriginal actors in Canada and in the world or with economic organizations unimaginable in ancient doctrines. Aboriginal peoples may even avail themselves of such contemporary economic organizations. They may properly demand that adaptive measures be their own, but adapt they must, and in ways that will subject them not only to modernity but to Canada's position as a nation among nations – to Canada's sovereignty.

In sum, the Canadian constitutional order should be flexible enough to enable Canadians to confront Aboriginal rights and self-government. However, procedural obstacles exist in parallel with obstacles related to interests and perspectives. In the aggregate, these obstacles call for sincere and sustained effort if a satisfactory conclusion is to be found.

To recapitulate, Aboriginal peoples have participated fully in Canadian politics over the past twenty-five years or so. Correspondingly, the response from Canadian governments has been comprehensive and has been seen in constitutional and Charter politics, in judicial treatment of cases brought to national and provincial courts about Aboriginal matters and in legislation and administration. Additionally, in 1991 the national government launched an ongoing attempt to formulate a systematic strategy through the Royal Commission on Aboriginal Peoples, an effort that the Aboriginal Action Plan of 1998 claims to pursue. The government's response has been not just to seek reconciliation with Aboriginal peoples but, in a prior sense, to encourage Aboriginal peoples to articulate their preferences. In this sense, we have argued, Canada's approach has been legalistic and moralistic.

Canada's approach will continue to be legalistic and moralistic, we expect. In politics, it has been said, the best indicator of what will be is what is. In the hands of Canadians, this approach may yield good results. While treaties come most readily to the Canadian mind as the medium for formal arrangements, legislation at national and provincial levels remains a good avenue, as do judicial decisions in the cases brought to court. The bottom-up approach called for by Franks in chapter 4, below, might have greater potential than settler and Aboriginal Canadians have so far conceded, corresponding well with prevailing (if not historic) currents in Canadian politics. Masterstrokes such as the Royal Proclamation or megaconstitutional politics, while conforming to the strategy advocated by the Royal Commission on Aboriginal Peoples, would seem to hold less potential.

One hesitates to assess the results or prospects in Canada. With mobilization of Aboriginal peoples has come a richness and diversity in their demands. With efforts to accommodate have come fresh problems to be solved. With megaconstitutional politics has come the prospect of national disintegration, which has reduced the priority of Aboriginal issues. The problems are far from being solved, and despite the political and legal energy applied, an agreed strategy has not emerged. Yet the doors remain open, and the resources of a civil society may yet arm Canadians to press forward with recognition and accommodation of their Aboriginal citizens.

Mexico

Two different proposals for autonomy emerged in Mexico during the mid-1990s.[39] One, propounded by the Party of the Democratic Revolution (the PRD) – the centre-left opposition in Mexico – originally proposed to establish autonomous regions. Because of the presence of nonindigenous people in indigenous regions these autonomous regions would be "pluri-ethnic" and would occupy an administrative hierarchy between municipal governments and state governments. The specific role and functions of such regions was rather poorly defined, although their end was the decentralization of power and the construction of greater indigenous control over cultural, educational, and juridical matters. A second proposal was the construction of autonomy at the local community level based on the recognition of local customary law, as occurred during the colonial period. This approach has the virtue of building on an established administrative structure – the municipality – and it also more truly reflects indigenous identification with and loyalty to the community.

This latter approach, which soon became dominant, received the fullest and most extensive elaboration in the San Andres Accords between the government and the Zapatista rebels. The accords were the culmination of a first phase of negotiations aimed at ending the conflict in Chiapas. In 1994 and 1995 a cycle of armed conflict, repression, tense ceasefires, failed peace talks, and low-intensity warfare finally led the government to pass the Law for Dialogue, Reconciliation and a Just Peace in Chiapas. The law called for a suspension of military operations and for peace talks. It also established the Commission of Pacification and Agreement (COCOPA) to coordinate the dialogue between the government and the EZLN. Over the next several months the seemingly irreconcilable differences between the government and the EZLN, especially over the negotiability of national issues, prevented the initiation of peace talks. In September 1995 the EZLN proposed the creation of working groups to deal with six major themes: indigenous rights and culture, democracy and justice, welfare and development, reconciliation in Chiapas, rights of women in

Chiapas, and the cessation of hostilities. A few weeks later, in October 1995, talks began in San Andres on the first of these areas, the polity's treatment of indigenous rights and culture, and agreement in this area was seemingly concluded in February 1996 with the signature of the San Andres Accords. Talks on the other areas proposed by the Zapatistas, including democratization and alterations in the provision of justice, remained stalemated or did not occur.

The San Andres Accords promised a new relationship between indigenous people and the state, asserting that "The State respects the self-determination of indigenous people at every level in which they prefer a differentiated autonomy within the norms established for indigenous peoples, provided national sovereignty is not compromised. This implies the recognition of their identities, cultures and forms of social organization." In pursuit of this goal, the San Andres Accords called for the drafting of national legislation, including constitutional reforms, that would recognize the collective rights of communities and permit the redrawing of municipal boundaries to reflect areas with majority indigenous populations. They recognized indigenous rights to ancestral lands and established the granting of concessions to communities that would give them control of their natural resources. Furthermore, the agreement required the promotion and protection of indigenous cultures and customs and the creation of bilingual and culturally sensitive education in indigenous communities. In addition, the accords provided for the equal status and treatment of indigenous women, enshrined the principle of indigenous control over municipal affairs, and encouraged the promotion of sustainability.

However, despite seeming agreement on these points, the San Andres Accords had still not been implemented several years later. Although the accords were scheduled to be submitted to the Mexican Congress "sometime after March 1996," the Mexican government had not presented them for ratification several years later. Simultaneously, the talks on democracy and justice stagnated. In August 1996 the Zapatistas announced their unwillingness to engage in further negotiations until five conditions were fulfilled: liberation of Zapatista prisoners, designation of a government negotiating team with decision-making capacity, activation of the Implementation and Verification Commission (COSEVE) established by the San Andres Accords, implementation of the agreement on indigenous rights and culture, presentation of serious government proposals in the talks on democracy and justice, and an end to military and paramilitary prosecution of indigenous people in Chiapas. Although some prisoners were subsequently freed and COSEVE was activated at the end of 1996, the lack of movement in other areas prevented the resumption of dialogue.

During the same period, COCOPA, the legislative commission that, as mentioned, had participated in negotiation of the San Andres Accords, tried to reactivate the peace process by drafting a set of legislative and constitutional reforms designed to implement the accords. Both the Zapatistas and the government were invited to comment on drafts of these proposals. In November 1996 COCOPA announced that it would receive "final" comments from the two sides. It would then elaborate a final proposal that each side could either unconditionally accept or reject. Acceptance by both parties would lead to immediate Congressional approval, given the participation of all major political parties in COCOPA.

COCOPA's proposal included reforms to articles 4, 18, 26, 53, 73, 115, and 116 of the Mexican Constitution. Most significantly, the proposed new language for article 4 of the Constitution would legally define the scope of indigenous autonomy:

The indigenous peoples have the right to free determination and, as an expression of this, to autonomy as part of the Mexican State, such that they may:

I Choose their internal forms of social, economic, political and cultural organization;

II Apply their traditional [judicial] systems of regulation and solution for internal conflicts, respecting individual guarantees, human rights, and, in particular, the dignity and integrity of women; their proceedings, trials, and decisions will be validated by the jurisdictional authorities of the State;

III Elect their authorities and exercise their internal forms of governance, in accordance with their own norms and within the scope of autonomy, guaranteeing the participation of women in conditions of equity;

IV Fortify their political participation and representation in accordance with their cultural specificities;

V Collectively agree on the use and enjoyment of the natural resources of their lands and territories, understood as the total habitat used or occupied by the indigenous communities, with the exception of those lands whose domain corresponds directly to the Nation;

VI Preserve and enrich their languages, knowledge, and all the elements which form part of their identity and culture; and

VII Acquire, operate, and administer their own means of communication.

Of almost equal significance, COCOPA's proposal also amended the language of article 115 of the Constitution regarding municipalities, giving them much greater scope and power.

The Zapatistas objected to what they saw as only a partial reflection of the San Andres Accords but reluctantly accepted COCOPA's proposal. In contrast, the government, despite having agreed to a simple acceptance or rejection, insisted on studying the proposal. In December 1996 it sent a list of twenty-seven objections to the EZLN and COCOPA. Because of their number and scope, these objections effectively amounted to a counterproposal. The government's objections to the COCOPA proposal were summarized by President Zedillo's (1994–2000) assertion that its language on autonomy would "create little States within a State."

The Zapatistas rejected the government's counterproposal, which led to a stalemate that lasted throughout most of 1997 and was accompanied by a steady rise in paramilitary violence against indigenous people in Chiapas, leading to hundreds of deaths and culminating in the Acteal massacre. Simultaneously, a number of municipalities in different areas of the state began putting autonomy into practice. By 1998, thirty-eight municipalities had established "autonomous municipal councils" that were functioning according to the provisions of the San Andres Accords.

Throughout this period, tense, acrimonious relations continued between the government, the EZLN, and COCOPA. The government maintained a hard line in Chiapas, deporting foreigners whom it accused of supporting the Zapatistas, while maintaining a large and intrusive military presence.

In January 1998 the government suddenly presented a new proposal for constitutional reforms on indigenous rights and culture, which included a host of "observations" on and modifications of the November 1996 COCOPA proposal. This government proposal was met with hostility by the Zapatistas and lacked support from a number of the parties represented in Congress and in COCOPA. Nonetheless, the government announced its intention on 1 March 1998 to unilaterally seek Congressional approval of its proposal.

However, the polarization between the government and the Zapatistas and the growing differences between the different parties represented in COCOPA, especially between the PRI and the PRD, continued to make agreement unlikely. Instead, the long stalemate promoted an increasingly unilateral and intractable environment. As a consequence, the situation in Chiapas remains volatile and unstable.

Thus, several years after the signature of the San Andres Accords, attempts to implement the agreement and construct a measure of formal indigenous autonomy in Chiapas have foundered, although the de facto construction of this autonomy has occurred in a number of municipalities throughout the state.

OVERVIEW OF THE CHAPTERS
THAT FOLLOW

Contributors to this volume apply the tools of political philosophy, political science, and jurisprudence to the analysis of Aboriginal self-government. Based on his reading of both Western and (North American) Aboriginal principles, Tully (chapter 2) advances the argument that recognition and accommodation of Aboriginal peoples is possible. He reviews the chief points of the Canada-Mexico comparison, the deficient forms of the settler-Aboriginal relationship (treaty and colonial), and then explains the principles of a new just relationship. Stavenhagen (chapter 3) examines the activation of indigenous peoples in Latin America and the articulation of a new "Indianist" ideology. This ideology revolves around questions of self-definition and legal status, land rights, cultural identity, social organization, customary law, and political participation.

Franks, in chapter 4, reviews the Canadian propensity for macro-solutions and the measures attempted or implemented under this heading, which he calls a top-down approach. He then goes on to outline a bottom-up approach, essentially municipal-style government, which in his view is where experience actually lies. While more legal-istic than the later approach of Esteva's chapter on Mexico, Franks's approach does pose an intriguing correspondence to Esteva's localism and may be seen as contrarian by Canadian standards. Turner's chapter 5 offers a trenchant claim that whatever is done in Canada must recognize that Aboriginal peoples are in fact sovereign and not subject to Canada's sovereignty, because the Aboriginal peoples of Canada have never given up the sovereignty they had when Europeans arrived in North America. He takes liberalism to task for attempting to treat Aboriginal rights as a form of minority rights, when in fact Aboriginal peoples can justly be seen only as a founding people of Canada, rather than as a minority. Asch, in chapter 6, follows this same reasoning, that Aboriginal peoples in Canada are in fact sovereign, and he critiques the several legal doctrines that have supported conclusions about loss of Aboriginal sovereignty. He especially attacks the *terra nullius* doctrine, under which North America was seen as uninhabited at the time the European explorers arrived. Lajoie et al. (chapter 7) offer a highly jurisprudential analysis of case law, backed up by content analysis of debates in Quebec's legislative assembly, to show considerable diversity in the conceptions of rights throughout Canadian and Canadian-Aboriginal practice.

Returning the narrative to Mexico in chapter 8, Esteva extends and locates Stavenhagen's analysis by examining the form and nature of indigenous activation in Oaxaca, a heavily indigenous state adjacent to Chiapas, and the remedies indigenous peoples seek. His chapter also contrasts nicely with Franks's, as pointed out above, and parallels Turner's in examining indigenous discourse on autonomy.

Franks, in the concluding chapter, turns to the comparison of Canada and the United States, first framing a model for policy and then tracing the development of Indian policy in the two countries according to the model. We get some surprises.

Canada and the United States have much in common, of course, reflecting their common colonial experience. But they also have differentiating core values that appear in their assessments of the community and the individual. That is, Canada, owing to Tory influence, places more emphasis on the community while the United States gives priority to the individual. One would expect, taking these core values alone into account, that Indian policy in Canada would be more tolerant of Indian communities and respectful of their culture. The United States, in contrast, lacking a good doctrinal basis for recognition of persons as members of a distinct group, would be more assimilationist. That Indian policy in the two countries did not correspond well with these expectations, at least up until 1970 or so, is explained by political facts rather than core values: differing frontier, leadership, and political influences.

What strikes Franks about the frontier experiences is not just the conventional observation that Canada brought law and order to the frontier *as* it was opened up, while the United States initiated this policy only *after* settlement. More importantly, the result was that in Canada Indians were pacified and thus effectively removed from the policy agenda for a long time. Pacification in America was a more painful and drawn-out experience, preventing decision makers from removing Indians so completely from the political agenda. Franks also draws highly revealing comparisons of two figures of great significance in Indian policy in the two countries. In the United States, John Collier was President Franklin Roosevelt's commissioner of the Bureau of Indian Affairs and the proponent of sympathetic, accommodating reforms in Indian policy. He kept Indian policy on the agenda in Washington. In Canada, Duncan Campbell Scott, in contrast a dedicated assimilationist, was a significant lifelong figure in the Department of Indian Affairs from 1879 to 1932. His influence, enduring after his retirement, was to bar Indian policy from the agenda in Ottawa.

The period of change in Canada's Indian policy after the unexpected (at least by the government) opposition among Aboriginal peoples to the white paper of 1969 was in the direction that Canadian core values would predict. Driven by constitutional politics and the demands posed by Quebec, as well as by Aboriginal peoples, Canada's Indian policy moved toward multiculturalism and self-government. America's Indian policy, which at the outset of this period had a firm legal basis for progress in Indian self-government, continued to move in that direction, as well, but at a slowing pace, especially for want of resource allocations.

In sum, the chapters that follow are linked not solely as a common effort to understand rights and self-government for Aboriginal peoples in North America but also as an inquiry into the sources of their relatively sudden mobilization and political emergence after a long period of marginalization, deprivation, and subjection to alien government. Why they gained access to the political consciousness and governing institutions of the majority population is not readily explained by ordinary calculations of the resources for political influence. Even in Mexico, where the violent confrontation of the Zapatistas compelled attention, the government has been forced, however ambivalently and partially, to confront indigenous demands. And Canada's persistent search for accommodative solutions sets a standard for the world.

Yet solutions are elusive. The authors in this collection seek principles through inquiry about legitimacy and rights and devise options for structural and institutional arrangements. Regardless of whether incremental or radical reform is best, we hope this book's analysis of the North American experience will strengthen the discourse about Aboriginal rights and self-government.

PART ONE

Overview

2 A Just Relationship between Aboriginal and Non-Aboriginal Peoples of Canada

JAMES TULLY

INTRODUCTION

The Colorado conference was a unique opportunity for scholars from Mexico, the United States, and Canada to meet and discuss the struggles of Aboriginal or indigenous peoples of North America for self-government. Two major themes emerged in the discussions. First, Aboriginal peoples in Canada and Mexico are engaged in three similar types of struggle: a struggle to free themselves from internal colonisation by the Canadian and Mexican governments,[1] to govern themselves democratically by their own laws and ways on their territories, and to establish a just relationship between Aboriginal and non-Aboriginal peoples of Canada and Mexico. Moreover, they have a long history of struggle stretching back to when Europeans arrived, reduced their population by 90 percent, took their territories, and subjected them to colonial rule. This history provides a profound narrative in terms of which they understand their task today and imagine a future when they will be free and equal to the peoples who have dominated them for half a millennium.

The second theme of the conference was the dissimilarity in specific detail of the struggles in the two countries. The characteristics of the invasions, taking of territories, usurpation of governments and cultures, and strategies of internal colonialism have varied considerably. The ways in which Aboriginal peoples have suffered and resisted extermination, marginalisation, and assimilation; preserved elements of self-rule, languages, and cultures; and fought for freedom are also various. One might say that there is a common agonic struggle between the overwhelming power of the two imperial states, Canada and Mexico, and the unconquerable freedom of the original peoples of this continent; a struggle that takes markedly different forms over time and place.[2] To understand these differences, there is no alternative to specific historical studies, and one can only hope that a discipline of the comparative politics of the Aboriginal peoples of the Americas will soon be established to carry out and coordinate these indispensable studies.

In the meantime, we must work in a provisional way with our own piecemeal research and the available interdisciplinary scholarship. Of the three types of struggle Aboriginal peoples are engaged in – struggles for decolonisation, self-rule, and a just relationship – I wish to take up only the third, and only in Canada. I will describe two major types of relationship between Aboriginal peoples and (non-Aboriginal) Canadians[3] over the last four centuries and argue that one of these should be the prototype for a new and just relationship between them. The reader will then be in a position to compare and contrast this account with the chapters by Esteva and Stavenhagen on the analogous struggles in Mexico.

A note of caution. Any generalisation about the relations between Aboriginal peoples and Canadians is fraught with danger. There are several hundred Aboriginal peoples or nations on the northern half of North America whose histories and cultures over the last ten thousand years are diverse. The length of time and the manner in which they have had to interact with Canadians are also various. The visions of different Aboriginal peoples of a just relationship with Canadians are also diverse and in a continuous process of reinterpretation. My sketch of two major types of relationship and of arguments for one of them is not comprehensive or definitive. It constitutes an opening and fallible attempt to articulate an *intermediate* description that is not too dissimilar to the ways many Aboriginal people express their relationship with Canadians, on the one hand, yet that is understandable to non-Aboriginal readers on the other. That is, by offering for critical response a first approximation of a sketch that might mediate our differences, it attempts to initiate an intercultural dialogue between Aboriginal peoples and Canadians in which they can gradually reach agreement on the just form of associating together.[4]

TWO TYPES OF RELATIONSHIP: TREATY AND COLONIAL

The relationships between Aboriginal peoples and Canadians have varied over the last four centuries from mutually beneficial association

to war, dispossession, and extermination; from consensual negotiations between equal nations to the coercive imposition of a structure
of domination. Whenever relations have passed from consent to coercion, Aboriginal peoples have refused to submit and have resisted in
a number of ways: with tactical compliance in residential schools and
prisons, substance abuse and suicide on reserves, open confrontation
and battle, and legal and political challenges.[5]

In this complex history of interaction, two main types of relationship
have persisted. The first is the treaty relationship. In it, Aboriginal
peoples and Canadians recognise each other as equal, coexisting, and
self-governing nations and govern their relations with each other by
negotiations based on procedures of reciprocity and consent that lead
to agreements that are then recorded in treaties or treaty-like accords
of various kinds, to which both parties are subject. Treaty-making
developed in the early modern period as a way of settling differences
and governing trade, military, and land-sharing arrangements by
means of discussion and consent, without interfering in the internal
government of either society. Treaty relations were surrounded by a
sea of strategic relations of pressure, force, and fraud, and the treaty
system itself was constantly abused. Nevertheless, from the first
recorded treaties in the seventeenth century to the land-base and off
land-base agreements of the Métis from 1870 to the present, the
Nunavut Agreement with the Inuit of the eastern Arctic in 1993, and
treaty negotiations with the Nisga'a nation of the Pacific Northwest
today, the treaty relationship has survived and evolved, comprising
over five hundred treaties and other treaty-like agreements. For most
Aboriginal peoples, including those who live off Aboriginal reserves,
it provides the normative prototype of the just relationship they aim
to achieve by their struggles. Let us set it aside for a moment and turn
to the second type of relationship.

During the nineteenth century a different relationship was imposed
over the Aboriginal peoples without their consent and despite their
active resistance. Their status as equal, coexisting, and self-governing
nations was denied. Their governments were displaced, and they were
forcibly subjected to the Canadian political system by the establishment of a structure of domination administered through a series of
Indian acts.[6] This colonial regime has gone through several phases.
Aboriginal peoples have been treated as obstacles to Canadian settlement and expansion who could be removed from their territories,
relocated on Crown reserves, and governed by the Indian Act; they
have been treated as primitive wards incapable of consent whose
religions, languages, cultures, and governments could be eliminated
and who could be coerced into the superior Canadian ways by their
civilised guardians; they have been treated as disappearing races who

could be marginalised and left to die out; and they have been treated as burdens on the Crown who could be off-loaded and assimilated to Canadian citizenship by extinguishing or superseding their Aboriginal and treaty rights. More recently, they have been treated as minorities with a degree of legal autonomy, self-government, and claims to land within the Canadian political system. What has remained constant through these phases is the colonial assumption that Aboriginal peoples are subordinate and subject to the Canadian government, rather than equal, self-governing nations subject to the agreements reached through the treaty system. (For the contrast between these two views, see Franks, chapter 4 and Turner, chapter 5, below).

The colonial relationship was set in place as the settler population increased and spread across Aboriginal America in the nineteenth century, changing the demographic balance and disrupting Aboriginal ways of subsistence. The end of the British and French wars rendered the military alliances with the First Nations irrelevant. The shift from trade to settled agriculture and manufacture caused the trading treaties to decline, and the new technologies led to the over-exploitation of wildlife, undermining Aboriginal economies and forcing Aboriginal peoples into relations of dependency. These factors and others upset the balance of power that underlay the rough equality of the treaty relationship.

The prevailing view of the world of (English and French) Europeans and European-Canadians in the nineteenth century served to legitimate the colonial relationship. This "stages" view ranked cultures and peoples hierarchically in accord with their stage in a purported process of world historical development. Modern European nations were taken to be at the highest and most developed stage, and their institutions and cultures provided the norm against which all others could be ranked. As the process of modernisation spread around the world from the European centre, the colonies and lower nations would develop into uniform nations like those in Europe. Aboriginal peoples were ranked at the lowest and most primitive stage, in a state of nature without governments or territorial rights, and thus beneath, or earlier than, relations of nation-to-nation equality and consent on which the treaty system had mistakenly been founded. Rather, they were taken to be under the sovereignty of the superior imperial power that discovered them and established effective control (as Asch explains in chapter 6, below). Since Aboriginal people were assumed to be subject to the Crown, the treaties were reinterpreted as domestic contracts to settle them on land the Crown reserved for them, to grant them hunting, gathering and fishing rights under Canadian law – subject to the pleasure of the Crown – and to extinguish whatever precontact rights they might have had.

In the twentieth century, the Eurocentric biases of the stages view that legitimated the colonial relationship in the heyday of European imperialism have been exposed by scholars in the human sciences as the imperial system has been partially dismantled in practice. Former European colonies have gained their freedom and equality as self-governing nations. In the case of Canada, it was only in 1982 that the last vestiges of British colonial rule were removed by the patriation of the Constitution (until then, amendment of the constitution was still subject to Imperial consent). In their many struggles, the indigenous peoples of the world are demanding that the process of decolonisation be extended to them, and for the same reasons. As a postcolonial attitude spreads, Aboriginal peoples are beginning to be seen, not as lower and subordinate, but as contemporary and equal; not to be ranked in Eurocentric stages but to be seen for what they are – as "diverse": that is, as exhibiting cultural similarities and dissimilarities. These monumental changes are beginning to have effects in court cases, constitutional negotiations, international law, the United Nations, and in the attitude and behaviour of citizens who wish to free their society from the disgraceful vestiges of internal colonialism and to recognise Aboriginal peoples as equals.[7]

At the present time, this enlightened trend is confronted by a powerful backlash that seeks to reassert the colonial relationship and justify it by uncritically repeating the discredited assumptions of the stages view and court rulings based on them and by playing on the fears of the consequences of equality.[8] If this dangerous confrontation is to be overcome, two questions need to be answered. What is the just form of recognition of Aboriginal peoples? and What is the practical form of accommodation of this recognition by the former colonising society? I would like to argue now that Aboriginal peoples should be recognised as equal, coexisting, and self-governing nations and accommodated by renewing the treaty relationship.

A NEW RELATIONSHIP

From the discussions between Aboriginal and non-Aboriginal people over the last fifteen years, as well as from the extensive research and dialogue carried out under the auspices of the Canadian Royal Commission on Aboriginal Peoples, a relationship that would meet the demands of justice and utility on both sides appears to consist of the following five principles: mutual recognition, intercultural negotiation, mutual respect, sharing, and mutual responsibility. Mutual recognition means that Aboriginal peoples and Canadians recognise and relate to each other as equal, coexisting, and self-governing peoples throughout their many relations together. Once mutual recognition is achieved, they engage in intercultural negotiations with the aim of reaching agreements on how they will redress past injustices and associate together in the future. Mutual respect, sharing, and mutual responsibility inform the relations of association and interdependence to which they agree. These principles constitute an Aboriginal-Canadian charter that should govern relations between Aboriginal and non-Aboriginal peoples. If they were adhered to, the distrust and confrontation would give way to trust and civility.

These principles are not my own. As I mentioned above, they are an attempt to restate what Aboriginal and non-Aboriginal people have said about the relationship. For each principle, I explain below its meaning in both cultures, the respective values associated with it, the injustices it redresses, and the mutual benefits it bestows on both partners in the relationship. In this way I hope to show that each principle is drawn from and in accord with both Aboriginal and Western values. Indeed, these principles are the norms implicit in the ways Aboriginal and non-Aboriginal peoples have acted together in the past when these ways have been just and fair, and they have withstood critical examination in the present. The relationship will be proven to be valid if these principles come to be accepted in the course of further critical discussion by all Aboriginal and non-Aboriginal people affected by them. These are, it seems to me, the rather exacting demands of justice in a postcolonial age.[9]

Mutual Recognition

The first and most difficult question in engaging in a just relationship is for the participants to agree on how they should recognise each other at the outset and relate to each other throughout. The first principle of mutual recognition as equal, coexisting, and self-governing peoples and cultures answers this initial question. It means that Canadians recognise the distinctive presence of First Peoples in Canadian life and, at the same time, that Aboriginal people recognise that non-Aboriginal people are also of this land by birth and adoption, with histories, institutions, rights, and enduring interests having their equal legitimacy. This form of mutual recognition replaces the unilateral recognition of the colonial relationship, where Canadians recognised themselves as self-governing and Aboriginal peoples as subject to Canadian governments as either a persisting or extinguishable minority.

Mutual recognition consists of two steps: the acceptance of this form of recognition by both peoples and its public affirmation in the basic institutions and symbols of Canada. When people enter into a relationship, they always recognise each other under some description. Recognition is usually habitual and unreflective, part of one's customary cultural understanding of, and attitude towards, self and others. The taken-for-granted form of recognition sets the horizon within which one envisions and relates to oneself and others. Up to the 1960s the stages view provided the unquestioned horizon of recognition for many Canadians, and it was inscribed in the institutions of Canadian society. Since then, it has been called into question and criticised, and the movement to a mutually acceptable form of recognition initiated through public discussions, court challenges, curriculum reform, constitutional negotiations, and film-making.

The transformation in the way Canadians and Aboriginal peoples recognise and relate to one another is difficult because it involves freeing oneself, and each other, from deep-seated prejudices and habits of thought and behaviour inherited from the imperial past. However, the change can be put in its proper perspective if placed in the wider context of analogous changes in self-understanding that Canadians are undergoing as they free themselves from captivity to other inegalitarian relations of the imperial age. Over the last sixty years Canadians have learned to recognise themselves, not as colonials subordinate to the British people, but as members of a self-governing confederation, different but equal to the peoples of the world. This new form of postcolonial recognition has been publicly affirmed by a Canadian flag and the patriation of the Constitution. European Canadians have recently learned to recognise non-European Canadians, not as inferiors unfit for the rights of citizenship, but as citizens equal to themselves with cultures worthy of preservation and to affirm this recognition in the Constitution. After centuries of exclusion and subjection, Canadian women have been recognised as equal citizens. This gender equality has been affirmed in the Constitution and the enormous changes in mutual recognition and relations between women and men this will involve have been initiated. The mutual acceptance and affirmation of Aboriginal and non-Aboriginal peoples as equal, co-existing, and self-governing and the public acknowledgement of this in the Constitution should be seen as part and parcel of these analogous transformations in the way Canadians recognise and relate to each other.[10]

Before we turn to the justifications of this form of mutual recognition, let me briefly explain its three features: equality, coexistence, and self-government. The desire for the equality of the two peoples, their cultures, and their governments, has been an important theme historically, best symbolised in the ceremonies and speeches surrounding the negotiation and signing of treaties over the last three centuries.

These sentiments are repeated by contemporary Aboriginal leaders seeking modern treaties to resolve outstanding tensions over lands, to recognize a nation-to-nation relationship and to assure a seat at the constitutional negotiating table.

As we have seen, this vision of a relationship between equals competed with, and was eventually overshadowed by, a colonial vision in which Aboriginal peoples and their cultures were treated as unequal and ranked as inferior. North America was retrospectively seen as either uninhabited at the time of European arrival or as inhabited by primitive peoples who, because they did not have European state formations and institutions of property, lacked government and jurisdiction. These ethnocentric assumptions have no place in a postcolonial civilisation or in the new relationship.

The second feature, coexistence, means that the governments and cultures of Aboriginal and non-Aboriginal peoples coexist, or continue, through all their relations and interdependencies over time. This involves abandoning the strategies of the past that have been rejected by the Aboriginal peoples and whose remnants are still with us. These strategies include the dogmas that Aboriginal peoples became subject to Canadian sovereignty without their consent and that treaties extinguished, and Canadian laws supersede, Aboriginal rights to govern themselves by their own laws. Strategies of assimilation, such as the 1969 white paper, and tactics of integration, whereby the traditions of Aboriginal peoples and Canadians are melded into a common whole, should also be abjured as unjust.[11]

Coexistence is a relationship in which Aboriginal peoples and Canadians live side by side, governing their own affairs in a relationship that values this form of political diversity. However, this is not a relation of separation and isolation. Natives and newcomers have interacted for centuries. Their identities and cultures have been shaped by these interactions, and a dense set of intercultural relations of interdependency and shared histories has developed on the middle ground wherever interaction takes place. Although many of the interrelations are unequal and dominating, they cannot be disentangled and separated from the peoples who have associated within them for so long. The objective of a new relationship is rather to lay the guidelines for the reform of these interrelations and the formation of egalitarian relations of interdependency. Nevertheless, no matter how interdependent the partners become, the recognition of coexistence ensures that Aboriginal cultures and governments will continue throughout. Third, Aboriginal and non-Aboriginal peoples should recognise each other as equal peoples who govern themselves and their lands by their own laws and cultures. They, in turn, govern their common relations in accord with the five principles on equal footing. The treatment of Aboriginal peoples as unequal and therefore subject to the laws and ways of the Canadian peoples constitutes the injustice of usurpation on which the Canadian colonial system rests. Recognition brings decolonisation and freedom to Aboriginal peoples and to Canadians as well, who long to free themselves and their children of any further complicity in a democratic society that contains a regime of inequality within.

In sum, there are no more basic values in Aboriginal and Western traditions than the right of peoples to govern themselves by their own laws and ways; for their laws and cultural ways to coexist and continue through their interrelations with others; and for them to be treated as equals.

What, then, are the justifications for this form of mutual recognition? Why should Aboriginal and non-Aboriginal peoples accept and affirm this self-description as equal, coexisting, and self-governing peoples as the basis of their acting together? The form of recognition I recommend can be justified, first, by the arguments that justify the recognition of any self-governing nation: the basic principles of political theory, international law, the common law of the Commonwealth and former Commonwealth countries, and the conventions of the Canadian and American constitutions.

Aboriginal people were the first inhabitants of this continent. As the result of long use and occupation they have continuing rights to the land, unless they are properly relinquished. Further, they have the status of independent, self-governing nations, in virtue of prior sovereignty, grounded in the practice of governing themselves by their own laws and ways and of entering into international relations with other Aboriginal nations and with Europeans when they arrived. Their status as self-governing nations was acknowledged in many early relations, and it was not surrendered by the establishment of settler governments or by treaties. The rights of a people to self-determination and the preservation of their cultures, rights that are increasingly but not completely recognised at the international level, are a further source of justification.

Legal support is found in the common law tradition established by the Crown, settler governments, and Aboriginal nations around the world in the early period of European colonialism. The first nations were recognised as independent, self-governing nations, equal in status to the Crown, in the early treaties and land negotiations, in landmark appeals to the Privy Council, in the Royal Proclamation of 1763, in the rulings of John Marshall, the early Chief Justice of the United States, and, by implication, in the constitutional amendments of 1982 that reaffirmed the Royal Proclamation and Aboriginal and treaty rights.[12]

However, as we have seen, after the balance of power shifted to the settlers, Aboriginal governments were suppressed by colonial laws that claimed to supplant their rights to hunt and fish, to educate their children, to move about freely, to associate together, to worship, to speak their languages. The policy of successive Canadian governments has been to continue the subjection of Aboriginal people to Canadian law without their consent. In the negotiations over the last decade, Aboriginal peoples have insisted on recognition of the inherent right of self-government. They have sought to reestablish public recognition of their long-suppressed but never-relinquished identity as first nations by tabling the following justifications which can now be drawn together in order to present a synoptic sketch of the new relationship and its principles.

When Europeans arrived, the Aboriginal peoples they encountered were independent, self-governing nations equal in status to European nations.[13] Their status as self-governing nations rested on exactly the same criteria in international law, then and now, as the status of European nations: the proven ability to govern themselves on a territory over time and to enter into international relations with other nations. These are the universal criteria of the inherent right of self-government on which nationhood rests in the modern world. The Aboriginal peoples had every right to recognise the Europeans as immigrants subject to their laws (perhaps granting them some sort of minority status), as nations did then and do now. The only valid way, therefore, in which Canada and the United States could acquire sovereignty in North America was by gaining the consent of the sovereign nations that were already here, as would be the case anywhere else in the world. The Aboriginal peoples agreed to recognise the settlers as coexisting, self-governing nations equal in status to themselves, with the right to acquire land from them over which the settler governments could then exercise jurisdiction and sovereignty by means of nation-to-nation treaties based on mutual agreement. This is the basis of the treaty relationship.

Accordingly, in treaty after treaty down to this day, the Aboriginal peoples have recognised the European settlers and their successor societies as equal, self-governing nations in North America on the condition that they recognise the equal, yet prior, status of the nations who were already here. Hence the phrase "First Nations." The Aboriginal peoples recognised the settler communities as nations because it fit in with their customary way of recognising and governing relations with other Aboriginal nations. The French and British officials participated in this system of mutual recognition because it fit in with their familiar way of recognising and governing relations with other nations and because they needed the First Nations as allies.

Therefore, the international legitimacy of Canada as a self-governing federation actually rests on its recognition by the Aboriginal peoples, not the other way round. Their consent to recognise Canada is, in turn, conditional, first, on Canada's acknowledgement of the Aboriginal peoples' equal yet prior status as nations, and, second, on Canada conducting relations with the First Nations by consent gained through the treaty system. There is no other valid justification of Canada as a sovereign federation and no way of avoiding this one. The other purported justifications reduce to might makes right, which is no justification at all; to specious misrecognitions of the status of the Aboriginal peoples at the time of contact, such as the imperial fiction of a state of nature; or to begging the question by presupposing the sovereignty of the Crown, as in the colonial relationship.

If Canadian governments fail to recognise the status of the Aboriginal peoples as equal yet prior nations, then they violate the inherent right of self-government, the ground on which the legitimacy of the global system of nations rests. Canada would then be an illegitimate state, founded on usurpation. This structural injustice would become increasingly glaring as the light of post-imperial civilization gradually exposes the colonial relationship with its unsupportable presumption of Crown sovereignty. If, conversely, Aboriginal and non-Aboriginal peoples mutually recognise and relate to each other as equal, coexisting, and self-governing nations bound together by treaty relations that rest on the consent of those governed by them, and if they affirm this form of recognition in the constitution and basic institutions of Canadian society, then they will dissolve the underlying cause of the current confrontation. Canada will then be a just confederation, and an exemplary member of the postcolonial age.

If this is a fair sketch of mutual recognition of the partners in the treaty relationship, I want to turn to the relationship itself and its basis in the consent of those governed by it. I will speak of Canada and the first nations as "partners" in treaty relations and of the relationship itself as a "partnership." Before doing so, however, I would like to clarify the partnership by drawing an analogy to the similar relationship between the provinces and federal government.

When the colonies confederated in 1867, they were recognised as having equal and inherent rights to govern themselves by their own assemblies, laws, and cultures, in virtue of their long prior development of responsible government. This right was further recognised to coexist or continue through all the relations they were later to engage in with each other and with the federal government. The federal government, for example, is not understood to have the right to extinguish or discontinue the political and legal institutions of the provinces or to alter the constitution, which sets out the relations between them, in ways that affect them without their consent. The relations between them are understood to be based on consent. Due to these universal, liberal principles of equality, continuity, and consent, this kind of confederation is called a liberal or "contract" confederation. It is simply the application of the same liberal and democratic principles governing the relationship between citizens and government in social contract theories to the relationship between provinces and the central government in federal theory.

Accordingly, the principle of mutual recognition that defines a just relationship between provinces and the federal government analogously defines a just relationship between First Nations and the confederation of provinces and federal government. The first difference is that the right of the federal and provincial governments to exercise jurisdiction over their respective territories is based on their recognition of the prior right of the Aboriginal nations and, consequently, the acquisition of land from them through treaties based on the consent of both parties. This was understood at the time of Confederation and the numbered treaties were made to meet the requirement.[14] For the provincial and federal governments to deny the treaty relationship between Aboriginal and Canadian governments would be to violate the conditions of their own legitimacy. For them to acknowledge it is to live up to their own principles. The second difference, which is not as great as it seems, is that the relations of interdependence between the provinces and the federal government are based on intergovernmental delegation, first ministers' negotiations, and referenda, and they are recorded in the Constitution and its amendments, whereas Aboriginal-Canadian relations are based on treaty negotiations, recorded in treaties and treaty-like agreements, and given constitutional protection under §35 of the Canadian Constitution.

There is one further similarity between the two confederations that rounds off this discussion. When the Aboriginal peoples agreed to share land and jurisdiction with non-Aboriginal peoples through treaties, one of the conditions of the agreements was that Aboriginal peoples living on the (now) non-Aboriginal lands could continue to be governed to a large extent by Aboriginal laws and customary practices. Indeed, this is one of the first and most famous recorded agreements in the early period. It follows that this condition applies in the present to the one-half million Aboriginal citizens living in non-Aboriginal Canada.

The Confederation of 1867 embodies a similar agreement. Federal law does not apply only to the provincial governments, as it would if Canada were a pure confederation. Rather, the citizens of the provinces govern themselves in a number of areas by federal laws and institutions, and they carry these federal relations with them from province to province. We may say that the Aboriginal people living off their territories, in an analogous way, carry their federal laws and ways with them. So again, once the false assumptions of the colonial relationship are set aside, the new relationship appears to be the reaffirmation and renovation of the principles informing the best of past Aboriginal and non-Aboriginal practices, rather than a strange departure from our history, as some have charged.

To summarise, I am suggesting that Canada should be seen as comprised of two confederations rather than one. The "first" confederation (or federation) is the treaty confederation of the First Nations with the Crown and later with the federal and, to some extent, provincial governments. The second confederation (or federation) is the constitutional confederation of the provinces and federal government.[15] The basis of the first confederation is the set of relations that the First Nations, Inuit, and Métis have established with the Crown, federal government and provincial governments over the centuries by mutual agreement.

The term "Canada" is usually taken to refer to the second confederation only (the federal-provincial confederation) and Aboriginal peoples are treated as if they were part of it. But Aboriginal peoples have never been a part of that confederation, and it is a travesty of history to pretend otherwise. Therefore, let us use the term "Canada" from now on to refer to the political association of the two confederations and abandon the narrow, colonial use of the term. This is, after all, how the term was originally used. Canadiens and Canadiennes were those who lived alongside the independent Aboriginal nations, adapted to indigenous ways, and identified more with this new association than with France. Aboriginal peoples are "Canadians" in this broad sense of the word: that is, members of Aboriginal nations and members of the confederation of the Aboriginal nations and the federal-provincial confederation. Furthermore, if the Assembly of First Nations gains democratic legitimacy among Aboriginal peoples, it could take on a role analogous to the federal government.[16]

The problem of Aboriginal-Canadian relations is that Aboriginal peoples have been treated as if they were within the second, federal-provincial, confederation, and subject to its laws, either as individual citizens, minorities, or quasi-autonomous governing units analogous to municipalities or provinces (as, for example, in the Charlottetown

Accord). Not only is this colonial relationship unjust, for the reasons I have sketched out, it is impractical. Aboriginal peoples are brought into a confederation they had no role in setting up and in which they are overwhelmed by non-Aboriginal laws and ways, as well as by the greater power of the provinces. They have struggled against it in each of its phases.

A recent example of this is the current federal government's pragmatic policy on Aboriginal self-government.[17] They refuse to engage in so-called abstract questions of justice related to the inherent right of Aboriginal self-government. Instead, they assume it is a right within Canadian law and then proceed to negotiate land claims and self-government as a package of minority rights under Canadian law. Although some of the agreements might be roughly the same in practice as agreements that would be reached under the five principles, the policy has two defects that may generate perverse effects in practice. First, because it finesses rather than faces the first principle of mutual recognition, it is unjust and serves to perpetuate the colonial relationship. The Aboriginal people involved do not gain the decolonisation and recognition they seek and deserve and, as a result, feel done down and dissatisfied with the agreement, as well as alienated from other Aboriginal nations who hold out for proper recognition. Nevertheless, the Aboriginal people involved feel constrained to agree because they fear that if they hold out, a future government, riding the backlash, will give them no recognition whatsoever. Consequently, the negotiation is a modus vivendi rather than a just agreement.[18] Second, because the status of Aboriginal peoples as equal, coexisting, and self-governing nations and the process of decolonisation are not explained to non-Aboriginal peoples, these ad hoc negotiations look like the granting of special status to a minority and the violation of the principle of equality before the law. Non-Aboriginal Canadians feel their interests have not been properly represented and justice has not been served. This fuels the backlash and further confrontations, as the federal government should have learned from the last one hundred years of similar policies.

If the two confederations were acknowledged, Aboriginal peoples would gain the recognition they deserve, yet they would still form part of Canada in the broader sense of a political association of two confederations. Very little change to the Canadian Constitution would be required. Section 91(24) of the Constitution can be read as recognising the existence of the first confederation. Section 25 specifies the treaty character of the relations of the confederation, and §35 could be amended to recognise and affirm an inherent right of self-government.

There are two practical advantages to this arrangement. First, most Canadians wish to affirm the Aboriginal presence *in* Canada, and most Aboriginal peoples wish to affirm their status as equal, coexisting, and self-governing peoples *and* their attachment to Canada. The only way these reasonable demands can be reconciled is to expand our postcolonial horizons and think of Canada and Canadians in the broad, two-confederation sense. Second, Aboriginal peoples would no longer be erroneously assimilated to some sort of minority or unrealistic province-like status. They would not be seen as competing with multicultural groups on the one hand or with provinces on the other. If Aboriginal peoples were regarded in this distinctive and historically accurate way, their relationship *with* rather than *within* the federal-provincial confederation, as well as their place in Canada in the broad sense, would be seen for what it is: sui generis (of its own kind).

Intercultural Dialogue

Once the way Aboriginal and non-Aboriginal peoples should recognise each other has been established, the next question will be how should they work out their relations together. The answer is through dialogues of negotiation in which they meet as equals. Dialogue is the form of human relationship in which mutual understanding and agreement can be reached and, hence, consent can replace coercion and confrontation. Between Aboriginal and non-Aboriginal people, it is an intercultural dialogue in which the partners aim to reach mutual understanding and uncoerced agreements by contextually appropriate forms of negotiation and reciprocal questioning on how they should cooperate and review their relations of cooperation over time. Specific types of relations are agreed to, written down as treaties, put into practice, and reviewed and renewed. It is not a once-and-for-all agreement, as in social contract theories, nor an accord frozen in a constitutional document. It is a conversation between the members of Aboriginal and non-Aboriginal cultures in all walks of life over the time they live together and share this land.

An intercultural dialogue is different from a dialogue within Aboriginal or non-Aboriginal cultures. Here the participants discuss and act in the customary practices of their culture. They acquire the abilities to think and act in these customary ways, and to reflect on and revise them, by growing up in their cultures. This implicit cultural sociability, or shared cultural understanding, of how to speak and act together is just what it means to be a member of a dynamic culture, or cultures, and to have a cultural identity, or identities, whether one is Haida and Canadian or Prince Edward Islander and Canadian.

When Aboriginal and non-Aboriginal partners engage in a dialogue to reach agreement on something or other, they unavoidably bring their cultural understandings with them, yet they enter a space where their cultures overlap – a middle ground. The dialogue is therefore intercultural, and more difficult for that reason. All sorts of misunderstandings arise just because the partners act implicitly in accordance with their different cultural understandings and expectations. There is a temptation for the more powerful to overcome these difficulties by forcing their cultural ways of speaking and acting on the other and to justify this by their presumed superiority. This was the role of the stages view discussed earlier.

The new relationship has no place for the injustice of non-Aboriginal people speaking for Aboriginal people, either in the imperial monologue of command and obedience or in the more subtle injustice of permitting Aboriginal people to speak, but only in the languages, traditions, and institutions of the dominant society. Justice demands a democratic dialogue in which partners listen to and speak with, rather than for, each other. Each speak in their own languages and customary ways, on equal footing, in order to reach fair agreements. This principle of self-identification, of listening to the voices of others in their own terms and traditions, is now widely recognised as the first step in a just dialogue.

This seems like an impossible task only because of another false assumption of the imperial age: that cultures are independent, closed, and internally homogeneous. As we have learned over the last sixty years, cultures are interdependent, overlapping, and internally complex. Cultures exist in dynamic processes of interaction, negotiation, internal challenge, and reinterpretation and transformation. As a result, humans are always members to varying degrees of more than one culture. They experience misunderstandings and differences within their first cultures – such as between genders, generations, and classes – that are not completely different in kind from misunderstandings and differences across cultures. Cultural understanding and identity is thus enormously more complex, open-textured, interactive, and dynamic than the old vision of closed and homogeneous cultures presupposed.

So, when Aboriginal and non-Aboriginal partners meet on the middle ground, they are not trapped in closed and mutually incommensurable worldviews. They have been interacting for over three hundred years. Interaction has shaped the cultural identities of both in complex ways (even giving rise to a distinctive intercultural people, the Métis), and it has brought into being a multitude of intercultural ways of discussing and acting together. The treaty system is perhaps the best known of these practices, woven together out of customs from many cultures, but there are innumerable others. An intercultural middle ground thus already exists, where the cultural understandings of the partners, while not the same as their first cultures, are not completely foreign. There is enough shared ground for them to find their feet together.

It is important not to misunderstand this inherited intercultural middle ground on which Aboriginal and non-Aboriginal people must begin to discuss their ways of cooperating in the future. It is far from an ideal speech situation. It is shot through with relations of inequality, force and fraud, broken promises, failed accords, degrading stereotypes, misrecognition, paternalism, enmity, and distrust. Notwithstanding, there is also a multiplicity of paths and ways Aboriginal and non-Aboriginal people have walked together in peace and friendship over their long history, with good intentions and mutual respect. They have shared goods and knowledge, made treaties and traded together, built bridges, airlines, and computer systems, managed resources, learned about ecology and language, defended Canada together through many wars, fallen in love, and stood in mutual awe of each others' art and spirituality. The resulting intercultural institutions and practices, as distorted as they are, provide the starting ground for a new dialogue of equality. There is no alternative, no ideal speech situation, no esperanto language of discussion that transcends Aboriginal and non-Aboriginal cultures, no one universal language.

As Aboriginal and non-Aboriginal people begin to converse on the distorted intercultural middle ground by trying to recognise each other as equals and accord mutual respect to each other's cultures, they can exchange their different stories, and, through the long process of question and answer, free each other from their deep-seated misunderstandings. In this way, dialogue itself will gradually transform from within the distorted intercultural practices, in accordance with the demands of justice. One example of this is the intercultural dialogue that has developed around recent constitutional and treaty negotiations and the Canadian Royal Commission on Aboriginal Peoples. Aboriginal and non-Aboriginal speakers have broken down the hegemony of the old imperial languages of European political traditions and gradually developed forms of expression that are faithful to their own traditions yet understandable to others.

Intercultural dialogue has deep roots in Aboriginal cultures, in diplomatic relations among nations, in the exchange of stories at public feasts, in the consensus forms of government, and in elder-child relations. In non-Aboriginal cultures undistorted dialogue is the norm implicit in many of the most-valued practices and institutions, from parliamentary democracy and free speech to relations of mutual understanding and criticism in the sciences. Dialogue with the aim of uncoerced agreements is thus the implicit norm of free relationships in both Western and Aboriginal cultures.

Furthermore, there is a special bond that holds the partners, and indeed the country, together in an intercultural dialogue. For many Aboriginal and non-Aboriginal Canadians, the history of their association with members of the other community has become part of their identity as Canadians. The bond is not one of unity of purpose but of a partnership in a shared history with people whom they recognise as different. The understandings of the shared history are of course very different. Nevertheless, for many people this is one vital aspect of their identity as Canadians; not just that there are members of the other group present in Canada but that there is a partnership, a shared life.

One purpose these Canadians share is sustaining the partnership, the historical conversation between them, as part of their sense of identity as Canadians. It cannot be the aim of a partnership of this kind to reduce one partner to the image of the other, for the partnership exists in virtue of the recognition and maintenance of their differences. This is a unique form of association that has developed in spite of the long struggle to reduce the relationship to a unity. In many respects it resembles the partnership between many English-speaking Canadians and Québécois and Québécoises. Its disappearance would be experienced as an irreparable loss, like the loss of a close friend. This fragile bond, this tangled sense of being woven together like different yet inseparable rows of wampum beads in an ancient belt that have rubbed themselves smooth over long use, is often overlooked. Yet, after all is said and done, it is the sort of bond that holds a confederation together. This shared sense of a destiny together, for better or worse, provides the element in which intercultural dialogue has its life and hope.

Mutual Respect

Once Aboriginal and non-Aboriginal peoples recognise each other as equals, it is necessary that they go on to show respect for each other – for their languages, cultures, laws, and governments – in their dialogue and in their conduct together if their relations are to be harmonious.

Respect has a somewhat different significance in Aboriginal and non-Aboriginal cultures. In many Aboriginal groups, particularly those adhering to traditional ways, great respect is shown to an elder who has lived long and acquired wisdom. Here respect is accorded in virtue of the specific worthiness of the individual person. This kind of respect relative to specific worth is common in many Aboriginal relations. However, there is another sense of respect in which it is bestowed on all members of the circle of life just in virtue of their *being* members of the circle of life: to animals, plants, waters, spirits, as well as to human beings. Failure to show respect to humans or other-than-humans means violating spiritual law and is likely to bring retribution in some form or other.

Respect is a valued aspect of relationships in non-Aboriginal cultures as well. Respect is often thought to be earned by personal effort and is therefore withheld from someone who fails to meet society's standards of behaviour. Demonstration of respect can also be demanded by persons and institutions of authority. However, there is another sense of respect that is similar to the circle of life sense in Aboriginal culture. Here, human beings are said to warrant a certain respect just in virtue of being human, of being of equal dignity and of being ends rather than means. This general sense of respect is often extended beyond the human species to all living things, to god's creatures, and to nature.

There is also a kind of mutual cultural respect that is akin to the more general, circle-of-life sense of respect in both Aboriginal and non-Aboriginal ethics. This kind of respect needs to be cultivated if mutual recognition of the two partners is to be effective and their relations harmonious. It is a public attitude of mutual respect for each other's cultures that undergirds individual self-respect, and so the ability to act freely and responsibly in public and private life. One can say that the well-being of members of both cultures is dependent on each other's attitude of cultural respect.

If a public attitude of mutual cultural disrespect prevails, as with the colonial relationship, then cultural difference is seen as a deficiency or disability. The child who enters an exclusively English- or French-language school speaking only Cree is treated as linguistically deficient. The industrial worker who goes hunting to help provide food for his extended family is treated as a delinquent worker. The teacher and boss see the attachment of the pupil and worker to their cultural differences as a sign of disrespect towards their culture and authority. Each thinks the other a bigot, intolerance and racism escalate, commands and the giving of orders replace dialogue. The sense of the pupil's and worker's self-worth is undercut, the strength of their conviction in learning and working dissipates, and self-abuse and dependency follow. This result is then pointed to by the teacher and boss to warrant and reinforce their initial disrespectful attitude, thereby closing the vicious circle. Of course, the other members of Aboriginal cultures can and do seek to shore up the self-confidence of the pupil and worker by affirming the respectability of their language and hunting. But because non-Aboriginal Canadians outnumber them to such an extent, their public attitude of cultural disrespect corrodes their cultural self-assurance as a whole.

Therefore, a public attitude of mutual cultural respect needs to accompany the mutual recognition and public acknowledgement of the equality of Aboriginal and non-Aboriginal peoples and governments. This attitude includes respect on both sides, in virtue of the membership of all Canadians in the circle of life. The justification for this attitude is partly economic self-interest, the realisation that it will provide the social basis for lives of individual initiative and economic self-sufficiency. There is also a dimension of moral consistency in extending to Aboriginal people the same kind of culture respect that European Canadians have enjoyed in their own case and that has always been the unacknowledged spring of their self-respect and initiative.

In addition to the way mutual cultural respect beneficially empowers both partners to live free and responsible lives, rather than experiencing the mutual detriment of a climate of disrespect, the experience of living in a society where a variety of languages, forms of government, economic organisations, and religions thrive and intermingle enriches each person's life, enabling them to see their own culture as one among many, and so gaining a self-critical, and tolerant attitude, rather than the haughty intolerance and stultifying dogmatism of the colonial vision. This is good in itself, but it also develops the kind of character that is needed to live and compete in the culturally diverse global market of the twenty-first century. Mutual cultural respect thus creates the positive and mutually supportive climate that enables relations among cultures to be harmonious, rather than the acrimonious and strife-ridden relations of the colonial culture of disrespect. The mutual respect for cultural diversity needs to be affirmed and taught as a fundamental characteristic of the civic ethos of Canada.

Sharing

The relations of interdependency between Aboriginal and non-Aboriginal peoples are also characterised by the principle of sharing. For relationships between the partners to evolve and develop, they must involve an element of sharing, the giving and receiving of benefits. Although sharing sustains all relations, I want to discuss its application to economic, political, and legal relations, since these are the most important and the most contested.

The practice of sharing is at the centre of many Aboriginal cultures. The harmony and balance among all living things is sustained by a chain of benevolence and gratitude. An animal that is asked to give up its life for the benefit of humans, for example, should be treated with reciprocal gratitude, usually in a ceremony of thanksgiving. The sharing of gifts accompanies commercial and treaty agreements. A person will share his goods and home with a visitor in need, who, in turn, will express the appropriate gratitude by returning the gift in kind at a later date to some other needy person. Sharing is not just one relation among many; it is seen as the basis of all relations. The bonds that hold many Aboriginal cultures together are created and renewed in great public ceremonies of sharing through the giving and receiving of gifts, such as the Potlatch among the West Coast nations.

Canada is founded on an act of sharing that is almost unimaginable in its generosity. The Aboriginal peoples shared their food, hunting, and agricultural techniques, practical knowledge, trade routes, and geographic knowledge with the needy newcomers. Without this sharing the first immigrants would have been unable to survive. As we have seen, the Aboriginal peoples formalised the relation of sharing in the early treaties in the following form: they agreed to share this land with the newcomers on the agreement that the newcomers would neither attempt to govern them nor use their land without their consent. The treaties involved other exchanges as well, such as trade, military, educational, and medical benefits, and political and legal interrelations, but the sharing of land and trade on this understanding were at the heart of the relationship.

In the early period, many of the newcomers, especially the Canadiens and Canadiennes, entered into these relations of sharing, acquiring land by agreement, exchanging gifts at treaty ceremonies and annually at trading posts in Aboriginal country, expressing gratitude to their Aboriginal hosts by practices such as thanksgiving, and developing a global trading system in which both partners shared their technologies and knowledge without assimilation. This partnership is the foundation of the Canada's economic development and wealth, a partnership that the Aboriginal peoples seek to renew.

When the colonial system was erected in the nineteenth century, government was imposed and land taken without Aboriginal consent. The original sharing of their goods and knowledge, the gift of the land, and their contribution to the trade and settlement economy were eliminated from most history books and Canada's collective memory. This act of greed and ingratitude was legitimated by the specious justifications mentioned earlier. Within the social Darwinism and racism of the colonial ideology, the Aboriginal practices of gift-giving and sharing were outlawed and classified as primitive and communistic, obstacles to the exchange and saving relations of a market economy. Aboriginal people were said to waste and squander their goods and to have contributed little if anything to Canada's growth. If they remained faithful to their ethic of sharing, this was taken as proof of their backwardness and the justification for policies of forced removal and assimilation. Despite this attempt to bury the sharing relation that is at the base of Canada's prosperity, non-Aboriginal Canadians continued to reciprocate by providing some support for the generous people who had been so ungratefully dispossessed and displaced. Unfortunately, within the distorted colonial relationship, this support was now seen as a burden and welfare, rather than a woefully unfair return, and channelled into relations of economic and social dependency, rather than the older relations of economic interdependency.

The justification for the attack on Aboriginal sharing practices was the assumption that relations of economic cooperation can evolve and be maintained on calculations of immediate self-interest alone. If this were true, then the "gift form" would be a pre-market relation and a threat to modernisation. This assumption, which prevailed for about a century, has been, however, shown to be erroneous. The older view, which the early administrators shared and learned from classic authors such as Aristotle and Cicero, has been shown to be correct by contemporary game theorists and economists. This is the view that forms of economic cooperation can evolve and be sustained only if an element of sharing or gift-giving is involved, that is, if the partners look out for their long-term shared interest to some extent and act towards each other accordingly. The people in the exchange see themselves not only as calculators of immediate advantage but as partners who share in relations of mutual benevolence and gratitude over time. If this dimension of sharing is overlooked, then, as Shakespeare classically explored in *King Lear*, the acids of ingratitude corrode the social fabric. This dimension of "sociability," as it is called, is a necessary condition of the highly complex relations of modern economic and political cooperation.

This insight is incorporated, for example, in the social policies of the European Union, in the social network of Canada and other modern societies, and in the policy of equalisation that is seen by many as a necessary bond of the Canadian confederation. The sharing involved in equalisation is partly a consideration of long-term interest; for the regions that are better off today were worse off yesterday and can reasonably expect to be again in the future, so it is in their long-term interest to be benevolent today in the expectation of gratitude tomorrow. But equalisation also goes deeper than this and closer to the Aboriginal understanding of sharing. It is the acknowledgement, essential to any cooperative partnership over the long term, that the Canadian economy is a shared enterprise to which all contribute and from which all should benefit, as a necessary condition of its overall social harmony and balance. The distribution mechanisms of the economy acting alone fail to deliver these benefits equitably (to put it mildly) and so fail to provide the conditions that enable the economy to survive.

The great question now is, how can sharing be built into a new, postcolonial relationship in order to generate mutually beneficial economic interdependence and ecologically benign forms of resource management? The answer is that, first, as in any modern cooperative relation, the partners must recognise and respect the rights of each – their rights of self-government and equality as peoples – and they must acknowledge and manifest mutual cultural respect. Under the heading of sharing, there must be a recognition and public acknowledgement of the presently unacknowledged and suppressed relation of sharing at the foundation of the Canadian confederation and economy, in our histories, narratives, and public institutions. As a long-overdue act of justice and gratitude to initiate the new relationship, Aboriginal peoples should have access to the ancestral lands that were unjustly taken from them. They should be assisted in developing economic self-reliance through new relations of economic cooperation, resource development, and the sharing of knowledge and technologies, just as they once helped non-Aboriginal people. For the partners to engage in productive relations together – and as an act of reciprocal justice – the appalling social and economic inequalities of Aboriginal peoples need to be levelled up to the Canadian equalisation norm by channeling public funding into policies of economic cooperation and self-reliance, rather than dependency, welfare, and despair. These mutually agreeable policies should aim at the development of Aboriginal economic self-sufficiency, through partnership arrangements in resource management and development, and so also the phasing out of federal financial support.

These policies will vary widely for Aboriginal nations with different land bases and for Aboriginal peoples living in urban areas and participating in the non-Aboriginal economy. However, the principle is the same in both cases; the long-overdue recognition that our present prosperity rests on an unacknowledged and unreciprocated relation of sharing extended by the Aboriginal people to all and the realisation that our future prosperity and well-being rests on equitable relations of sharing in the future.[19]

The second dimension of sharing is a just means of sharing legal and political powers. Aboriginal nations vary greatly in their ability and desire to govern themselves by their own laws. Some wish to delegate several of their powers to the federal or a provincial government and voluntarily subject themselves to those laws. Others wish to repatriate many of their legal and political powers and to govern themselves in accord with their own laws and traditions. Aboriginal peoples living off the reserves require another form of relation. One of the immense advantages of the treaty relationship over any other possible system is that it can handle this range of interdelegation of powers in a way that is responsive to local differences.

For the relations of sharing of legal and political powers to be just, they need to be based on the principles laid out above. The interdelegation relation must be based on negotiations involving intercultural dialogue between equals, based on mutual consent, recorded in treaty-like agreements, and open to review and amendment in the future. Most important, no matter how many powers an Aboriginal nation agrees to delegate to, or leave with, the federal or a provincial government, its status as an equal, self-governing nation must continue. It is worth noting that Chief Justice Marshall insisted on this in the early treaties. Citing Emeric de Vattel, he stipulated that no matter to what extent Indian nations came under the "protection" of the United States government through treaties of interdependency, they retained their "sovereignty."[20]

At the present time many laws are applied to Aboriginal peoples without their consent, many treaties have been violated, and in some cases, such as that of British Columbia, treaties have never been made. While Aboriginal peoples protest this, very few are in a position to govern themselves immediately. This dilemma is at the centre of the current expensive and destructive impasse. Aboriginal and non-Aboriginal people have a strong interest in establishing a system that is acceptable to both sides, flexible, and dependable.

The best way to deal with the transition to degrees of self-government, economic self-sufficiency, and political and economic relations of sharing is to set up a decolonisation commission, much as the League of Nations did earlier in the century for the former European colonies. Composed of Aboriginal and non-Aboriginal members and guided by the report of the Canadian Royal Commission on Aboriginal Peoples, the commission would start from the status quo and monitor the transition over the next decades.

Non-Aboriginal Canadians have, I believe, two major concerns that the commission should address. The first is that Aboriginal self-government should not involve a large sum of public money in a time of acute recession. It should, in fact, decrease the amount of public money currently distributed to Aboriginal people. The only way to meet this concern is for Aboriginal peoples to become economically self-sufficient, for which they would need a land and resource base to support Aboriginal government and economic development with the rest of Canada. This could be done by returning to the Aboriginal nations a sufficient amount of the lands that have been unjustly taken from them. As these lands and resources were developed in cooperation and Aboriginal people are employed, federal payments and exemptions could be decreased accordingly.

The size of the land base and the degree and type of self-government should be tailored to the size and locale of the Aboriginal nations. Traditional nations that have been divided into tiny bands should be encouraged to join together. The commission must ensure that, in accord with the principle of mutual recognition, the interests and rights of non-Aboriginal peoples are equally represented in the negotiations and agreements. For Aboriginal people living off the reserves, policies designed to enable them to participate in the Canadian economy would serve the same purpose. If this were explained as a matter of redress for past injustices and of decreasing federal payments, I believe most Canadians would accept it. Presumably Canadians would like to see Aboriginal people become economically independent and contribute to the Canadian economy, rather than remain a burden on it.

The second concern widely expressed by non-Aboriginal Canadians is the assurance that Aboriginal governments will not become uncontrolled dictatorships. I believe there are two related points here. One is that Aboriginal leaders be made accountable to Aboriginal people: that their rule be based on the agreement of Aboriginal citizens. The fear expressed is that as the Indian Act is dismantled, a class of Aboriginal male elites will seize power and rule despotically against their own people.[21]

This concern is shared by many Aboriginal peoples as well, especially Aboriginal women. To meet this concern, it is neither necessary nor practical that Aboriginal peoples set up representative governments modelled on non-Aboriginal governments. One of the advantages of defining Aboriginal governments as a distinct confederation is that different forms of responsible Aboriginal governments are to be expected, based on Aboriginal traditions, customs, and innovations. These forms will vary across Aboriginal nations, with their different traditions, circumstances, and needs. However, the condition of democracy must be met: Aboriginal governments must be dependent on and answerable to the people they govern in a manner appropriate to their ways. The decolonisation commission should be responsible for ensuring that this condition is met. Once it is, non-Aboriginal

Canadians should be not only satisfied but also proud of the political diversity Canada embodies.

The second point is that there should be constitutional limits on Aboriginal governments. For non-Aboriginal Canadians, the Canadian Charter of Rights and Freedoms is the most obvious example of such a limit. Consequently, this point is often expressed as a demand to impose the Charter on Aboriginal peoples. However, there are two objections to doing so that follow from the principles of mutual recognition. The federal government has no right to impose the Charter without the consent of Aboriginal peoples and although it embodies basic, cross-cultural values, it does so in a specific manner that is shaped by the cultures, history, and circumstances of non-Aboriginal Canadians. Aboriginal governments require Charter limits that Aboriginal peoples agree to and that derive from Aboriginal cultures, history, and circumstances.

The basic limits are the rights and freedoms of due process, the ability of citizens to participate in their governments, freedom of speech, gender equality, security of the person, and so on. These values, shared by Aboriginal and non-Aboriginal peoples, are given constitutional expression in a wide variety of forms in different countries. Even within Canada, the Charter is applied differently in different regions. Therefore, these shared values need to be formulated in a manner that is appropriate to Aboriginal cultures and ways, just as the Charter is appropriate to the distinctive ways of non-Aboriginal Canadians. There are numerous methods by which this could be done. For example, an Aboriginal Justice on the Supreme Court, an Aboriginal interpretive clause in the Charter, and changes to the Charter similar to those proposed in the Charlottetown Accord have been suggested. Another alternative, favoured by many male and female Aboriginal citizens, is for Aboriginal peoples to develop their own Charters and appeal to them in their own courts.

In addition, Aboriginal governments will be constrained by a variety of United Nations agreements and the evolving international law of indigenous peoples. The negotiations between Aboriginal and non-Aboriginal partners concerning health care, justice, resource development, environmental protection, and employment will involve yet more limitations. The decolonisation commission should ensure that these limitations are established in the transition to self-government.[22]

Mutual Responsibility

The final principle of a just relationship is that the partners act responsibly towards one another and towards the habitat they share.

Aboriginal Elders explain that the identity of their people is related to the places they live in; that the Creator has placed them here with the responsibility to care for all the ecologically interrelated forms of life in all their harmonious diversity. This timeless responsibility involves looking back to the wisdom of one's ancestors and forward to the seventh generation in the future. This unshakeable sense of responsibility to the source and network of life is at the core of Aboriginal identity. As noted earlier, it is coupled with a strong sense of self-, or individual, responsibility. A person learns to take up this responsibility to others and the environment through an individual quest for understanding of, and attunement to, his or her place in nature, a quest that marks the passage to adulthood. (This idea is familiar to many Canadians through the song by Susan Aglukark entitled "Shamaya.")

It would be idealistic to hold that this twofold ethic of responsibility finds perfect expression in the organisation and administration of the everyday affairs of Aboriginal peoples. Still, the Elders who emphasise responsibility more than rights to do as one pleases are speaking from an ancient and powerful understanding of the nature of humankind and its place in the larger community of life on this planet. Younger people, in positions of leadership as well as in positions of dependency and despair, are turning to them for guidance and inner strength.

Non-Aboriginal people of European extraction have their own cultural understanding of responsibility. A high value is placed on individual responsibility, and individual freedom is associated with responsibility in many traditions. The sense of individual responsibility extends out to care for one's family and friends and care for the common good of one's communities, from local associations to the Canadian federation, and to a sense of responsibility for endangered peoples and species around the globe.

Although an exploitative stance of irresponsibility towards nature prevailed over the last century, on the assumption that nature was a limitless resource for the use and abuse of the human species, this faustian presumption has been discredited. Many people, especially in the environmental sciences, argue that this stance has caused enormous damage to the environment and threatens to render the planet uninhabitable. There is a dawning awareness of the environment as a living system of interdependency in which humans, as one member among millions, have responsibilities of caretaking for its delicately balanced ecological diversity. In this view, we should be responsible for the caretaking of ecological diversity for the same reason that we should be responsible for cultural diversity, as the very condition of our existence and well-being.

The change in attitude from the earlier, exploitative stance is even deeper than this for many Canadians. It is the sense that the diverse ways of life of Canadian peoples have their history and their being in this encompassing and awe-inspiring ecological diversity. To act irresponsibly is not just short-sighted but a spiritual failure; an act of sacrilege and desecration against the source of being of the peoples we are.

This broader vision of Canada as a harmonious confederation of cultural and ecological diversity and of Canadians as caretakers of this irreplaceable dwelling place of endless beauty can be understood to some extent in the spiritual traditions of non-Aboriginal Canadians. However, there is something distinctively Canadian about this emerging sense of identity, as if Canadians have finally freed themselves from their colonial habit of defining themselves in traditions derived from Europe and have taken responsibility for defining themselves. It is not surprising, therefore, that many have turned to the indigenous Canadian wisdom of Aboriginal Elders for guidance and cooperation in working out an ethic of responsibility appropriate to this new vision of Canada. Mutual responsibility, then, provides the final fibre for weaving a just and inspiring partnership between Aboriginal and non-Aboriginal peoples.

ABORIGINAL SELF-GOVERNMENT AND LIBERAL DEMOCRACY

The arguments given above show that a just relationship between Aboriginal and non-Aboriginal peoples embodies familiar principles. I would now like to argue that the relationship preserves, and indeed enhances, the goods that citizens expect from a liberal democracy. For there would be a deep conflict in values if removing the colonial relation between Aboriginal and non-Aboriginal peoples in the name of justice, equality, and self-government led to a society in which other values associated with liberal democracies were thereby compromised. It is important to see that this is not the case. Indeed, the new relationship preserves the values of a liberal democracy in a way appropriate to a just, culturally diverse society, and thus it will be an exemplar for other plural societies in the twenty-first century.

Aboriginal and non-Aboriginal peoples expect a political association to provide the basis for the individual freedom and dignity of its members in both the public and private spheres. It should enable them to participate freely and with equal dignity in governing their society and to live their private lives in accordance with their own choices and responsibilities. The first good, civic participation, cannot be achieved by seeking to assimilate Aboriginal peoples to non-Aboriginal forms of government. This is not only unjust, for the reasons given, it is the cause of the alienation, anomie, and defiance that come to any free people who are forcibly governed by alien laws and ways. Self-government enables Aboriginal peoples, just as it enables non-Aboriginal peoples, to participate in governing their societies in accord with their own laws and cultural understanding of democracy, to overcome alienation, and to regain their dignity as equal and active citizens. This, in turn, generates a strong sense of pride in, and allegiance to, the Canadian confederation as a whole, because it is the protector, rather than the destroyer, of self-government and citizen participation.

The crucial feature of democratic participation and citizen dignity is not a canonical form of institutions. This assumption was one of the mistakes in the stages view of historical development. Rather, the practice of government should rest on the sovereignty of the people, enabling them to exercise their powers of self-rule in culturally appropriate ways and to amend or overthrow the government if it thwarts their powers. Accordingly, the forms of democratic participation and citizen dignity appropriate to Aboriginal and non-Aboriginal peoples are similar but not identical.

Aboriginal peoples, with their smaller societies, tend to place greater emphasis on direct participation and government by consensus. In many cases, political authority rests on the ability of the person or council to sustain the actual consent of each citizen over time. When ongoing consent is lacking, the people often form sovereign bodies, such as healing circles, to reform defective practices. The inequalities of rule imposed through the Indian Act, such as that of men over women, are being dissolved as the colonial system is dismantled and these democratic forms are revitalised and renovated, in a way analogous to the reform of gender inequalities in non-Aboriginal governments. Although these forms of face-to-face self-government have always been an ideal in Western traditions, non-Aboriginal governments, due to their size and degree of institutionalisation, place more emphasis on representative government and majority rule, with compulsory obedience even if citizens dissent from the outcomes. And, alas, reform is not as easy in these large forms as in the smaller and more consensual Aboriginal governments.[23]

The second good, individual freedom and responsibility, is equally important. It too is understood in slightly different ways in both cultures. Aboriginal peoples in general have a strong sense of responsibility to their communities, combined with an equally strong commitment not to interfere with but only to provide suggestive role models for the freedom of the individual in taking up these responsibilities

in an autonomous way. As a result, there is in general a larger commitment to individual freedom in parenting, friendship, and work
than in non-Aboriginal societies, where a greater degree of intervention and conformity are seen to be necessary and valuable.

The protection and enhancement of both civic and individual freedom and responsibility has always been the primary concern of liberalism. In recent years liberal theorists have asked how these values can
be preserved in the more culturally diverse, postcolonial societies of
today.[24] They have argued that the social condition of being able to
exercise civic and individual freedom in pursuing and revising one's
life plans is that people should be members of viable cultures that
provide the necessary and partly constitutive context for individual
autonomy and choice. Consequently, viable cultures are now seen as
a primary good of a liberal society.

Previous liberal theorists agreed with this view but presumed that
modern European cultures were superior cultural bases for individual
freedom. Since they presumed that these "superior" cultures developed as a result of modernisation itself, they held that governments
need not be concerned with cultural preservation once non-Europeans
were drawn or coerced into the process of modernisation. They could
therefore look on the extinguishment of cultural diversity and the
inculcation of European culture with indifference or moral approval.

In hindsight, theorists now see that this line of argument of liberalism during the imperial age not only misunderstood the relation of
cultural diversity to modernisation but also overlooked another condition of individual freedom and responsibility: self-respect. A person
can engage in citizenship and personal freedom only if she or he has
a threshold of self-respect; a sense of his or her own value and the
secure conviction that what he or she has to say and do in politics and
life are worthwhile. The social basis of self-respect is that others recognise the value of one's activities and goals, that there is an association in which individuals can acquire a level of confidence in the worth
of what they say and do. Since what individuals say and do and the
plans they formulate and revise are partly constituted by their cultural
identity, the condition of self-respect is a society in which their culture,
or cultures, is recognised and affirmed by others, both by those who
do and those who do not share that culture, or cultures.

Consequently, a society whose members view the disappearance of
the cultures of other members with indifference or moral approval or
treat them with indignity, derision, and contempt destroys the self-
respect of those members and, in so doing, undermines their abilities
to be citizens and autonomous individuals in work and private life.
The disastrous effects of successive policies of cultural destruction and

assimilation on the self-respect of Aboriginal peoples proves this obvious but overlooked point beyond reasonable doubt. Thus, if a liberal democratic society is to provide the basis for its two most important liberties, civic and personal liberty, it must protect the cultures of its members and engender the public attitude of mutual respect for cultural diversity that self-respect requires.

There are many ways this can be done: by protecting all Canadian cultures from Americanisation, by accepting each province's right to govern in accordance with its distinct laws and ways, and by recognising official language minorities, multiculturalism, and the special role of Quebec in protecting its culturally diverse, predominantly French-speaking society. For Aboriginal cultures there is only one just way this can be done: by recognising their inherent right to govern themselves in accordance with their own cultures and engendering among both Aboriginal and non-Aboriginal people respect for each others' cultures. Consequently, the mutual recognition of Aboriginal and non-Aboriginal peoples as equal, coexisting and self-governing peoples is not only just but also preserves and enhances the values of liberal democracy in a manner appropriate to a culturally diverse and post-colonial age.

CONCLUSION

There are two major objections to the relationship I have recommended. The first is that it is incompatible with individual equality and rights. I have responded to this by showing that the opposite is the case. Individual equality and rights enable citizens to participate in government and to exercise their individual freedom in the private sphere. The mutual recognition of and respect for Aboriginal and non-Aboriginal peoples as equal, coexisting, and self-governing peoples provides the conditions for equality of civic participation and individual freedom in a culturally diverse society. In addition, this proposal complements Canada's long liberal, common-law tradition of accommodating individual rights and equality with the preservation and promotion of the various cultures of its citizens.

The second objection is that this kind of legal, political, and cultural pluralism will lead to the disunity of the confederation. Again, the opposite is the case. The assumption that the unity of a political association requires the uniformity of its members derives from the early-modern period of national consolidation and centralisation, when cultural differences were experienced as a threat to one's own insular identity and treated as inferior. It has no place in the world of today.

The proof is in the dismal record in practice. The attempts to gain unity through uniformity have failed. The Aboriginal peoples have suffered centuries of policies designed to assimilate or integrate them, on the assumption that the unity of a political association requires uniformity. These concerted efforts have caused resistance, despair, and confrontation. Other cultural members of the Canadian confederation have suffered analogous forms of suppression in the name of national unity. None of these efforts have succeeded, except in the case of the extinction of a number of Aboriginal peoples of Canada. Rather, these imperious attempts to impose a uniform and homogeneous Canadian identity have led to one crisis of unity after another. The record is abhorrent and intolerable.

On the contrary, the recognition and accommodation of cultural, legal, and political diversity historically has eased the confrontations and conflicts in Canadian society and enabled the members of the confederation to work together on their common problems and aspirations. We must draw on these rich sources of plural government and mutual respect, beneath the dead machinery of uniformity, and show to ourselves and others that unity and strength derive from the love of a confederation that protects and harmonises, rather than assaults and denigrates, our diverse identities.

I would like to conclude with a description of the end or goal of this relationship: the mode of life Aboriginal peoples are struggling to bring into being by transforming the colonial relationship into one of mutual recognition, intercultural dialogue, mutual respect, sharing, and responsibility. The Aboriginal narratives I am familiar with are emancipatory. They provide a history of their people, the relatively recent period of European-Canadian arrival and domination, and a path of possible liberation. As we learned at the colloquium from which this volume originated, these narratives provide a "profound history" in terms of which the original inhabitants of North America understand where they are coming from, where they are, and where they are headed. Not surprisingly, Aboriginal emancipation does not involve a new or higher stage of history, as in many Western narratives, but, rather, the restoration of an indigenous harmony among peoples and between humans and nature that existed before the arrival of Europeans. Harmony is seen as working through the diversity of things and the endless play of differences, as the spirit that informs the whole.[25]

In many Aboriginal narratives this harmonious diversity was disrupted by the invasion and occupation of strangers whose restless mode of life is out of tune with the ways of this continent. Nonetheless, harmony will be restored in the long run. It will win out because it is "indigenous," both in the descriptive sense that it is embodied in the ecology, Aboriginal peoples, and ways of North America and in the normative sense that it is appropriate or fitting for this place. Harmony will be restored by gradually infusing the diverse ways of both Aboriginal and non-Aboriginal peoples and the relations among them. So, someday, we all, Aboriginal and non-Aboriginal, will be indigenous. One cannot understand the miraculous endurance of so many Aboriginal people in the face of so much power expended to dispossess and efface them unless one grasps this profound orientation in the world, which, generation after generation, provides the aim and ethical source of their refusal to surrender. The relationship I have sketched in this chapter is a poor attempt to give academic expression to this sense of harmony that animates the struggles we are trying to understand.

The indigenous way of being in the world, of harmony in diversity, requires a great symbol to give it expression. In 1991 a black bronze canoe, six metres in length, was placed in the courtyard of the Canadian embassy in Washington, DC, as a symbol of Canada as it enters the uncertain waters of the twenty-first century. Called *The Spirit of Haida Gwaii*, this awe-inspiring work of art by the Haida and Canadian artist Bill Reid contains thirteen distinct crew members from Haida mythology: the raven, grizzly, eagle, frog, mouse woman, dogfish woman, beaver, a human paddler named "the ancient reluctant conscript," and, standing among this diverse crew of partners, a chief who bears the wonderfully enigmatic name of "who is he going to be?"[26]

The myth creatures all struggle for and receive recognition in the canoe in different ways. Each has their own cultural history and identity in Haida mythology, and each has a competing story about their long travels together. In spite of all their obvious distinctness and differences, they overlap and criss-cross with each other in inexhaustible and unheard-of ways. The chief stands in the middle, recognising and listening to each and providing guidance. Raven is at the helm to remind you that their diverse cultural identities and tangled forms of self-rule are important but even more complex than they appear at first sight. In the great raven stories one learns too that the partners in this wonderful confederation get over their occasional conflicts and quarrels because they have a sense of humour and know how to laugh at themselves. Yet, for all this seemingly impossible diversity, the oars and paddles of the partners are in unison, and the canoe glides harmoniously into dawn of the new century.

3 Indigenous Movements and Politics in Mexico and Latin America

RODOLFO STAVENHAGEN

THE RETURN OF THE NATIVES

The emergence in recent years of indigenous peoples as new social and political actors in Latin America can be seen as an instance of the transformation of the state and the transition to new and more democratic forms of existence. During the colonial period indigenous peoples had a fixed status in society, but since the emergence of independent republics in the region almost two hundred years ago, indigenous peoples have been involved in an uneasy and ambiguous relationship with the state and its institutions. As Latin American countries approach the new millennium, they are now faced with the task of reassessing this relationship in the light of the new emerging Indian identities that articulate old grievances and express new demands. The once fashionable theories of social change, modernization, and nation-building that dominated social science thinking for over half a century are now being challenged by the new social movements of indigenous peoples and their developing political ideologies. The peace accord that the government and the revolutionary insurgency in Guatemala signed in December 1996 to end a thirty-year-long civil war included among its first points the issue of indigenous peoples' culture and rights. One of the pebbles in the shoes of the Sandinista government in Nicaragua during the 1980s was the unresolved issue of autonomy for the indigenous peoples of the Atlantic Coast. Bolivia's new political constitution refers to the country as being multiethnic, plurilingual, and multicultural. The Zapatista Army of National Liberation, which declared war on the Mexican national government in a spectacular uprising on 1 January 1994, is made up of Indians and strives for the recognition of indigenous demands. Politics in Latin America can no longer ignore "the return of the natives," long neglected by politicians and power brokers, as well as by intellectuals and policymakers.

To the extent that this problematique is common to various countries in the region, I will refer in this chapter both to issues specific to Mexico as well as to some of the more general processes that are relevant to a better understanding of the situation of indigenous peoples in Latin America. The starting point of this story might well have been the formal beginning of a continent-wide Indianist policy (better known as *indigenismo*) at the Inter-American Indianist Congress held in Pátzcuaro, Mexico, in 1940. It was here that the assembled government delegates decided to pursue policies designed to improve the lives and livelihoods of the continent's indigenous populations, mainly through measures intended to assimilate them into the so-called national mainstream. As defined by the then-prevailing nationalist ideologies that had arisen during the preceding century, the urban *mestizo* middle-class intellectuals and their political offshoots usually rejected the indigenous components of the national culture. They actually saw no future for them, except in an idealized past whose privileged locus turned out to be the museums, and more recently as an instrument for earning foreign exchange in the form of tourism and handicrafts. *Indigenismo* evolved into a set of social policies intended to "integrate" the numerous Indian communities and tribes into the life of the nation as defined by the governing elites. It has always been the instrument of the national state for dealing with the Indians, rather than a process whereby the Indians themselves could achieve greater freedoms, rights, and participation in the political and economic system.

WHO ARE THE INDIANS?

Indigenista policies, while undoubtedly well-intentioned, actually turned out to be ethnocidal and quite ineffectual even by the standards of their own declared objectives. At the periodically held Inter-American Indianist Congresses (the eleventh such congress took place in Nicaragua in December 1993), delegates routinely decried the sorry state of the continent's indigenous peoples. While governments would report on their programs and development plans, often in self-congratulatory language, indigenous peoples were given only a token presence at these congresses, even as their socioeconomic situation deteriorated noticeably. A recent World Bank study concludes that poverty among Latin America's indigenous populations is pervasive and severe. Moreover, it considers that the living conditions of the indigenous population are generally "abysmal," especially when compared to those of the nonindigenous population.[1] Long before the World Bank took notice, Indian spokespeople and their advocates had been insisting, with little success, on the need to combat the poverty and "marginalization" of indigenous communities in the Americas. Although Mexican presidential candidates routinely promise to redress the "historical lag" (*rezago histórico*) of their Indian compatriots when their campaign trips bring them into contact with them, Indians have learned to distrust this public rhetoric and have long relied on traditional patron-client relationships with local politicians and bureaucrats to obtain small gains or redress specific grievances. Since the Mexican revolution, the corporate structure of the political system has been able to maintain a certain degree of control over the indigenous populations. But this picture was abruptly challenged by the armed uprising of the Zapatista Army of National Liberation in the jungles of southeastern Mexico at the beginning of 1994, even as official Mexico proclaimed its entry into the "First World" through the North American Free Trade Agreement (NAFTA).

Who are the Indians in Latin America, and how many are there? Whereas criteria used in definitions vary from country to country and census data are notoriously unreliable, knowledgeable estimates consider that there are over four hundred different identifiable Indian groups, with a total population of close to forty million, that range from some numerically insignificant, almost extinct jungle bands in the Amazon to multimillion-strong peasant societies in the Andes. Mexico has the largest number of indigenous people in Latin America, about ten million, but they represent only between 12 and 15 percent of the total population. According to census information, in 1990 almost six and a half million people spoke an Indian language, representing almost 8 percent of Mexico's total population. But given the notorious deficiencies in census gathering, particularly in the rural areas, and considering that the linguistic criterion is not the only one that defines Indian identity in Mexico, scholars estimate that the actual Indian population is at least 50 percent higher than that given by census figures. Fifty-six different linguistic groups are officially recognized, ranging from small communities on the verge of cultural extinction, to the million-strong speakers of the Nahuatl and Maya languages.[2]

By way of contrast, in Guatemala and Bolivia Indians constitute the majority of the national population, and in Peru and Ecuador they come close.[3] Although Brazil's Indians represent less than one-half of

1 percent of the population, as the original inhabitants of the Amazon basin they have played a significant role in recent years, resisting encroachment upon their territories, claiming land rights and political representation, struggling for the preservation of the Amazon environment, and achieving their incorporation into the new Brazilian constitution adopted in 1988.

The substantial body of *indigenista* legislation usually placed the indigenous peoples at a disadvantage in relation to the rest of society, even when many laws were of a protective and tutelary nature. While formal citizenship to all nationals was granted in most states after independence, in some nations Indians continued to be treated until very recently as minors and as legally incompetent. It was not until the last decade or so that Latin America's basic laws were modified in a spate of constitutional reforms. These reforms not only include norms regarding native languages and cultures but in some cases also address indigenous communities and their territories as specific forms of social organization: Argentina, Bolivia, Brazil, Colombia, Ecuador, Guatemala, Mexico, Nicaragua, Panama, Paraguay, and Peru have all undertaken such constitutional reform in recent years. Some observers place this restructuring within the framework of the "wave of democratization" that has occurred in Latin America during the 1970s and 1980s; others recognize the active role that indigenous organizations themselves played in stimulating these changes.[4]

Mexico was an early proponent of *indigenista* policies, and for many years around the middle of the century its handling of state-Indian relations through the federal National Indianist Institute (Instituto Nacional Indigenista) was considered a model for other countries. The INI had been set up in the 1940s by a group of dedicated officials who had the ear of the national authorities. Scholars-cum-politicians such as Alfonso Caso and Gonzalo Aguirre Beltrán developed a theory of *indigenista* action that had wide repercussions in the ensuing debates over the relations between the state and its indigenous populations.[5] Mexico, however, was a latecomer to the wave of constitutional reform taking place in Latin America. In fact, shortly after political independence in the early nineteenth century, Mexico proclaimed the equality of all of its citizens, and special reference to Indians in legal documents was avoided. The 1917 Political Constitution refers to the rights of peasant communities in article 27, which deals with agrarian matters, but avoids any ethnic identification. By 1992, however, things had changed and the new amendment to article 4 of the constitution, adopted by the Congress that year, recognized that the nation's pluricultural makeup is based on its original indigenous inhabitants. Article 27, a mainstay of peasant agrarian demands, which had previously been changed to allow for the privatization of communal property, now included a reference to "the lands of indigenous communities." However, these changes have not had any practical effect. By 1998 no secondary legislation deriving from the new article 4 of the constitution had been enacted, and the project of a new law on indigenous rights and culture, to have been presented jointly by the government and the Zapatistas (as a first result of preliminary peace talks between the two antagonists), had become bogged down in the Congress. In contrast, the local Congress of Oaxaca passed a law in 1998 that recognized the specific rights of the state's Indian peoples.[6]

THE RISE OF INDIGENOUS ORGANIZATIONS

The rise of indigenous organizations over the last three decades may be considered both cause and effect of the transformations regarding indigenous peoples in Latin America occurring in the public sphere. In the 1960s there was only a handful of formal organizations created and run by indigenous persons and pursuing objectives of interest to indigenous peoples as such. By the mid-1990s there were many hundreds of such associations of all types and kinds: local-level organizations, intercommunal and regional associations, formally structured interest groups, national-level federations, leagues, and unions, as well as cross-national alliances and coalitions with well-developed international contacts and activities. Truly, it can be said that indigenous organizations, their leadership, objectives, activities, and emerging ideologies, constitute a new kind of social and political movement in contemporary Latin America whose detailed history and analysis has still not been undertaken.[7]

An earlier organization, frequently considered as the prototype of others, is the Shuar Federation, established in the early 1960s to protect the interests of the various dispersed Shuar communities in the Amazon lowlands of eastern Ecuador. The Shuar decided to form their federation to defend their land from encroachment by outside settlers and commercial interests and in the process discovered that the struggle over land rights could not be separated from their survival as an ethnically distinct people with their own traditions and cultural identity. They also discovered, as so many oppressed peoples have throughout history, that only by joining forces and uniting efforts would they be able to achieve their purpose. Though motivated by economic and social considerations (preservation of ancestral lands, access to productive resources), the struggle of the Shuar cannot be described strictly as a "class struggle," in distinction to the conflicts over land between peasants and landowners that took place more or less at the same time in the Andean highlands. To the extent that the Shuar and other lowland indigenous peoples were not inserted clearly in an agrarian class structure, their organization took on a more communal and ethnic character than the more class-oriented movements of indigenous peasants elsewhere in Latin America.[8]

While occasional associations including the label "indigenous" or "Indian" did arise in Mexico, the birth of the contemporary Indian peoples' movements can be traced in that country to the mid-1970s. In 1974, to commemorate the 500th anniversary of the birth of Bartolomé de las Casas, Bishop of Chiapas and known to history for his public denunciations of the atrocities committed by the Spanish invaders against the Indians in the Americas, a national Indian congress was organized in Chiapas under the auspices of the government and with the participation of the local bishop, Samuel Ruiz. At this meeting indigenous participants were highly critical of the paternalistic, authoritarian "indigenist" policies of the government and vividly denounced the insufferable living conditions to which they were usually subjected. One year later the national government promoted the creation of the National Council of Indigenous Peoples (CNPI), which it hoped to control and manipulate, as it did with so many of the "popular" organizations grouped within the corporate structure of the PRI, Mexico's official ruling political party. By that time, however, a new generation of articulate indigenous representatives was taking control of these organizations, and at the 1975 Indigenous Congress in the historic location of Pátzcuaro, which was promoted by the national government, they refused entry to nonindigenous participants (including sympathetic indigenous advocates, as well as government representatives). Meanwhile, in response to increasing criticism, the Mexican government's indigenous affairs department, the Instituto Nacional Indigenista (INI), proclaimed a new policy of indigenous "participation" (*indigenismo de participación*), but in fact nothing much changed in the government's handling of its relations with indigenous peoples. During the ensuing years, in the 1970s and 1980s, a feverish process of organization and mobilization resulted in the emergence of numerous local-level indigenous associations, as well as in efforts at regional and national articulation. Some of these were short-lived, others went through numerous phases and transformations, and only a few survived into the 1990s. Truly, this process of social mobilization falls within the domain of the "new social movements" that have taken place in many countries during the second half of this century.[9]

Organizations similar to those in Ecuador and Mexico emerged during the 1970s in several other countries, and they consolidated their activities during the 1980s. They soon managed to break out of the cocoon of "community centred" activities to which state-sponsored development projects so frequently tried to limit them. While "community development" programs, some of them financed by multilateral donor agencies and nongovernmental organizations, did generate increasing involvement by local people, it became obvious to the emerging indigenous elites that local-level activity by itself was politically limited. Like the Shuar, they were able to build a transcommunal indigenous identity involving an increasing number of local communities and emphasizing ethnic identity as a unifying bond and mobilizing agent. A number of ethnic organizations began to appear on the political scene whose leaders would speak in the name of the ethnic group as such rather than for this or that particular rural community. This level of organization was soon followed by region-wide associations involving several ethnic groups. Thus arose the Confederation of Indigenous Nationalities of the Ecuadoran Amazon (CONFENAIE), the Indigenous Association of the Peruvian Jungle (AIDESEP), the Regional Indigenous Council of the Cauca Valley (CRIC) in Colombia, the Indigenous Confederation of Eastern Bolivia (CIDOB), and many others. They all held their congresses, published their manifestos and platforms, addressed petitions to state and national governments and to the international community, and often organized militant actions such as protest marches, demonstrations, sit-ins, land occupations, and active resistance, or they initiated legal proceedings and lobbied legislatures and public officials to further their various objectives.

A more recent level of organization became the country-wide indigenous confederation. Again, the Ecuadoran Confederation of Indigenous Nationalities (CONAIE) has been at the forefront of political activity by organizing two major peaceful indigenous "uprisings" in Ecuador in 1990 and 1993 that practically paralyzed the country and forced the national government to negotiate with the indigenous peoples over agrarian and other issues. The Brazilian Union of Indian Nations (UNI), which congregates numerous Amazonian tribes, played a crucial role in the political discussions leading up to the drafting of the constitutional article devoted to indigenous peoples in the new Brazilian constitution (1988). Similarly, the Organización Indígena de Colombia (ONIC) took an active part in the national political debates that resulted in Colombia's new constitution of 1991.

Indigenous organizations have also reached out beyond their countries' borders to become involved in international activities. In Central and South America, indigenous activists attempted to set up cross-national regional organizations, with mixed success, and since the late 1980s a number of international, regional, and continental meetings have taken place in an attempt to coordinate indigenous activities surrounding the commemoration of the Quincentenary of The Encounter of Two Worlds (or 500 Years of Indigenous Resistance), the United Nations Year of Indigenous Peoples (1993), and the UN Decade for Indigenous Peoples, starting in 1995. Indigenous representatives from Latin America are active (but not quite as active as their colleagues from North America) in the discussions of the UN Working Group on Indigenous Populations that has been drafting a Declaration on Indigenous Rights (to be considered, it is to be hoped, by the General Assembly at some future time), and they have also taken part briefly in the debates leading up to the adoption of Convention 169 on Indigenous and Tribal Peoples by the International Labour Organization (ILO) (1989). Indigenous representatives sit on the governing bodies of the recently established (1992) Fund for the Development of Indigenous Peoples of Latin America and the Caribbean. Again, indigenous representatives are participating in consultations with the Inter-American Commission on Human Rights concerning a future inter-American legal instrument on indigenous peoples' rights. International activity of this kind has brought indigenous representatives from Latin America into contact with representatives from other parts of the world, in addition to helping them become familiar with international law and the mechanisms and proceedings of human-rights protection in the international system, a relationship that in turn promotes their cause and helps bolster their political bargaining power at home.[10] Mexican indigenous participants have been increasingly seen at these regional and international conferences.

IDENTITIES AND IDEOLOGIES

A careful analysis of the declarations, resolutions, and statements produced by these different organizations and congresses (which is beyond the scope of this chapter) would show a progression of ideas and a sequence of issues over time. In earlier years indigenous manifestos would remind the public at large of their historical victimization and their secular poverty and demand some kind of overall retribution and justice from governments. At the same time, a persistent theme in many of these documents was a certain idealization of the Indian, pre-Columbian past, depicted as a kind of golden age, a period without exploitation, discrimination, and conflict, just as Indian cultures were (and often still are) described as morally superior to so-called Western civilization.[11]

In later years, the demands put forward by indigenous organizations became more focussed on specific issues such as land, agricultural credit, education, health, technical aid, investments in infrastructure, and so forth, issues that were addressed to governments, which were expected to solve them. More recently, specific socioeconomic demands have been coupled with calls for autonomy and self-determination. Ethnic identity has become a rallying point for many such organizations, concern over ecology is now a major source of contention, particularly in the Amazon lowlands, and increasingly there are demands for legislative changes and compliance with recent international legal instruments, such as the ILO's Convention 169 and the draft UN declaration on the rights of indigenous peoples. At international meetings indigenous representatives are increasingly putting forward constructive proposals involving new legislation and promoting social and economic policies.

Indigenous organizations do not only hold meetings and disseminate their programs and ideas; they also negotiate with public authorities, send representatives to international conferences, and often receive financial aid from donor agencies for specific activities. Who represents these organizations and, in general, how representative are they of the indigenous population? This is a question that governments frequently raise when they wish to challenge the authenticity of indigenous representation at the national and international levels; or it becomes an issue between rival factions and groups that compete for official recognition or access to resources. It is true that in numerous cases existing indigenous organizations were structured from the top down and initiated by indigenous intellectual elites who lack a real popular base, but more and more indigenous organizations are being built from the bottom up, through a painful process of mobilization and organization, in which new leaderships emerge who have a grassroots base and who express the true concerns of their affiliated members.

The issue of representation will no doubt continue to be raised for some time to come. Traditional community-based leadership generally is in the hands of an older generation of local authorities who, while well immersed in the ethnic culture of their group, are not always well prepared to deal with the challenges of "modern" organizations and political negotiations. These traditional authorities are increasingly being replaced by a younger generation of indigenous activists, many of them professionals who have lived and honed their skills in a non-Indian environment. While there may be tensions between these two generations, their roles are often complementary: the older traditional authorities concern themselves with local community matters; the younger leaders are involved in building organizations and alliances, and they deal with the outside world. This process is taking place among Mixtec highland communities in the Mexican state of Oaxaca, as well as in the states of Chiapas and Guerrero.

As more and more indigenous youngsters make their way through the formal educational system and achieve professional status as agronomists, teachers, doctors, lawyers, and so forth, an indigenous intellectual elite has emerged in several Latin American countries that is becoming the life-blood of the new organizations. Indigenous intellectuals are actively engaged in developing the "new indigenous discourse" that gives these organizations their distinctive identities. They are not only involved in formulating the political agendas of their movements, they are also rediscovering their historical roots, are concerned with language, culture and cosmology, and become actively engaged in "inventing traditions" and building new "imaginary communities."[12] To the extent that the new indigenous intelligentsia participates in national and international networks and is able to get its message across to other sectors of the population and to the extent that it is able to mobilize resources and obtain certain collective goods (material and political resources, recognition, and so on), indigenous intellectuals have become indispensable links in the process of organization and mobilization.

In Mexico, for example, the first formal indigenous associations beyond the local level were organized by Indian schoolteachers working for the federal Ministry of Education. They had been trained to teach in bilingual grade schools in Indian villages. The National Association of Writers in Indigenous Languages brought together native students of indigenous oral traditions as well as creative writers, most of whom were and are at the same time employees of the government or active academics.[13] During the tragic years of civil war and military repression in Guatemala, Indian mobilization frequently took place through innocuous-sounding associations for the preservation and study of Maya culture, by which an emerging Maya identity became crystallized.[14]

On the other hand, the indigenous leadership also draws support from the grass roots, from local activists engaged in struggles against human rights abuses, or for land rights, or over environmental concerns, issues in which indigenous women are often especially active. Sometimes there appears to be a tension between the grass-roots activists and the intellectuals, because the former are concerned with more immediate issues and push for concrete solutions, whereas the latter are more involved in long-term institution-building. Moreover, whereas indigenous intellectuals are contributing to the development of an "Indianist" ideology and weltanschauung and also at times find themselves engaged in discussions with various other ideological tendencies in Latin America (nationalism, Marxism, liberation theology, Christian democracy, evangelical Protestantism), grass-roots activists do not have much patience for intellectual debates and are more interested in negotiating specific issues with the powers that be rather than aspiring to ideological coherence or purity. These various approaches, as well as other factors, have led to not a few disputes over organizational matters, strategy, and tactics that sometimes give the impression of a very fragmented and factionalized indigenous movement.

Many of these issues came to the surface among Indian organizations after the appearance of the Zapatista Army for National Liberation (EZLN) in Chiapas in January 1994. This armed uprising, which took Mexico and the world by surprise on the day the North American Free Trade Association (NAFTA) came into being, was soon able to convince public opinion (as well as the Mexican authorities) that it did indeed have a strong social base among Indian communities in the state of Chiapas, as well as widespread sympathy and support elsewhere. However, despite their tacit and often vocal agreement with the Zapatistas' demands, many indigenous organizations in Mexico were split over how much to support it actively, and some of them were careful to distance themselves from armed struggle as a desirable way to push their demands. The government swiftly attempted to divide the Indian movement even further by trying to buy off and co-opt the leadership of numerous organizations, even as the more radical associations suffered various forms of harassment and selective repression, such as the umbrella organization the Consejo de los 500 Años in the state of Guerrero and the Frente Independiente de Pueblos Indios (FIPI), which began a nation-wide organizing effort in the early 1990s.

The Zapatista uprising and its aftermath exemplifies the ambiguous relationship among indigenous peoples, social organizations, political parties and the national government. The first Declaration of the Lacandon Jungle, in which the EZLN made its objectives public in January 1994, mentions eleven basic grievances, none of which can be considered especially indigenous: land, labour, shelter, food, health, education, independence, liberty, democracy, justice, and peace. These are issues that concern all of Mexico's population. Moreover, the fact that the EZLN's principal spokesman, Marcos, was obviously an urban mestizo intellectual prompted the government and some early critics to label the uprising as anything but indigenous. Some commentators in the national press voiced their opinion that the Zapatista uprising was not an authentic indigenous movement because it did not stick to specific indigenous demands, whereas others suggested that it had no national implications because it resulted from specific local conditions in Chiapas. Both positions were proven wrong as the movement unfolded: rooted in local conditions, the success of the Zapatistas was based on the fact that their political analysis had national implications. In fact, other indigenous groups, as well as numerous peasant, urban, and popular movements, saw their own situation mirrored in the Zapatistas' proclamations.

As the conflict continued, public opinion as well as government officials recognized that the social base of the Zapatistas was indeed almost exclusively indigenous. After the first Peace Accord of San Andrés, covering essentially indigenous demands, was signed in February 1996 between the federal government and the EZLN, the former proceeded to carry out an extensive national "consultation" among indigenous peoples regarding the issues on which agreement had apparently been reached: indigenous culture and rights, including the thorny issue of autonomy. The results were announced in May, and they showed that the demands raised by the Zapatistas had widespread support among indigenous groups across the country. The government admitted as much, and though it backtracked subsequently on its commitment to the results of the consultation and the agreement it had signed with the EZLN, it could no longer deny the essentially indigenous component of the Zapatista uprising.

Indeed, in successive public statements the EZLN insisted increasingly on the question of indigenous rights and culture, participation of indigenous people in the political process, legal recognition of indigenous peoples and communities, as well as territorial, political, and legal autonomy at the local and regional levels (the latter demand being rejected adamantly in official circles). In a 1996 interview, Subcomandante Marcos, the EZLN spokesman, admitted that the indigenous leadership of the movement had not wished to identify the uprising with exclusively indigenous demands at the beginning, so as to avoid being labelled as purely local in character and thus becoming marginalized and set apart from the rest of the country (especially in the electoral year of 1994). Hence the insistence, in the earlier documents of the EZLN, on the larger, "national" issues. As the EZLN recognized the sympathy and support it was receiving at the national and international levels because of its mainly indigenous component, its discourse changed accordingly, and indigenous issues were increasingly emphasized.[15]

The EZLN sponsored an important National Indian Congress that was held in Mexico City in 1996 with the participation of indigenous representatives from various parts of the country. This is now one of the major indigenous organizations in Mexico.[16] However, except for activities related to the peace negotiations between the EZLN and the Mexican government (stalled since January 1997), Mexico's principal social organizations and political associations devote little attention to indigenous issues, a neglect that indigenous organizations do not cease to point out with a certain bitterness. During the legislative campaign in the first half of the electoral year 1997, political parties had very little to say about indigenous issues. As the media impact of the Zapatistas waned and the peace negotiations faltered, public opinion became less concerned with these problems.

As in Mexico, so also in a number of other Latin American countries. Inasmuch as most indigenous communities in Latin America are rural peasant societies, Indian demands have much in common with the concerns of all peasants about land and water rights, agrarian reform issues, agricultural credit, technical assistance, access to markets, farm prices and subsidies, and so on. These have been particularly burning issues in the Andean highlands, as well as elsewhere, since the 1960s, when numerous militant peasant movements emerged in Latin America. Furthermore, while Indian organizations are apprehensive about their identity and their independence, they also know that their scope and impact will be limited if they isolate themselves from other social movements. Thus, indigenous organizations have had to grapple with two related problems: the role of indigenous movements within the wider framework of conflict and interest articulation in the national society and the crucial issue of building strategic alliances with other organizations.

On the first point, I shall not refer to the earlier debates, common in the nineteenth and early twentieth centuries, about the supposed inferiority of the indigenous "races" in Latin America, nor to the national elites' objective of doing away with the "barbarous" natives who threatened the survival of civilization. Rather, over the last few decades the debate has centred on two alternative conceptualizations. On the one hand, there was the idea that indigenous cultures were not integrated into the national mainstream culture and that modern nation-building required the rapid incorporation of the Indians and therefore their disappearance. For the indigenous organizations this idea presented the options of either accepting the state's assimilationist policies but negotiating their terms, of rejecting them altogether, or of putting forward alternative possibilities. Each of these three positions has at some point been taken up by one or another indigenous organization.

On the other hand, ever since the 1930s a long-running debate has posed the question of whether the indigenous peoples should be considered as an exploited subordinate social class (subsistence peasantry, agricultural workers) or as culturally distinct oppressed peoples (nationalities) who may, in fact, also be internally differentiated in socioeconomic terms. This is the "ethnie-class" debate, and it has implications for the objectives and strategies of indigenous and other social movements. In the early 1960s an attempt was made to bridge this conceptual dichotomy through the introduction of the concept of "internal colonialism," later applied in other contexts as well.[17]

If Indian populations were considered to be but a segment of the exploited peasantry, then the solution to their problems would be found in class organizations and struggle (peasant unions, land reform). Moreover, emphasis on ethnic identity would dilute class consciousness and attendant political attitudes. If, however, Indian identity was pivotal, then class-related issues would be of secondary importance. If Indians see themselves as a "colonized" people, then collective "liberation struggles" leading to decolonization would appear to be in order. It would appear that most indigenous organizations in recent years have opted for the second position, rather than for a strictly class-based approach. While not denying or neglecting class-related issues, they have emphasized ethnic identity and the "ethnic-national" aspects of their struggles, which has also brought them prominence both at home and abroad. One of the reasons for adopting this position can be found in the rather biased approaches to the "Indian question" taken by traditional leftist parties in Latin America, who for many years fostered a pure class approach to social conflicts, thus alienating many potential Indian supporters who did not see their own concerns reflected in the Marxist discourse of these political parties. Instances of this can be found in the conflict between the Sandinistas and the Miskitos in Nicaragua during the 1980s and in the evolution of revolutionary ideology and warfare in Guatemala over the last four decades.[18] While indigenous intellectuals have not been overly concerned with these debates, academic social scientists have been deeply involved in them in Mexico as elsewhere.

The controversy over "class" vs "ethnie" has had wider implications for political strategies and tactics as well, because it relates to the possibility of indigenous movements forging alliances with other social and political organizations. Early on in the process of organization and mobilization, indigenous activists realized that in order to achieve their wider objectives and to prevent encapsulation, they would have to seek allies among other sectors of society, particularly labour unions, peasant organizations, students, and urban intellectuals, as well as established institutions such as the Catholic Church (or at least among some of the supporters of its current tendencies, such as the promoters of liberation theology), and under certain circumstances, some political parties as well. Some indigenous organizations got their start as offshoots of a political party: in Mexico the ruling PRI attempted to establish and control a number of indigenous organizations in the 1970s; in Bolivia the various political parties had, and some still have, indigenous organizational affiliates, and a clearly indigenous party, the MRTK (Tupac Katari Revolutionary Movement), has openly and successfully vied for political power (the MRTK's former presidential candidate, Victor Hugo Cárdenas, an Aymara Indian, was vice-president of the Bolivian Republic in a coalition government between 1993 and 1997).[19] The national congress and the senate of Mexico have several indigenous members, elected on national party lists, although this is a fairly recent phenomenon. In general, however, indigenous organizations (though not necessarily their individual members) have shied away from political party affiliation as such, and their leaders usually reject the overtures of political parties to incorporate or co-opt them into established party structures. As a result of the public debate on indigenous rights in Mexico that was stimulated by the emergence of the Zapatistas, some sectors of the PRI have announced their renewed interest in indigenous causes, but they are a minority. Within the left-of-centre Party of the Democratic Revolution (PRD), while there is much sympathy for the Zapatistas, there is so little debate about indigenous issues in general that one of the PRD's principal members, a former federal congressman, stated his disappointment publicly during the electoral campaign of 1997.

Nevertheless, the need for tactical alliances with other social organizations has become more obvious to the indigenous leadership, particularly when the objectives of social struggle – such as defending human rights under repressive governments like Guatemala's successive military regimes – are shared. At international congresses attended by indigenous and other organizations the issue of alliances has become overt. Participating organizations underline the fact that widespread, all-inclusive popular mobilization will have greater political impact than isolated actions by smaller, fragmented groups. On the other hand, indigenous leaders argue that their particular agendas (ethnic identity, recognition of historical rights of indigenous peoples) get easily sidetracked and subordinated to the more general concerns of the larger popular organizations. In general, they fear (with some justification) that indigenous organizations will become minor players in a game dominated by the established mestizo organizations, and that they will risk being manipulated by more experienced mestizo politicians.

Indigenous organizations would not have achieved as much as they have without external support over the years. In fact, many of these organizations got their start with the aid of outside agents, to which some of them are still beholden. Both Catholic and Protestant missionary organizations helped some of the indigenous associations of the Amazon lowland to organize in the 1960s and 1970s. Schoolteachers, agronomists in government service, anthropologists from academic institutions, health workers, and other non-Indian professionals, as well as activists from different kinds of political groups, have also been instrumental in helping organize the indigenous movement. Many of these organizations now receive financial aid or subsidies from numerous international donor agencies and nongovernmental organizations of various kinds that have set up shop over the last few years in Latin America. One of the reasons why the Zapatista uprising has so far been successful (and, one suspects, why it took off there and not elsewhere) is that for many years Christian Base Communities associated with the Theology of Liberation and accountable to Bishop Ruiz of San Cristóbal las Casas, have been actively involved in community organization among the Indian peoples of Chiapas. Not surprisingly, Bishop Ruiz, soon after the start of the uprising, became first an unofficial mediator between the Zapatistas and the Mexican federal government and later the head of the National Mediation Commission, which was established by law, to help broker the peace negotiations. But after continuing attacks in official circles and by the political right accusing him of being actually the "inspirator" if not the instigator of the Zapatista uprising, Bishop Ruiz chose to resign in June 1998 as president of the mediation commission, after which it was dissolved by the other members.

WHY AND WHEREFORE

Is the rise of the indigenous movement only a temporary phenomenon or is it here to stay and does it represent some deeper changes in the societies of Latin America? Only time will tell, but for now it is clear, at least to this writer, that the indigenous movement does express fundamental social forces that underlie some of the transformations that have been occurring on the continent during the latter half of the present century.

Several factors may account for the rise of indigenous awareness and the emergence of these new social movements on the public scene. In the first place, mention could be made of the overall disenchantment with, and the failure of, traditional development policies that were assiduously pursued by national governments and multilateral organizations since the end of the Second World War. "Economic development" was the magic slogan wielded by generations of government planners and academics that would bring improved living standards and burgeoning incomes to the poor, the marginalized, the backward populations of Latin America. This did not happen, as the "lost decade" of the 1980s so clearly showed. Indigenous populations were indeed drawn into the "modern" sector of the economy through market mechanisms, labour migrations, and an expanding communications and transportation infrastructure, but they saw the benefits of growth going, as always, to the elites. Except for a few show-case projects, the situation of indigenous peoples deteriorated, if anything, during the period, as they increasingly lost their autonomy and means of subsistence and became more and more dependent on market capitalism. In the process of unequal development, indigenous populations everywhere were victims rather than beneficiaries, the most vulnerable and fragile populations caught up in the maelstrom of rapid, unstable social and economic changes. This fact was not lost on the emerging Indian intelligentsia who soon became skeptical of upbeat economic projections, government promises, and predictions about their imminent accession to progress and civilization. Disillusionment with mainstream development strategies was shared widely, beginning in the 1970s, and the search for development alternatives often focussed on the local, grassroots level, which would naturally include indigenous communities.

A second factor accounting for the rise of indigenous movements that is closely related to the previous one was the increasing awareness by the emerging Indian intellectuals that the modern nation-state that the mestizo elites had been building so assiduously ever since the nineteenth century was fundamentally flawed. Instead of being all-inclusive, it was in fact exclusionary: Indian cultures were denied; Indians were victims of subtle or open racism and discrimination; indigenous peoples (even when they constituted demographic majorities as in Bolivia and Guatemala and in numerous subnational regions elsewhere) were excluded from economic well-being, from social equality, from political decision-making processes, and from access to justice in the legal system. Indians could not recognize themselves in the prevailing model of the "national" state, as fashioned by the mestizo and white, upper-class elites.[20] The indigenous roots of Latin America had long been considered a burden by the European elites, and government assimilationist policies (*indigenismo*) made it clear that indigenous cultures had no future in the modern nation-state. Despite formal citizenship rights granted to Indians in most Latin American countries, indigenous peoples have in fact been treated more frequently as second-class citizens when they have not been denied such rights altogether (in some countries they have been treated as minors, wards of the state, and legally incapacitated). Representative democracy, institutional political participation, equality before the law, due process, and respect for their languages, culture, religion, and traditions, as well as dignity accorded by the rest of national society, were not for Indians. Many indigenous persons in fact internalized the stereotypes and stigmas imposed on them by the dominant sectors and resorted to self-denial and self-denigration in order to become accepted by non-Indians. Others developed a "culture of resistance," turning inward and avoiding contact as much as possible with the outside world (a reaction that in recent years has become increasingly difficult to uphold). Still others, realizing that the existing model of the nation-state denies them their identity and their very survival as viable cultures, have begun to challenge the dominant mainstream notion of the nation by proposing alternative conceptions of a multicultural, polyethnic state. This is one of the demands that the new indigenous movement has been putting forward in recent years.

There is no doubt that the indigenous movement has in turn been inspired by the anticolonial liberation struggles of the postwar years. Indigenous intellectuals have identified with national liberation movements, often considering that their own struggles are anticolonial as well because their peoples were the victims of an earlier external colonialism that turned into internal colonialism during the post-independence period. As they witnessed the achievements of the anticolonial and national liberation movements, it is likely that they would have posed the question, "why not us?" Indeed, in many indigenous manifestos and proclamations, the Indian peoples of Latin America are presented as victims of colonialism and their struggle as one of anticolonial resistance. This was clearly stated and repeated in many national and international fora during the commemorations of the 500th Anniversary of The Encounter of Two Worlds, an event that further stimulated the constitution of indigenous organizations on the continent.

The rise of this movement also mirrors the emergence of an indigenous or "Indianist" worldview that is not as yet a structured and coherent political ideology but that contains elements that clearly distinguish it from other ideologies that permeated social thought for many decades. It would appear that because the hegemonic ideologies of the times did not address the problematique of indigenous people and the national state, or did so inadequately, they were rejected as theoretical guideposts by the burgeoning indigenous intellectuals, who then went on to construct their own ideological texts.[21]

Closely related to the ideas of economic development and nation-building is the concept of "modernization," which was at one time widely hailed as an all-encompassing, universalizing social process that would eventually subsume the traditional, backward, or premodern, forms of society. Indigenous communities and cultures were "traditional and backward" and therefore doomed to disappear. Modernization policies, touted as remedies for underdevelopment and poverty, were designed to help accelerate this process, considered by many as inevitable and desirable. The modernization paradigm, still wielded by policymakers as synonymous with progress and therefore morally legitimate, is today considered by many Indian activists and advocates as little less than ethnocidal. The emergent Indianist ideology finds little support in it and does not, in turn, support it. Indeed, in many instances, it explicitly rejects "modernization" as a viable objective for indigenous peoples. This tension is expressed clearly in the conflicts surrounding environmental changes, particularly in tropical rain forest areas. In these regions, modernization is often identified with vast ecological transformations that destroy forest biotic resources, the habitat of numerous indigenous groups.[22]

Modernization theory (one of the intellectual fads associated with the sociology of development) also posited the need for far-reaching changes in cultural values among the "backward" and "traditional" populations. Schools of applied social scientists applied their skills to telling indigenous populations around the world that their ways of life were morally wrong (the missionary approach) or dysfunctional to the modern world (the technocratic approach). Indigenous peoples who fell for these arguments soon found themselves morally bereft, culturally impoverished, and materially destitute. Current indigenous (or Indianist) ideology therefore challenges the modernization paradigm as irrelevant at best and as potentially destructive of indigenous values. Bolivia's former vice-president, Aymara Victor Hugo Cárdenas, likes to say that Indians are not against modernization as such but insist on their own view of modernization rather than accepting a Western-imposed model.

For decades the modernization approach to social and cultural changes among indigenous peoples competed with the worldview of Marxism, not only as a cognitive map of the real world in which indigenous peoples were caught but also as a revolutionary guide for action and historical transformation. Marxist political groups, with their various tendencies (communist, Trotskyite, Maoist, Fidelista, and the like), had their "indigenist" platforms (when they thought about indigenous peoples at all, which was not very often). Usually this meant exhorting Indians to shed their indigenous identities and to join the class struggle as poor, exploited peasants. Sometimes, it meant simply rejecting indigenous peoples outright as too backward to understand the class struggle and concentrating on revolution among the "advanced" classes of Latin America, particularly the urban proletariat. It was held that once the struggle had been won, an enlightened revolutionary government would bring progress to the backward Indians.

Indian intellectuals recognized that orthodox Marxist views of the "Indian problem" were not so different from the modernization approach discussed above. Some of them rejected both as being products of the colonizing West. Indigenous skepticism increased as a number of Indian groups found themselves literally in the cross-fire between leftist guerrillas and repressive military establishments in a number of Latin American countries during the 1970s and 1980s (Bolivia, Colombia, Guatemala, Peru). In Nicaragua they were pressed between a leftist revolutionary government and the u.s.-organized *contras*. Thus, the Indianist ideology emerged as an alternative to the ideological vacuum regarding the role of indigenous peoples of established mainstream political philosophies of both the liberal and Marxist varieties. Subcomandante Marcos of the EZLN admits that the orthodox Marxism embraced by many of his generation in the heady 1960s and 1970s turned out to be irrelevant to the indigenous struggles of the 1980s and 1990s.[23]

Although it would be difficult to speak of a finished, well-rounded, self-contained Indianist ideology at the present time (it may, in fact, never be developed), there are a number of issues and strands that persist and reappear in the various currents of Indianism as expressed in the documents of indigenous organizations, groups, seminars, conferences, caucuses, journals, and periodicals. These issues are frequently coupled with specific demands addressed mainly to governments but sometimes also to the society at large. They can be grouped under five major headings.[24]

Definition and Legal Status. While bureaucrats, legal scholars, and anthropologists (as well as an occasional missionary) have wrangled over who is and who is not an Indian (or what is "indigenous") – which is why the definition and quantification of indigenous peoples in Latin America is an ambiguous task – the right to self-definition has become one of the recurring demands of indigenous organizations. It has now become a question of cultural identity and quite often a matter of honour (regardless of such "objective" criteria as use of language, dress, or active participation in communal life). Even more than an individual choice, it is collective identity and group recognition that many organizations crave. As long as being Indian was stigmatized, self-identification did not offer particular incentives; but with changing times, Indian self-identification has become a political tool in a contested social space.

To the extent that social and cultural labels often imply specific legal status and that the attribution of legal status has typically been a prerogative of governments, indigenous organizations that demand the right of self-definition (now considered to be a fundamental human right) also question the government's authority to impose such status unilaterally (which is what, in fact, has occurred from the beginning). The Indian movement strongly demands new legal status for indigenous peoples in a democratic polity, a demand that in the last few years has been heard increasingly by politicians and lawmakers and that finds expression in the legislative and constitutional changes referred to above.

Land and Territorial Rights. Although no longer receiving much attention in the era of economic globalization, land rights and agrarian issues are central to the survival of indigenous peoples in Latin America and constitute one of their principal demands. The loss of land is one of the constants in the indigenous history of Latin America. Consequently, the struggle for the preservation or the restitution of agrarian rights lies at the base of many of the recent efforts at indigenous organization. Land and its various resources (forests, water, game, even minerals) are viewed mainly as a collective, communal good, even though the notion of individual property rights has made headway after decades of capitalist expansion. Agrarian struggles have occurred among the Mapuche in Chile, in the Andean highlands in Peru and Ecuador, and among the Maya of Guatemala, and they are at the root of social conflicts in Mexico, including the Zapatista uprising in Chiapas.[25] The land issue has not been resolved for the Indian peasantry in Latin America, and its neglect by governments – after the heyday of land reforms in the 1960s – imposes severe economic and social burdens on indigenous peoples.

Whereas land rights in the strict sense refer to productive resources, indigenous peoples also insistently demand territorial rights, that is, the recognition and legal delimitation of ancestral homelands, territories that have been occupied continuously by an indigenous group over a period of time and that usually represent the geographical space necessary for the cultural and social reproduction of the group. Indian territories have suffered severe losses through outside colonization or government-induced expropriation, and there is consensus that without their own territory the social and cultural survival of indigenous peoples is seriously threatened.[26]

As a result of the changes in article 27 of the Constitution introduced by the Salinas government, land tenure reform in Mexico now allows communally held land to be turned into private properties, under certain circumstances. In the coming years, indigenous communities that had received collective land titles under the agrarian reform program from the 1920s onward may be forced, through market pressures, to relinquish these rights as privatization in all economic sectors proceeds. Numerous indigenous organizations have now taken up the defense of their traditional land tenure rights as a major objective, and some of them demand a return to the earlier formulation of article 27. The national government, as well as Mexico's principal business interests, is adamantly opposed to any such change, arguing rightly that the earlier land tenure legislation had been openly flouted through all sorts of illegal arrangements and bureaucratic imbroglios. Still, the defense of collective or communal land and territorial rights ranks high on the agendas of indigenous organizations. After the enactment of the amendment to article 27 of Mexico's constitution in 1992 (concerned with land reform), landless peasants, including Indians, lost all hope of ever being able to receive a plot of land. The EZLN has stated that this was also one of the factors impelling them to rebel.

Cultural Identity. Spontaneous cultural change and acculturation and state policies of assimilation have been widely considered as detrimental to the survival of Indian cultures, in other words, as *ethnocidal.* Through a passive culture of resistance, numerous indigenous peoples have been able to preserve elements of their cultures and maintain their ethnic identity, which in recent years is being strengthened by a conscious cultural revival undertaken by indigenous elites and cultural militants. Thus, Maya culture is actively being fostered in Guatemala by numerous indigenous organizations; Aymara and Quechua languages and traditions are being revived in the Andean countries, while in Mexico, as noted above, an organization of indigenous writers and intellectuals is promoting indigenous literature. Sometimes these activities receive governmental support, but indigenous organizations usually have to rely on their own resources, perhaps with some help from sympathetic nongovernmental organizations (NGOs).

Ever since the nineteenth century, Spanish (or in Brazil, Portuguese) was the official and national language of Latin American states, and indigenous tongues were labelled "dialects" at best, unworthy of preservation. Thus, official and private (usually missionary) education among indigenous groups traditionally imposed on them the state language, often prohibiting the use of the vernacular in any public instance (in legal proceedings, in municipal administration, and so forth). Because indigenous peoples were thus disadvantaged in the use of their own tongues, their rights were easily and systematically trampled. In recent years, as a result of indigenous demands and the reassessment of *indigenista* policies by teachers and social scientists, some governments have implemented bilingual educational programs in indigenous areas. Indigenous organizations now demand educational services in their own tongues, teacher-training programs for their own people, and curriculum content geared around indigenous cultures. In some states (Peru, for example) indigenous languages have now been given status as national languages; in others, legal and administrative proceedings involving indigenous peoples must allow for the use of indigenous languages.

Mexico's Ministry of Public Education (Secretaría de Educación Pública) has run a program of bilingual indigenous education for three decades. Instruction in the vernacular language is carried out in the early years of primary school education among all the indigenous linguistic groups in the country. After the third grade, however, instruction is only in Spanish. Indigenous teachers' organizations have insisted not only upon bilingual but also upon intercultural education, whereby emphasis would be placed on a curriculum adapted to the needs of the local indigenous culture. As the federal government is responsible for the official unitary curriculum in all of the country's primary schools, intercultural education is still more a hope than a reality.

Social Organization and Customary Law. Indigenous community life, and therefore the viability of indigenous culture, depends upon the vitality of the group's social organization and, in many instances, upon the active implementation of local customary law. This has recently become an important demand of indigenous organizations, insofar as the failure of the state legal system and the public administration to recognize local social organization and customary law also contributes to the weakening and eventual disappearance of indigenous cultures.

In Mexico there has been renewed interest in the customary law of indigenous peoples. Article 4 of the Constitution now states that the Indians' customary law will be taken into consideration in all matters concerning agrarian disputes and administrative procedures (there is no mention of civil or penal law). Local judges and government attorneys have been asked by INI and the National Commission of Human Rights (CNDH), among other agencies, to be sensitive to indigenous traditions and customs, and indigenous organizations have placed this issue high on their agenda. Further federal legislation will no doubt deal with this complex issue, though it is by no means certain that it can be resolved satisfactorily at the level of the national congress. Both conservative and liberal legal scholars, trained in the tradition of positivist legal doctrine, have come out staunchly against any kind of recognition of legal pluralism, arguing that the modern sovereign state needs to integrate all its citizens in only one legal system. The issue will probably be debated for a long time to come. (See chapter 7, below, for a comparable debate in the government of Quebec.)

No Latin American state formally recognizes legal pluralism, but a certain degree of tolerance for local "uses and customs" has always existed (in colonial times a distinct Indian legal domain was in fact established by the Spanish Crown). The formal recognition of customary law and of traditional forms of local authority, dispute resolution, inheritance practices, land use patterns, and so on, is nowadays a stated objective of many indigenous organizations.[27] This is clearly a political demand that is often expressed in the indigenous objective of achieving a higher degree of political participation.

Political Participation. Indigenous organizations now ask not only for increased political representation in existing bodies of government (municipal councils, state legislatures, national parliaments) but also seek the right to self-determination (as guaranteed in international law),[28] which is expressed through local and regional autonomy and self-government. Many states are still wary of these demands, because they believe them to be stepping-stones towards secession and the territorial fragmentation of the nation-state. Indigenous organizations, however, are usually quite firm in that they ask only for *internal* self-determination and for greater participation in national politics, not as some excluded minority, but as the descendants of the original inhabitants of the country. They claim to be the "true" representatives of the "nation": "first nations."

The demand for autonomy has been voiced insistently by numerous indigenous organizations in Mexico, particularly since the Zapatista uprising in 1994, and the federal government has offered to deal with the issue. Just how this demand might be handled is not clear, since different conceptions of autonomy are used rather loosely by the various actors. One approach, which has been formally tabled in Congress by the Party of Democratic Revolution (PRD), suggests the establishment of "autonomous regions" as a new administrative level somewhere between the municipality (which is the smallest formal territorial unit in Mexican law) and the state. How such pluriethnic regions (including Indians and non-Indians) might be constituted is anybody's guess. Most grassroots indigenous organizations insist rather on communal autonomy at the local level, leaving open the possibility of subsequent integration into wider regional units. In fact, attempts at the implementation of local-level autonomy, without government authorization, have already taken place in areas of Oaxaca and Chiapas over the last three or four years. New legislation will have to be crafted on these complex problems in the future, but as of mid-1998 no action has been taken by the Congress.

Autonomy statutes for indigenous regions have been adopted in Brazil, Colombia, Nicaragua, and Panama and are being considered elsewhere. This is probably the policy area in which more controversy will take place in the coming years.

International developments in the field of indigenous rights in recent years have had a deep influence on the posture and evolution of indigenous organizations in Latin America and may have influenced the evolving positions of governments as well. The United Nations Working Group on Indigenous Populations has been drafting a Declaration of Indigenous Rights since 1982. Latin American governments at first ignored its work, but as the years went by, they began taking an active interest in it. In the beginning, indigenous representation from Latin America was scant, but in recent years more and more indigenous organizations from the region have taken part in the working group's yearly debates in Geneva. This has become a *Bildungsreise* for many an indigenous leader, an obligatory stop on the road to effective leadership and influence in a regional or national-level organization. Whatever the eventual outcome of the draft Declaration (possibly approval by the General Assembly in modified form), indigenous organizations already refer to its various provisional articles as a necessary point of reference in their own political discourse. Thus, indigenous leadership will say that indigenous peoples, like all peoples, have the right to self-determination.

On the other hand, indigenous representation was not particularly numerous in the debates leading up to the adoption of Convention 169 of the International Labor Organization (ILO) in 1989. Indigenous points of view were expressed mainly by labour delegates who were not always as well informed as they might have been. Convention 169 has now been ratified by a number of Latin American states. Indigenous organizations rightly refer to it as one of the obligatory existing legal instruments binding governments, and they are actively promoting its ratification in those countries that have not yet done so. Mexico was one of the first states to ratify Convention 169 in 1989, but it has virtually been a dead letter in that country. Accusations by indigenous organizations and by occasional international officials of the ILO that Mexico has violated provisions of Convention 169 have been indignantly denied by government representatives. To the extent that there is an emerging international law of indigenous rights, indigenous organizations in Latin America will make use of it both legally and politically.[29]

The indigenous discourse occurs at the crossroads of issues regarding human rights, democracy, development, and the environment. It has become increasingly clear that indigenous demands concern not only indigenous peoples but the entire national society. Since 1994 nobody has expressed these demands more clearly than the Zapatista Army of National Liberation in Mexico. Indigenous peoples demand not only more and better democracy, or the improved implementation of human rights protection, or greater participation in the presumed benefits of development programs, they are also actually challenging the very premises upon which the nation-state in Latin America has been built over more than a century.

PART TWO

Problems and Remedies

4 Rights and Self-Government for Canada's Aboriginal Peoples

C.E.S. FRANKS

Of all the difficult questions that modern governments and political philosophers have to deal with, none have more complexities and competing viewpoints and arguments than issues of rights.[1] And of rights issues, few are more difficult to disentangle than those dealing with the rights of Aboriginal peoples, whether their rights within their own community or the rights of their community against the dominant external society and government. Issues of Aboriginal rights and self-government include problems of individual versus group rights, of the meaning and utility of rights in different cultural contexts, and of conflict between minority and dominant cultures, of small versus big.

To examine the issues of Aboriginal rights and self-government in a comprehensive way would demand a thorough understanding of the complexities of arguments about rights, for rights are essentially contestable concepts and there is no agreement over their meaning or their utility. It would also, if Canada is to be the focus, demand a close study of the history of native rights in Canada, of the jurisprudence related to native rights and self-government, of the legislation, the constitutional provisions, the royal proclamations, government statements, constitutional negotiations, negotiations for self-government, other authoritative edicts dealing with self-government, and all the other multifarious and complex paraphernalia of the modern state and the citizen's quest for autonomy and meaning in relationship to it. Self-government is also an essentially contestable concept. There is no agreement over what it means, what powers a self-government should have, whether a self-government is subordinate to, equal to, or superior to, the other levels, provincial and federal in particular, of government in Canada.

Such a study, of course, is impossible within the limits of a brief chapter, tempting though it is to try. Here I shall confine my examination to three key issues in the intimidating and enormous field of rights and Aboriginal self-government. First, I shall consider the question of what rights Aboriginal self-governments should have against other governments, in particular against the larger governments of the dominant society. Second, I shall take a brief look at the question of further entrenching Aboriginal rights, such as the right to self-government, in the Constitution. Third, I shall look at the question of what rights citizens of Aboriginal self-governments should have against their self-governments. The first and second of these issues have received the most attention in discussions of Aboriginal self-government in Canada, though arguably the third is at least as important.

Before I begin, I must make a disclaimer. In considering, in particular, the question of rights within self-governments and Aboriginal communities, I write as an outsider, and as a result my comments are offered from that perspective, with all the cautiousness and awareness of issues avoided or ignored for other reasons, including ignorance, that an outsider inevitably brings to complex questions inside different cultures. I have not, for example, presented in any serious way the arguments of some Aboriginal leaders and others that Aboriginal cultures and traditional forms of government are so different from the Western tradition that the Western conceptions of rights have no meaning within them. Nor have I explored in any detail how western rights in practice might be adapted to the potentially very different circumstances of Aboriginal self-governing bodies.

What I have tried to do is to consider the questions of rights within the context of some of the economic, political, legal, and social forces affecting Canada's Aboriginal communities. Modern western conceptions of human rights, after all, emerged from the economic, legal, and political forces that transformed European and North American societies in recent centuries. Modern rights discourse would sound as strange to an inhabitant of medieval Europe as the medieval conceptions of rights and the just society sound to a modern ear. Economic and social change has affected Canada's Aboriginal communities just as it has affected the rest of Canada. These sorts of change often demand political and legal changes to accommodate the needs of citizens. Here I offer some thoughts on what I consider crucial rights issues affecting Aboriginal self-governments.

CANADA'S ABORIGINAL PEOPLES

According to the Constitution Act, 1982 (§35), Canada's Aboriginal peoples include "the Indian, Inuit and Métis peoples of Canada." Not explicitly mentioned in the constitution are the non-status Indians who have formed a significant group in decennial census surveys. Presumably they now fit within the "Métis" or status Indian categories, or are not considered Aboriginal peoples. This constitutional terminology masks a welter of confusing legal and other categories. The key distinction lies between "status Indians" and those without such status, the "non-status" and "Métis." Status Indians and Inuit are recognized as a federal responsibility, while Métis and non-status are not. This division between federal and provincial spheres of responsibility is a crucial one in many aspects of Canadian politics and government including Aboriginal rights and self-government.

An act of Parliament in 1985 (Bill C-31) opened up eligibility for status to many who had either lost it through choice or marriage or whose parents had so lost status. In addition, designation as non-status or Métis is a matter of individual choice, and it is quite possible that many persons who had previously not chosen to consider themselves as of Aboriginal heritage reversed their choice in the more sympathetic atmosphere of 1991. In addition, of course, Canada's Aboriginal peoples have a generally very high rate of population growth.

The Department of Indian Affairs calculated a total of 511,791 status Indians in 1991.[2] Of these, 284,649, or 55.6 percent, lived on reserves; 20,110 lived on Crown land; and 207,032, or 40.5 percent, lived off-reserve. The proportion of status Indians living off-reserve, particularly in Canada's large cities, is steadily increasing. In 1994 there were 617 Indian bands in Canada. The largest of these bands are the Six Nations of the Grand River in Ontario and the Kahnawake of Quebec, both of which are located in the settled south and not far from Canada's largest cities. Three-quarters of the on-reserve Indians, however, live on reserves of fewer than 1,000 people, many of which are in remote northern areas of Canada. Approximately 30,000 of the status population belong to the Inuit of the far north.

The economic and health statistics for Canada's Aboriginal people are consistently worse than those for the general population. Aboriginal people are more likely to be unemployed, have low education, suffer from disabilities, die as infants, be subjected to violence, be incarcerated in penal or other institutions, have a low level of educational achievement, live in substandard housing, or have a below-subsistence income.[3] Their life expectancy is ten years less than the

Canadian average.[4] Statistics Canada found that of the 388,900 adults aged 15 or older who identify with an Aboriginal group, 36 percent reported that they can speak an Aboriginal language well enough to carry on a conversation, but only 21 percent of the 148,155 children under 15 made this claim. At the same time, 51 percent of adults reported that they participate in traditional Aboriginal activities, compared with 44 percent of children. The Inuit have the highest retention of language and traditional lifestyle, the Métis the lowest.[5]

These gross statistics mask enormous variations among Aboriginal groups. Some bands, for example the Sechelt of British Columbia, have a lower rate of unemployment and higher per capita income than the average of that province. Indians in Quebec have a lower rate of incarceration in penal institutions than the average for that province. Some bands are prosperous and well-managed; others, even though they have large revenues, often from oil and gas developments, are prosperous in aggregate but distribute benefits unevenly.

Overall, regardless of whether a band has its own resources or not, regardless of whether it is located in the remote north or near a large city in the south, regardless of whether it is a reserve in the south or a community in the northern territories, the band (or community) and its government are heavily subsidized by the federal government. In 1997 this financial support amounted, in aggregate, to approximately $20,000 for every status man, woman, and child. Most of these funds are not given directly to status Indians. Rather, they are transferred either through programs like medical care and housing or through financial transfers to band, community, and territorial governments. Non-status Indians and Métis, because they are not legally considered the responsibility of the federal government, do not enjoy this federal financial support. Whatever special support they get comes from their province and is generally much less than that given by the federal government to status Aboriginals.

Canadian status Indians since 1960 have been able to vote in federal elections and, in effect, are full citizens of the federal polity, though ones with a particular legal status that gives them different rights and entitlements from ordinary citizens. Whether they are full citizens of the provinces depends on the measure of citizenship used: many provincial governments refuse to extend their normal services to off-reserve Indians, and they are even more likely to refuse them to on-reserve Indians, on the view that Indians are constitutionally a federal, not a provincial, responsibility.

Residents on the land base of a reserve or self-governing unit could be status Indians who are band members and full citizens of the self-government; status Indians who are not band members (perhaps persons who regained status under Bill C-31 but are excluded from full membership because of the band's membership code, or members of other bands who have married into the band or for some reason reside on the reserve); non-status Indians who are accepted as band members under the band's membership code; non-Indian band members accepted under the band membership code; non-Indians who are not band members; or children of status Indians who are not eligible to achieve status under Bill C-31. In addition, there may be nonresident band members. These members can be important: Bill C-31 required the approval of a majority of *all* band members eligible to vote, whether resident or not, for the approval of a membership code. In Canada, 236 bands have their own membership codes authorized under Bill C-31. Some of these codes exclude Indians who gained status under Bill C-31 and their children from full band membership.

The right of citizenship – to be a member of the community – has become one of the key issues in some Aboriginal communities. On the one side are the persons, or the children of persons, who lost their membership for whatever reason, such as personal choice or marriage. Many of these people have close kinship and other ties with the band. On the other side are band leaders faced with the problem of meeting urgent needs for housing, schooling, and public services, but with a limited budget that does not grow with the population. Some of the wealthy Western bands are reluctant to bring back persons who chose to leave but now want to return to share the new-found wealth. The Indian Act does not allow band members who are not resident on a reserve to vote for band leadership. This provision effectively disenfranchises a high proportion of members of some reserves.

Discussions of self-government and the rights of self-government appear often to concentrate on the "pure" case of a band with its own reserve land base and a population exclusively composed of status band members. In actual fact, Aboriginal people living in these conditions comprised only slightly more than half of status Indians and much less, approximately 20 percent, of the total Aboriginal population. Discussions often also seem to assume that the reserve in question exists in isolation from the broader Canadian community; this is true for the numerous and generally small northern native communities, but it is certainly not true for the large reserves near big cities in the south.

Just as the social, cultural, economic, and political conditions of Aboriginal communities vary greatly, so also do the possibilities for self-government and the attendant rights. This paper will for the most part deal with the issues as though they related to the "pure" case of the isolated, status community. This approach best highlights the issues. At the same time, the rights issues of other Aboriginal peoples, whether off-reserve, non-status, or on reserves near big cities with mixed Aboriginal and non-Aboriginal populations, have added complexities and, perhaps, a weaker argument for a drastically different rights regime from the "pure" case. To examine the "pure" case is to go a long way towards addressing the issues relating to the others.

WHAT RIGHTS SHOULD ABORIGINAL SELF-GOVERNMENTS HAVE AGAINST OTHER GOVERNMENTS?

The question of the rights of Aboriginal self-governments against other governments concerns autonomy and what freedom from interference by other governments an Aboriginal self-government should have. The United States example is instructive on the rights of Aboriginal governments against other levels of government. Indians are an anomaly to the American constitutional order because they are self-contained and self-governing entities to a large extent insulated from interference by the dominant governments. In the mid-nineteenth century Chief Justice John Marshall incorporated ideas stemming both from the British tradition and from the writings of Francisco de Vitoria in a doctrine of tribal sovereignty.[6] In the 1832 decision in *Worcester v. Georgia*, Marshall held that Indians retained their character as a distinct political community of a national character.[7] This was an elaboration of a decision he made in the preceding year, *Cherokee Nation v. Georgia*, in which he found that the Cherokee Nation was a nation, defined as a distinct political society separated from others, capable of managing its own affairs and governing itself.[8] American Indian tribes, according to Marshall, were not foreign nations; rather, they were domestic dependent nations. Later, in *Johnson v. McIntosh*, Chief Justice Marshall advocated a much attenuated doctrine of Indian tribal sovereignty and nationhood, but his earlier judgements still stand as foundations of constitutional understanding of Indian self-government in the United States.[9] The principles of sovereignty and nationhood were confirmed in *United States v. Kagama*, where the Supreme Court ruled that Indian tribes are self-governing entities within the United States and that they are immune from state legislation but subject to federal jurisdiction when the government chooses to exercise it.[10]

Tribal sovereignty is thus recognized in the United States, but it is a sovereignty exercised by the tribe only where Congress has not legislated or where treaties preclude Congressional action. The legal existence of American Indian tribes is contingent upon federal recognition, and Aboriginal title is subject to extinguishment by Congress. There are no constitutional provisions that protect Indian self-governments or property from encroachment by Congress (although article 1, §8, identifies Congress as the proper body empowered to regulate commerce with Indian tribes), nor are there limits to the exercise of its powers by Congress apart from those that the Supreme Court might consider contrary to the general provisions of treaties, the Constitution, or the Bill of Rights. The exercise of sovereignty can also be limited when Congress chooses to delegate authority to the states. In short, Congress does not grant powers of self-government to Indian tribes. The tribes already have this. However, Congress retains the power to restrict sovereignty and the scope and structures of self-government through legislation. Congress has exercised these powers on many occasions and in many areas.

Consequently, although American law and constitutional interpretation treat Indians as both "sovereign" and "nations," neither term has had much force in practice. This seemingly powerful legal position did not prevent the loss of lands through allotment, the interference in almost every aspect of band management by the Bureau of Indian Affairs, or the espousal by the federal government of a policy of termination. Nor did it prevent a drastic reduction in expenditures on Indians during the Reagan administration. Legal and constitutional terminology in itself is not enough to guarantee full recognition in practice, nor do abstract statements bring rights policies.

Nevertheless, American Indian tribes have, at least since the Indian Reorganization Act of 1934, enjoyed in law more autonomy than Canadian Indian bands. A system of tribal courts in the United States has alleviated many of the problems of Aboriginal peoples in confrontation with the justice system. Indian bands enjoy a measure of self-government. At the same time, the Bureau of Indian Affairs has proven itself to be even more adept than the Canadian Department of Indian Affairs in creating monitoring and accountability mechanisms that reduce much of the true meaning of self-government and political responsibility. Neither Canada nor America has gone far in accepting the right of a self-government to make its own mistakes and then live with these mistakes and their consequences within a regime of freely elected representative government, open debate, and transparency and accountability.[11]

In Canada the British North America Act of 1867 clearly assigned responsibility for "Indians and Lands reserved for the Indians" to the federal government (§91(24)). At the same time, "Property and Civil Rights" were assigned to the provinces (§92(13)), and the provinces retained ownership and control over Crown lands within the provincial boundaries. This division between federal and provincial spheres has caused many problems over the years, including the issues of the extent to which Indians would be regarded by provincial governments as citizens of the province and entitled to benefit from programmes of provincial governments and the conundrum in land claims that the province owns the lands outside reservations, while much of the claim by band or tribe is directed against the federal government for failure to live up to treaty or other federal obligations. In effect, the level of government that owns the resources necessary to resolve the claim is not necessarily a party to the dispute.

The constitutional rights of Canada's Aboriginal peoples were given formal constitutional recognition in the Constitution Act, 1982, which in §35 states:

35(1) The existing Aboriginal and treaty rights of the Aboriginal peoples of Canada are hereby recognized and affirmed.
(2) In this Act, "Aboriginal peoples of Canada" includes the Indian, Inuit and Métis peoples of Canada.
(3) For greater certainty, in subsection (1) "treaty rights" includes rights that now exist by way of land claims agreements or may be so acquired.
(4) Notwithstanding any other provision of this Act, the Aboriginal and treaty rights referred to in subsection (1) are guaranteed equally to male and female persons.

In addition, §25 contains an interpretive clause that stipulates that

25. The guarantee in this Charter of certain rights and freedoms shall not be construed so as to abrogate or derogate from any Aboriginal, treaty or other rights or freedoms that pertain to the Aboriginal peoples of Canada including
(a) any rights or freedoms that have been recognized by the Royal Proclamation of October 7, 1763; and
(b) any rights or freedoms that now exist by way of land claims agreements or may be so acquired.

There is no doctrine for Aboriginal peoples in Canada like the American doctrine of domestic dependent nations, and in fact the Canadian government has explicitly rejected the notion that Indian nations are sovereign. The Royal Commission on Aboriginal Peoples, on the other hand, found that "Aboriginal people asserted constantly that their inherent rights of sovereignty and self-determination have never been extinguished or surrendered but continue to this day. They said this fact must be recognized and affirmed by Canadian governments as a basic pre-condition for any negotiations on self-government."[12]

Discussion of the sovereignty and nationhood of Aboriginal peoples in Canada is coloured by concerns over the larger question of Quebec separation. (As I write, the Parti Québécois, whose main platform is Quebec independence, is the government in Quebec and has held two province-wide referendums on separation, the most recent, in 1995, being defeated by only the narrowest of margins.) The strong nationalist and separatist movement in that French-speaking province now prefers to describe its goal as "sovereignty" rather than using its earlier term of "separation" because "sovereignty" leaves a better taste in the voters' mouths. By analogy, federal government recognition of Aboriginal people as sovereign nations might be taken by sovereign-tists to justify equivalent recognition of Quebec as a sovereign nation. The Canadian government is not likely to change its mind on its opposition to recognizing Aboriginal peoples as sovereign nations.

Canadian courts have been more responsive to rights claims by Aboriginal people – whether for traditional hunting and fishing rights, the fiduciary responsibilities of government, or land claims – than the provincial or federal governments. Starting in the early 1970s, a series of judicial decisions has significantly increased the scope and power of Aboriginal rights and forced governments to respond to Aboriginal claims.[13] The constitutional entrenchment of Aboriginal rights in the 1982 constitution gave the courts further grounds for clarifying these rights and has expanded them to far beyond what governments were willing to recognize or accept only a few decades ago. Both provincial and federal governments are now obliged to recognize traditional fishing and hunting rights and the need to resolve land claims before allowing the Crown lands under dispute to be used for non-Aboriginal purposes. These issues are especially important in the northern terri-tories and in the province of British Columbia where most Indian bands have never signed treaties. At the least, these cases have given added powers to Aboriginal groups in their negotiations with the two levels of government and have given an added inducement to govern-ments to negotiate a settlement to land claims so that orderly develop-ment can proceed for both the Aboriginal and non-Aboriginal people. Even without recognition as sovereign nations, Aboriginal peoples have far more powerful weapons at their disposal in negotiations with other governments now than they had only a few decades ago.

There have been fewer items of legislation dealing with Aboriginal people in Canada than in the United States. This is perhaps not surprising, because in general Canada has fewer statutes governing programs than the United States, and comparable Canadian statutes tend to be less detailed, less specific, and couched in much more general terms than American statutes. This difference is partly a product of the difference in systems of government: detailed and specific legislation in the United States is an instrument through which Congress controls the executive in a system of separated powers; general and broad enabling legislation in Canada is a convenience to the executive in a system where the same body, the cabinet, controls both executive and legislature. The Indian Act of 1876 still remains the act that authorizes the activities of the Indian Affairs department, and although it has been amended over the years, its fundamental provisions relating to the governance of Indian communities and their control by the department have not been substantially altered.

The Indian Act gives the Department of Indian Affairs comprehensive powers over government on reservations. Band governments have much less power than municipal governments (which themselves are not very powerful in Canada), and what powers band governments do have are constricted by, and subject to review and reversal by, the federal government. Perhaps another reason for the paucity of legislation on Aboriginal affairs in comparison with the United States is that the original Indian Act was so comprehensive that the federal government found that it could do most of what it wanted within the act and did not need additional legislative powers. As long as Indians were not a political force and as long as Indian issues were not important politically, all that was needed and done over the years was minor tinkering to the original heavy-handed structure. The ability of Aboriginal communities to bring actions against the federal government was limited. At present, however, with the demands and momentum for self-government increasing year by year, and with Indian issues becoming prominent, the Indian Act, which in many sections is out of date and unwieldy, is in urgent need of substantial revision, perhaps even repeal and replacement by new legislation. The capacity of the Indian Act to be bent to allow for self-government is limited, though the Manitoba bands and the federal government, for one, have reached an agreement on the establishment of self-government within that province.[14]

The Royal Commission on Aboriginal Peoples concluded that self-governments would draw upon Aboriginal traditions of governance, including the centrality of the land, individual autonomy and responsibility, the rule of law, the role of women, elders, and the family or clan, leadership, consensus in decision making, and the restoration of traditional institutions.[15] The core jurisdiction of Aboriginal self-governments would include "all matters that are of vital concern to the life and welfare of a particular Aboriginal people, do not have a major impact on adjacent jurisdictions, and are not otherwise the object of transcendent federal or provincial concern."[16] Core and periphery jurisdictions would include Constitution and governmental institutions; citizenship and membership; elections and referendums; access to and residence in the territory; lands, waters, sea ice, and natural resources; preservation, protection, and management of the environment, including wild animals and fish; economic life, including commerce, labour, agriculture, grazing, hunting, trapping, fishing, forestry, mining, and management of natural resources in general; the operation of businesses, trades, and professions; transfer and management of public monies and other assets; taxation; family matters, including marriage, divorce, and adoption and child custody; property rights, including succession and estates; education; social services and welfare, including child welfare; health; language, culture, values, and traditions; criminal law and procedure; and the administration of justice, including the establishment of courts and tribunals with civil and criminal jurisdiction."[17] In some areas, criminal law, for instance, these proposed powers exceed those of Canada's provinces.

The Royal Commission proposed three models for self-government.[18] The first, the "Nation" model, would have an identifiable land base, parts of which might be shared with non-Aboriginal governments under co-jurisdiction or comanagement arrangements. Citizenship would be defined by the nation through a broad range of criteria though these criteria, unlike the Indian Act, would not include a blood quantum (some minimum proportion of Aboriginal ancestry). Non-Aboriginal residents would not be citizens. The nation government would exercise a broad range of powers, including powers over land, justice, education, welfare, public works, and other services. Internal government procedures and structures would vary from nation to nation and would build upon a particular nation's traditions. Nation governments could be centrally or federally organized and could be composed of a series of geographically separated communities. They could have urban components or extensions. A nation government would be more powerful than municipal governments, which in Canada are creatures of the province, and would, in fact, be more like a provincial than a municipal government. The Commission did not identify a list of Aboriginal nations that would be eligible for this sort of government. It thought the number of distinct Aboriginal nations might be as high as eighty, although at the time of first European contact there were between fifty and sixty Aboriginal nations inhabiting the territories now making up Canada.[19]

The second model, a "public" government, would be one like the one proposed for Nunavut (the new territory in the Eastern Arctic to be created out of the Northwest Territories for the Inuit of the region) or for the Inuit government of Makivik in Northern Quebec. All residents of the area would be citizens.[20] A public government would serve as the government for both the resident Aboriginal peoples and non-Aboriginals alike. The important factor would be that the Aboriginal peoples would form the majority. Some land could be public, for the peoples as a whole, while other land could be owned by the Aboriginal peoples for their uses, and still other comanaged. A public government would be organized to serve both Aboriginal and non-Aboriginal people who live in a defined territory. It would differ from a non-Aboriginal public government in that the rights of residents might be differentiated to allow the Aboriginal majority to retain treaty and other rights, including the right to self-government, certain economic rights, for example in the harvesting of renewable resources, and rights in the protection of their cultural heritage and languages. The powers of a public Aboriginal government might, like those of Nunavut, be like those of a territory. Or, like that of the Inuit in Northern Quebec, they might have enhanced municipal jurisdiction.

The third, "community-of-interest" model, would not be land-based or territorial, though it might have access to a specific area of unoccupied Crown land.[21] Membership in a community-of-interest government would be based on Aboriginal identity and voluntary affiliation. These individuals and families of Aboriginal heritage might or might not have political, cultural, or family affiliations with a particular nation. Unlike nation or public Aboriginal governments, a community-of-interest government would not exercise the right of self-government, and its jurisdiction and authority would be limited and would be assigned, delegated, or transferred by other Canadian and Aboriginal governments. It would focus on matters of immediate human impact, such as education, culture, language, social services, child welfare, housing, and economic development. The main functions of community-of-interest governments would be service delivery to Aboriginal people in large cities, though the functions might apply in some nonurban areas as well. They would relate closely to those of municipal governments in their regions.

What the Commission did not propose was self-governments like most of those now existing, agreed to, or under discussion in Canada. These latter are primarily of the municipal model and do not exercise many functions beyond those of municipal governments. These include the Sechelt band of British Columbia, which was established by federal statute of 1985; the governments of the James Bay Cree and the Inuit of Northern Quebec, which were established by federal and Quebec statutes; and the agreements for self-government of the Indian bands of Manitoba and elsewhere. The exception is Nunavut, which, like the present Northwest Territories, will have powers approximating those of a province. The Commission's focus, stemming as it did from notions of sovereignty and of Aboriginal nationhood, was primarily on the government of an Aboriginal nation. Self-government as a sort of enhanced municipality living under the laws of the province was scarcely considered as an option, despite the indisputable fact that such a municipal type of structure and power has proven to be the norm in self-government as actually implemented.

There is a seemingly unbridgeable chasm here between the aspirations of Aboriginal leaders and what other levels of government are willing to grant. Aboriginal leaders demand that tribes be formally recognized as sovereign nations, a demand that was repeated by the Royal Commission. But the federal government, for very powerful political reasons, is not likely to grant this recognition. Quite the opposite to what Aboriginal leaders demand, virtually all self-governments negotiated and agreed to by the federal government and Aboriginal communities are of the enhanced municipal model that the Commission did not even consider and that has been rejected by national Aboriginal leaders. Clearly the aspirations and demands of national Aboriginal organizations are out of sync with what is actually happening in the self-government project.

It is not likely that in the foreseeable future Aboriginal peoples will be recognized as sovereign, nor are their governments likely to be of the nation model. But, it might be wondered, does this really affect the possibilities for their future development in any serious way? The answer is that it probably does not. The most successful Indian tribes in Canada, such as the Sechelt in British Columbia or the James Bay Cree of Quebec, have self-governments on the enhanced municipal model. Whether they are formally recognized as sovereign nations or not is irrelevant to their economic development, their capacity for self-government, or, for that matter, the capacity to retain their culture, language, and lifestyle. Content is more important than labels.

The experience of the United States shows that designating Aboriginal self-governments as "sovereign" and as "nations" is no guarantee either that their sovereignty or their nationhood will be recognized by the dominant society or make any difference to how governments act (see chapter 9). The labels are not important; what are important are the processes by which the rights of self-governments are affirmed and the commitment of other levels of government to the recognition and achievement of these rights. Canada's explicit constitutional recognition of Aboriginal rights is already greater than that of the United States, and at present the political will appears to exist in Canada to ensure that effective self-government of the enhanced municipal type becomes a reality.

In the long run, the economic base of Aboriginal communities will be a more important determinant of the viability and success of an Aboriginal self-government than recognition as a sovereign nation. At present virtually all Indian bands rely on massive transfers of funds from the federal government for their economic survival. Potential alternative sources of economic resources include a self-government's land base, the economic rents it is entitled to from resource and other developments, the natural resources it owns, the skills and entrepreneurial spirit of its citizens, and its capacity to raise income through taxation and other means. Few of Canada's Indian bands now have the economic resources to be self-sufficient. Resolution of land claims will help to create a stronger economic base. But even accommodation of the full land claims of many bands would not provide an adequate economic base for their existing population, let alone the much larger one they will have in the future.[22]

One of the least satisfactory aspects of the report of the Royal Commission on Aboriginal Peoples is its discussion of economic development. On the one hand it states that self-reliance is a goal and that "a government cannot be truly autonomous if it depends on other governments for most of its financing." Therefore "first and foremost, effective government depends upon a sound economic base. Without an adequate land and resource base, and without flourishing economic activity, Aboriginal governments will have little access to independent sources of revenue." On the other hand, fiscal autonomy apparently means unconditional grants from other levels of government, not that self-governments should raise their own revenues through taxes: "financial arrangements should reflect the principle that for Aboriginal self-government to be meaningful, fiscal autonomy and political autonomy should grow together. This relationship should be reflected in the proportion of transfers to Aboriginal governments from the federal and provincial governments that are unconditional. The nature of transfers from other governments, for example, should reflect this principle." Most funding now is "of a highly conditional nature."[23]

The Royal Commission proposed to resolve the social and economic problems of Aboriginal peoples through massive increases in expenditures by federal and provincial governments: "governments should commit significant additional resources to resolve historical claims, restructure the political relationship, and improve living conditions and economic opportunities for Aboriginal people."[24] They calculated that governments should increase their annual spending "so that by year five, expenditures are between $1.5 and $2 billion more than they are today." These higher expenditures would need "to be sustained for a number of years," but the economic costs would result in a substantial economic gain for all Canadians. "They will lead to greater economic self-reliance for Aboriginal people and restore health and vitality to Aboriginal individuals and communities." The positive results would begin to be realized in terms of the economy and government finances by about the tenth year following the adoption of this recommendation, and after about year twenty there would be a net gain.

The federal government did not respond to this proposal with any enthusiasm. For some years the federal government had been engaged in severe cost-cutting measures, especially in transfers to other governments, to cope with a huge and mounting deficit. At the same time as other groups suffered from these cutbacks, federal expenditures on Aboriginal people were one of the few programs for which spending was increasing. There was little evidence that bands with greater economic resources were resolving their problems more successfully than those with lesser, and the Commission did not defend their proposal by offering evidence that more expenditures were a proven solution. The official opposition in Parliament, the Reform Party, had proposed reducing, not increasing, expenditures on Aboriginal peoples.

Regardless of how serious these problems of rights in relation to other governments appear to be for status on-reserve Indians, they are much more serious to non-status and off-reserve Indians and Métis. The federal government does not consider these peoples to be Indians under the terms of the Constitution and the Indian Act. They are considered to be a provincial responsibility, and provincial governments have been far less sympathetic to claims of special status, needs for massive funding, land bases, and sources of support other than the federal government. The Royal Commission recommended that these non-status Aboriginal peoples be accepted by the federal government as Indians and as a federal responsibility, but this is not likely to happen, not least because of the horrendous cost implications to the federal government of accepting this more than doubling of the Aboriginal population that it would be responsible for. The inequalities in legal status and in government support are enormous within the broad collectivity of Aboriginal peoples. They are exacerbated by continued out-migration to large cities, where at present Aboriginal people form an underprivileged underclass, with problems seemingly as intractable as those of the reserves they left behind.

SHOULD THE RIGHTS TO
SELF-GOVERNMENT BE EXPLICITLY
ENTRENCHED IN THE CANADIAN
CONSTITUTION?

The Royal Commission on Aboriginal Peoples argued that "the inherent right of self-government was recognized and affirmed in §35(1) of the Constitution Act, 1982 as an existing Aboriginal or treaty-protected right."[25] The federal government has also stated that it accepts that the right to self-government exists within present constitutional provisions. Nevertheless, the aborted Charlottetown Accord would have added, to §35 of the 1982 Constitution, the statement that "The Aboriginal peoples of Canada have the inherent right of self-government within Canada." One may wonder what might be added, by further constitutional entrenchment, to a right that both sides accept to be already recognized in the Constitution.

The Constitution Act, 1982 provided for a series of constitutional conferences on matters that directly affect Canada's Aboriginal peoples, including the identification and definition of the rights of those peoples to be included in future constitutional amendments. Aboriginal leaders put an enormous amount of time and energy into preparing for these conferences, and they were left with no small residue of bitterness and resentment when their efforts came to little. At the final of these constitutional conferences, provincial premiers were unwilling to accept the possible impositions that constitutional entrenchment of further rights, especially the right to self-government, might place on their governments. Not the least result of this impasse was that Elijah Harper, its sole Aboriginal member, prevented the Manitoba legislature from voting in support of the Meech Lake Accord. The demise of the Meech Lake Accord caused massive resentment in Quebec and in turn paved the way for a grave constitutional crisis in Canada, which the Charlottetown agreement, because of its defeat in a nation-wide referendum, failed to resolve.

The Royal Commission carefully avoided recommendations requiring constitutional amendment. (The one exception was their recommendation that the Alberta Métis Settlements Act be constitutionally entrenched.)[26] At the same time, the Commission felt that in future discussions of constitutional change Aboriginal peoples should participate on all aspects of the Constitution, not just the ones that apply explicitly to them. "The moral legitimacy of any future constitutional amendment would be brought into question if Aboriginal people did not have a say in its content."[27] Areas of explicit concern to Aboriginal peoples would include, first, those that would ensure greater certainty in such matters as self-government, where at present the right is inferred rather than explicitly stated. Aboriginal governments would be entrenched as one of three orders of government, along with the federal and provincial levels.[28] Métis would also be constitutionally recognized as being included in the term "Indian" as it is used in the Canadian Constitution. Second would be "consequential amendments that become necessary as a result of amendments of the first sort." Third would be institutional amendments relating to Aboriginal participation in the House of Commons and Senate, and possibly a third, Aboriginal, House with its own role in the legislative process.[29] In addition would be other amendments, such as to make Aboriginal peoples formally part of the processes of constitutional amendment, to clarify such things as exactly who constitutes a Métis person, and to entrench a proposed Royal Proclamation that would state the principles governing relationships between Aboriginal peoples and other governments. This is by no means a trivial list. To consider where these amendments would fit into the Canadian Constitution and constitutional amendment processes, it is necessary to look more broadly at the Canadian Constitution.

Statements of rights exist at many different levels, with widely varying degrees of legal power and significance. The constitutions of many democratic countries contain statements of fundamental rights that have no legal power but simply represent ideals for the government and the polity to bear in mind. Great Britain has no formally entrenched statement of rights. Rights in Great Britain exist in the common law, in acts of Parliament, and in documents like the Magna Carta, which, in effect, was a treaty between the king and wealthy nobility. Most key aspects of the British constitution are unwritten. Prime Minister Diefenbaker's Canadian Bill of Rights of 1960 was an ordinary act of the Canadian Parliament. Its legal force was as a statute for construction and interpretation by the courts of other acts of Parliament. The American Bill of Rights is part of the written American Constitution, and the principles in it are enforceable by the courts. The American Constitution itself is brief, difficult to amend, and for the most part contains very general statements of principles and rights that the courts and legislatures must then define and interpret.

The Canadian Constitution partakes of both British and American practices. The original British North America Act of 1867, which was a simple statute of the British Parliament, allocated powers between the federal and provincial jurisdictions and stated that its intention was to create a dominion "with a constitution similar in principle to that of the United Kingdom." In effect, the principle of the supremacy of Parliament, which underlies the British system of government, was to be adopted in Canada. Within their spheres of jurisdiction both federal and provincial legislatures were sovereign and free to legislate as they saw fit, with judicial review for the most part confined to the question of whether a particular piece of legislation was "intra vires" or "ultra vires" – within the competence of that level of government and legislature or not.

Prime Minister Trudeau, soon after being elected in 1968, began a determined push towards constitutional entrenchment of a bill of rights along the lines of the American model. It took fourteen years to achieve, the result being the Constitution Act, 1982. This act itself is a curious mixture of both general statements of rights and principles and specific negotiated compromises between the ten provinces and the federal government. As a consequence of this mixed heritage, the Canadian written Constitution contains some strange provisions.

It is the only constitution in the world that mentions sawdust (a provincial responsibility). The British North America Act of 1867 in a similar vein of minutiae made Sable Island off Nova Scotia a federal responsibility. Among the most contentious parts of the 1982 Constitution was the amending formula. The very complex and cumbersome formula that was finally agreed to demands that some provisions, like the Charter of Rights and Freedoms, require agreement of the federal Parliament and all ten provincial legislatures to amend. (Abbreviated amending procedures are available for less important matters.) Experience has shown that major amendments are very difficult to make. Although there have been a few post-1982 amendments dealing with provisions that affect relatively unimportant clauses, or a single province, the two efforts at comprehensive amendment (Meech Lake and Charlottetown) failed. Not only did they fail, but the efforts themselves were immensely destructive in terms of creating bitter feelings and harming their intended goal of national unity.

Any Canadian government that wants to amend the constitution in any serious way must be prepared to put much of its energy and political resources into the amending effort over a period of many years and, in so doing, perforce neglect other urgent concerns; it must be prepared to enter into a process of barter and negotiation with provincial governments and other groups (four national Aboriginal peoples' associations participated in the negotiations leading to the Charlottetown Accord); it must be prepared to see the issues considered in amendments escalate and expand to cover totally unforeseen and unexpected details not related to the original purposes of amendment; it must be prepared for major political leaders and others to articulate extreme demands and positions and to utter threats to divide the country; it must be prepared to submit the final document to a national referendum in which the currently accepted decision-rule means that a majority in every province must approve; and it must in the end be prepared to accept failure as the likely outcome, with all the disappointment, anger, and estrangement attendant upon the frustration of so many hopes and the waste of so much energy. Not surprisingly, the likelihood of a Canadian government wanting to subject itself and the country to this traumatic process in the near future is low.

Even when a right is entrenched in a constitution and subject to judicial review, this by no means guarantees how the right will be defined by the courts. The courts can be full of surprises – as, for example, the federal government and the government of British Columbia have learnt to their cost in many cases dealing with Aboriginal rights. The process of transmuting abstract statements of rights into actual policies and programs involves legislatures that create the laws that express the trade-offs, that find the balance, and that make specific the general. It involves the cabinet ministers and public servants who, in the process of changing provisions of a statute into a working program, have as much influence over the actual policy as the legislature – and often more. It involves the courts, to which appeals can be made and which have their own biases and predilections and can reach conclusions desired by either, both, or neither party to a dispute.

In the British parliamentary tradition, Parliament is supreme, and legislation passed by Parliament is the main source of explicitly defined rights. The parliamentary processes of representative and responsible government are expected to assure that fundamental rights are recognized. In Canada the supremacy of Parliament is constrained by a constitution that limits the powers of each level of government, and it is even further constrained now by the Charter and other provisions of the Constitution Act, 1982. At the same time, Parliament (or the provincial legislature) remains supreme within its field of competence. Judicial rejection of statutes can be overridden by Parliament and the provincial legislatures through the "notwithstanding" clause (§33), which gives them the power to protect legislation from a judicial review (or disallowance) finding that provisions in the legislation contravene the Charter of Rights and Freedoms. Rights in the Charter can be further constrained by such limitations as are demonstrably justified in a free and democratic society (§1).

With all these qualifications to the strength of entrenchment and obstacles against achieving it, one might well wonder what could possibly be the value of entrenching further Aboriginal rights, such as making explicit the right to self-government, and why any politician in her or his right mind would want to begin the exhausting, convoluted, and high-risk process of seeking constitutional amendment. The advantages of recognition in the Constitution appear to be both symbolic and tangible. They are symbolic because the Constitution, sawdust and Sable Island notwithstanding, is the most authoritative, prestigious, visible, and powerful statement of the highest political ideals of the country. They are tangible because as long as rights and powers are specified, governments cannot claim that they do not exist. It was only after entrenchment of the right to self-government was rejected by political leaders that the Royal Commission found the right to be already implicit in existing constitutional provisions.

Constitutions around the world divide into those that are couched in general terms, like the American, and those that are detailed and specific, like the Swedish. They also divide into those that are difficult to amend, like the American, and those that are relatively easy to amend, like the Swiss or Swedish. Successful constitutions divide into two groups: those that are brief and general but difficult to amend, like the American, and those that are detailed and long but easy to amend, like the Swedish. Canada finds itself in the worst of constitutional worlds, with a constitution that is long and detailed, but very difficult to amend.[30] As a result of the tendency towards length there is a strong desire among groups, interests, and provincial governments to have detailed and specific provisions and rights recognized in the Constitution, but the amending process is so difficult (probably more difficult in practice than the American) that the likelihood of success in getting new rights or other provisions entrenched is very low.

Entrenchment of the right to Aboriginal self-government is not likely to happen in the foreseeable future.[31] In at least the short-term future, the bottom-up approach to self-government, of federal and provincial government negotiations directly with Indian bands and groups of bands, is the only feasible one. The bottom-up approach could be enhanced by a statute of the federal Parliament enlarging the range of issues to be discussed and determined in negotiations leading to self-government, ensuring that the process is fair, ensuring adequate resources to Aboriginal participants in the process, and in general speeding up what is now a lengthy, obstacle-ridden, and largely unsuccessful process. Statutory change is far more likely to happen than entrenchment and would probably be more useful.

RIGHTS OF CITIZENS AGAINST ABORIGINAL SELF-GOVERNMENTS

The question of the rights citizens should have against Aboriginal self-governments is not normally asked. The more usual question is what rights and powers Aboriginal self-governments should have, particularly against other levels of government. But the question of citizens' rights within self-government still needs to be looked at. After all, self-governments, whatever their particular form, will be recognizable as governments in the Western sense of the term. Self-governments will have citizens and leaders. They will have legal powers over citizens and others in their area of jurisdiction. They will perform police, judicial, and law-making functions. They will allocate resources and administer crucial programmes in education, welfare, housing, and economic development. They will likely have the power to tax. Citizens' rights against government in the West have evolved as a means of protecting citizens against arbitrary and abusive use of these sorts of powers and as a way of controlling governments and holding them accountable.

Perhaps even the term "citizens" is not appropriate, because it draws on liberal-democratic discourse (using the term "liberal-democratic" as in political philosophy) of human rights and freedoms. Certainly many Aboriginal writers on self-government have objected to the entire liberal-democratic rights terminology as being ethnocentric and inapplicable.[32] "Members" and "membership" are commonly used terms, but these, with their heritage from the Indian Act, also have potentially offensive connotations of imperialism and colonialism. But regardless of terminology, the issue remains the same: Aboriginal self-governments have and will have a designated and legally defined set of human beings who are members of the band, or tribe, and as such are citizens and members of self-governments. Self-governments will also have powers over their citizens/members.

Like other statements of fundamental rights, the Canadian Charter of Rights and Freedoms includes basic rights to liberty and equality. The Charter applies equally to federal and provincial governments but is silent on its application to Aboriginal self-governing units, perhaps because in 1982 the possibility of such self-governments becoming legally recognized entities with special rights and powers had not been contemplated. As the Royal Commission on Aboriginal Peoples pointed out, "The drafters of the *Constitution Act, 1982*, did not provide in explicit language for Aboriginal governments or attempt to describe their exact position in the Canadian federation."[33]

There is by no means universal agreement, particularly within Aboriginal leadership, on whether the Charter should apply to self-governments. The Royal Commission on Aboriginal Peoples found that there were two opposing viewpoints. On the one hand was the approach that "as a matter basic constitutional principle, it would be highly anomalous if Canadian citizens enjoyed the protection of the Charter in their relations with every government in Canada except for Aboriginal governments."[34] Freedom of speech, for example, should be enjoyed by all Canadians, including Aboriginal peoples. "According to this approach" the Commission concluded, "it is hard to imagine that Aboriginal governments are exempt (or would want to be exempt) from this fundamental guarantee, as enshrined in the *Canadian Charter of Rights and Freedoms*."[35] On the other hand was the view that "some Charter provisions reflect individualistic values that are antithetical to many Aboriginal cultures ... According to this view, then, if the Charter applied to Aboriginal governments, it could hamper and even stifle the efforts of Aboriginal nations to revive and strengthen their cultures and traditions. As such, the Charter might operate as the unwitting servant of the forces of assimilation and domination."[36] If there is to be any sort of statement of rights, it should be one developed by Aboriginal people in the context of Aboriginal traditions of governance and culture, so this argument goes.

The Commission itself chose an intermediate approach that it claimed combined the strength of both views while avoiding the extremes they represent. Its main components were, first, that all people in Canada are entitled to enjoy the protection of the Charter's general provisions in their relations with governments in Canada, no matter where in Canada they are located or which governments are involved, and second, that Aboriginal governments should occupy the same position relative to the Charter as the federal and provincial governments. Aboriginal governments should thus have recourse to notwithstanding clauses under §33 to the same extent as the federal and provincial governments (additionally, the "opting out" section can be used to exempt governments from some provisions of the Charter). Third, the Commission stated that the Charter, in its application to Aboriginal governments, should be interpreted in a manner that allows considerable scope for distinctive Aboriginal philosophical outlooks, cultures, and traditions.

The Commission thought that their conclusions on notwithstanding powers should be

tempered by a basic consideration. The power to pass notwithstanding clauses belongs only to an Aboriginal nation and, in the absence of self-governing treaties, can be exercised only in relation to matters falling within the core areas of Aboriginal jurisdiction. This means that the governments of local Aboriginal communities do not have the power to pass notwithstanding clauses. It also means that for an Aboriginal nation to pass notwithstanding clauses in relation to matters falling within the periphery, the power to pass such clauses must be acknowledged specifically in self-government treaties or agreements with the Crown.[37]

Further, the Commission observed,

The Charter is a flexible instrument, one that gives governments a significant measure of latitude in implementing its terms. In particular, §1 enables governments to enact reasonable limits on Charter rights so long as these "can demonstrably be justified in a free and democratic society." This section is, of course, available to Aboriginal governments. Section 25 of the Charter gives an Aboriginal government an alternative way to justify its activities when these are challenged under the Charter. This section enables an Aboriginal government to argue that certain governmental rules or practices, which may seem unusual by general Canadian standards, are consistent with the particular culture, philosophical outlook and traditions of the Aboriginal nation, and as such are justified. This approach is consistent with the contextual approach that the Supreme Court of Canada has adopted more generally in applying the Charter.

The courts, the Commission felt, would be sensitive to the particular requirements of Aboriginal self-governments and would ensure that the Charter would be interpreted in a manner deferential to and consistent with Aboriginal cultures and traditions. The Commission offered, as an example of where this sensitivity might be needed, an Aboriginal charter of rights containing a series of provisions dealing with the treatment of accused persons in an Aboriginal justice system. Here, the non-Aboriginal courts should "take these provisions into account in determining the effect of the legal rights provisions of the Canadian Charter with respect to the Aboriginal government in question."[38] Aboriginal juvenile justice systems might also deviate from the non-Aboriginal norm as to rights to legal counsel. On the other hand, the Commission observed that it was clear in the Charter that Aboriginal self-governments, like other Canadian governments, should recognize and accept legal equality of the two sexes.

The Commission was obviously trying to find a middle ground between complete subordination to the Western ideals and values of the Canadian Charter, on the one hand, and complete disregard of the Charter in favour of an unspecified but pure Aboriginal structure of rights, on the other. The examples it gave of where Aboriginal versions of rights might differ from the non-Aboriginal norms are so narrowly focussed on problems of legal proceedings as to be unhelpful in considering the question of where Aboriginal governments might properly deviate from western norms of, for example, representative government or of equal access of all citizens to the benefits of government programs.

To explore these important areas on which the Commission was silent, some sense of the nature of rights in modern non-Aboriginal society is necessary. In modern rights discourse, rights are classified into three categories.[39] The first is that of negative rights, which the citizen claims against government. These include the right to participate in government through elections, voting, political activism, speech-making, and so forth. They also include freedom from interference with liberty, including the right to free speech; freedom of conscience and religion, of thought, belief, and artistic expression, of association, and of the press; the right to enter into contracts, to own and dispose of property, and so on. Citizenship, the right to be a member of the community, is one of these basic rights. Important also are the rights to freedom of person, of protection against arbitrary arrest, imprisonment, punishment, or sequestration of property. These rights are negative in the sense that they set limits on the extent to which government can interfere with the activities of citizens, and they also give citizens the power to influence the decisions of government that affect them. In the category of negative rights belong also the democratic rights of voting for representatives in an elected government, of standing for office, and of having elections at reasonable intervals. These rights say that governments should be freely chosen and effectively held accountable and responsible.

The second class is that of positive rights, or statements of what citizens are entitled to get from government. Positive rights are a more recent addition to the panoply of human rights than negative rights, and they are largely associated with the arrival of the positive, activist state in the late nineteenth and twentieth centuries. Positive rights include such rights as the right to housing, food, and clothing, to education, to a minimum standard of living, to medical care, to economic security, to pensions in old age and for the disabled; and so on. Clearly they are a more expensive proposition to government than negative rights, and they imply a standard of living and general level of economic productivity sufficiently high to enable government to provide these costly benefits to all citizens.

The third class of rights is procedural, including the sort that the Commission mentioned in its discussion of rights that might differ from the Canadian norm under an Aboriginal self-government. Some of the most important procedural rights define the circumstances in which, and the procedures by which, government can take away or infringe upon the freedoms of the citizen against the state. The most formally established of these define due process and fairness in the courts of law. Western states are not in complete agreement as to what due process and natural justice mean. For example, the rules of evidence vary from country to country. Hearsay evidence is admissible in many European countries, while it is not in the British common law tradition; the British tradition of the jury has no counterpart in many European countries; and there is also a pronounced split between British-style courts, where the judge is an impartial presiding officer over a contest between two teams of legal adversaries, and the continental style where the judge is more actively engaged in the pursuit of truth, in an inquisitorial rather than an adversarial format.[40] Other procedural rights involve the methods available to citizens for claiming both positive and negative rights. These would include the administrative procedures by which a citizen can claim welfare assistance, housing, support for business development, free education, or benefits from universal medical-care insurance.

The ways rights are affirmed in practice vary from country to country, just as in practice there are different and contradictory definitions of natural justice in courtroom and other procedures. Recognizing this helps to ensure that discussion of rights for Aboriginal peoples is not so bound by what is familiar to Canadians that it fails to appreciate that many other styles than those most familiar to North Americans are possible and defensible for achieving procedural justice and recognizing negative and positive rights. The same argument, of course, holds true for negative and positive rights as well. Western countries vary enormously in their forms of representative government, their instrumental definitions of civil liberties, and the policies and programs that define the positive rights to which citizens are entitled.

Definitions of rights arose in specific places and times, under specific systems of government, and in specific cultures. It is wrong to make the assumption that one particular definition of a right, or for that matter one particular list of rights, is universal, and applies to all people, in all places, at all times. In fact, societies that formally espouse the western style of human rights have been relatively few. Compare those that espouse some other form of ideals, such as that the purpose of the state is to ensure that the will of God or the Creator is observed on this earth or that revealed or scientific truth (such as the revolution of the proletariat or the leadership of the master race) should be achieved or that the traditional order, hierarchy, and structure of society and politics are justifiable simply because they have always existed and are what is fit and proper. The Royal Commission on Aboriginal Peoples came close to espousing a revealed truth approach to human laws in such comments as: "For many Aboriginal people, the law is grounded in instructions from the Creator or, alternatively, a body of basic principles embedded in the natural order. Thus basic law is viewed as the 'law of God' or 'natural law.' This basic law gives direction to individuals in fulfilling their responsibilities as stewards of the earth and, by extension, other human beings. The law tells people how to conduct themselves in their relations with one another and with the rest of creation ... Since the law ultimately stems from God, any failure to live by the law is to turn one's back on the Creator's gifts."[41] To modern rights theorists, the key difficulty with these claims for justification by revealed truth and tradition is not that they are wrong or that people disagree on what God or the Creator want but that they foreclose argument and discussion and prevent consideration of the possibility of change and new directions.

The questions that must be asked about citizens and Aboriginal self-government are, first, are there good grounds for insisting that this broad range of negative, positive, and procedural rights should be recognized within self-governments; and, second, if so, then in what form should they be recognized? Is the standard form of right as expressed in non-native society appropriate or are there other options that might seem unfamiliar but that could equally well, or preferably better, achieve the principles of freedom, equality, and justice? I shall consider these together.

Many philosophers in the past treated human rights as "natural," which can logically be, and often has been, interpreted as meaning that these rights existed in some state of nature. The noble savages of Enlightenment thinking come from these roots. Many discussions of Aboriginal rights in Canada use this kind of argument and claim that there was a golden age in the past where all members of the culture shared in a blessed and nonalienated existence and the relationships between humans were conducted on a basis of civility and respect that ensured that the ideals embodied in fundamental rights were recognized.[42] The challenge, if this approach is accepted, is to recreate the past, so that the traditional virtues are once again made manifest and citizens once again live in a state of harmony and fulfilment. As the Royal Commission on Aboriginal Peoples noted, some commentators believe that the structures and processes of long-ago traditional native government need only be reclaimed and recreated for the values and ideals of the society to be revived and create a better world.[43] If this argument is accepted, there is no need for the Western type of rights in self-government.

In opposition to this optimistic vision stands a crueller and more pessimistic view. This line of argument leads to the conclusion that Aboriginal societies need to be moulded to fit the Western model, so that they can prevent the worst excesses of unregulated human behaviour. Non-native observers of traditional native societies in North America have fallen into both camps. Some have seen the Aboriginal peoples as representatives of a golden and blissful state of nature before the intrusions of an artificial state, while others have seen them as living in a Hobbesian world of cruelty and violence. The dominant government policies for most of the nineteenth century and well into the twentieth century followed the latter course and looked at Aboriginal peoples as "in tutelage," training to emerge from their unpleasant past and reap the benefits of the "more advanced" western civilization.[44] These observations and policies were biased, ethnocentric, racist, and based on bad science and erroneous observation. But they were also very influential.

The domninant school of thought in Canada now argues for a Westernized version of self-government, where the rights and freedoms articulated in liberal-democratic statements of rights are accepted as essential to Aboriginal self-government as for other Canadian governments.[45] The Charlottetown Accord concluded that the self-governments should come under the Charter of Rights and Freedoms, and so did the Royal Commission on Aboriginal Peoples.[46]

In considering this question of the applicability of Western types of rights to the relationships between citizens and Aboriginal self-governments, one trap that must be avoided is the assumption that because many traditional native societies did not have the formal structure of government and courts separated from the rest of society and identifiable as discrete institutions, as they are in Western societies, no such institutions and processes existed in traditional societies. They did exist. For the most part they were embedded in the broader structure of society and family. A characteristic of traditional society, as Tönnies and many who followed him have observed, is the lack of differentiation in structures and institutions and processes: family is government, economy, system of justice, society, education, and culture; clan and extended family are community and polity.

Modern Western societies are the unusual ones in the amount of differentiation of functions and processes into many institutions and the division of tasks among specialized bodies and countless varieties of technically competent people. In many ways small traditional societies and communities can operate on a more sensitive and personally aware basis than modern mass societies, where impersonality and consistency of treatment of categories are the bureaucratic norms. But they can also be cruel and unable or unwilling to change.

In a modern Western society constitutional statements of rights are pitched at a very abstract level and must be refined and made more concrete before they can be implemented in any meaningful way. Rights like "liberty" and "equality" are not self-defining. Quite the contrary, they are highly contestable and amenable to many different and often conflicting meanings.[47] One of the most important issues in modern politics, for example, revolves around the meaning of equality, whether it has the very limited meaning of equality before the law or a more expanded meaning of equality of opportunity, in effect a level playing field, or whether it should have the even more expanded meaning of equality of condition, such as is intended by some programs for affirmative action. This last meaning is entrenched for some groups in the Canadian Charter of Rights and Freedoms.

Fundamental rights often and inevitably conflict with one another. A great deal of the argument over rights is about the trade-offs between freedom and equality. An excess of freedom leads to great social inequalities. Some laws, for example the prohibitions against indenturing oneself or one's children, exist to prevent the inequalities that excessive freedom, and the domination of some by others, creates. On the other hand, an excessive zeal in working towards equality can lead to severe constraints on personal freedom by insisting on conformity. The most fundamental conflict in liberal democracy lies between democratic rights – the power of a majority to legislate as it sees fit – and the rights of minorities to be protected against the majority, in effect, the conflict between liberal principles and democratic processes. With an entrenched charter of rights and freedoms the courts become the adjudicators of these conflicts. Further, rights are not absolute. Each has boundaries outside of which behaviour is against the law. For example, freedom of speech is limited by laws on libel, slander, false news, hate propaganda, treasonous utterance, pornography, and many other prohibitions.

The legislative processes in Western democracies can quite properly be viewed as an effort to define fundamental freedoms, to establish appropriate limits to them, and to resolve the trade-offs and conflicts between them in a way that is satisfactory to the polity.[48] Changes to legislation, and new legislation, come as a result of changes in the economy and society or as a result of changing emphasis on and interpretation of fundamental ideals and values. In this way, the meaning and practical interpretation of rights, as well as the emphasis given to one right over others, alters over the years. The rights themselves, in a very abstract sense, remain as constant ideals and symbols. For rights in Aboriginal societies also, whether formally articulated or embedded in practices, their meaning, the trade-offs between them, and their limits will change over the years. So also will the way they are expressed in practice and the means established to ensure they are recognized.

The key question on rights and self-government is whether or not Aboriginal societies, economies, and polities have become modern enough so that they should, like other modern Western societies, adhere to the sort of rights espoused in the Charter of Rights and Freedoms. Aboriginal societies have been adapting and changing since the coming of the first Europeans and doubtless were adapting long before the arrival of Europeans, as the Ice Age waned and the era of megafauna drew to a close. In the western plains of Canada the now traditional culture of buffalo hunting on horseback is itself an innovation derived from the Europeans. Horses had not existed in North America before the Spaniards first brought them, and horses reached the Canadian plains and changed Aboriginal culture long before the first Europeans got there. The fur trade caused a first wave of cultural adaptation, as changes came to the woodland Indian culture through the introduction of metal implements for hunting, cooking, sewing, and other tasks. Native cultures and societies continue to change in response to external and internal pressures as new technologies are adopted and make their mark.

Despite these changes in the centuries since the beginning of the fur trade, the traditional economy and culture of Canada's Inuit and remote northern Indians were largely intact until after the Second World War. Beginning in the 1950s, however, government began to provide more welfare, health, education, public works, and other services to native communities. Provision of these services required massive cultural and economic changes, including the relocation of seminomadic people into settled communities, disruption of the traditional hunting and gathering economy, the breakdown of traditional learning and acculturation patterns because of the demands of the school year, the creation of a cash economy through welfare and other transfer payments, and the extensive intrusion of government administration (whether by the band or the Department of Indian and Northern Affairs) into community life and the economy. At the same time, large-scale developments through government (the military, hydroelectricity, and so on) or business (mining, oil and gas, timber) began to limit and intrude upon traditional Aboriginal pursuits and communities.

These transformations of the economy and culture, loss of traditional life-style, and expansion in the role of government have forced the most profound changes ever experienced by many northern native communities.[49] Aboriginal peoples in Canada, like Canadians generally, now live for the most part in a cash economy, where the standard form of economic transaction is through a cash exchange. This is true for labour, where employment income is in money, which in turn is used for the purchase of goods. The traditional subsistence economy, based on noncash transactions of hunting and gathering and frequently relying on bartering and the gift relationship for the distribution of goods, is by no means extinct. But it forms only a small part of the economy of most Aboriginal societies, even in remote northern communities where country food and fur trapping still prominently contribute to subsistence. The fastest growing parts of the northern economy are outside the traditional economy. One is the modern sector, in both government and private spheres, where transactions, through wages and employment, are on a cash basis. Government forms a far bigger part of the economy in the Canadian north than it does in the south, and a bigger proportion in native communities generally than in non-native. In the Northwest Territories, for example, 40 percent of direct employment is in the public service, while government-related employment accounts for an additional 20 percent.[50] Comparable figures in the south and in nonnative Canada, would be under 20 and 10 percent respectively. The other fast-growing sector is the welfare economy, which also is based on monetary transactions and which is controlled by government.[51]

Aboriginal cultures have changed so much over the centuries that past practices, even if they were known (and many are not because they have been lost in the dislocations faced by Aboriginal communities), are not a good guide to what might and should happen in the drastically changed present. Most traditional societies, for example, were composed of highly mobile small groups. Membership in these groups was fluid and voluntary; families would come and go as parts of larger agglomerations, and groups of all sizes were peripatetic, with close contacts, including family ties, with numerous other groups. If a particular household did not like the way one camp was led, they could and would pack up, go, and join another.

The settlement of these formerly nomadic groups into permanent communities with stable membership was one of the biggest changes to Aboriginal cultures in the north in recent years. No longer could dissidents or variety seekers easily leave and join another group. Membership in a group, or band, has become a form of legal identity, and membership in one band does not guarantee membership in another if a person or family moves. For many bands, band membership and band membership codes are closely controlled by band leaders.[52] Sanctions of the loss of legal rights associated with band membership affect mobility between native communities and reinforce the inward clustering associated with relocation to settled year-round communities.

Government plays a much more dominant role in Aboriginal communities than in the past. With the bulk of the economic activity in a community being government or government-related, whether in terms of employment in the public service, contracts with government, or the distribution of welfare, housing, and other government programs, the government itself has become the dominant decision maker affecting the economic well-being of citizens. As long as native communities relied on the subsistence economy and as long as the main economic activity was in the fur trade and in transactions with outside firms, band government was not a major influence over the economic situation of individual families and community members. In a traditional community, government had little if anything at all to say about economic matters, except perhaps to resolve disputes over rights to hunting and gathering in a given area or to decide when and how communal hunting and fishing activities would be managed. The rest was left to tradition and individual efforts. Within present-day native communities, particularly in the north but also elsewhere to a large extent, because of the enormous role it plays in the economy of the community, government has a much greater influence over its citizens than do the governments of comparably sized nonnative communities.

In crucial and fundamental areas of the economy, economic relations, and the role and power of government, Aboriginal societies have been modernized and have moved far beyond the practices and relationships of the past. These changes increase the need for citizens to have rights against Aboriginal self-governments. The liberal-democratic political rights of representative and accountable government, of citizen participation, and of due process for guaranteeing these rights are a product of a literate, cash-based transactional society.[53] They are a way of recognizing important social values in a society in which barter, gift, and family relationships no longer dominate the economy. Citizens' rights now extend to the positive sphere and include the distribution of resources within the community through employment, welfare, and other programs. Each of these programs has a means of appealing administrative decisions associated with it. Decisions can also be appealed in the ordinary courts of law. These appeal processes affirm the principles of due process and equity in the assertion of positive and negative rights.

In small-scale traditional Aboriginal societies there was no need for the paraphernalia of courts, rules of justice, representative and accountable government, and formal rules of due process found in Western culture. The economic and social transformations of Aboriginal communities in the twentieth century have been so profound, however, that now Aboriginal self-governments need them as much as governments in the larger nonnative society. These rights and rules are there to protect the citizen against the state, against the arbitrary use of state power, and against the domination of power by one group or family, and to ensure that principles of fairness and equity are followed by government in its handling of collective resources. This is a powerful argument for the recognition of a liberal-democratic style of rights in Aboriginal self-governments.

There are other arguments as well. Liberal democracy does not necessarily make the assumption that government and governors are going to misbehave, but it does make the assumption that misbehaviour is possible and that a political system must ensure that such misbehaviour is exposed and corrected and that the citizen can be assured, through due process, of the redress of grievance. There is increasing evidence that, regardless of traditions and culture, Canadian

Aboriginal governments are as vulnerable to these sorts of abuses as non-Aboriginal governments. One journalist has argued in the *Globe and Mail* that taxpayers pour millions of dollars into reserves but on some reserves the result has been good only for the well-connected few. While some prosper, most band members live in abject poverty. Indian reserves, like non-Aboriginal communities, have been torn apart by battles over power and money. And in these battles some people win, some lose.[54] The Royal Commission on Aboriginal Peoples recognized the potential for this sort of problem in discussing the lack of legitimacy of band governments, the tendency of political leaders to interfere inappropriately in the day-to-day management of economic development, and the problems of concentrating power in the hands of a small political leadership or a single individual.[55] These sorts of abuses are not the norm in Aboriginal governments any more than they are in non-Aboriginal governments.[56] But abuses can exist in Aboriginal self-governments, just as they can in non-Aboriginal governments, and safeguards against abuses, and remedies, are needed in both kinds of governments. Procedural rights against government that are so much part of politics that they are normally taken for granted in the nonnative society – especially accountability, transparency, and open and free elections – would solve most of these problems.

Rule by the Department of Indian and Northern Affairs (DIAND) and its predecessors was colonial and paternalistic. Self-governments, in effect, will be attempting to create new governments for which leaders and followers alike have had limited previous experience. Their experience is better than in most postcolonial countries because the broader context of Canada partakes of reasonably successful representative government. Nevertheless, the lessons from the many countries that have got out from under the colonial umbrella in the postwar period show that the practice of representative government is not usually well taught in colonial regimes and that the postcolonial euphoria all too often changes when authoritarian governments do not recognize fundamental human rights.

Just as in non-Aboriginal communities, there will be many different views on rights issues within self-governments. Some differences have already arisen. In the discussions leading up to the Charlottetown Accord of 1992, the Native Women's Association of Canada (NWAC) disagreed with the other national Aboriginal organizations over the issue of whether or not the Canadian Charter of Rights and Freedoms would apply to Aboriginal governments.[57] The dispute reached a point where NWAC applied to the Federal Court of Canada for an order prohibiting the government of Canada from disbursing funds to the other national organizations and giving NWAC a comparable place in the constitutional discussions. Although the first decision went against NWAC, on appeal the Court decided in favour of NWAC, observing that "There is ample evidence that ... native women as a class remain doubly disadvantaged in at least some Aboriginal societies by reason of sex. The uncontradicted evidence is that they are also seriously disadvantaged by reason of sex within the segment of Aboriginal society residing in or claiming the right to reside on Indian Reservations."[58] The federal government and the other national Aboriginal organizations ignored this ruling, proceeding with the final stages of talks on the Accord. NWAC then attempted to have the nation-wide referendum on the Accord halted, but failed. The Accord also failed in the referendum, being defeated even in Aboriginal communities. These events not only illustrate strong divisions within Aboriginal communities, but suggest as well a lack of confidence in the ability of their national leadership to represent these divisions.

Canada's Aboriginal peoples have within their traditions many mechanisms and procedures for achieving substantive and procedural rights against their governments. Some of these are quite different from the standard Western political and legal structures and procedures, but this does not make them less effective. Quite the contrary, many traditional dispute-resolving mechanisms, for example, possess a sensitivity to local culture and circumstances and a flexibility that ensures appropriate responses and outcomes and that makes the courtrooms of non-native society seem clumsy, rigid, insensitive, and crude in comparison. But these traditional structures need to be revived and operated in a context that also affirms fundamental human rights in the perennial confrontation between citizen and state. Not the least of the concerns of native women, for example, is that the sentencing circles, which are increasingly being used as a traditional substitute for sentencing by the courts, operate against the interests and needs of native women.

Citizens of self-governments need guarantees of rights against their governments that recognizably meet the standards of representative democratic government, of transparency and accountability, of equality and freedom, and of due process in procedural justice. This is not to say that Aboriginal self-governments must look and behave like non-native local governments. Democracy can appear in many different forms, as can courts of law and processes of justice. But the political and judicial processes of self-governments must meet basic standards, and these are the standards articulated in a very general and abstract

way in the Charter of Rights and Freedoms. There is enormous room
for variation and sensitivity to local traditions, needs, and concerns in
the affirmation of rights.[59] But modern circumstances are not traditional ones, and modern Aboriginal self-governments cannot be limited to the same small role as traditional ones, nor can they observe
rights in the same undifferentiated and unexplicit way.

A crucial addition and limitation must be made to this argument.
Sometimes liberal democracy is made to appear to be an all-
encompassing ideology that affects and defines the bulk of human
relationships, both economic and political. I do not believe that to
be a correct understanding of liberal-democracy, and my discussion
relates only to a very restricted area of economics and politics, and
especially to the relationships between citizens and governments.
Liberal-democratic principles impose constraints on what government
can do and establish procedures for making legitimate decisions and
selecting and dismissing leaders. The principles also establish criteria
for assessing the adequacy of processes and decisions. Liberal democracy says nothing about the "cosmic ultimates" (to use J.A. Corry's
phrase)[60] to which groups or individuals make personal commitments.
Rather, the rules and principles of liberal democracy establish the
framework in which individuals and groups can resolve the conflicts
and disagreements between them and their pursuit of more profound
goals. In effect, liberal-democratic rights define the ground rules that
permit as much freedom and tolerance as possible in the political
sphere. Liberal democracy makes room within itself for many varieties
of human experience, belief, and aspirations. One of the strengths of
liberal democracy lies precisely in the fact that it says nothing about,
and does not intrude into, many of the most vital areas of human
existence and meaning. But this is also a weakness that makes liberal
democracy a limited, incomplete, and, in some ways, unsatisfying
ideology.

Aboriginal communities face difficult choices in balancing the
desires of traditionalists with those of modernists, in allocating scarce
resources among competing demands, in coming to terms with the
greater society in ensuring economic development while at the same
time preserving their culture and important traditions. Human rights
charters, including the Canadian Charter of Rights and Freedoms, do
not tell governments how they should solve these problems and issues,
any more than they tell individual citizens how they should run their
private lives and businesses. What a charter of rights does is set the
ground rules for these discussions and procedures, so that basic standards of equality and fairness are recognized and met by all parties.

5 Liberalism's Last Stand: Aboriginal Sovereignty and Minority Rights

DALE TURNER

> We have discarded our broken arrows and our empty quivers, for we know
> what served us in the past can never serve us again ... It is only with
> tongue and speech that I can fight my people's war.
>
> Chief Dan George, *My Heart Soars*

> Whatever else he denounces in our culture he is certain that it still
> possesses the moral resources which he requires in order to denounce it.
> Everything else may be, in his eyes, in disorder; but the language of
> morality is in order, just as it is. That he too may be being betrayed by
> the very language he uses is not a thought available to him.
>
> Alasdair MacIntyre, *After Virtue*

INTRODUCTION

Aboriginal rights as they are entrenched in the Constitution Act, 1982 can be interpreted as rights that are accorded to Aboriginal peoples in virtue of their membership in minority cultures.[1] In this characterization of Aboriginal rights, endorsed by various forms of political liberalism, there is no need to recognize Aboriginal political sovereignty, because it simply does not exist in any serious fashion or Aboriginal sovereignty simply does not play an important role in determining the content of Aboriginal peoples' special rights.[2] Legitimate political sovereignty in its most robust form within political liberalism is accorded only to the provincial and the federal governments. Aboriginal rights, then, if they exist at all, are subsumed within the superior forms of sovereignty held by the provincial and federal governments.

The purpose of this chapter is to argue against this liberal characterization of Aboriginal rights. I will argue that most Aboriginal communities claim that their so-called special rights flow from their legitimate political sovereignty.[3] In other words, I want to take issue over the source and meaning of Aboriginal rights and sovereignty. I shall take a closer look at the liberal claim that Aboriginal rights imply a type of minority right, and I shall offer an explanation why most Aboriginal peoples themselves do not subscribe to political liberalism's justification of their rights as minority rights. I will argue that justice demands that Aboriginal understandings of their political sovereignty oblige contemporary and future policymakers to include Aboriginal voices in drafting legislation and policies that concern the welfare of Aboriginal peoples.

Unfortunately, an investigation into the meaning of Aboriginal sovereignty must begin with an examination of political liberalism. This is because Aboriginal conceptions of sovereignty are not fully recognized as legitimate by the federal and provincial governments in Canada. As Kymlicka states in *Liberalism, Community, and Culture*:

For better or worse, it is predominantly non-aboriginal judges and politicians who have the ultimate power to protect and enforce aboriginal rights, and so it is important to find a justification of them that such people can recognize and understand. Aboriginal people have their own understanding of self-government drawn from their own experience, and that is important. But it is also important, politically, to know how non-aboriginal Canadians – Supreme Court Justices, for example – will understand aboriginal rights and relate them to their own experiences and traditions ... on the standard interpretation of liberalism, aboriginal rights are viewed as matters of discrimination and/or privilege, not of equality. They will always, therefore, be viewed with the kind of suspicion that led liberals like Trudeau to advocate their abolition. Aboriginal rights, at least in their robust form, will only be secure when they are viewed, not as competing with liberalism, but as an essential component of liberal political practice.[4]

I agree with Kymlicka that Aboriginal rights "in their robust form" do not have to compete with liberalism; however, for Aboriginal peoples it is not simply a matter of waking liberals from their dogmatic slumbers in order to see how Aboriginal sovereignty makes sense in the language of political liberalism – Aboriginal peoples have tried for over five hundred years to make colonial governments recognize the legitimacy of Aboriginal sovereignty.

Rather, I will take on board Kymlicka's classification of Aboriginal rights of governance as a special class of minority rights to show that his theory of minority rights necessitates the inclusion, and recognition, of Aboriginal explanations of political sovereignty. So, in one sense I am contributing to the rich tradition of Aboriginal voices that have presented arguments in favour of Aboriginal sovereignty. Where my contribution differs from others is that I am not justifying or generating a theory of Aboriginal sovereignty at all; rather I am going to engage a generous version of political liberalism to show that it fails *unless* it recognizes Aboriginal conceptions of political sovereignty. But my goals are not solely philosophical: the importance of Aboriginal conceptions of political sovereignty finding their way into political liberalism's justification of Aboriginal rights is ultimately to change the racist and oppressive public policies that have held Aboriginal peoples captive for over 130 years. One way of renewing a just relationship, and, more importantly, of renewing hope in Indian Country, is for non-Aboriginal peoples to understand better the significance of Aboriginal sovereignty. The precise content of a theory of Aboriginal sovereignty, however, will remain open, as indeed it should; Aboriginal sovereignty is best understood by listening to the diverse voices of Aboriginal peoples themselves.

My discussion will fall into two parts. I shall begin with a brief discussion of Will Kymlicka's liberal theory of minority rights. For Kymlicka, Aboriginal rights are considered to be a special class of rights within a general theory of minority rights. Therefore, he argues, Aboriginal rights do not pose a problem for political liberalism, as they can be subsumed within a more general liberal theory of rights. Kymlicka's liberalism arguably offers the most generous accommodation of Aboriginal rights within contemporary political liberalism; in fact, Kymlicka is a strong advocate of Aboriginal self-government. In the second section I will examine more closely Kymlicka's characterization of Aboriginal communities as "national minorities," that somehow became "incorporated" into the Canadian state. Kymlicka himself points out that this notion of incorporation is problematic and fraught with historical injustice, but I shall emphasize that developing a thorough understanding of what I call "Aboriginal incorporation" goes to the heart of our understandings of Aboriginal sovereignty and especially of how we ought to characterize the historical relationship between Aboriginal peoples and the European newcomers.

While I cannot provide, in the limited space of this chapter, a fully developed account of Aboriginal sovereignty, I shall suggest what I take to be a more fruitful way of approaching the complex issue of Aboriginal sovereignty without discarding Kymlicka's political liberalism. Essentially, I will take Kymlicka up on his idea of Aboriginal incorporation to show that a thorough investigation of the meaning of this concept requires a radical shift in our understandings of historical interpretation, political sovereignty, and, most importantly, Aboriginal peoples' place within their colonial societies.[5]

KYMLICKA ON THE LIBERAL THEORY OF MINORITY RIGHTS[5]

Kymlicka begins *Liberalism, Community, and Culture* by stating that he will examine the "broader account of the relationship between the individual and society." In other words, he is interested in the individual's sense of belonging to a community and, therefore, to a culture. He proposes to defend a brand of liberalism influenced by Rawls and Dworkin against communitarian objections that it possesses only a "thin" theory of culture.[6] Communitarians mean by this objection that contemporary liberal theorists attach little value to the role that culture plays in shaping an individual's moral and political identity. This brand of liberalism is supposedly unable to deal with a rich, or "thick," theory of culture, especially given the diversity of cultures prevalent in most constitutional democracies.[7] There are two distinct problems within the liberal-communitarian debate that Kymlicka wants to examine: first, there are communitarian critiques demanding thick theories of culture and, second, both liberals and communitarians have failed to deal with the diversity of cultures.

Furthermore, Kymlicka focusses on liberalism as a normative political philosophy, and he will provide what he takes to be the fundamental moral commitments made by a liberal political theory. The philosophical issue at hand is to determine what an individual's essential interest is when she deliberates about her moral status in the world. For Kymlicka our essential interest is the fact that we attempt to live a good life; that is, we value most those things that a good life contains. However, the current set of beliefs we hold to be of most value may be the wrong ones. Therefore, it is imperative that we be able to deliberate so that we can change our minds if we consider certain beliefs that we hold to be inimical to the good life. So for Kymlicka our essential interest is living *the* good life – not the life we currently believe to be good.[8] Next, according to Kymlicka, we must revise these beliefs from "the inside." An individual can lead a good life only if she makes choices according to the values that she holds to be true. Kymlicka has two preconditions for what he takes to be the necessary conditions for the fulfillment of our essential interest in leading a good life. First, we must lead our life from the inside, that is, from the set of beliefs we value as the best for our pursuit of the good life. Second, we must be free to question these beliefs.[9]

Kymlicka introduces culture into his theory because we must evaluate our beliefs from within the context of a culture. In his earlier *Liberalism, Community, and Culture* he does not offer a substantive understanding of culture, because he is not interested in exploring culture per se, but rather in establishing a set of rationally devised cultural conditions: "individuals must have the cultural *conditions* conducive to acquiring an awareness of different views of the good life, and to acquiring the ability to intelligently examine and reexamine these views."[10] These cultural conditions must allow individuals to live their lives from the inside; further, these individuals must have the freedom to question their beliefs in "the light of whatever information and examples and arguments our culture can provide." The culture Kymlicka is referring to as "ours" is the one that has shown great concern for the rights of individuals. The liberal's explicit interest in the individual has forged the traditional liberal concerns for, as Kymlicka states, "education, freedom of expression, freedom of press, artistic freedom, etc."[11]

Kymlicka offers a more substantive discussion of culture in his recent *Multicultural Citizenship: A Liberal Theory of Minority Rights*:

The sort of culture that I will focus on is a *societal culture* – that is, a culture which provides its members with meaningful ways of life across the full range of human activities, including social, educational, religious, recreational, and economic life, encompassing both public and private spheres. These cultures tend to be territorially concentrated, and based on a shared language.[12]

Further, a societal culture is one that is "institutionally" embodied. It is clear that Kymlicka has the same type of community in mind here as he offered in *Liberalism, Community, and Culture*; specifically, a legitimate societal culture is one that is "modern" and shares a common identity with an underlying commitment to individual equality and opportunity.[13] This type of societal culture's public policies are guided by three imperatives: first, the government must treat people as equals; second, the government must treat all individuals with equal concern and respect; and, third, the government must provide each individual with the appropriate liberties and resources needed to examine and act on his or her beliefs. These criteria constitute a liberal conception of justice. So for Kymlicka it is of the utmost importance that an individual choose what is best for the good life and that she be free to act on these choices: "for meaningful individual choice to be possible, individuals need not only access to information, the capacity to reflectively evaluate it, and freedom of expression and association. They also need access to a societal culture. Group-differentiated measures that secure and promote this access may, therefore, have a legitimate role to play in a liberal theory of justice."[14]

Cultural membership, then, is a primary good in Kymlicka's liberalism.[15] Because culture is a primary good for all individuals, governments ought to protect, or preserve, the integrity of the plurality of cultures from which individuals make their choices. Kymlicka identifies "two broad patterns of cultural diversity." In the first instance, "cultural diversity arises from the *incorporation* of *previously* self-governing, territorially concentrated cultures into a larger state. These incorporated cultures, which I call 'national minorities,' typically wish to maintain themselves as distinct societies alongside the majority culture, and demand various forms of autonomy or self-government to ensure their survival as distinct societies."[16] The second pattern of cultural diversity arises out of "individual and familial immigration." Essentially, groups that fall into this category came into Canada under the assumption that they were going to become part of the existing societal culture; in a sense, they left behind their own societal cultures in order to join another. One of the main arguments of *Multicultural Citizenship* is that national minorities have stronger claims to group-differentiated rights than cultures that have immigrated to Canada from other parts of the world. In the Canadian context, the national minorities consist of the English newcomers, French newcomers, and Aboriginal peoples.

Kymlicka claims that national minorities, as *previously* self-governing cultures, *incorporated* to form the Canadian state. He adds, "the incorporation of different nations into a single state may be involuntary, as occurs when one cultural community is invaded and conquered by another, or is ceded from one imperial power to another, or when its homeland is overrun by colonizing settlers."[17] From an Aboriginal perspective the Canadian state came into existence by means of all three practices: some Aboriginal communities were conquered,[18] some communities ceded powers to the British Crown and later the Canadian governments, and many communities were simply overrun by colonial newcomers. Of course, the three practices were not exclusive to each other, since most Aboriginal communities experienced all three forms of incorporation. I shall return to the issue of Aboriginal incorporation later, but first I shall take a closer look at Kymlicka's justification for the special rights held by national minorities.

In chapter 6 of *Multicultural Citizenship*, "Justice and Minority Rights," Kymlicka provides what he takes to be overlapping arguments for the justification of minority rights, or group-differentiated rights, within a liberal-democratic state. He discusses three arguments for the recognition of minority rights: the equality argument, the argument from historical agreement, and the diversity argument. As we shall see shortly, Kymlicka's theory is driven by the equality argument, since the historical agreement and diversity arguments, although meritorious on their own, ultimately depend on the equality argument for normative support.

Kymlicka's major motive in providing three overlapping justifications is to show that the concept of "benign neglect" is untenable for political liberalism. Advocates of the benign-neglect view argue that recognition of universal individual rights resolves any problems associated with demands for special cultural recognition – on this view, substantive differences between cultures are unproblematic because the state grants the same package of rights to all individuals. Group-differentiated rights advocates, however, argue that there are substantive differences between the diversity of cultures and that legitimate recognition of this diversity requires the state to allocate accordingly different packages of rights. Kymlicka argues that "the state unavoidably promotes certain cultural identities, and thereby disadvantages others. Once we recognize this, we need to rethink the justice of minority rights claims."[19] The equality argument is intended to resolve the conflict between the benign-neglect view of rights and the group-differentiated rights view.[20]

The normative role of equality in Kymlicka's equality argument now functions on the level of the national minorities. Since cultural membership is a primary good *and* Aboriginal peoples constitute a national minority, they are accorded special rights by the state – where the state is implicitly understood as *the* ultimate legitimate expression of political sovereignty. Aboriginal rights are a legitimate class of rights, since liberals give credence to the intuition that prior occupancy has at least some normative weight in a theory of justice; indeed, this intuition generates the legitimacy of a national minority in Kymlicka's theory.[21] The special rights that Aboriginal peoples possess are rights of governance, one of three forms of group-differentiated rights in Kymlicka's theory of minority rights. These rights – the inherent rights that are legitimate from the initial formation of the Canadian state – are the strongest form of group rights in Kymlicka's classification of minority rights. The other forms of group-differentiated rights – ethnic rights and special representation rights – are allocated to certain groups who arrived after the formation of the Canadian state, and they do not entail rights of governance.[22]

Kymlicka's equality argument can be briefly summarized as follows. National minorities (Aboriginal peoples, the English newcomers, and the French newcomers) are the fundamentally privileged sovereign groups in Kymlicka's characterization of the Canadian multinational state. National minorities have rights of governance because they were the initial legitimate entities that formed the multinational state of Canada. However, for various reasons the national minorities relinquished, or transferred, certain powers to the larger political union. Kymlicka notes that the creation of the multinational state may not have arisen from a just context; however, this poses no significant problem for his theory because his view of the political relationship *today* is premised on the fundamental political recognition of equality among the incorporating national minorities. I believe that this assumption goes to the core of our understandings of the meaning of Canadian sovereignty and especially Aboriginal sovereignty.

I want to point out, though, that there are two normative dimensions to Kymlicka's theory of minority rights, and it is important to keep them separate. First, there is the cultural dimension. Aboriginal cultures, because they are unfairly vulnerable to the cultural influences of the dominant culture, are afforded special rights in order to protect the integrity of their societal cultures. Aboriginal peoples happen to constitute a kind of collective (a minority one at that), so their special rights are premised on the fact that cultural membership is a primary good *and* that Aboriginal cultures are vulnerable to the unfair influences of the dominant culture. This is largely the context from which liberals have discussed the legitimacy of collective rights for groups. However, the second normative dimension to Kymlicka's theory of minority rights involves the language of political sovereignty. Although Kymlicka does not use the word "sovereignty," the language of political sovereignty is nonetheless brought into his theory by introducing the concept of a national minority. This is because national minorities, that is, communities that were self-governing at the time of incorporation, are eligible for rights of governance. Aboriginal communities constitute national minorities because normative weight is given to the fact that Aboriginal peoples occupied Canada first, and therefore they were self-governing societies.

Recognize that both of these normative dimensions are at work in Kymlicka's justification for Aboriginal rights of governance. However, liberals have discussed Aboriginal rights mostly in the language of cultural protection, rather than in the language of Aboriginal sovereignty.[23] Kymlicka is right to bring into the discussion the fact that Aboriginal peoples constitute a national minority, but it does not follow that Aboriginal sovereignty, which is implicit in their status as a national minority, has to disappear from the discussion of Aboriginal rights of governance in a contemporary context. If we take seriously the claim that Aboriginal peoples were self-governing nations before contact, then we must reexamine our understandings of Aboriginal incorporation, because Aboriginal incorporation calls into question the nature of the formation of the Canadian state. Although Kymlicka appreciates the fact that Aboriginal peoples have suffered greatly throughout the history of the relationship, he nonetheless sidesteps the issue of determining the meaning of Aboriginal incorporation.

Interestingly, both the normative dimensions of Kymlicka's theory relating to culture and those relating to sovereignty yield interpretations that advocate Aboriginal rights of governance. But I claim that the second interpretation offers a more fruitful approach for capturing Aboriginal understandings of their sovereignty.

The first interpretation begins by recognizing that Aboriginal peoples constitute a national minority. Once this status is bestowed upon Aboriginal peoples, it follows that if our theory of justice deems it necessary, then rights of governance can be distributed to them. Since culture is a primary good for all individuals, including Aboriginal peoples, the state ought to ensure policies that protect the integrity of all cultures. Since Aboriginal cultures are unfairly vulnerable to decimation by the overpowering dominant culture in Canada, justice demands that they be accorded special rights. Because Aboriginal peoples constitute a national minority, the possibility exists, within a distributive theory of justice, that these special rights *may* be rights of governance.

Importantly, the rights accorded to Aboriginal groups are justified only "if there actually is a disadvantage with respect to cultural membership, and if the rights actually serve to rectify the disadvantage." Kymlicka adds:

One could imagine a point where the amount of land reserved for indigenous peoples would not be necessary to provide reasonable external protections, but rather would simply provide unequal opportunities to them. Justice would then require that the holdings of indigenous peoples be subject to the same redistributive taxation as the wealth of other advantaged groups, so as to assist the less well off in society. In the real world, of course, most indigenous peoples are struggling to maintain the bare minimum of land needed to sustain the viability of their communities. But it is possible that their land holdings could exceed what justice allows.[24]

The point behind this passage, as Kymlicka goes on to explain in the accompanying footnote, is that he places Aboriginal rights squarely in a theory of distributive justice. Aboriginal cultures, as national minorities, can exercise their rights of governance only to the extent that they do not offset the balance of fairness between the remaining cultures in Canada. This added proviso leads to a weaker form of Aboriginal sovereignty, because the rights of Aboriginal governance are recognized only to the extent that they do not trump the sovereignty of the Canadian state. Aboriginal peoples argue that to characterize their rights in this ahistorical way is to fail to recognize the source of their rights of governance.[25]

ABORIGINAL INCORPORATION AND
ABORIGINAL SOVEREIGNTY

I suggest that there is another way to interpret Kymlicka's argument
for Aboriginal self-government – one in which Aboriginal perspectives
are included in the discourse about their rights. We retain Aboriginal
communities as national minorities but then focus on the problem of
Aboriginal incorporation in order to determine the *current* political
status of *particular* Aboriginal communities. This is because many
Aboriginal communities maintain that they are *still* self-governing
nations and that Aboriginal peoples have not, in fact, relinquished, or
ceded, any powers to the state.[26] Aboriginal incorporation calls into
question our understandings of Aboriginal peoples' political relationships with the Canadian state. On this view, Aboriginal rights of governance can be recognized in a much deeper sense than in the first
interpretation. This is because Aboriginal sovereignty does not have
to dissipate after the formation of the Canadian state; more importantly, it lies in the forefront of any current discussion about Aboriginal rights.

This second approach differs from the first in that it facilitates a
stronger conception of Aboriginal sovereignty. I take a stronger conception of Aboriginal sovereignty to be something like that provided
by the Gitksan people mentioned in note 2. That is, "the ownership
of territory is a marriage of the Chief and the land. Each Chief has
an ancestor who encountered and acknowledged the life of the land.
From such encounters come power. The land, the plants, the animals
and the people all have spirit – they all must be shown respect. That
is the basis of our law." The "voice" that arises within a strong conception of Aboriginal sovereignty arises directly from the community
itself; that is, from the people who hold the traditional knowledge of
their community and are recognized by their citizens as legitimately
expressing the meaning of their political sovereignty.[27] However, for
Canadian governments, recognition of a strong conception of Aboriginal sovereignty entails acceptance of the possibility that there are
Aboriginal communities in Canada that remain sovereign. Canadian
governments have failed miserably to recognize Aboriginal sovereignty
in any form; until Aboriginal peoples participate as equals in the
discourse that determines the meaning of their political sovereignty,
and the rights of governance that follow from that sovereignty, legislative instruments and the meaning of rights as found in §35(1) of
the Constitution will remain mysterious and elusive for policymakers.[28]

Of course this does not bring us any closer to the meaning of
Aboriginal sovereignty. However, the first step we must take to better

understand what Aboriginal peoples mean by sovereignty is to investigate the historical relationship itself.[29] But it matters significantly how we go about this investigation. Kymlicka uses the word "incorporation" to capture the historical significance of the early period of the relationship. Interpretations of history, then, find themselves playing pivotal roles in determining the meaning of Aboriginal sovereignty. The frustrating problem for Aboriginal peoples is that their interpretations of history have not been recognized as legitimate. For now, I want to focus on contemporary political liberalism and emphasize that a liberal theory of rights, in the context of Aboriginal peoples, functions ahistorically: it begins from a rationally constructed theory of distributive justice that bestows a set of fundamental rights on all individuals and, as a consequence, a set of special rights to individuals who belong to minority cultures. As I have tried to show by looking at Kymlicka's theory of minority rights, it is possible for a version of political liberalism to recognize that some Aboriginal communities are self-governing nations, but there remains a substantive difference over the meaning of Aboriginal sovereignty. This difference may not mean much to liberals and Aboriginal policymakers, since a liberal theory of justice has, in some sense, distributed fairly special rights to Aboriginal peoples. However, sovereignty lies at the very core of Aboriginal existence, and history is the main source for understanding the meaning of the complex nature of Aboriginal political sovereignty.

Kymlicka, however, makes room for historical interpretations to find their way into a liberal theory of justice by invoking his second argument in favour of group-differentiated rights. The argument from historical agreement is meant to provide additional normative support to the more fundamental equality argument, while addressing the issues surrounding the dissolution of Aboriginal sovereignty. Kymlicka points out that proponents of group-differentiated rights have had difficulties convincing opponents with historical arguments. He states that "Those people who think that group-differentiated rights are unfair have not been appeased by pointing to agreements that were made by previous generations in different circumstances, often undemocratically and in conditions of substantial inequality in bargaining power." He goes on to ask, "Why should not governments do what principles of equality require now, rather than what outdated and often unprincipled agreements require?"[30]

Kymlicka's answer is to question a fundamental assumption underlying the equality argument. "The equality argument assumes that the state must treat its citizens with equal respect. But there is a prior question of determining which citizens should be governed by which states." Here he raises, I believe, the most serious problem for political liberalism. If we invoke the equality argument without looking at history, we gloss over the fact that Aboriginal peoples became citizens in many different ways, most of them unjust. More importantly, in some communities, Aboriginal peoples simply are not citizens of the Canadian state.[31] Canadian political leaders, policymakers, and especially judges of the Canadian state have unilaterally assumed that, for better or worse, Canada's Aboriginal peoples have become citizens of Canada in the fullest sense of its meaning. Essentially, this is how Kymlicka uses the term incorporation, since his theory implicitly subsumes the fact that Aboriginal peoples have become citizens of the Canadian state and, more importantly, that they *may* have relinquished their original sovereignty in this process of incorporation.[32]

This is where Kymlicka's concept of incorporation becomes most important and useful for my investigation of Aboriginal sovereignty. If the incorporation process was unjust, as Kymlicka suggests was the case for many Aboriginal communities, we have to reassess in a much fuller investigation the validity of Aboriginal incorporation. It is not enough to leave the investigation with the claim that the incorporation was unjust, and therefore the Canadian state should accord Aboriginal peoples special rights to rectify past wrongs. This leads to Waldron's view of "superseding" injustice, which, along with Melvin Smith's views of "one law for all people," treats Aboriginal peoples with a fundamental disrespect, in that it does not allow them to speak for themselves.[33] The relevant issue for Aboriginal peoples is, not whether we ought to rectify past injustices in order to balance the scales of a liberal distributive justice system, but how governments can come to recognize the legitimacy of Aboriginal sovereignty in order to renew the political relationship on more just foundations.[34] Kymlicka's theory can be interpreted in a way that at least makes room for Aboriginal peoples to speak for themselves, and this is an important first step for political liberalism. History has not been kind to Aboriginal voices, so it matters how Aboriginal voices ought to be listened to and respected as philosophically legitimate participants in the discourse about Aboriginal sovereignty.

In summary, I have attempted to argue in this chapter that political liberalism's characterization of Aboriginal rights of governance does not require the participation of Aboriginal peoples in order to characterize the content of their "special" rights. This is because Aboriginal rights of governance are justified within a theory of distributive justice that does not recognize the legitimacy of Aboriginal sovereignty. Aboriginal peoples argue that their rights of governance flow from their political sovereignty and that those rights ought to be recognized by the Canadian governments. (This is the significance of §35(1) of the Constitution.) It is precisely this fact of Aboriginal experience that the Canadian governments have refused to recognize in any serious fashion. Kymlicka's theory of minority rights, however, can be reformulated in a way that brings the Aboriginal voice into the dominant, non-Aboriginal discourse about Aboriginal rights of governance. However, to do so in a just way involves a reexamination of Aboriginal incorporation by Aboriginal peoples and the Canadian state. The meaning of Aboriginal incorporation is problematic because Aboriginal interpretations have not been recognized by their dominant colonial governments; therefore, it matters how we go about understanding its meaning.

6 First Nations and the Derivation of Canada's Underlying Title: Comparing Perspectives on Legal Ideology

MICHAEL ASCH

I am aware that some writers have, by a system of artificial reasoning, endeavored to justify, or rather excuse, the encroachments made upon Indian territory, and to denominate these abstractions the law of nations, and, in this ready way, the question is dispatched.

Senator Thomas Frelinghuysen, 1830[1]

INTRODUCTION

Canada is formally an independent state. It is certainly not a colony for, as *Webster's Third International Dictionary* clearly states, a "colony" is "a body of people settled in a new territory, foreign and often distant, retaining ties with their mother or parent state."[2] Canada is recognized by other states as independent and free of all British authority. Hence, it is formally not a colony. Nonetheless, to understand Canada, especially in relation to the Aboriginal fact, it is reasonable to suppose Canada is something like a colonial state, for it is founded on political institutions and values that derive solely from the history and culture of the original colonizers and defines its origins as a radical departure from an indigenous past in which the appearance and then the formal independence of the original colonists represent the formative historical events. Thus, while Canada, like many other settler states where the former colonists have now become the majority of the population, may have achieved its formal independence from its former "parent" state, at a most basic level it finds itself nonetheless a creature of the very colonial institutions and values that formed the fabric of the political culture of the colonizers. It is therefore not as much postcolonial as it is "colonial" in its own political ideology and composition.

The primary objective in this chapter is to examine the premise that Canada is a colonial state by discussing in particular the way in which legal reasoning is used to justify how it legitimately holds underlying title and sovereignty in the face of prior Aboriginal sovereignty and then to outline an alternative form of reasoning that might provide a better means to ground Canada's title within contemporary ethical principles. Through this process the chapter, primarily by implication, attempts to explore the broader question of the nature of underlying title as it is justified in other supposedly postcolonial settler states, of which the United States and Mexico are but two examples.[3]

CANADIAN LAW AND SOVEREIGNTY

An analysis of Canadian legal ideology provides an appropriate means to understand how Canada retains its colonial mentality when justifying the legitimacy of its underlying title in the face of prior Aboriginal sovereignty. As has been indicated in a number papers I have recently completed, this ideology may be understood by reference to decisions in leading Canadian court cases, precedents followed in Canadian courts, constitutional history and scholarly writing on relevant Canadian law.

As Slattery has pointed out, English law provides four primary means by which Canada or another state could justify the acquisition of new territories.[4] These are conquest, or the military subjugation of a territory over which the ruler clearly expresses the desire to assume sovereignty on a permanent basis; cession, or the formal transfer of a territory (by treaty for example) from one independent political unit to another; annexation, or the assertion of sovereignty over another political entity without military action or treaty; or the settlement or acquisition of territory that was previously unoccupied or is not recognized as belonging to another political entity.

As an analysis of leading contemporary court decisions indicates, Canadian legal ideology at present relies, in particular, on the settlement thesis as a justification for Canadian sovereignty.[5] This thesis rests on the concept that the territory claimed by the colonists was previously a *terra nullius*: a territory without people, one that was, to reiterate, either previously unoccupied or not recognized as belonging to another political entity. When looked at from a strictly logical perspective, the settlement thesis, then, may safely be presumed to be unproblematic in the colonial context only where it can be presumed there were no inhabitants at the time the colonists first arrived. While it is perhaps reasonable to make such a presumption about Antarctica, certainly it cannot be presumed about the whole territory that was later to become known as Canada.

Relying on the settlement thesis when colonists claim sovereignty and underlying title to lands where indigenous peoples already live, as in Canada, has proven difficult and has required a certain flexibility of logic. It is to this flexibility, I believe, that Senator Frelinghuysen was referring when he decried "artificial reasoning" in the quote cited above. The rationale has been to rely on the presumption that the territory was not "recognized as belonging to another political entity." The first premise of this approach has been to assert that, in law, the original inhabitants did not possess political rights or underlying title that required recognition by the colonizers.

This form of legal reasoning dates back at least to 1608 and the beginning of the British colonial period. In that year, the English court was called upon to decide, in *Calvin's Case*, whether the Scots kept their lands after their conquest by the English. In it, Judge Cook determined conditions where the original inhabitants' rights were to be protected and where they did not need to be. Given that the decision was rendered during the Elizabethan era, it is not surprising that the division rested on religious grounds. As the court said:

And upon this ground there is a diversity between a conquest of a kingdom of a Christian King, and the conquest of a kingdom of an infidel; for if a King come to a Christian kingdom by conquest, seeing that he hath *vitoe el necis potestaiem*, he may at his pleasure alter and change the laws of that kingdom: but until he doth make an alteration of those laws the ancient laws of that kingdom remain. But if a Christian King should conquer a kingdom of an infidel, and bring them under his subjection, there *ipso facio* the laws of the infidels are abrogated, for that they be not only against Christianity, but against the law of God and of nature.[6]

As the case was directed toward the Scots, the rationale of the decision held in favour of the conquered. However, by implication the case also provided precedent for the view that Aboriginal people in "Canada," not being Christian at the time of first contact, did not have rights that required recognition. Hence, a unilateral assertion of sovereignty and underlying title by the colonizers would be considered legitimate in the eyes of the law.

Similar forms of "artificial" reasoning, although based on different terms, have been used in subsequent periods to justify the unilateral assertion of sovereignty and underlying title by colonists in the face of indigenous sovereignty. For example, in the nineteenth century the division of the world between cultivators and noncultivators was crucial. Based on this reasoning, Australia, at least prior to the 1992 *Mabo* decision, which recognized the repugnant nature of such reasoning, presumed that the land was a *terra nullius* precisely because the Aborigines did not practise agriculture. The agricultural form of the *terra nullius* thesis was popular to justify unilateral assertions of underlying title by colonists in other settler countries, such as the United States. As well, it also proved to be repugnant to Senator Frelinghuysen and perhaps many other contemporary commentators.[7]

By the second decade of the twentieth century, British colonial law had come to rely on a presumptive division of the world into "civilized" and "primitive" in order to justify unilateral assertions of sovereignty by colonists. Seminal for this version was the 1919 decision in *Re: Southern Rhodesia* of the Law Lords of the Privy Council of Great Britain, the highest judicial authority in the Empire. In it, the Law Lords stated:

The estimation of the rights of aboriginal tribes is always inherently difficult. Some tribes are so low in the scale of social organization that their usages and conceptions of rights and duties are not to be reconciled with the institutions or legal ideas of civilized society. Such a gulf cannot be bridged. It would be idle to impute to such people some shadow of the rights known to our law and then to transmute it into the substance of transferable rights of property as we know them. In the present case it would make each and every person by a fictional inheritance a landed proprietor "richer than all his tribe." On the other hand, there are indigenous peoples whose legal conceptions, though differently developed, are hardly less precise than our own. When once they have been studied and understood they are no less enforceable than rights arising under English law. Between the two there is a wide tract of much ethnological interest, but the position of the natives of Southern Rhodesia within it is very uncertain; clearly they approximate rather to the lower than to the higher limit.[8]

It is the division between "civilized" and "primitive" found in *Re: Southern Rhodesia* that has been adopted by the Canadian courts as the precedent upon which to determine the extent to which Canada is required in law to recognize Aboriginal rights and, in particular, to determine the original sovereignty and jurisdiction of the Aboriginal peoples who were present prior to the arrival of the first colonists.[9] Specifically, as will be discussed below, the courts have held that, notwithstanding the existence of certain Aboriginal rights, the indigenous people who lived in Canada prior to colonization were too primitive to have a form of sovereignty and underlying title that required recognition by colonial authorities. Therefore, despite the fact that people lived here and had certain rights, with respect to sovereignty and underlying title Canada had been a *terra nullius* prior to the arrival of the colonists.

CANADIAN ABORIGINAL RIGHTS AND THE *TERRA NULLIUS* HYPOTHESIS

There is good evidence to indicate that the *terra nullius* thesis regarding Canadian sovereignty may be an innovation that resulted from events beginning as recently as 1969.[10] In that year, the Canadian government issued a white paper on Indian policy that was premised on the presumption that Aboriginal peoples were simply ordinary "Canadians" and that the special status that had resulted from treaties and policy was discriminatory and would be terminated in favour of economic development funds so that Aboriginal people could find their rightful place in Canadian society.[11] In that same year the Nishga (now Nisga'a) who reside in British Columbia advanced the first contemporary court challenge (known as the *Calder* case, 1973) for legal recognition that Aboriginal peoples had rights that had existed prior to contact with colonists and that these rights continued to exist to the present.

In the first contemporary application of the *Re: Southern Rhodesia* reasoning to reject Aboriginal rights assertions, Chief Justice Davey of the British Columbia Appeals Court stated that

the Indians on the mainland of British Columbia ... were undoubtedly at the time of settlement a very primitive people with few of the institutions of civilized society, and none at all of our notions of private property ... [Therefore] I see no evidence to justify a conclusion that the aboriginal rights claimed by the successors of these primitive people are of a kind that it should be assumed the Crown recognized them when it acquired the mainland of British Columbia by occupation.[12]

However, in January 1973 the Supreme Court of Canada, while not describing the nature or extent of the rights of the Nisga'a and splitting 3–3 on whether those rights continued to exist, did agree that in law Aboriginal people lived in organized societies in the period prior to colonization.

Given that the Supreme Court recognized in 1973 that "organized societies" existed prior to colonization, Canada could not be considered an absolute *terra nullius*. The legal question to be determined became the description of the nature and extent of these rights in the period prior to colonization and subsequently to the present time.[13]

This question has been addressed both by the political system and by the courts. The former acted, ultimately, to recognize "existing" Aboriginal rights in the Constitution Act, 1982, thereby protecting these rights from extinguishment by normal legislation. However, despite a number of constitutional conferences devoted to finding agreement among all political actors on the nature and extent of these rights, no substantive agreement was achieved.

At the same time, the courts, through jurisprudence, have started to flesh out answers to the question. Speaking broadly, the courts have determined that in law Aboriginal rights related to the use and occupation of the land, such as hunting and fishing rights, existed prior to colonization and, because legislatures did not pass acts expressly disallowing them in the period prior to the Constitution Act, 1982, continued to exist after the assertion of sovereignty and up to the present. At the same time, the courts have asserted that Aboriginal peoples did not hold sovereignty, jurisdiction, and underlying title with respect to their lands and peoples and/or that the unilateral assertion of sovereignty, jurisdiction, and underlying title by colonizers was sufficient to extinguish those held by Aboriginal peoples. As will be seen by the few illustrations cited below, the crucial element in this "artificial reasoning" has been the application of the division between "civilized" and "primitive" that is derived from the *Re: Southern Rhodesia* precedent.

The first incorporation of *Re: Southern Rhodesia* reasoning into Aboriginal rights law following the Supreme Court's decision in *Calder* (1973) was by Mr Justice Mahoney in *Baker Lake* (1979).[14] In this case, Inuit (formerly known as Eskimos) applied for an injunction to stop mining exploration activities, on the grounds that they interfered with the Inuit Aboriginal right to hunt and fish. In rendering his judgement, Mahoney had occasion to determine who might legitimately bring forward an Aboriginal rights claim. Following the reasoning in *Calder,* Justice Mahoney asserted that one of the requirements was "that they (the plaintiffs) and their ancestors were members of an organized society."[15] As a result, in order to determine whether they had standing to request the injunction, Mahoney provided a description of what might constitute an organized society in relation to the Inuit. To this end, after citing a number of authorities and, in particular, *Re: Southern Rhodesia*, he stated: "The fact is that the aboriginal Inuit had an organized society. It was not a society with very elaborate institutions but it was a society organized to exploit the resources available on the barrens and essential to sustain human life there. That was about all they could do: hunt and fish and survive."[16]

In short, Mr Justice Mahoney asserted that it was possible to have an organized society in the sense used by the Supreme Court in *Calder* that had institutions respecting occupation and use of land ("hunt and fish and survive") that were sufficiently civilized for recognition by colonists, but that may not have had institutions sufficiently elaborate to incorporate any form of sovereignty, jurisdiction, and underlying title that required recognition. However, as Mahoney's judgement favoured the standing of the Inuit plaintiffs, the logical refinement of the *Re: Southern Rhodesia* reasoning to the disadvantage of Aboriginal peoples when making assertions about their legal rights respecting those matters remained implicit.

Over the past two decades the theory of *terra nullius* embedded in Mahoney's decision has been used in a number of judgements on themes related to Aboriginal rights issues. For example in *Apsassin et al v. Canada* (1988), the trial judge, Justice Addy, stated that even in the 1940s the Dunne-za, who live in British Columbia and were the plaintiffs in the case, "had no true organized system of government or real lawmakers. They also lacked to a great extent the ability to plan or manage, with any degree of success, activities or undertakings other than fishing, hunting and trapping. It seems that many of their decisions even regarding these activities, could better be described as spontaneous or instinctive rather than deliberately planned."[17]

This view is repeated by Mr Justice McEachern, who in deciding in *Delgamuukw* (1991) that the Gitksan-Wet'suwet'en did not hold underlying title, jurisdiction, or sovereignty over their traditional lands that was sufficiently significant to warrant recognition by colonists, stated, "I do not accept the ancestors 'on the ground' behaved as they did because of 'institutions.' Rather I find they more likely acted as they did because of survival instincts which varied from village to village."[18]

More crucially, in a number of recent decisions, the Supreme Court of Canada has raised the idea that, while Aboriginal people did possess rights from before colonization, Canada, because of the relative primitiveness of Aboriginal peoples, was still a *terra nullius* with respect to sovereignty and underlying title to the nearly explicit level. For example, the Court, in *Sioui v. the Province of Québec* (1990), judging in favour of the Huron claims to certain treaty rights in part, stated a doctrine that required the Courts to "adopt a generous and liberal interpretation" of these rights.[19] However, in constructing the reasons for this doctrine, the Court had occasion to refer to *Jones v. Meehan*, an 1899 decision of the Supreme Court of the United States, where the judges stated:

In construing any treaty between the United States and an Indian tribe, it must always ... be borne in mind that the negotiations for the treaty are conducted, on the part of the United States, an enlightened and powerful nation, by representatives skilled in diplomacy, masters of a written language, understanding the modes and forms of creating the various technical estates known to their law, and assisted by an interpreter employed by themselves; that the Indians, on the other hand, are a weak and dependent people, who have no written language and are wholly unfamiliar with all the forms of legal expression, and whose only knowledge of the terms in which the treaty is framed is that imparted to them by the interpreter employed by the United States; and that the treaty must therefore be construed, not according to the technical meaning of its words to learned lawyers, but in the sense in which they would naturally be understood by the Indians.[20]

And they then went on to say that "The Indian people are today much better versed in the art of negotiation with public authorities than they were when the United States Supreme Court handed down its decision in *Jones.* As the document in question (the Treaty with the Huron) was signed over a hundred years before that decision, these considerations argue all the more strongly for the courts to adopt a generous and liberal approach."[21]

The doctrine, however, is expressed more succinctly in *R. v. Sparrow.* In this 1990 decision, the Supreme Court upheld that Aboriginal peoples have rights respecting the use and occupancy of lands for hunting and fishing that derive from the period prior to contact, rights that remained in place despite the establishment of colonial and, later, Canadian and provincial legislation respecting such subjects. At the same time, they asserted that "It is worth recalling that while British policy toward the native population was based on respect for their right to occupy their traditional lands, a proposition to which the Royal Proclamation of 1763 bears witness, there was from the outset never any doubt that sovereignty and legislative power, and indeed the underlying title, to such lands vest in the Crown."[22]

As Patrick Macklem and I indicate, the presumption that Crown sovereignty and underlying title arise "from the outset" of colonization must derive from the premise that prior to colonization Canada is considered in law to be a *terra nullius.*[23] Therefore, sovereignty and underlying title were acquired by "settlement," which, as was stated above, is a thesis in English law that refers "to the settlement or acquisition of territory that was previously unoccupied or is not recognized as belonging to another political entity." Given that Aboriginal people lived here prior to colonization, the territory was occupied. Thus, the thesis rests on the presumption that the territory "is not recognized as belonging to another political entity." Given the reliance by the courts on the artificial reasoning found in *Re: Southern Rhodesia,* the basis for the lack of recognition, as is demonstrated by the court decisions cited above, must be that, while they had occupancy rights, Aboriginal people were not sufficiently civilized that their prior sovereignty and underlying title required recognition by the colonists.

PROBLEMS WITH THE *TERRA NULLIUS* DOCTRINE

I hope it is self-evident that there is something wrong in relying on a doctrine to legitimate sovereignty and underlying title that presumes members of another culture were sufficiently primitive that, in law, the land was a *terra nullius*. It is nonetheless instructive to provide some evidence to support such sensibilities. For this purpose, I choose the following. First, the doctrine has been discredited by the High Court in Australia – another settler state that arose from British colonization. Initially, in *Milirrpum*, a case decided in 1970, the trial judge asserted that, notwithstanding any factual evidence that might be produced by Aborigines, in law Australia was a "settled or peaceably occupied colony," and as such in law the territory had been a *terra nullius* prior to colonization.[24] Later, however, in *Mabo v. Queensland*, a 1992 decision of the High Court of Australia, the judges rescinded this premise because, as Justice Brennan stated, it relies on "a discriminatory denigration of indigenous inhabitants, their social organization and customs."[25] He then continued, "it is imperative in today's world that the common law should neither be nor be seen to be frozen in an age of racial discrimination."[26] Two other members of the High Court were even more explicit and argued to reject the *terra nullius* doctrine because it treated "the Aboriginal people of the continent ... as a different and lower form of life whose very existence could be ignored for the purpose of determining the legal right to occupy and use their traditional homelands."[27]

Second, the doctrine has been rejected by the world community. For instance, the Declaration on the Granting of Independence to Colonial Countries and Peoples implicitly suggests this where it states, "[i]nadequacy of political, economic, social or educational preparedness should never serve as a pretext for delaying independence."[28]

The *terra nullius* doctrine was rejected directly for circumstances similar to those found in Canada by the International Court of Justice in their 1975 "advisory opinion" in *Western Sahara*. Here, the Court was asked to determine specifically the following question: "Was Western Sahara (Rio de Oro and Sakiet El Hamra) at the time of colonization by Spain a territory belonging to no one (*terra nullius*)?"[29] They responded by saying that it was not, largely because "the information furnished to the Court shows that at the time of colonization Western

Sahara was inhabited by peoples which, if nomadic, were socially and politically organized in tribes and under chiefs competent to represent them."[30] And Spain entered into treaty arrangements with local inhabitants in the late nineteenth century and therefore did not treat the indigenous peoples as living in a *terra nullius*.[31] The situation in Canada, with some important exceptions, is highly similar. The Crown entered into treaties, the texts of which indicate that the Crown recognized the existence of political authorities who could negotiate on the behalf of collectivities.[32] Furthermore, the British Crown entered into such treaties much earlier than the nineteenth century and continued the practice into the twentieth. Therefore, regardless of whether the texts are accurate with respect to the "extinguishment" of Aboriginal title – and there is good reason to doubt whether this was always correct[33] – the British Crown did recognize that the land was not a *terra nullius* and ought to have made treaties prior to settlement in all areas of what is now Canada.[34]

Third, the doctrine of *terra nullius* has been rejected as a matter of fact. It is true that in 1919, when *Re: Southern Rhodesia* was written, there was a presumption that there could be people "so low in the scale of social organization that their usages and conceptions of rights and duties are not to be reconciled with the institutions or legal ideas of civilized society." However, anthropological evidence had produced sufficient results on this topic that, by 1930, the pseudo-evolutionary view had been completely discredited.[35] Rather, the evidence accumulated from that period on indicates that there are very few, if any, societies that existed at the time of colonization that would not have concepts about jurisdiction reconcilable to "rights arising under English law."[36] As the late Mr Justice Hall sagely pointed out in *Calder,* "The assessment and interpretation of historical documents and enactments tendered in evidence must be approached in the light of present-day research and knowledge, disregarding ancient concepts formulated when understanding of the customs and cultures of our original people was rudimentary and incomplete and when they were thought to be wholly without cohesion, laws, or culture, in effect a subhuman species."[37] It is therefore inappropriate for Canada to rely on a doctrine that is factually incorrect.[38]

Finally, Canada has played a significant role in the decolonization process by supporting United Nations' declarations and by providing aid to newly decolonized countries, and through its readiness to engage as a peacekeeper in situations where colonialism or its aftermath have caused significant problems for local populations. Therefore, at least by implication, Canada has rejected theories, such as *terra nullius*, that had been used to justify continued colonial rule in such situations. It is therefore an affront to its own self-understanding as a player internationally for Canada to justify its sovereignty and underlying title on the very same doctrine, *terra nullius*, used by colonial powers to legitimate their occupation of colonial territories.

ALTERNATIVES TO *TERRA NULLIUS*

For the reasons cited above, it is inappropriate to maintain that Canada, in law, was a *terra nullius* prior to colonization. The alternative, then, is to accept the premise that the Aboriginal peoples who lived in Canada held underlying title and sovereignty. Were this simple fact accepted, the questions in law would become, Did Canada legitimately acquire sovereignty and underlying title from the indigenous peoples and if so how was this accomplished?

There is evidence to suggest that at least the following four approaches have been considered in response to these questions. The first resolves the issue by asserting that the determination of sovereignty and underlying title does not turn on issues related to the rights and holdings of indigenous peoples. One example of such an approach is the appeal to the liberal-democratic value of "majority rule."[39] In this view, the legitimacy of a state is to be determined not by reference to origins but rather by an appeal to "self-determination" as an aspect of "universal suffrage" by the citizens of an internationally recognized state. The appeal of this approach is likely that, by avoiding origin issues, it avoids referring to enthnonationalism. As ethnonational cleavage within a state is manifestly a singular cause for world strife, it defuses the most likely form of tension that will lead to conflict within and between states. Certainly, the development of such conflict in places like Bosnia and the former Soviet Union bears witness to stark reality of this danger.

At the same time, the appeal to majority rule on its own has very serious limitations. Protests regarding proper representation within liberal-democratic states made by those marginalized by gender, ethnicity, national identity, race and, to some extent, class show some possible areas of weakness contained in the concept of majority rule for the construction of an equitable political culture, even where true ethnonational cleavage may not be present.[40] Further, where such cleavage is present, the universalizing tendency of the state and the inevitable public nature of the majority culture create conditions where minority cultures are perpetually under threat to assimilate.[41] Such is the case in Canada where, despite certain consociational arrangements, even the French-speaking population in Quebec feels such assimilative pressures. Finally, in cases such as Canada, where the descendants of the original colonists have become the majority, the principle of majority rule delegitimizes the otherwise unassailable claim to sovereignty and underlying title held by the indigenous people, on the grounds that they now constitute a minority. In short, in such situations the appeal to majority rule can be seen as constituting a justification for legitimizing the fruits of colonialism. Therefore, it is likely not an account of the legitimacy of Canadian sovereignty and underlying title that addresses adequately the questions of whether Canada legitimately acquired sovereignty and underlying title from the indigenous peoples and, if so, how it was accomplished.

A second approach resolves the issue by asserting that the exclusive underlying title and sovereignty that was held originally by Aboriginal peoples became lost or diluted through a process that, in its main characteristics, did not require the assent of Aboriginal peoples. One specific form taken by those who espouse this approach is the conquest thesis cited above. It is a thesis that, as I have stated previously, dominates American thought on the topic of the acquisition of sovereignty and underlying title from indigenous peoples in the United States.[42]

The specific form of this alternative now developing within Canadian legal thought is much less confrontational than the conquest thesis. The specific thesis, which derives from international law, is entitled "prescription."[43] This thesis as to how a colonizing population may legitimately acquire sovereignty and underlying title is described by Slattery as follows: "[I]t may be argued that for reasons associated with other basic values and principles of justice, territories illegitimately acquired may sometimes, by passage of time, be transformed into legitimate dominions – a process traditionally termed 'prescription.'"[44] Slattery and, later, the Royal Commission on Aboriginal Peoples, in *Partners in Confederation*, have adopted a concept derived from prescription as a means to explain the acquisition of sovereignty and underlying title by the Crown in the Canadian situation.[45] In particular, *Partners* argued that Canada was not a *terra nullius*. Nonetheless, through conscious acts, as well as through long experience of living side by side, relations between Aboriginal peoples and colonists evolved in such a way that Aboriginal sovereignty and underlying title gradually became incorporated into what was originally a British Crown that was solely within the polity of the colonists. This was accomplished largely without the active assent of the Aboriginal parties. Nonetheless, because the Crown has been broadened to incorporate, rather than extinguish, Aboriginal sovereignty and underlying title, they exist in law whether or not they are explicitly recognized by constitutional provision. In this view, along with the provincial and the federal, the Aboriginal constitutes one of three constitutionally recognized "sovereigns" within Canada and finds its expression as an order of government that, like the other orders of government, possesses legislative authority in its areas of competence.[46] At the same time, because they have already been incorporated into the "Canadian" Crown, Aboriginal sovereignty and underlying title have been domesticated, in that they are in principle and practice to be expressed only within Canada and only with respect to those jurisdictions determined by the Canadian constitution and courts.

The approach taken by Slattery and the Royal Commission is to be commended for avoiding the absurdity of the *terra nullius* thesis, for providing an account that is historically contextualized, and for providing practical means to enable the expression of Aboriginal self-government within the existing constitutional frame. Nonetheless, the approach fails in that it does not adequately address two fundamental questions. The first relates to the issue of the legitimate acquisition of sovereignty and underlying title by the Crown mentioned above. To suggest that, notwithstanding the import of long social intercourse as well as certain conscious acts of alliance, Canada acquired its title through "the passage of time" begs the question. To make such an account adequate and convincing would require a detailed examination of the process by which it took place. It would also require confirmation by Aboriginal peoples that they accept that the process was legitimate and that the result legitimately defines the full scope of their title and sovereignty today. As evidence from Aboriginal peoples themselves attests, such a view is not shared universally and is rejected most clearly by First Nations, especially those with treaties. Rather, Leroy Little Bear has stated:

The Indian concept of land ownership is certainly not inconsistent with the idea of sharing with an alien people. Once the Indians recognized them as human beings, they gladly shared with them. They shared with Europeans in the same way they shared with the animals and other people. However, sharing here cannot be interpreted as meaning the Europeans got the same rights as any other native person, because the Europeans were not descendants of the original grantees, or they were not parties to the original social contract. Also, sharing certainly cannot be interpreted as meaning that one is giving up his rights for all eternity.[47]

The second fundamental question not addressed concerns the principle of prescription itself. As Slattery suggests, the case of prescription rests in particular on an appeal to "basic values and principles of justice" as the essential component to justify the legitimate acquisition of underlying title. Neither Slattery nor the Royal Commission provides any evidence to justify such an appeal in the Canadian case. Therefore, given the long history of colonization and the sorry history of relations between Aboriginal peoples and Canada, it is clearly not self-evident how an appeal to "basic values and principles of justice" could be applied convincingly to legitimate the Crown's acquisition of underlying title in the Canadian situation.

The third approach to resolving whether Canada legitimately acquired sovereignty and underlying title and, if so, how this was accomplished rests on the "cession" thesis or "the formal transfer of territory from one independent political unit to another." It presumes that one party through a conscious act, such as a treaty, willingly agreed to cede its underlying title and sovereignty to the other.

Crucial to deciding on the appropriateness of the application of this thesis to the Canadian case is evidence that indigenous peoples did willingly cede territories to the Crown by means of treaty or other formal act. There does appear to be such evidence, at least for portions of Canada, in the written versions of a number of treaties signed between the Crown and various First Nations. For example, the text of Treaty 4 states: "The Cree and Saulteaux Tribes of Indians, and all other Indians inhabiting the district hereinafter described and defined, do hereby cede, release, surrender and yield up to the government of the Dominion of Canada, for Her Majesty the Queen, and Her successors forever, all their rights, titles and privileges whatsoever, to the lands included within the following limits."[48] This text is then followed by a detailed description of the territories included within the "cession." On the basis of this type of evidence, it could be asserted that, at least where similar treaties have been signed, underlying Aboriginal title and sovereignty were lawfully transferred to the Crown and hence to Canada.

There are two major problems with the application of the cession thesis to the Canadian context. First, there are clearly large regions of Canada, of which British Columbia is now the primary example, where no treaties of any sort have yet been negotiated. Therefore, the application of the cession thesis to these regions is prima facie inappropriate and certainly is not advanced.

The second problem pertains to areas where treaties were signed that include clauses related to cession of lands to the Crown. Here, serious doubts have been raised about the legitimacy of the clauses themselves on at least two grounds. The first is that cession requires two willing parties. In the Canadian case there may be instances where the government party created conditions that coerced the indigenous party to agree to a cession that otherwise would not have achieved an agreement. The second refers to times when the Crown did not even raise cession as a matter for the negotiations or when it had any such request rejected by the indigenous party.[49] Hence, in at least some cases, the written versions of the treaties may be "unfaithful," "inaccurate" and/or even "fraudulent" in reporting agreement by indigenous peoples with respect to clauses concerning the cession of their underlying title and sovereignty to the Crown.[50] Thus, the legitimacy of cession is in doubt even in those regions of Canada where, by following the terms of the written versions of treaties negotiated with indigenous peoples, it would appear that a lawful transfer of underlying title and sovereignty to the Crown had taken place.

In sum, it is clear that the cession thesis cannot be applied to certain important regions of Canada and for other regions the cession clauses that appear in treaties at least require further clarification. Hence, the broad application of the cession thesis raises doubts as to the legitimacy of Canada's acquisition of underlying title and sovereignty from indigenous holders.

At the same time, it is fair to ask whether the application of the cession thesis provides in principle an adequate method to legitimate the acquisition of underlying title and sovereignty from indigenous peoples. The answer, I believe, is yes. Provided that a cession has been made willingly and through democratic means, it would, doubtless, be considered as legitimate in international law and as complying with international morality as reflected in United Nations' doctrines on colonized peoples. And indeed, despite the practical difficulties with applying the cession thesis in the present, there is good evidence to indicate that Canada would prefer to see the underlying title issue ultimately resolved by reference to the formal cession of lands by Aboriginal parties.[51] Hence, in this view the application of the *terra nullius* hypothesis may represent an interim solution that is to be replaced in time by lawful cession.[52]

It is also clear that the resolution of the underlying title issue through cession will meet with much resistance by indigenous peoples, especially from First Nations. For example, Chief Harold Turner of the Swampy Cree Tribal Council stated during the hearings of the Royal Commission on Aboriginal Peoples that "[T]he treaties were signed as our symbol of good faith to share the land. As well, the treaties were not signed to extinguish our sovereignty and our form of government."[53] Alexander Christmas, president of the Union of Nova Scotia Indians similarly told the hearings of the Royal Commission that "In our view, if future agreements are to provide for coming generations and reflect our unique constitutional relationship with the Crown, they must be based on the recognition of our aboriginal and treaty rights, not on their extinguishment."[54] And the Union of British Columbia Indian Chiefs stated in "Treaty-Making and Title" that "What is negotiable in treaty-making are the *ways in which our Indian Nations will exercise our rights and jurisdiction* - i.e., the manner in which Indian and non-Indian jurisdictions will accommodate each other in BC" (emphasis in original).[55]

These statements and others from all regions of Canada provide an insight into the strength of the First Nations' opposition to cession as a goal of negotiations with Canada. It is therefore reasonable to presume that without using coercive measures, it will prove extremely difficult, if not impossible, for Canada to extract agreement concerning cession from indigenous peoples and, in particular, First Nations.

The fourth approach, as detailed elsewhere, is premised on a thesis that which I will call "affirmation."[56] This thesis asserts that the legitimacy of Canada's sovereignty and title derive from an acceptance by Canada of the continued legitimacy of the underlying title of indigenous peoples. Like the cession thesis and like prescription, this approach concedes that underlying title and sovereignty were held by indigenous peoples prior to colonization. It also accepts that in law their title continues in the present. It differs significantly from the other approaches and, in particular, from the cession thesis in that it is premised on the view that Canada affirms that indigenous peoples will continue to hold underlying title in perpetuity. Therefore, the goal of negotiations with indigenous peoples is not to seek the cession of their underlying title as the basis for the origin of Canada's title. Rather, the objective is to derive Canada's title from the on-going underlying title of indigenous peoples and to ground its legitimacy by negotiating its recognition by the affirmed holders of on-going underlying title. It is an approach that has been favoured by many indigenous peoples in Canada.

The affirmation thesis, like cession, advances an approach that, since it represents a recognized means to achieve sovereignty in a colonial situation, would find favour internationally. It is also clear that the resolution of the underlying title issue through affirmation, like the resolution by cession, will meet with much resistance. However, in this case it will be by governments and, likely, by the descendants of the colonists, rather than by indigenous peoples. For example, negotiations would likely involve an agreement that indigenous peoples, who indisputably have had less than their fair share from Canadian wealth in the *terra nullius* period, would now gain access to what many in Canada would consider more than their fair share. In some instances, negotiations might give rise to the return of some lands that, from Canada's viewpoint, are held by "third parties,"[57] rather than the Crown.

Certainly, negotiations will lead to a reshaping of jurisdictional powers in a manner that would give much more clout to Aboriginal governments than now exists. Each of these matters, and many others, will likely lead to strong resistance by individual Canadians, as well as provincial and federal governments. Hence, given the relative power differential between indigenous peoples in Canada and the descendants of the colonists, it is clear that a resolution of the issue on the basis of affirmation is easily at least as remote as one based on cession.

DISCUSSION AND CONCLUSIONS

Of the four alternatives discussed here, two in principle do not provide appropriate ways to resolve the problems associated with the *terra nullius* thesis. An appeal to liberal-democratic values, such as majority rule, avoids the issue completely. As such, it fails to explain the fundamental question to be addressed in any claim to the lawful holding of underlying title and sovereignty: how, absent the *terra nullius* thesis, indigenous peoples became incorporated into the state in a manner that convincingly validates the presumption that their participation is legitimately limited to their right to vote as members of its body politic. While the appeal to prescription or conquest provides a form of explanation for the incorporation of indigenous peoples into the state, it presumes that the legitimacy of the underlying title and sovereignty of a state founded by colonists can occur without the consent of the original holders of title and sovereignty.[58] As such, it runs counter to certain central tenets of the United Nations' Declaration on the Granting of Independence to Colonial Countries and Peoples[59] and of other current international codes with respect to colonized peoples.[60]

Inasmuch as they rely on the assent of indigenous peoples to legitimate Canada's underlying title, only the cession and affirmation theses meet international standards in principle. But because it is strongly resisted by many First Nations, in practice the cession thesis, while advocated by Canada and pursued strongly, is not likely to be accepted universally in the uncoerced form essential to meeting international standards. At the same time, because of presumed and realized resistance to it on the part of governments and many Canadians, the affirmation approach, notwithstanding its acceptability to indigenous peoples and international standards, is not being pursued by Canada. In short, there is no approach that is, at present, acceptable to all parties. When, then, will result?

As one contemplates the future, it seems clear that until there is a change in political will, the Canadian government will continue to pursue a long-term policy based on the premise that eventually all indigenous peoples will agree to "cede" their underlying title to the Crown.[61] This policy will likely be bolstered in the short term by a court system that, notwithstanding the absurdity of the thesis, will maintain that indigenous peoples have no lawful claim to underlying title because in law Canada was a *terra nullius* with respect to it.[62] Given the power differential between the Canadian governments and non-indigenous Canadians on the one hand and indigenous peoples on the other, Canada likely takes the position that, eventually, indigenous peoples will willingly "cede" their territories. It is a position that, given political realities, appears unassailable.

Still, there is merit in examining the possibilities that would likely derive from a change in political will that would allow Canada as well as indigenous peoples to advocate negotiations on the basis of the affirmation thesis. A Canada built on the cession thesis, even when cession was obtained legitimately, would be forever weak in the area of the symbolism of the country as a unique place. Canada, as I stated above, remains captured in current ideology by a colonial imagination that represents the country as a radical departure from an indigenous past. In that sense, Canada has still not achieved postcolonial status. I believe that a Canada based on the cession thesis would never get beyond a colonial vision of itself. For example, it is likely that such a Canada would perpetuate the proposition that the public and general history and culture of Canada are those of the colonists and their descendants, while the histories and cultures of indigenous peoples represent only private and specific histories and cultures, somewhat akin to those of "ethnic" groups. In short, Canada would be a state that, on the one hand, accepted legitimacy through the cession of underlying title from indigenous peoples while, on the other, it treated with disrespect the cultures and histories and, indeed, those very peoples whose cessions gave Canada legitimacy.

In contrast, a Canada founded on the affirmation thesis would conceptualize itself as originating in a past that begins at "time imme-morial." It would likely necessitate a country that would understand itself as one based on the association of two streams of peoples; one with ancient roots here, the other with equally ancient roots from various parts of the world. It would locate indigenous peoples at the centre rather than the periphery of the story of this place and would understand the colonists as more recent arrivals whose stories become added to, rather than depart radically from, the stories of this place. In this sense, the affirmation thesis creates a Canada with an ancient and historically connected history, a history that differentiates it from all other places. To paraphrase the words of J. Edward Chamberlin, at present non-indigenous people see Canada as chapter 15 of the story of another place and see the original people of this place as latecomers who enter the story only at that chapter.[63] Instead, non-indigenous people need to see their presence in Canada as chapter 15 of the story of this place as well as a chapter in the story of other places, and to realize that to find out about the earlier chapters of this place, they must address and learn from those whose stories reach back to that time. That would be a benefit of the affirmation approach.

At the same time, there is no escaping a conclusion that the difficulties associated with pursuing this approach would be massive. Possibilities of strong potential conflict, including the possibility of civil disobedience on the part of non-indigenous Canadians, abound. For example, it is very hard to imagine that negotiations between the parties on how wealth would be shared "fairly" or on a host of other economic and financial matters would be anything less than painstaking. One must anticipate even more difficulties concerning matters on the political side. For example, it is virtually impossible to imagine federal and provincial governments willingly participating in negotiations whose aim would be to redistribute jurisdiction in a manner that would result in the diminution of their power.

There are, however, at least two matters of a fundamental nature where, despite what might appear to be the potential for an intractable dispute, none is likely to occur. The first concerns areas where treaties have already been negotiated. Here, indigenous peoples understand that the original negotiations with the Crown have already led to treaty rights for non-indigenous Canadians and the Crown. In such cases, then, negotiations are likely to focus specifically on ensuring that the original terms of the treaties as had been agreed to by both parties come into force.

The second concerns the status of non-indigenous peoples and the Crown in areas where treaties have yet to be negotiated. There is evidence to support the view that Western peoples, as well as indigenous peoples, derive the legitimacy of underlying title by reference to a relationship between a territory, a people, and the Creator. However, there is a significant difference between the dominant method of Western conceptualization and the ways in which at least some indigenous cultures understand that title. In the former case, the territory is considered to have been given exclusively to a people (or more recently a state). Those who do not form a part of the people to whom the territory has been gifted are often assimilated or removed from the territory of that people. Were this the Aboriginal understanding, then the status of non-indigenous peoples, once they conceded underlying title, would be in jeopardy. However, there is strong evidence to indicate that many indigenous peoples, at least within a particularly important train of thought, understand underlying title on a slightly different basis. As they describe it, while the territory given by the Creator is, in a sense, given to a people, the gift includes an encumbrance. This encumbrance is that the legitimacy of the underlying title depends on how the people to whom it is given share it with the other species to whom it was given, with the past and the future generations and, most crucially, with those human beings who request an opportunity to share in it. Thus, indigenous peoples would be required by the nature of the gift to negotiate political relations, in good faith, with non-indigenous people and Canada.

Notwithstanding the fact that there will be some other pleasant surprises, it is clear that negotiations based on the affirmation thesis will be slow and very difficult.[64] Because of their wealth, power, and strength of numbers and because of the difficulties associated with that thesis, Canada and Canadians are now strongly inclined to insist on the actualization of their rights through the negotiation for the cession of title by indigenous peoples. Yet, for Canada to truly become a postcolonial state, it is necessary for Canadians to treat indigenous peoples with the respect required of those who now legitimately hold underlying title and to work to build a country together with them. For that process to unfold, it is important to agree to negotiate on the basis that the legitimacy of Canada's title is to be derived by the affirmation by both parties, in the first instance, that the underlying title of indigenous peoples shall remain unceded.

7 Quebec's Conceptions of Aboriginal Rights

ANDRÉE LAJOIE, HUGUES MELANÇON,
GUY ROCHER AND RICHARD JANDA*

Constitutions are not known for the precision of their wording, especially when they entrench rights. The Canadian constitution is no
exception, entrusting judges with the interpretation of such expressions as "reasonably demonstrable," "free and democratic society,"
and, certainly not least, "Aboriginal rights."[1] This study is part of an
ongoing research endeavour comprising several successive projects
aiming at a better understanding of the role of the judges in the
production of law through the interpretation of open-ended constitutional wording. In this chapter we analyze Quebec's conceptions of
Aboriginal ancestral rights so as to allow a comparison, in subsequent
research, with the respective meanings that both Mohawks and
Candians give to the same expression.

In order to construct these meanings – for we have no illusions
about "objective" interpretations – we wanted to start from their
most characteristic expression in each culture: in Canadian judicial
and political discourse (in that order) of the common law tradition,
in political and judicial discourse (in that order) in the legicentrist
context of Quebec, and in interviews in the oral culture of the
Mohawks. From these differing starting points, however, the data
thus gathered is analysed using a linguistic method whereby any
mention of an Aboriginal right, either in text or in oral discourse,

* *Jean-Pierre Koch and Judith Harvie contributed to research in this chapter relating to the political
sources of Quebec conceptions of Aboriginal rights. First published in *Canadian Journal of Law and
Society* 13(1):63.

is rephrased to put that right in the position of subject in the sentence considered, so as to list complements or attributes ascribed to it.[2] Summations of meanings for each group can then be achieved to allow later comparisons.

In this chapter, we apply this analytical method to Quebec's conceptions of Aboriginal rights. These conceptions are taken here as separate entities not yet in their comparative framework. They are derived from reports of recent debates of the Quebec legislature bearing directly or indirectly on Aboriginal rights and from case law on the same subject from Quebec's courts and Quebec judges of the Supreme Court of Canada. Our analysis shows several different judicial conceptions since the British Conquest, making it necessary to put them in an evolutionary perspective and to present them before presenting data gleaned from political discourse in the National Assembly and its standing committees, since the latter source became available only at the end of the last of the four periods considered here.

In political discourse within the standing committees, the split between different conceptions is partisan – although this split is less important than one might have expected – and also driven, as we shall see, by other trends crossing party lines. But insofar as case law is concerned, the relevant classification is by time period. The meaning of "Aboriginal rights/ *droits ancestraux*" that one can extract from judicial discourse has evolved over time: major changes have coincided with landmarks such as the Royal Proclamation of 1763, the *St Catherine's Milling* decision of the Privy Council of 1888, the Supreme Court decision in *Calder*, the Constitution Act, 1982, and more recently the *Van der Peet* trilogy and such cases as *Pamajewon, Adams, Côté,* and *Delgamuukw*.[3] Higher court decisions were followed universally in Quebec. We have not attempted a classical legal analysis of cases and precedents, far from it. However, the meanings, content, and scope given to Aboriginal rights by Quebec judges, as well as their vocabulary, cannot be understood if they are not not seen as some sort of reaction to these landmark cases.

JUDICIAL DISCOURSE OF QUEBEC JUDGES

At the risk of distortion, we would summarize the views held by Quebec judges – except for a few – as follows: operating within civil law from a strictly positivist perspective, they hold property rights to be no part of Aboriginal rights. However, they have recently nuanced this position, distancing themselves from a former definition of Aboriginal rights in reference to partial beneficial rights such as usage, usufruct, possession, and occupation.

Indeed, the concept of an Aboriginal title, vaguely defined as a *sui generis* relationship of the Aboriginal peoples with the land and based on first occupancy of the territory, was present in the early cases and was expanded after 1973. This is also true for the right to legal and political autonomy – not rooted in land title – in European continental law, from which the Quebec tradition stems. Legal and political autonomy are acknowledged increasingly, if incidentally, throughout the whole era, although in variable degrees and most often in *obiter dicta*. These conceptions find their explanation in the positivist perspective of which they are the product, as evidenced by the meanings given by judges during the four periods stretching between the British Conquest to the present time.

Before undertaking a description of the Quebec judges' conceptions of Aboriginal rights, however, it should be noted that it is obviously possible to arrive at readings of the same legal data that are quite different from theirs. This can be done not only by looking at it from the pluralist perspective, through the lenses of Aboriginal legal orders, but also, even within the Canadian and Québécois legal orders, through theoretical approaches other than positivism, such as constructivism or *analyse systémale,* or even merely through adopting a critical standpoint.[4] But it is the views of Quebec judges with which we are concerned here. Generally, in the writings of these judges Aboriginal rights refer to Aboriginal title, on the one hand, and to certain forms of political and legal autonomy, on the other, two categories comprised of several variable elements with which we shall deal for all four periods.

First Period (1763–1888):
From the Beginning of the English Regime
to the St Catherine's Milling *Case*

The period from 1763 to 1888 was characterized by a denial of Aboriginal title as collective property and the beginnings of what would prove to be a more open – although at times ambivalent – attitude toward political and legal autonomy.

Indeed, Indian title – as it was then known – had been recognized as an individual right of property in *Nianentsiasa*.[5] In that case the judge relied upon the testimony of a notary who recognized the existence of a custom at times acknowledging such proprietary rights. But a few years later, Indian title was flatly denied as a collective exclusive ownership right in *Bastien*, on the basis of legislation.[6] What emerged instead was the inclusion in "title" of partial beneficial rights: usage, usufruct, possession, and occupation. This inclusion was based on custom in *Bastien* and on first-occupant doctrine in *Connolly*.[7] It was also based on the alternate affirmation of surface rights (hunting, fishing, trapping, lumbering) without any express grounds in *Picard*, but the denial of surface rights in *St-Onge* was justified on the grounds of absence of title.[8]

With regard to legal and political autonomy, the denial of title as collective property did not have the consequences in civil law that a common lawyer might fear: in the continental legal tradition of the Quebec legal community, land ownership and political jurisdiction over territory have been distinguished ever since the end of feudalism and, consequently, can be severed more easily in Quebec judges' minds than in common law discourse.[9] This could explain two related judicial decisions rendered around the time of Confederation that recognized the autonomy of Aboriginal legal orders from Quebec law. At the trial level, this recognition, independent of title, was based on sovereignty, rights of first occupant, and even pluralism,[10] which grounds the Court of Appeal would later narrow to a special kind of pluralism linked to the extraterritoriality of Quebec law. Yet this pluralist recognition of the autonomy of the Aboriginal legal orders, however mitigated, was too hard to swallow for some judges, such as Loranger J.A., who stated, "Même si l'on reconnaissait la coutume indienne du mariage comme règle de droit étranger, un tribunal chrétien du Bas-Canada ne pourrait pas la reconnaître, car elle heurte les principes de notre droit et ne comprend pas les caractères essentiels du mariage en droit canadien."[11]

Second Period (1888–1973): From St Catherine's Milling to Calder

The trends discerned in the first period would be largely maintained – albeit in a somewhat restricted way – during the second period (1888–1973): no new case bore on legal and political autonomy, except indirectly through the application of Quebec law to reserves.[12] The courts' attitude toward Aboriginal title remained largely unchanged, at least where conclusions were reached. However, from 1888 on judges' decisions would be based on other grounds, subject to a narrower interpretation, than those previously invoked.

Indian title as collective exclusive property rights thus continued to be denied in all cases where it was in question: *Corinthe, Bonhomme, Star Chrome,* and *Lazare*.[13] However, the basis for this denial came mainly from the interpretation given to the Royal Proclamation of 1763 given by the Privy Council in the *St Catherine's Milling* case.[14] In the *Star Chrome* case, the fact that such rights had not been expressly recognized during the French regime led the Privy Council to the conclusion that they did not exist in 1763 and thus could not have survived the Proclamation, which confirmed existing rights only. Other grounds were also invoked in the decisions: absence of first occupancy, lack of permanent occupation of the land for Aboriginals living on the Sulpicians' reserve, or seigneurial tenure.

This is what we refer to when we conclude that these judges operated within civil law from a strictly positivist perspective, an approach that denies – at least implicitly, as outside the purview of legal imagination – the existence of Aboriginal legal orders before the arrival of the French and their maintainance in the absence of surrender during the French or English regimes.[15] However, this attitude did not prevent the judges deciding these cases and others from recognizing partial beneficiary rights, as they had before, rights such as usufruct[16] (although they stopped short of perpetual usufruct[17]) or occupation and possession,[18] or even new rights like fiduciary rights.[19] But when it came to surface rights, such as woodcutting and grazing rights, which were confirmed in the prior period, the Court of Appeal denied them,[20] and reversed the decision of the Superior Court on the basis of the absence of title.[21] With regard to personal rights, which the courts were coming to consider in those years, their record was ambivalent. Judges were willing to recognize residence or instruction rights that had been expressly granted by the Sulpicians to Indians,[22] or the standing of Aboriginal individuals in civil courts.[23] However, influenced by a positivist reading of the Indian Act,[24] they were less open to granting other rights linked to legal capacity, such as the right to contract[25] or to be named a legal guardian.[26]

Third Period (1973–82):
From Calder *to the Canada Act, 1982*

In the third period (1973–82), the courts followed the trend concerning the autonomy of Aboriginal legal orders set in the first period, except where criminal law was concerned. But it is regarding Aboriginal title and related rights that a new paradigm then started to displace the previous one, amplifying the ambivalence of the Quebec judges concerning the concept of Aboriginal rights.

Indeed after recognition in *Calder*[27] of Aboriginal title based on rights of first occupancy – at least in principle in the *obiter dicta* of Supreme Court Justices Hall and Judson – judges in Quebec wavered much more in matters of Aboriginal rights. In turn they affirmed, restricted, or denied collective ownership, partial beneficiary rights, and surface rights, depending on whether they thought the French regime in Quebec had an effect on Aboriginal title that could not have been taken into account in the *Calder* case because that case dealt with British Columbia. Thus in *Groslouis*, Judge Malour, from the

Superior Court, applying Judge Hall's reasoning in *Calder*, recognized that Aboriginal title encompassed an "Aboriginal right to land" *sui generis*, quite different from the positivist concept of private property, and he based his decision on first occupants' rights and a new interpretation of the statute of 1912 extending the frontiers of Quebec.[28] However, the following year the Court of Appeal reversed that decision, applying the *St Catherine's Milling* and Royal Proclamation rationale to deny the same rights[29]. Likewise, partial beneficial rights of possession and occupation were alternately recognized on the basis of first occupancy (in *Groslouis*), or restricted, on the basis of the supremacy of Quebec law over the Royal Proclamation (in *Paul*), while usufruct was denied on the basis of the restricted territorial application of the Royal Proclamation (in *Kanatewat* and *Dumont*[30]). Surface rights followed the same pattern: they were recognized on the basis of title in *Groslouis* and on the basis of the James Bay Agreement in *Naskapis*, merely discussed in *Duchesneau*, but denied in *Kanatewat* and *Pinette*, respectively on grounds of lack of title and custom.[31]

On matters of legal autonomy, the lower courts continued to be open to certain forms of pluralism, taking Inuit custom into consideration in *Deer*,[32] an adoption case, and recognizing a different concept of property for Aboriginals in *Groslouis*. However, on appeal from this latter case, Justice Turgeon reversed this decision, going as far as to conclude that the Crees and Inuit had already been assimilated and therefore could not claim their own concept of property.[33] However, the Court of Appeal stopped short of setting limits to the application of criminal law, rejecting the request from Mohawk defendants that all Quebec courts be declined jurisdiction over criminal acts committed on Indian reserves.[34]

Fourth Period (since 1982): Post-Entrenchment

If 1982 was indeed a landmark for Aboriginal rights in Canada, the Canadian Charter of Rights and Freedoms itself had little to do with it formally. In fact, the constitutionalisation of Aboriginal rights is contained in a section of the Constitution Act, 1982, outside the Charter.[35] The Charter refers to Aboriginal rights only in an interpretive clause.[36] This might have had an impact on remedies available for violations of Aboriginal rights had not the Supreme Court decided in *Sparrow* to deal with such violations through a process analogous to that available for Charter violations.[37]

Until a flurry of recent decisions,[38] Quebec judges – despite the constitutionalisation of Aboriginal rights and its liberal interpretation by the Supreme Court – followed the trend they had previously established. That is, they remained more open to restricted forms of legal autonomy than to title and territorial rights, which were almost always recognized in principle, often in rhetorical language, only to be denied, entirely or almost entirely, in their application to the case at hand. The grounds for denial would vary somewhat in time, perhaps to adjust appearances for the purpose of *stare decisis*, but without apparent consistency. Quebec courts had a slight tendency to rely more on §35 of the Constitution Act, 1982 after *Sparrow*, although this ground had been used before. The other variations in rationale appear to be related to the facts of the particular case, such as the presence or absence of treaty or evidence of traditional practice.

The recognition in principle of Aboriginal title on the basis of the Royal Proclamation was accompanied by its denial in practice, given the circumstances of the case under consideration, in *Adams, Côté*, and *Ross*.[39] In these three cases the grounds invoked were the territorial limits of the Proclamation, the absence of exclusive possession, and the effect of provincial statutes of general application within the province. After *Sparrow*, the pattern of affirmation in principle but denial in the case at hand did not change. Rather, the grounds invoked shifted from first occupant, treaty, or cession to absence of treaty, cession, or effects of the French regime. The latter grounds were voiced by Court of Appeal Justices in both *Adams* and *Côté*.[40] However, on appeal from these two decisions in October 1996, the Supreme Court of Canada rejected the argument that the French regime had any bearing on the existence or survival of Aboriginal rights in Quebec. Thus, in both cases Justices Lamer and L'Heureux-Dubé decided that the object of §35(1) of the Constitution Act, 1982, was to protect traditional Aboriginal activities, regardless of the "formal gloss of legal recognition from French colonial law."[41] Moreover, although Chief Justice Lamer had once affirmed that Aboriginal title amounted to ownership in an *obiter*,[42] he more recently stated unequivocally that he saw a difference between *sui generis* Aboriginal title and fee simple.[43]

However, before these recent decisions, it was the reasoning of the Appeal Court that was used in this period by Quebec judges regarding surface rights, recognized in theory both before and after *Sparrow*, without noticeable difference as to rationale, except in denial of application. Such rights as hunting, fishing and trapping were then affirmed as an accessory to Indian title in *Sioui, Ross*, and *Côté*, and by the majority decision of the Court of Appeal in *Adams*.[44] These rights were found by the trial judge, the Superior Court, and the dissenting appeal judge in *Adams* (an opinion confirmed by the Supreme Court of Canada in the *Adams* and *Côté* appeals) to be independent from Indian title but rooted in immemorial usage.[45] Surface rights were also recognized as derived from treaties in *Sioui* and *Côté*. But even if some of the grounds invoked to justify not applying these principles were the same throughout this fourth period – limited territorial application of the Royal Proclamation, precedence of provincial statutes, absence of treaty, interpretation of treaty, renunciation – new ones appeared as a direct consequence of *Sparrow.*

In that case, the Supreme Court opened the door to constitutional modulation of Aboriginal rights along similar lines to those set out in the "*Oakes* test" for the curtailment of Charter rights.[46] The threshold test adopted by the Supreme Court of Canada in the *Sparrow* case, dealing with the infringement of constitutionally protected Aboriginal and treaty rights, is similar to the test that was set out in *Oakes.* Once the individual or group challenging the legislation has demonstrated a *prima facie* infringement of his or their Aboriginal rights, the state must first satisfy the courts that the legislation or regulation can be justified by a valid legislative purpose. Then, on the question of justification of the legislative measure itself, due regard must be had to the fact that Aboriginal rights are constitutionally protected and to the special fiduciary relationship that exists between the Crown and Aboriginal peoples.[47] Hence, taking the contrary view to that of the Quebec Court of Appeal, the Supreme Court of Canada held that the provisions of a federal fisheries law subjecting the Aboriginal right to fish to the discretionary powers of a minister could not be justified under the two-tiered *Sparrow* test.[48]

In contrast to territorial rights, political and legal autonomy of Aboriginal nations fared better than in the preceding periods, albeit in restricted forms. Such autonomy was denied only by the Superior Court in *Sioui,* on the argument of the effects of the French regime on law applicable to Quebec. Later, certain residual forms of autonomy were recognized in *Eastmain* and *Adams,* respectively on the strength of the James Bay Convention and the 1701 peace treaty.[49] But self-government as an Aboriginal right faced a major setback as a result of *Pamajewon.*[50]

In the field of criminal law, the courts started to struggle with the notion that Aboriginal peoples have a right to a certain form of legal autonomy, or at least a right to have their political and cultural beliefs taken into account in the judicial process. In one case involving an incident in an Aboriginal community, a Youth Court judge, fearing invalidation of the decision for discrimination, refused to take into account any cultural factors that could have affected the required legal criminal intent for a sexual assault conviction.[51] Unlike their colleagues from R.O.C., Quebec judges have traditionally been reluctant to consider any such cultural factors at the sentencing level, other than the fact that imprisonment in a federal penitentiary is a particularly harsh punishment for an Aboriginal offender from an isolated community.[52] However, one Superior Court Justice did find that the political and cultural beliefs of Aboriginals were of importance in sentencing. In *Cross*, a case that dealt with events surrounding the Oka crisis of 1990, it was ruled that the honesty and sincerity of the accused Mohawks' beliefs had to be taken into account as a mitigating factor.[53]

More recently, the role of Aboriginal communities at the decision-making level in the criminal sentencing process was also recognized by a Quebec judge working the circuit court in the Arctic, in cases involving the use of community sentencing circles.[54] It can be argued that in these cases of community sentencing, the circuit court judge relaxes the axiom of uniform application of the criminal law by giving Aboriginal communities a say about the fate of Aboriginal offenders. Legal autonomy is here defined as a form of power-sharing between the sentencing judge and more or less formalized community institutions whose role is to assist the judge in finding a just solution in each case. In Quebec, as in the rest of Canada – albeit at a slower pace – community sentencing is now used as a testing ground for Aboriginal self-government initiatives such as traditional and neotraditional conflict resolution mechanisms.[55]

Operating within civil law from a strict positivist perspective, Quebec judges have thus generally held property rights to be no part of Aboriginal rights, although their position has evolved somewhat over time in reaction to landmark Canadian cases. From the beginning of the English regime, they denied the collective character of Indian title, as it was then known, and this trend has been maintained until most recently, while its grounding evolved. First based on statute, after *St Catherine's Milling*, it shifted ground to the Royal Proclamation instead, until a new paradigm started to uproot the previous one: Quebec judges, no doubt moved by *Calder* towards recognition of first occupant's rights, now wavered much more on matters of Aboriginal rights, affirming, restricting, or denying collective ownership. Yet the Quebec courts maintained their reluctance towards Aboriginal title even after entrenchment in 1982, despite the fact that Quebec judges on the Supreme Court of Canada recently rejected the view that the French regime had any bearing on the survival of Aboriginal rights in Quebec.

However, because political autonomy is more easily distinguished from land ownership in civil than in common law, the narrow positions held by Quebec judges regarding the latter did not prevent them from being more open regarding the former. Thus, even in the years immediately following Confederation, they recognized the autonomy of Aboriginal legal orders on the basis of sovereignty, rights of first occupants, and even pluralism, which grounds the Court of Appeal would narrow down to a special kind of pluralism linked to the extraterritoriality of Quebec law. This trend was maintained in lower courts up to the entrenchment of Aboriginal rights, after which it was

often affirmed, and denied only once, until recently when self-government as an Aboriginal right faced a major setback as a result of
Pamajewon.

Such, then, is the record of Quebec judges since 1763, now to be
compared to a much shorter and more recent period of political
discourse, as reflected in the National Assembly and its standing
committees.

POLITICAL DISCOURSE
OF THE NATIONAL ASSEMBLY
AND THE STANDING COMMITTEES

The primacy of legislation over case law in the Quebec tradition has
not been quantitatively reflected in the production of statutes relating
to Aboriginal questions, no doubt because the constitutional division
of legislative powers ascribes exclusive competence over "Indians" to
the federal Parliament. Yet, due to the inherent contradictions of
federalism, "exclusive" does not really mean *exclusive,* and some provincial legislation pertaining to other subjects, when read in the Canadian legal order, can validly affect Aboriginals.[56]

In order to analyse relevant Quebec legislative material, we have
therefore chosen to focus on the political discourse related to such
legislation in the debates of both the National Assembly and in its
standing committees in the First Session of the 34th Legislature,
between 28 November 1989 and 18 March 1992, during which time
the Oka crisis occurred. This choice offers the advantage of illustrating
the views of all political parties in Quebec before, during and after
the crisis. The debates bore on Aboriginal affairs immediately predat-
ing the crisis but also reflected earlier views, because MNAs referred
to former debates from 1983 and 1985 on that question.

Indeed, throughout the period covered by the 34th Legislature, a
great variety of subjects of interest to Aboriginals was broached both
in the National Assembly itself and in the standing committees that
dealt indirectly with Aboriginal affairs within their more general mandate. Thus, the Committee on Planning and Infrastructures discussed
negotiations with the Atikamekw and Montagnais on hunting, fishing,
and forestry and the construction of a provincial road going through
a reserve; the Committee on Labour and Economy discussed negotiations with the Atikamekw and Montagnais, as well as Algonquins,
regarding the planning of resources development; the Committee on
Social Affairs heard the Regional Council of Kativik and the Grand
Council of the Crees and Naskapis on the adoption of amendments
to the Health and Social Services Act;[57] the Committee on Culture
received a memorandum on the *Arpin Report on Culture* from the

Crees;[58] and the Committee on Institutions, which studies the budget of each department, discussed on these occasions not only spending by the Minister of Aboriginal Affairs and negotiations with Aboriginals but also the accessibility of the Human Rights Commission and the ombudsman to the Aboriginals and, most prominently, the administration of justice and public security in Aboriginal communities.

We applied two separate analyses to this material. The first dealt with explicit mentions of Aboriginal rights, which we treated in the same analytical manner as their equivalents in judicial discourse.[59] The second analysis attempted to explicate the implicit meaning of these rights. The latter method consisted in identifying the postulates underlying, and essential to, the statements issued by participants in the Assembly and its standing committees in relation not only to Aboriginal rights but also to the legal system deemed applicable to Aboriginals living in Quebec, in order to ascertain the scope of the affirmation of such rights. The results of those analyses show a cleavage along party lines, quite evident in the explicit discourse – where the Parti Québécois' (PQ) stand is clearly more favorable to Aboriginal autonomy than the Quebec Liberal Party's (PLQ) – but much less sharp, if not blurred, in the implicit discourse, where we see through to the personal ideological inclinations, uncensored by conscious partisanship.

Explicit Mentions of Aboriginal Rights

The use by all parties of the term Aboriginal rights was more often generic, without specification as to content or scope of the rights. During debate the PLQ would, for example, quote Aboriginal rights as an "important preoccupying question."[60] Rémillard, then Liberal Minister of Justice, mentioned that the Quebec government's position on the "rights and freedoms of our Aboriginal friends" was well known; they are historical rights constitutionalised in 1982, and the same general norms of rights and liberties should be enforced where Aboriginals are concerned.[61] (See table 7.1 for a list of the full names, party affiliations, constituencies represented, and cabinet posts, if applicable, of contributors to the debates.) Ryan, then Minister for Public Security, would later reaffirm this position,[62] even to the extent of taking Aboriginal traditions and customs into account in applying Aboriginal rights.[63] Yet in the same breath, Rémillard said that because one person's rights end when others' begin, no distinction in their application should be based on culture or ethnicity, and he refused to distinguish between collective and individual rights.[64] For other members of that government, Aboriginal rights – although specified by the Supreme Court to a certain degree in *Sparrow* –

Table 7.1

Members of Quebec National Assembly Participating In Debates on Aboriginal Rights,
18 November 1989 to 10 March 1992

M.N.A.	Party	Constituency	Cabinet Post
Gaston Blackburn	PLQ	Roberval	Minister for Recreation, Fish and Game
Jacques Brassard	PQ	Lac-Saint-Jean	
Neil Cameron	PE	Jacques-Cartier	
Guy Chevrette	PQ	Joliette	Parliamentary Leader
John Ciaccia	PLQ	Mont-Royal	Minister for Aboriginal Affairs (prior to the Oka crisis)
Christian Claveau	PQ	Ungava	
Francis Dufour	PQ	Jonquière	
Sam Elkas	PLQ	Robert-Baldwin	Minister for Public Security (prior to the Oka crisis)
Jean Filion	PQ	Montmorency	
Louise Harel	PQ	Hochelaga-Maisonneuve	
Richard Holden	PE	Westmount	
Denis Lazure	PQ	LaPrairie	
Robert Libman	PE	D'Arcy-McGee	Leader
Gérard R. Morin	PQ	Dubuc	
Denis Perron	PQ	Duplessis	
Gil Rémillard	PLQ	Jean-Talon	Minister for Justice and Minister for Canadian Inter-governmental Affairs
Claude Ryan	PLQ	Argenteuil	Minister for Public Security (after the Oka crisis)
Raymond Savoie	PLQ	Abitibi-Est	Minister for Revenue (after the Oka crisis)
Christos Sirros	PLQ	Laurier	Minister for Aboriginal Affairs (after the Oka crisis)

remained unclear in certain areas,[65] or awaited discussion with Aboriginals themselves.[66]

The PQ also talked about Aboriginal rights in a generic sense, mainly by referring to the motion adopted by the cabinet in 1983 (and voted on in 1985 when the PQ formed the government), which proclaimed fifteen principles of Aboriginal rights based on first occupancy.[67] The PLQ opposed this motion, claiming it failed to meet the expectations of the Aboriginals, since it did not constitutionalise the rights it recognized.[68] But even though these mentions of that motion seemed to be about rights in generic terms, they referred in fact to the fifteen principles and thus contained references to quite specific rights.

Discourse on specific rights was indeed more characteristic of the PQ, both when it was in power and later in opposition, according to evidence from the debates under study here. So, even if only a small number of MNAs affirmed Aboriginal rights during the debates –

Perron, Lazure, Harel, Trudel, and Chevrette – this affirmation was
not merely the product of this small group's ideas but rather a settled
party position derived from the aforementioned cabinet decision and
parliamentary motion.[69] This party position was contradicted only
once, as regards the recognition of a distinct legal system for Aboriginals in Quebec, by an MNA who had never held a cabinet post in his
whole career.[70]

The fifteen specific rights were mostly collective rights: political
rights such as the right to maintain and develop an Aboriginal identity,[71] to self-government within Quebec,[72] and to retain Aboriginal
customs and traditions,[73] including the right of Aboriginals to retain
their own legal system[74]; to cultural rights such as rights to culture
itself[75] and to Aboriginal languages[76]; to economic rights, both large
in scope, like the right to participate in the orientation and benefits
of the economic development of Quebec and to "possession and
control" of the land,[77] and the more specific rights (akin in fact to the
surface rights recognized by the judiciary) of harvesting,[78] fishing,[79]
hunting,[80] trapping,[81] and participating in the definition of policies
relating to the preservation of wildlife.[82] However, these rights also
comprised some individual social rights, such as benefits from services
offered to the general population,[83] including health and social services and specifically child protection,[84] delivered in their own language,[85] not to mention a timely right to be compensated for damages
flowing from the Oka crisis.[86]

As for the Liberals, one would have expected less emphasis on
collective rights on their part, especially after their justice minister
refused to distinguish collective from individual rights. Yet he and his
colleague from Aboriginal Affairs also affirmed the right to constitutionalised self-determination.[87] Other Liberal ministers and MNAs
affirmed other political rights, such as rights to Aboriginal customs
and traditions,[88] the right of Aboriginals to control their own
institutions[89] and to develop their communities,[90] as well as some
economic rights, such as tax exemptions[91]; and cultural rights – to
culture itself and to languages.[92] But, as most "small-l" liberal parties
would, they insisted somewhat more on individual rights: rights to
fundamental freedoms,[93] to peace and public security,[94] to arms,[95] to
standing in Court,[96] and, finally, "most probably" to compensation for
damages flowing from the Oka crisis.[97]

Implicit Discourse Pertaining to Aboriginal Rights

The express mentions of Aboriginal rights that we have just outlined
are included in a more general discourse on Aboriginals, which we
went on to analyse for its implicit meaning.[98] The implicit images of

Aboriginal rights resulting from this latter analysis are not more homogenous than the diversified conceptions that we found in explicit mentions of Aboriginal rights, but they are less partisan, being divided rather by ideological positions that crossed party lines.

Indeed these positions, although they form a continuum, can be summed up in three bundles that we call "restrictive," "intermediate," and "open." The positions were held by members and ministers of both the PLQ and the PQ, as well as the Equality Party (PE). The reason for these apparently "unnatural" convergences is precisely that they are unconsciously embedded in implicit discourse and that the speakers did not always realize with whom they concurred. The positions were mostly focused on the legal and political autonomy of Aboriginal nations, and they contribute very little to the meaning ascribed to Aboriginal title.

Restrictive Positions. For a first group, forming a majority of the contributors to the debates analysed here (Rémillard, Elkas, Blackburn, Bélisle, Savoie, and Claveau [PLQ] and Chevrette, Filion, Brassard, Dufour, and Morin [PQ]), Quebec laws should apply equally everywhere in Quebec, including reserves, which were taken to be part of Quebec. For this group, Aboriginals were assimilated to an ethnolinguistic minority. The PQ members of the group used the word "nation" almost universally to refer to them, although this term was generally absent from the PLQ discourse. This group's position is one of state-centric legal monism, implicitly based on a theory of law according to which only states have normative powers and only one state can have supreme authority on a given territory. According to this view, the federal and provincial authorities in Quebec alone should negotiate, and then only with elected, representative band councils, recognized by law, and not with warriors or traditionalists who have no legal status and do not respect Quebec and Canadian law.

In its most extreme form, the monological monism[99] held by this group (with one exception, Rémillard) implies a single supreme authority, that is competent for the application of the law. In this view, there is one territory, one state and one legal system within which all laws, but especially criminal and fiscal law or laws related to gambling, hunting, or fishing, apply everywhere *in the same manner* and are interpreted within the same logic, derived from the set of values dominant in that state at any given time. Rémillard excepted, this was the view of this group, which alternately based it on the rule of law, equality under the law, or the Indian Act.

Rémillard adopted an alternative, perhaps milder, version of monism that we call dialogical monism, according to which the authorities would sometimes apply the same law somewhat differently to different populations, in at least partial recognition of their specific values; they would "colour" the law differently in order to gain legitimacy. Then the minister for justice, Rémillard insisted on the universal application of Quebec laws, while sometimes allowing a degree of flexibility in police enforcement of criminal law on the reserves. In so doing, he nearly bridged the gap between the first and second groups and almost transformed their discrete relationship into an ideological continuum, barely marked by degrees of openness.

Intermediate Positions. A second, much smaller group (Sirros, Ryan [PLQ], Perron [PQ], Libman [PE]) maintained an intermediate position that we would characterize as still monist, but with a stronger dialogist flavour than the one we have just ascribed to Rémillard.

For them, Aboriginals are grouped into nations, not to be confused with mere ethno-linguistic minorities, and band councils are not municipalities. These facts should be reconciled with the supremacy of Quebec laws, in order to achieve peace, which is preferable to the integral application of all sections of the Criminal Code. Thus, police intervention must take into account the mentality, customs, and expectations of the Aboriginal populations. Because these expectations are legitimate, police forces should be hired from within their communities and controlled by the band council in order to make them acceptable to the Aboriginal population.

On this continuum, where differences are very subtle and gradations barely perceptible, Libman and Perron link the last-mentioned subgroup of those holding the intermediate position with the next, open group.[100] They frequently mentioned Aboriginal claims to self-government and even full sovereignty with implied approbation, and they considered such protection of Aboriginal culture to be legitimate. Before the Oka crisis, Perron even affirmed that we share the territory with the first occupants. Yet this pair considered Aboriginals to be citizens like any others and to have a right to urban integration and to the expression of their views on the Quebec constitutional question.

Open positions. A third and last group – or should we say duo – (Ciaccia [PLQ][101] and especially Harel [PQ]) crossed the bridge into legal pluralism[102] of a weak variety,[103] where several legal orders can coexist on the same territory, but under the hegemony of the state. The difference from the position of the previous group is that in this case we are not dealing with different applications/interpretations of the same law but with the recognition of an Aboriginal power of normativity as such.

The proponents of this conception of Aboriginal rights maintained that the Aboriginal peoples are entitled to the constitutionalisation of the rights of their choice, such as self-government and development in the context of their traditions, identity, and roots. This image holds that we share the territory with them but must not pretend to equal application of our laws to their lands: laws are based on culture and cannot be universal; only justice is universal.

According to Ciaccia and Harel, we must negotiate with the Aboriginal nations, both through the band council and the traditional Long Houses, and through the Confederacy. The Aboriginal population should not be integrated into the Quebec majority. Rather, their identity should be respected within a pluri-nation, as distinguished from a pluri-ethnic state, where different governments are competent to enact laws for their respective peoples.

Read separately in its implicit subtext, the discourse of the debates showed less partisan cleavage than the explicit mentions of Aboriginal rights would have led one to expect. A majority trend, equally divided between the Liberals and the PQ, sets a quite restrictive approach to the interpretation of the concept of Aboriginal rights by framing it into an implicitly monist background, where one state applies one law equally, to all, everywhere, on one territory. Also equally divided among major parties, several small minorities – one within and others outside that first trend – adopted an increasingly open position, growing from mild to strong dialogism, and on toward weak pluralism. The most advanced position did recognize a shared territory, thus perpetuating an oxymoron that has been with us since the French regime, by which autonomous legal orders would exercise self-government within Quebec. Thus, the whole picture is best characterized as more a continuum of increasingly open ideas as the number of proponents decreases than as a sequence of distinct positions.

In summarizing our analysis of the Quebec parliamentary discourse on Aboriginal rights and comparing it with that of Quebec judges on the same topic, we must emphasize the limits imposed on this exercise by both the time-frame and the context in which it was set. The time-frame, as we have mentioned, was that of parliamentary debates surrounding the Oka crisis; it was both short and focused by exceptional events, and it is entirely possible that a different picture could have emerged had we dealt with a longer or different period. The context, as we have also explained, was not legislative per se and therefore not closely representative of the opinions of the government or the opposition, as would have been the case for a statute. Yet, we feel that our choice of both period and material, although restricted by the unavailability of debate transcripts for earlier periods, is adequate to support the following circumscribed concluding comments.

Contextualized by the results of our analysis of the implicit discourse, the parliamentary discourse on Aboriginal rights, taken globally, does not show sharp contrasts, and the division on partisan lines is blurred but still present and meaningful. In its discourse, the position of the PQ remained more generous than that of the PLQ, both because it was more detailed as to the content of rights than that of its opponent and because the Liberal Party removed its more open minister, Mr Ciaccia, from the aboriginal affairs portfolio when the Oka crisis brought the subject up front in the summer of 1990, showing that the party sided (of course) with its majority. Various forms of Aboriginal legal and political autonomy within Quebec that were favorably considered in all judicial decisions (with one exception and one dissent) also constituted the main preoccupation in the debates, which rallied some important ministers from different governments, even some who adhered to the most restrictive conception of Aboriginal rights.

The impression that there is a more positive attitude towards basic autonomy than towards economic rights related to Aboriginal title is reinforced by the fact that specific rights recognized by both leading parties were – with one circumstantial exception – collective rights related to legal and political autonomy: self-determination within Quebec, customs and tradition, culture, and language. In contrast, the eight collective rights related to the common law concept of title and its economic components – rights to possession and control of the land and to participate in its economic development, to the definition of policies relating to the preservation of wildlife, as well as surface rights (harvesting, fishing, hunting, and trapping), which were expressly acknowledged by the PQ not only when it formed the opposition, but from the time it was in power in the eighties – were not only couched in more restrictive language in judicial decisions but also absent from the Liberal's express discourse and the implicit discourse of all parties. Silence is not always acquiescence, and sometimes it speaks loudly.

As for individual rights, they were, of course, more important for any liberal party insisting on traditional fundamental rights "of the first generation" – freedom, security, legal rights, and the right to arms. The PLQ is no exception. In contrast, the PQ stressed individual rights "of the second generation," social rights to health and social services. Yet individual rights are much less important in the political discourse than collective ones and, with the exception of property rights, absent from the judicial discourse.

A general pattern characterized by a few important common features thus emerged from within both judicial and parliamentary sources of the Quebec conceptions of Aboriginal rights. On the whole, a more liberal attitude was taken by the political class than by the judiciary, except perhaps on criminal law matters, even though neither the criminal courts nor the National Assembly ever seriously questioned the applicability of criminal law to Aboriginal peoples. Yet the different contexts in which criminal law was discussed are an important factor. Quebec courts seem to be awakening to restricted forms of legal pluralism at the sentencing level, while in the political arena pragmatism seemed to prevail over principle, at least in the context of the Oka crisis.[104]

But apart from this nuance, on the whole both groups held a more open position about legal and political autonomy – although a majority confined it within the boundaries of legal monism – than on economic rights linked with Aboriginal title, and both emphasized collective over individual rights. Beneath partisan diversity and rhetoric, there was a consensus on some basic issues, a core of specific elements common to all – or most – Quebec judges and legislators on the Aboriginal question.

8 The Revolution
of the New Commons

GUSTAVO ESTEVA

For centuries Indian peoples in Mexico attempted to retain or to reclaim their old commons, their *ejidos*.[1] This struggle of resistance inspired the Revolution at the beginning of the century and continued during the postrevolutionary regime. It is now becoming a struggle for liberation. Based on what they still have, both materially and spiritually, Indian peoples have abandoned the impossible enterprise, still desirable for a very few, of *restoring* or *reconstituting* their old commons. Instead, they are giving new expression to their contemporary aspirations. After enriching their vision with their own experience and that of other peoples, they have ceased to see the past as destiny, even though they are not breaking with their tradition. And they refuse to buy the escape to the future offered by modernity. Through new initiatives, they are trying to realize far-reaching dreams in their new or regenerated commons.

Some of them are trying "to recreate the Mexican State."[2] Others are abandoning the design of the nation-state in order to reorganize society: in going beyond democratic pluralism, with its ideal of a civilized attitude towards minorities, they want to advance towards *radical pluralism*, to promote the harmonious coexistence of culturally differentiated peoples.[3] Instead of a social pact among individuals, which is the premise of the current state, they hope to construct another society where fully individualized, Westernized Mexicans will coexist with people living in "commonality."[4] Far from being a reminiscence or a survival of the past or a return to a premodern condition, this ideal is a contemporary creation. It can be called postmodern, in spite of the confusion created by scholars and the media around this word, because it represents a rupture with the fundamental premises of the modern era, redefining the future.

SELF-GOVERNMENT

Oaxaca, a state neighbouring Chiapas in southwestern Mexico, has the largest concentration of Indian peoples in the country, and it is the only state where they represent a social majority. In 1986, for the first time in a century, an Indian was selected as a candidate for governor. The day he launched his political campaign, he met with representatives of the sixteen Indian peoples living in Oaxaca. For several hours they spoke in their own languages, without interpretation. Nobody else understood what they said. At the end of the meeting, a very old man crossed the big hall and told the candidate, pointing his finger towards him, "We want you to be for us like the shade of a tree." That was all. Surprised, like most of the people attending the meeting, I asked some of my Indian friends about the meaning of their ritual. They explained it to me without hesitation. How could he pretend to govern them if he was not even able to speak their languages, the supreme expression of their cultures? How could he govern if he was forced to address them in Spanish, the language of the colonizers? But they were not in rebellion. They wanted a governor, and better if he was one of them, an Indian. But they wanted the government he would lead to be well rooted in one place, where everyone would be able to see him – like a tree; they did not want a government trying to govern them all the time and everywhere, even against their will. And they wanted their government to have the capacity of helping them in case of calamity or conflict – to be able to offer them protection, like the shade of a tree.

This attitude is reflected daily in the struggle of the Indian peoples for control of local government, the municipalities created by the Europeans.[5] They have always resented this institution as a tool of domination, and they have attempted for centuries to put it at the service of their own ends and use it to settle their conflicts with the government and the society.

Oaxaca illustrates the meaning of this struggle. It has less than 5 percent of Mexico's population, but a fifth of its municipalities. In spite of the resistance of the authorities, who consider that this number is excessive, Indians are still struggling to increase it and to modify, at the same time, the structure and operation of the municipalities.

Differentiated political practices prevail in four-fifths of the municipalities of Oaxaca. Authorities are appointed in the tradition of the *cargo* system, in which citizens accept their responsibility to perform public duties for the community.[6] Elections are not procedures that appoint authorities through the majority vote but bureaucratic formalities to get external recognition for the decisions of the community concerning public duties, which are made in assemblies that ritually express the consensus obtained through complex procedures involving everyone. The length of the *cargo* is also based on consensus.

The way in which local authorities are appointed is opaque for outsiders. The following can be a typical procedure. Nobody knows how it starts, but when the name Juan appears in a conversation, everybody has something to say. Then, another day, someone brings up Epifanio's name, and an animated discussion starts. Step by step, new names are added, and others are eliminated. After some time, through procedures always mysterious to the outsider, there are only three names left, and the task now is to list them in sequence. On the day of the assembly, everybody knows what will happen. The ritual is performed, and the persons whose name was placed first in the list is appointed. The person who is appointed rarely gives a speech but always asks for the collaboration of everyone. Some people come subsequently, on the day of the "elections," to offer proof of the agreement. For a year the appointed person will be the head of the local council. At the end of that year, he will resign, and the person whose name was placed second on the list will occupy his place. The next year, the third will do the same.

This method has its own vices: it reflects the existing tensions between a structure of government that attempts to control the people and the struggle of the communities to freely exercise their capacities for self-government. It also reflects the struggle against *caciques*, local headmen supported from the outside, who bring oppression and control to the last corner of the communities and use conventional political practices to subordinate them to external decisions.

Political parties are also a source of tension. In most cases they have not represented a democratic advance in the communities: rather, they have divided them as much as religious sects. However, on 30 August 1995, after a long struggle, a new local law made it possible to do without political parties and use traditional methods, rather than elections, to constitute local governments. Of the 570 municipalities in the state, 412 opted for the new procedure. While violence and postelectoral conflicts appeared in the municipalities where political parties continued to participate in local elections, none emerged in the municipalities where people were now able to follow traditional methods and get legal recognition for them. In some of these municipalities, graffiti appeared at the entrances of the villages saying, "No place for political parties in this town." Some political analysts have argued that the new law represents a step back in the march to democracy, since the local bosses, the *caciques*, will use the communities' consensus to reaffirm their domination. The opposite seems to be true, however: the *caciques*, who were affiliated with the official party, had always used elections – which were usually manipulated by them – to strengthen their political power.

Recent events in Chiapas reveal the importance of this struggle for Indian peoples. The province has a population equivalent to Oaxaca's but only a fifth of its municipalities. After the rebellion of 1994 people not only obtained control over municipal governments but also started to divide them so that they would be of an appropriate size. The movement became contagious, and formal authorities, elected through fraud, have been replaced by representative councils. Reshaping the municipalities and making substantial changes in their operation are now a top priority on the political agenda of the people of Chiapas.

Meanwhile, in Oaxaca the struggle to widen and consolidate freedom inside the municipal structures has been intensifying. A New Agreement is being negotiated with the state government to establish a new basis of mutual respect and to recover for the people functions and power concentrated until now in national or state bureaucracies. Proposed in March 1994, the agreement includes a specific attempt to decentralize political and administrative decisions affecting the lives of the Indian peoples as they relate to the administration of justice, agrarian conflicts, and the allocation and management of public funds. These changes would be made through new organizations constructed by the peoples themselves at the level of the community, the municipality and the region.[7] They are described in more detail in the following sections.

"OPEN-EYED" JUSTICE

The administration of justice is a permanent source of tension between Indian peoples and the established regime. "Official" justice represents a clear threat, both because of its corrupted and discriminating practices against the Indian peoples and because of its opposition to their own traditions.

Human rights organizations have documented continual violations of human rights in Indian regions and have helped to liberate many unjustly imprisoned Indians. But perhaps the time has come to ask if their initiatives are not becoming counterproductive. The struggle for human rights has started to cause unforeseeable effects. Born to fight abuses of power, it is now a pretext for new abuses. Indian peoples have started to suspect that the struggle for human rights may be the last frontier of colonialism, because human rights are defined and established around the individual, under an assumption of universality based on colonialist premises. For many Indian peoples, duty, rather than right, is the basic principle of social order. Instead of the individual, the minimal unit of abstract categories, there is the person, a knot in a web of relations. While the Indian peoples intensify their struggle against individualization and affirm commonality, the claim for human rights affirms the former and dissolves the latter. The recognition of collective rights has not advanced much recently because collective rights are assumed to be a mere aggregation of individual rights or because those involved in the struggle for rights refuse to dissolve the latter and abandon any assumption of universality.[8]

The two systems of justice – official justice and the justice of the Indian peoples – are worlds apart. In the villages everyone, including the children, knows an offense and what to do about it; for the society at large and the government, crime is the business of lawyers and bureaucrats. The society at large emphasizes punishment and atonement, at great social cost. Indian peoples, in contrast, look for compensation and rehabilitation. In many indigenous groups, for example, if a person kills a man, he does not go to jail but assumes economic responsibility for the family of the dead man for the rest of his life, which usually transforms him into a dedicated citizen. The very fact that the "criminal" accepts this "punishment" in spite of his freedom to escape is a proof of the value Indians place on belonging to their communities and staying in them. Generalized knowledge of the concrete principles to be applied in the case of an offense and the conditions in which justice is administered further enhance its personalization, to a level that is impossible in the larger society. "There," an Indian leader told me recently, "they represent justice as a blindfolded woman; here, we want it with our eyes wide open." Who will dare to argue for the impartiality and universality symbolized by the bandage over the eyes? Given the distortions of the administration of justice in the real world, is it still meaningful to look for the universal application of a single legal system?

The system of justice in the villages can be plagued by vices and even atrocities. Periodically, excesses committed in the villages create a public scandal and are used as a pretext to defend the dominant system and the value of universal human rights. People distrust federal justice and react in an uncontrolled way against some criminals when many villages take justice into their own hands. Sometimes such reactions look barbaric. For example, at the beginning of 1995 in Ojitlán in the Sierra Chinanteca of Oaxaca, the whole village rose up against a *cacique* who had assassinated the people's leader. People were convinced that the authorities would protect him and that he would be a permanent threat to them. He was beaten and then raped in the plaza of the village by all the men, who planned to burn him and throw his remains to the pigs. The police did not dare to enter the village, because the residents had posted armed men at every access point. However, Bartola Morales a Chinanteca woman who possessed great moral authority, crossed a lake in a canoe to reach the village, hoisted white and red flags with two other women, and courageously challenged the crowd, demanding reflection. The end result was that the authorities committed themselves to putting the man in jail, removing him from his official position, and giving all his properties to the village. The life of the criminal was thus saved, preventing more atrocities.

For many, such excesses and vices could be avoided, correcting at the same time those of the established regime, through the improvement of the regime itself. They think that eliminating the corruption and distortions of the regime, establishing limits to "judiciary inflation" (the tendency to transform every daily incident into a legal suit), and encouraging more citizen participation will solve current problems. Indian peoples, however, are bringing a different approach to the public agenda. One that not only contradicts the Constitution – which bans exclusive tribunals, in the name of the universality of law and individual rights – but also challenges the conventional notions of justice. Empirical studies give good support to their approach. In Oaxaca, for example, the number of crimes is lower in the villages where Indian justice, tolerated by the authorities, prevails. When they are in charge of their own security, the Indian peoples are better protected. And the cost of official justice and the atrocities currently committed in the judiciary system and the prisons – which the Indian peoples see as contemporary, socially accepted venues of torture – are avoided.

The New Agreement between the Indian peoples and the state government, which will, as noted, decentralize the administration of justice, will demand great juridical imagination to give legal value, within the present framework, to mechanisms that will establish different spheres of competence for official justice and the Indian peoples' justice, as well as limits to what everyone can do and a basis for mutual respect. Rather than tolerating the current system, the problem now is to recognize the wisdom and effectiveness of procedures rooted in the peoples' traditions, that have been successfully adjusted to contemporary conditions. Increasing opposition to such an approach is jeopardizing the New Agreement, which will not be agreed upon in its entirety any time soon. But Indian peoples will not give up their struggle until they succeed.

AGRARIAN CONCILIATION

Through continual struggle the peoples of Oaxaca have acquired most of the arable land and all the forests. In that sense, agrarian reform has virtually come to an end: 7.4 million hectares of the 9.5 million hectares in the province are held under a form of social tenure; 73 percent of this is communal land; the size of private properties usually respects constitutional limits.[9]

In Oaxaca, however, as in the rest of the country, there are still intense agrarian conflicts. Most of them have been created by external interventions, which have exacerbated or stimulated confrontation among peoples, or among groups inside a village, about the land or forms of representation.

In the course of the last five hundred years, the law – the text – dismantled agreements among neighbours based on the word, mutual trust, and tradition. If an agrarian dispute starts in an illiterate village, the elder will run to his hut to produce the deed the village got from the Spanish Crown, often at a gold price, or the document of the Mexican government recognizing those deeds or the communal tenure. The mistakes in those documents, as a consequence of bureaucratic deficiencies, corruption, or bad faith, are a continual source of conflict and remove the solution of disputes from the hands of the people. When agreements are reached, after a long and difficult process, the agrarian authorities often refuse to recognize them.

During the last decade, a new procedure of direct conciliation has been successfully implemented, often based on the revaluation of traditional authorities and old customs. In the New Agreement, this matter has a high priority. The idea is to leave all agrarian conflicts in the hands of the people, reducing the function of agrarian authorities to technical support and legal validation of the agreements.

The story does not end there. The constitutional reforms to the land tenure regime introduced by the Salinas administration (1988–94) dismantle the fundamental basis of the land tenure system created by the Revolution, in order to transform the land into a commodity allocated by the market. Indian peoples, as well as many other peasants, wish to cancel these reforms, not to return to the old regime – which was plagued with vices and limitations – but to create a new one that would be better adjusted to their historical claims and contemporary conditions.

PUBLIC FUNDS

During the last decades, states and municipalities were stripped of their fiscal power, while the native peoples were exposed to the depredation of their cultures and environments by public and private developers. They thus became increasingly dependent on federal funds, which operated as the main tool for systematically dismantling the commons. Designed with a centralist and homogenizing vision and standard development criteria, federal programs inhibited or distorted the differentiated initiatives of the peoples. They also continually introduced into municipalities forms of organization which divided the people and undermined traditional patterns. In some cases they used old practices, like the *tequio* – unpaid work for the community – to cap the costs of public works, at the price of dissolving the original meaning of these practices.

For a long time Indian peoples have struggled to increase their access to public funds and adjust the design of the official programs to their local conditions and needs. They have made important strides in that direction, and now they are reorienting their efforts in order to recover their fiscal capacity and acquire control over the allocation and use of public funds. This struggle has been confronted with strong resistance, but it is part of the commitment already accepted by the state government in the framework of the New Agreement. Some advances have already been made, and similar processes are happening in other provinces.

RESTRUCTURING POWER

Since 1994, two main points on the Indian agenda have been receiving increasing attention: formal and practical recognition of the community and its autonomy and the creation of "autonomous regions."

The more frequent and generalized political conflict in Oaxaca, as in many other provinces, is a dispute between the main towns of the municipalities and their communities.[10] In the last few years, groups of communities have created formal or informal unions to promote their claims. Some of them are trying to become municipalities; many others now claim that the community, not the municipality, should become the basic unit of the political system and that many of the functions of the municipalities established in the Constitution should be transferred to it.[11]

This struggle now overlaps with the attempt to create new regional structures. The issue is still being debated, following different interpretations of the struggle for autonomy. Some are trying to structure both the municipality and the region "from the bottom up" as coordinating spaces for culturally defined communities. Others want to add a level of government, between the municipality and the state, for Indians.[12]

There are already some more or less informal regional structures of government that are not legally recognized but are tolerated by the authorities. None of them seems to be associated with separatism or fundamentalism. Their common denominator is the affirmation of traditional practices of self-government in the community, the municipality, or the region. There is no consensus, however, about their design.

Constitutional reforms now being debated need to give due consideration to such initiatives, both to define new spheres of competence and to recognize the plural and differentiated character of the political bodies to be established. One of the critical points will be to define levels of government that can operate as "hinges." They will juxtapose two radically different styles of government: the local government and the state or national government; direct democracy (government *by* the people) and formal democracy (government *for* the people); government rooted in the people, giving continuity to tradition by linking it to contemporary conditions, and government based on abstract principles, often alien to the people.[13]

BEYOND DEVELOPMENT

Some of the struggles and initiatives of Indian peoples are still associated with development: they try to get access to the goods and services defining the ideal of life that has shaped the contemporary notion of development since 1949.[14]

Among many Indian peoples, however, as well as among peasants and marginal urban dwellers, a new movement has emerged in recent years that goes beyond development. Many peoples have retained some conventional claims (more roads, schools, health centres, jobs), but they are also starting to *bypass* the dominant institutions, seeing them as bureaucratic requisites of an alien and hostile world or as a last resort for resolving some predicaments. The school diploma has started to play the role of a birth certificate or an identity card: it is needed for some negotiations but has ceased to be the symbol of the kind of useful learning that provides social mobility. The health centre or the hospital are desired for reasons of status or as additional medical options, but they are no longer symbols of healing or health. Many people are still looking for a temporary or permanent job, to get needed cash, but salaried work no longer defines a desirable destiny for everyone, and even less is it the only way to survive in a dignified way.

In the recent initiatives of Indian peoples, there is not yet a conceptual challenge to the institutions of development, which are still seen as requisites for social life or as rights that must not be renounced. But practices "bypassing" those institutions are now proliferating, and they advance according to different definitions of the good life. The following story suggests the direction of this struggle.

Don Marcos Sandoval is confused. He cannot discover a valid answer to a question put to him by his sons. When he complains that none of them is willing to come with him to the *milpa* (the traditional intercropping of corn, beans, and squash), which he can no longer work by himself, and asserts that what he knows about it will soon be lost forever, they react by blaming him: "Why did you send us to the school, father?" they say without hesitation. And he asks himself what it is that he did wrong.

For many years he was a great leader in San Andrés Chicahuaxtla, a little village of the Triqui nation. When he was appointed to the main *cargo*, his first action was to negotiate the limits of the lands of San Andrés with its neighbours. Since then, he has led the annual march, when the whole village participates in the clearing feasts of the boundary lines, singing and drinking, to celebrate with their neighbours the peace that subsequently reigned among them.

In the 1970s he was also a dignified representative of his people when a populist president wanted to have direct dealing with Indian peoples.[15] At that time he had the opportunity to go frequently to Mexico City and to give strong speeches before big audiences. Several times, his lucidity, firmness, and dignity brought him to the front page of the newspapers.

In the course of that experience, he acquired information about many government programs that were to bring "the benefits of development" to the villages. He consulted his people, who encouraged him to do something about those programs. After some years, San Andrés got electricity, a school, a health centre, and a new municipal building constructed with a lot of cement, the unmistakable sign of "modernity." Don Marcos well remembers the day when the road that reached the village was inaugurated.

His sons attended San Andrés' primary school. When they finished, Don Marcos made sacrifices to send them to continue their studies in the neighbouring town of Tlaxiaco, in Oaxaca, and even in Mexico City. He believed, like all members of his generation, that they would thus enrich the life of the village and create a better way of life for themselves.

His sons, for their part, soon faced great perplexity. Day after day they asked themselves how they would use what they were learning in the school, which tended to alienate them from their village. The promises of comfort and prestige implicit in their formal education were unrelated to the reality around them in both the village and the city. They observed the increasing difficulties of those who already possessed diplomas, and they did not understand how some of them claimed that the miserable jobs they got in the cities were proof of success. Their discontent began to grow, taking different forms in each of them: two abandoned their studies to start some initiatives in their own community; the remaining three followed the educational experience to the end and submitted their diplomas to the acid test.

One son, who became a teacher, succeeded in being commissioned to a village near Chicahuaxtla, which is also part of the Triqui nation. Because the formal institutions had abandoned the school, he was able to introduce changes in the curriculum. As in many Indian schools, he was the only teacher for all grades. Step by step, he involved all the children in workshops that he improvised. He got some equipment to help them learn skills that could be useful in the community. After a time only the three rs remained from the official program. In the end he was fired when the Ministry of Education discovered what he had done, but by then all his students were busy in activities learned in the school, and the workshops were flourishing.

Another son, Fausto, also a teacher, was confronted with a personal tragedy when the time came to return to the community: his wife refused to abandon the city and come with him. Fausto does bring his children to the village from time to time, but he has problems detaching them from their Nintendos and preventing them from wasting water. Anyway, along with Marcos, one of this brothers who had abandoned his studies, he has founded a very special cultural centre called, literally, "The house that hosts our way."

Before starting the centre, Fausto and Marcos interviewed all who had been in positions of authority in San Andrés since the 1940s to get their advice. They also did some research about the situation of the children. When they observed that those not attending school were more competent in everything the village needed than those who were schooled, they tried to organize alternative ways of learning for those attending school. One of their successes was associated with the annual feast of carnival. Through a simple contest, they involved young people in preserving the feast and renewing everyone's participation. As Fausto Sandoval said:

It would not be appropriate to say that our project has involved the whole community; the community is a whole and does not operate through specialized groups. At the beginning, for example, people resented our videos of the annual march; but they have started to enjoy them and discover that they can be useful. We have obtained support for some *cargos*; we have organized composting, looking for alternatives to the abusive use of chemicals; we have constructed dry latrines and many other things, but it is clear that we have not been able to do many other things included in our initiative. It was a big dream, and we did not have what was needed to realize it. But we persist, and we let it grow as a living being. It is an initiative that is part of our life here.

We, the people of Chicahuaxtla, are people that live in dignity. We are the owners of ourselves. Everyone has his land and access to everything in the community. After leaving the village for several years, I returned because this is my home, my family is here, my roots are here, and here I have everything.[16]

Some time ago, Fausto started a new venture. He used the opportunity created by some bureaucratic changes in the Ministry of Education to participate in the preparation of textbooks adjusted to regional conditions in Indian languages. The experience, which has just started, has already produced unforeseen results. Previously, when the children were doing their homework, their parents were impotent and uncomfortable: how could they help them describe the height of the Himalayas if they did not even know of their existence? In the new class on geography the children concentrate on the surroundings of Chicahuaxtla. As a result, the parents have discovered that they know more than the teacher about what their children are learning. They have recovered a feeling of dignity and importance by revaluing their own knowledge, and they have started to ask themselves new questions about the function of the school. When they bring their children to the *milpa* to help in the cultivation, they are no longer afraid that the teacher will complain; the new evaluations in the school appreciate the progress of the children in that area.

Marcos, who launched the "big dream" with Fausto, is slowly advancing in the hierarchy of *cargos* in the village. Two years ago he was designated to speak to the king and the queen of Spain during their visit to Oaxaca. Full of respect and hospitality, he welcomed them to these old lands "where different peoples conserve, coexist and resist with our own ways of life."

And he added:

We use this occasion to tell the Western world that our way of life has been essentially in community, with solidarity, with a profound respect for the land, our mother, which hosts us and nourishes us; that is why our heart is angry when we see how it is damaged, destroyed by ambition and greed, when it is denied to its ancestral owners, when the natural equilibrium is broken with so many industrial products.

We have been extensively studied from the view of the West, but we have not been understood. Its way of development, its civilization, its way of seeing the world, and its relation with nature are imposed on us, denying all the knowledge generated by our different peoples. We domesticated corn, our sacred food, which has given us our existence, and we are still improving it. Even so, every day, when an agronomist comes to the village, he tells us that the corn produced in their research centres is better; when we build our houses with our own knowledge and materials, an architect comes and says that to live in a dignified way we must have a house built with industrial materials; if we pray to our ancient gods, religious people come to tell us that our beliefs are superstitions. We can offer many other examples. That is why we want to tell the civilization of destruction that we offer our own civilization of conviviality; we only ask that they learn to see us.[17]

Under Don Marcos's leadership, people built a health centre, but no doctor ever came to it and for some time the new building had no use. However one day some friends of the Sandovals, who apparently resented the lack of urban facilities in Chicahuaxtla's houses, were hosted there. Since then, it has operated as a house for friends of the villagers.

When Zacarías Sandoval, the third son of Don Marcos to continue his scooling, concluded his studies to qualify as a doctor, he came to do his social service at Chicahuaxtla's health centre. He kept some rooms for guests, convinced that his patients would be better cared for in their homes, and he gradually modified some of the facilities. For example, he changed the surgical room to help the women give birth in the traditional squatting position. He discovered later that the women felt better if some other women, friends and relatives, were with them during labour. He invited them to attend, and discovered again that many of them knew a lot about labour. He told them that they must be in charge and that he would be available to help if needed. He was never called, but he became famous in the region for his success in assisting births.

Neither I nor the Sandovals like to talk about Otilia Sandoval, a magnificent young woman who was forced to abandon the community to follow her husband, who works in Mexico City, obsessed with the idea of offering a better education to his children. One day, when Marcos was explaining to me his frustration because Otilia's husband refused to come back to the village, he expressed great perplexity about the fascination that modernity still exerts on many of his friends and neighbours. Lunchtime came, and we entered the warm domain of Doña Refugio, whom we found sitting on the floor of her house, next to the open fire at the centre of the room. We sat on very small benches around the fire, and we talked with her and her sons for several hours. She offered us, one by one, a great bowl of squash flower soup made from squash that grows in the *milpa*. More dishes cooked with other vegetables from the *milpa* came later, while we were talking about her reasons for living in the village and preserving her customs. She usually refused to leave Chicahuaxtla, although from time to time, she did accompany her husband on an errand to Oaxaca, as she had on many trips to Mexico City a few decades ago. Her sons had offered her a new stove and other comforts of modern houses, but she refused all of them. She even rejected a Lorena stove made of mud, which would have eliminated the open fire.

We were asking ourselves what the reasons were for this rejection when Doña Refugio offered us a convincing answer. During the ensuing conversation she revealed how far her world is fully immersed in agriculture. Some of the reasons she offered for rejecting some comforts did not seem logical. She said, for example, that the stoves are bad for the back, because they force the women to remain standing. I do not know if she is right: many women prefer the stoves precisely because they allow them to stand. But by seeing Doña Refugio in her own space, I started to fathom her real reasons for saying what she said and to see why she does not see any reason to abandon her village.

That open fire is the centre of the warmest room of the house. Doña Refugio is there, every day, at the centre, surrounded by her family, talking with her sons or her husband, discussing personal matters or community affairs. That fire and Doña Refugio are the centre of the conversation, and in fact the centre of family life; and family life is the centre of the community. The life in the community is in fact organized around those fires, in the centre of the "kitchen," in the source of the *comida*. The very essence of the *milpa* is here, not in the corn growing in the fields – the only element perceived by the agronomists. It is here, around the communal fire, in the heart of the family.

In remembering Doña Refugio's reasons – to bring my memories to this essay – I again started, in retrospect, to enjoy every minute of my stay in San Andrés. But at the same time I did not feel comfortable. Was it appropriate to tell her story here? I have that experience in my skin. It is easy for me to share the joy and wisdom I found there; the skills I discovered among the Triqui; how, wisely, they have been able to overcome the challenges of modernity, to leave it behind, step by step. I could spend hours telling stories of San Andrés. But in doing so in this place, would I not be running the risk of alienating others from my argument, militating against my own cause?

Everybody knows such stories. Many enjoy and admire them. They recognize the quality of such a way of life – for those peoples, far away in the mountains. They even accept that it should be protected and supported. Some others think that a varnish of modernization will not harm them if their traditions are fully respected, a position that usually invites intense debate: how is one to find an ideal equilibrium between such different worlds? How is one to respect, for example, the world of Doña Refugio and at the same time move her away from the open fire, as many modernizers demand? Anyway, both those who want to protect those cultures and those who want to "improve" them through modernization do not find any inspiration for themselves in my stories. Thus, they could be counterproductive. They could present Indian initiatives as going back into history, or, even worse, as an idealization of misery and oppression.

I have dared to tell this story in spite of my reservations, however, because if I am to help us recover the soil under our feet, as I think we need to do, I cannot fail to allude to the cultures of the soil and to experiences that represent, in my view, a postmodern regeneration of tradition. I have never seen a nostalgic gaze in Doña Refugio. At some point in her life she felt the need to slow her pace and regain her own rhythm. Her sons did the same. They were able to take a look at the land promised by the modernizers, to smell what it would mean for their lives, and to decide to limit it. Doña Refugio can rise up from the open fire to enjoy the video filmed by her sons, and they can use this tool and other electronic gadgets. They do not live at the margin of "modernity," in a premodern world. But they are learning to limit modernity. The Sandovals were able, at some point, to transform Don Marcos's aim to bring development to his village into a critical awareness now recognizes some "deficiencies" of the village as privileges that should be protected and demands careful reflection before adopting any technical novelty. If she were cooking on a stove, Doña Refugio would become a servant of her family or would be encouraged to promote a new division of labour between the sexes. By the open fire in the soil, in a situation continually denounced by many feminists, Doña Refugio presides over the life of her family and her community. Daily she becomes the centre of the house, and she cannot avoid a magnificent smile of satisfaction when her sons and the friends of her sons sit surrounding her after a meal and talk for several hours. She usually follows every aspect of those conversations, intervenes whenever she finds it appropriate, and freely expresses her own views. Every day the magic of her fire brings before her eyes the incidents of a changing world, without taking her feet out of the ground.

Fifty years ago George Orwell warned us that in the long term we will discover that canned food is more lethal than a machine gun. I have been asking myself for a long time how it will be possible to perceive as deprivation not being able to experience the luxury of eating Mexican strawberries during the European winter or canned beans everywhere. How is it possible to be fully aware of what is lost in such a homogeneous, global assortment, which cannot be compared with the real diversity of eating according to the rhythm of the seasons in your own environment? I have no answer, but I suspect every time I go to Chicahuaxtla that the Sandovals have one. They have not shared it with me or with Don Marcos. And their case, anyway, is not an anomaly, an exception. Half of Oaxaca's peasants have worked and lived in the United States. Some of them do that regularly. They not only keep in constant touch with their communities while they are far away, but most come back to their own spaces, after they have had first-hand experience of what modernity and development mean for their daily lives.

A month ago the Sandoval family had a solemn meeting. All the sons and their wives were there. They had come to make a very special decision: each of them would made a specific commitment to accompany Don Marcos in the cultivation of the *milpa* in the plot he has cared for all his life. And Don Marcos is confused again: he does not know how and why after so many years of refusing to participate in the *milpa* and blaming him for such rejection his sons have suddenly decided to participate again when they have so many other things to do. I have the feeling that Doña Refugio knows why.[18]

Behind the current initiatives of Indian peoples, in Oaxaca and elsewhere, there is no intention to present their way of life as a model, or, even less, to force others to adopt it. They are primarily focused on gaining respect for it. But they now want something more. They know by experience that their struggles, peaceful or armed, may bring them land and freedom. But their successes are only ephemeral. After some time they discover that they have only substituted oppressors, without eliminating oppression. They now want something more. And this brings me to the Zapatistas, the movement that started in Chiapas and that the world discovered on their TV screens or through e-mail.

THE SURPRISE

The Ejército Zapatista de Liberación Nacional (EZLN) has received a lot of attention everywhere, and all of us in Mexico are still dazzled by the events surrounding it. Those discovering for the first time one side of Mexican reality that they completely ignored are as dazzled as those who were living in that dark side but were not used to the light.

Around May 1994 I came to the conclusion that the Zapatistas had already changed Mexican society and were changing it further. I like many others, asked myself how it was possible that such a localized, weak movement could have such an impact. In looking for an answer, I was forced to write a book, and I will not summarize my arguments here.[19] But there are two questions that deserve some elaboration: How much has Mexican society really changed? and Can we attribute any changes to the Zapatistas?

For many, Mexico has not changed much. They offer many proofs: the results of the 1994 presidential elections would show that the old regime is still in control; the fast reaction of the American government and the international institutions after what the IMF director called "the first financial crisis of the twenty-first century" and the almost immediate stabilization of some financial indicators would be a proof of both economic health and the appropriateness of the international decision to prevent any radical change in Mexico's policies and orientation. According to this position, we had a delay in our march, not a change of direction. After the turbulence of a special year (1994), we will continue our race to economic and political modernization, fully immersing ourselves in the global economy.

In my view, however, substantial changes have occurred. The whole *economic perspective* has been modified. The model that received universal praise was based on a fragile element: external confidence in internal stability. When internal stability was lost after the rebellion, everything else started to explode. The "crisis" not only produced the conventional sequel of devaluation, inflation, unemployment, and recession; it also revealed the weaknesses of the basic structures. From a framework of carefully constructed certainties, we came to a situation in which the only certainty is incertitude.

The *political perspective* has also changed. The conventional structures of political power and the conventional means of political control have been shaken. The dominant regime has been forced to make more concessions in twelve months than in the previous fifty years. Opposition parties have more influence now than in their whole history. The hypertrophied presidential regime has come to an end. All this is the result of a long process, but it was precipitated by the capacity of the Zapatistas to reveal that the emperor doesn't wear any clothes.

The *vision of the country* as a shared reference has also been profoundly modified. It has become evident that the image created by the government was illusory. Instead of living in a society rapidly advancing towards the First World, people are in acute distress, looking for their own way, while at least two opposite factions contend for leadership and create extreme polarization.

Even those who fully trust that the former path can be recovered recognize the volatility of the situation. Opposite political projects will continue struggling. The outcome will probably depend on the eventual articulation of an alternative that can be appropriately compared with the dominant project and its illusory promises.

WHEN THE WORD BECOMES THE VERB

Twenty years ago, on the last page of *Tools for Conviviality*, Iván Illich wrote: "Anguish takes me, when I discover that the only possibility of stopping the mortal swell is in the word, more precisely in the verb, which has come to us and can be found in our history. Only within its fragility, the verb can bring together the crowd of men to transform the wave of violence into convivial reconstruction."[20] The dominant view at the end of 1993 was that nothing could stop Mexico's accelerated incorporation into the globalized economy. It was a mortal swell that was devastating entire cultures and environments with dramatic violence. Words stopped it.

The Zapatistas never posed a military threat to Mexico's national security. The guerrilla warfare that the government wanted to force on them may cause severe turbulence, but it cannot modify, by itself, the course of Mexican society. Neither can the solid social and political organization of the Zapatistas, who are confined to a few hundred Indian communities in the south of Mexico. The word, shaped as verb, has done it.

No other declaration or gesture of the Zapatistas had the impact of their initial emblem: *Basta*, Enough! With that word they brought forth a latent attitude in millions of Mexicans. What many felt but did not dare to express or even think found immediate articulation in one word. Today it is an epidemic. It is constantly repeated in everyday life, nourishing the political positions of many forces and giving expression and guidance to a wide variety of unbearable incidents of daily life. Enough! has been incorporated into colloquial language to define unacceptable situations. It articulates an almost unanimous rejection of the current conditions of life in Mexico. For many, Enough! now defines an existential attitude.

The Zapatistas and their spokesman, Subcomandante Marcos, used the words masterfully. They did not use them to build a political or ideological platform, looking for affiliation, but to give a voice to those deprived of it and to articulate profound and generalized feelings.

Perhaps the Mexican experience of this period will be studied to reveal the nature of modern political power, that is, the extent to which it depends on general perceptions. The operation of power is associated with the institutional production of truth – truth being statements through which people govern themselves and others, no matter if they are true or false. Power changes with the changes in those statements. The transformation of Power thus depends on the institutional regime that produces truth, rather than on changes in political and administrative appearances.[21] The events in Mexico in 1994 deeply affected that regime: a good number of "statements" that had been governing the Mexican people have vanished. The Zapatistas, with genius, articulated general intuitions. Well-rooted in tradition, in the land, their Words – to repeat – became Verb. The Zapatistas have been very effective in dissolving existing statements, but not in constructing new ones.

We do not yet have new statements to govern ourselves on our own terms. As a consequence, power structures are increasingly empty, and they will continue falling apart, as the Berlin Wall did, until new statements give shape to new institutions.

ANOTHER REVOLUTION?

There is still the possibility that the one thousand communities that were the cradle and shelter for the Zapatistas will be exterminated. I hope that massive efforts of the people, inside and outside Mexico, will stop the massacre. But the communities are under a new threat that could exterminate whatever is still alive when the military leaves. A big program has been announced that was conceived by the government in the conviction that a group of "professionals of violence" manipulated the Indians, who only wanted development. The program will be administered to them on a fast track. The developers' army has already arrived in Chiapas, and the communities, perhaps, will not offer them the same resistance they showed to the government's army.

But the spirit of the Zapatistas is no longer confined to Chiapas. It is in the long march of a thousand miles that representatives of one-third of the Indian and peasant communities of Chiapas walked a few months ago to bring their claims to Mexico City. It is in the "autonomous regions" they created in Chiapas. It is in almost daily meetings being organized in Mexico City to discuss new mobilizations and political goals. It is everywhere. It has permeated many people. It is a revolution.

I hardly dare to use this word. Mexicans use it with a smile or a solemn gesture to underline that we are not really saying what we are saying. For sixty years the word was used in rituals dedicated to denying what we did at the beginning of this century. But I have no other word to say what I want to say. Revolutions are identified not so much by the violence that usually comes with them but by the fact that they substitute authorities, modify political relations, and substantially change the constitution and the law, as well as the economic and social situation.[22] We are in that process of change. We have made the first social revolution of this century. Perhaps we now have the responsibility for making the first of the twenty-first century.

SOCIOLOGICAL INNOVATION

Who are the Zapatistas? From the beginning, they have been a source of perplexity: none of the pertinent categories can describe them. They are not a group of discontented Indians, manipulated by a "hidden force." Neither are they a fundamentalist, ethnic, "millenarist" or "autonomist" movement. They are not professional guerrillas, nor do they comprise a movement that only presents some claims.

For many reasons, they can be characterized as constituting an *Indian and peasant rebellion*: this explains their guerrilla form and their struggle *against* an oppressor or an oppression, not *for* a collection of claims. But they are creating something different from all previous rebellions. Because of a lack of interest in central power, peasant and Indian successes have been ephemeral after their rebellions have ended. The Zapatistas have learned from that experience. They have challenged existing power, not to seize it for themselves – like guerrillas – but to change it: they have wanted to involve social majorities in its definition. A coalition of political parties, with full participation of those without partisan affiliations, would establish a democratic, transitional government. This government would open political spaces in which people would define by themselves the nature and shape of the new society they want to build.

Although rooted in tradition, the Zapatistas launched a contemporary movement with modern means and a postmodern political style. They believe that their regenerated commons, which are spaces for self-government, can exist and flourish in a democracy. They are thus catalyzing a revolution that may invert modern institutions and create a convivial society.

When the Zapatistas dared to challenge the dominant view, they instantly produced an "Aha!" effect in millions of Mexicans, who identified themselves with their awareness, their claims, their dignity. They applauded the humour, poetry, and intelligence of their spokesmen, who masterfully used the media for their own ends. New coalitions of the discontented were instantly formed, supporting the long, patient work of thousands of grassroots organizations.[23] Millions entered into an intimate revolt, full of doubts about the way to express their profound rebellion. Hundreds of thousands were mobilized. People started to win the streets.

These successes of the Zapatistas did not come from their very limited military strength but were the result of their capacity to articulate social discontent in a timely and precise fashion, in a way that the political opposition had been incapable of doing. "When the river floods," said an old man, "it is because water has been accumulating up in the mountains." The Zapatistas were living in the mountains; they saw the flood coming. *But they did not seek to control it.* They have avoided any temptation to lead or control the social forces they have activated. They have refused to change the very nature of their movement, to become, for example, a political party. "Nothing for us, everything for all," they say. This is not a slogan but a very effective political style that allows the Zapatistas to continually nourish the coalitions of discontents inspired by their actions while avoiding ideological and political rivalries and sterile polemics.

For those who consider that the political parties should have a monopoly over political activity, this position of the Zapatistas – affirming and challenging democracy – is both ambiguous and contradictory. But it acquires meaning in the context of "new" social and political movements that try to complement formal democracy with radical democracy.[24] It also corresponds to the situation of the country, where government and political parties have lost credibility and people can only trust the dialogue of facts.

THE QUESTION OF POWER

The state, including the democratic state, naturally tends to be unjust and arbitrary. Restricting it is the point of departure of many valid political positions. In the former Soviet Union, people believe that the market can limit the state; that means that they have not understood a thing. In the West, people are abandoning the ballot box and are looking for alternatives but finding only dead ends. One of them is to be found in the recognition that if people can express themselves democratically, most of them will vote for things that good socialists will call petit bourgeois preferences: a little more pornography and sports, more TV than reading, and soon. Both socialists and liberals have thus accepted the need for an elite to guide the people and decide on their behalf. But elites corrupt themselves. After the bankruptcy of state socialism and all the variants of the populist, liberal, or welfare state, the authoritarian option is now open: to govern by force and with the market is the new name of the Apocalypse. In Mexico, we are at the brink of falling into this abyss.

Communities appear as an answer to this dead end. True, they come to our attention because we cannot find another answer. But they also emerge because there is an increasing conviction that the future will be, one way or the other, a community fact. Socialism clearly carried a message of communitarianism, but it was translated as collectivism, "statism," and self-destruction.[25]

However, even those accepting the value and potentialities of communities do not think that they can simultaneously confront the forces of transnational corporations and the modern nation state. How to resist the blind and abstract logic of modern power, which seems to have escaped the possibility of human control?

Modern societies have abandoned the tradition that derived power from Heaven, but not its structure and imagery. The transition from the Pope or the monarch to a president or a prime minister eliminated church intermediation as a source of legitimacy, but it did not change the location of power. People's power has been reduced to the faculty of depositing it in someone, up there. Since political parties have sequestered democracy and political life is increasingly a media event, this regime has become a mechanism to concentrate power in an elite dedicated to reproducing itself and to protecting its own interests. The conception that pretends to construct power as a pyramid but shapes it as a mushroom is still common.

On the other hand, the emptiness of the paraphernalia of power is increasingly evident. Power is, in the end, the power of doing something, but the powerful can do less and less, everyday. The inertia of blind forces imposes itself over the powerful. They no longer have real *power*: they use the economic, military or political *force* that they still have, precisely because they no longer have power. Rather than being trapped in the illusion of changing the composition or orientation of those at the top, in the government or in business, people are trying to imagine alternative power designs capable of expressing the real power of people and condensing it strategically. And that is what the Indian peoples seem to have been doing. Power up there, concentrated at the centre, has suffered all kinds of transformations during the last centuries, but for the Indian peoples it has always meant oppression, domination, destruction. Rather than opposing it with another design of central, illusory power, they have concentrated their efforts on constructing another form of power more connected to their traditions and based on the community fabric.

A few years ago after the fall of Somoza in Nicaragua, I was examining political alternatives with five of the nine Sandinista commanders. I used the insight that I have just outlined in my suggestions to them. They viewed me with pity: "The power that you think is illusory," they said, "is precisely what we now have in our hands. And we will use it for the benefit of the people, in our revolution." What is it that they had in their hands? Somoza's power was threefold: the United States, the National Guard, and his money. When the Sandinistas entered Somoza's bunker, the American government was no longer supporting him, the National Guard had been dissolved, and his money was in Miami. While the Sandinistas were stubbornly trying to rebuild that power, to put it at the service of their ideology, people took away the trust that could have been used to construct another form of power.

This is our present challenge in Mexico. The Zapatistas revealed that the emperor was naked, thus precipitating the fall of our political regime. We still have a presidential regime and both the imagery and the structures of the old regime. But we know it is in agony. For the Indian people, and perhaps for the social majorities, the challenge now is to invent a new regime, juxtaposing a democratic power, constructed from the top down, with a power structure constructed from the bottom up, in which you command by obeying, as the Zapatistas say. Is this possible? Is it not trying to have your cake and eat it too?

Democratic governments could be dedicated to the common good if they linked real government with the social majorities organized in their own commons and if they were designed on a human scale so that the people could govern themselves and assume responsibility for their own behaviour. In Mexico agreements of this kind, governing events and behaviours *with* the citizens and *by* the citizens, could only be properly constructed by Indian peoples. Only they have the full community identity and ability for self-government and self-determination. Only among them is power not, as in a democracy, an *executive* function that orders and commands. Those who have authority among them are like the *Shu-tashá* of the Mazatec people, "the man who serves the people" and performs his function by obeying them. (The symbolic meaning of that word is "a flower that walks in the hands of the people"). Only the Indian people can wisely and effectively deal with their own justice and security, the conciliation of their conflicts, and the guidance of collective efforts towards the common good, the creative practice of the art of living and dying.

But it could be possible to learn from them. In the country there are many groups, both rural and urban, that still constitute a real commons. All of them reject the current situation, while affirming themselves in their differentiated initiatives and the rich diversity of their cultures. They could advance together, towards the articulation of new political options.[26]

CONVIVIAL COMMONALITY

If utopia is something that has no place in this world, then what is now being promoted by the Indian peoples is ambiguously utopian: the new era is already here as an alternative to industrial society, but it still does not have *its* place.

Rather than globalization, localization; rather than urbanization, "ruralization"; rather than modernization and individualization; recovery of the present and the commons; if that is what is happening among the social majorities, as I believe, it would imply that they have used the turbulence of a dying era to launch another, redefining the good life. If that is the case, they could have taken the most interesting cultural initiative of our time.

TAKING ROOTS AGAIN

The world has ceased to be a dream, a prophecy, a project. It has become real. Cultural isolation belongs to the past. There are no peoples, cultures, or societies without "contact" with the "external world": they are interwoven now. A kind of worldwide web makes interactions, interpenetration, interdependence ineluctable. In such a context, the propensity to unify and homogenize the world has intensified, no longer through ideology but through production: the global farm, the global factory, the global market. The new systems of transport and communication have created a novel sensation of belonging to the world – a form of common existence – captured in the emblem of the global village. Corporate transnationalization, what the experts called the internationalization of capital a few decades ago, creates the illusion of full integration, of a deep and complete subsumption of one's being in a globalized reality, confirmed by empirical experience: people wear the same jeans or smoke the same cigarettes (or stop smoking in response to the same campaigns). A Mexican soap opera sets audience records in Russia, and gossip about the English royal family reaches everyone.

This description, however, does not grasp what is really happening among the social majorities of the world, who, rather, confront their increasing *marginalization* from the "globalized" mode of living.[27] They are also increasingly aware of this situation: they know that they will not eat at MacDonald's, will not check into a Sheraton hotel, and will not have a family car; they know that those who are "globalized" will deplete the world's resources well before that could happen.

Being aware of their inevitable exclusion from a way of life proposed as an ideal for everyone, in whose name developers continue sacrificing their lives and environments, people in *barrios* and villages have started to react. Faced with the globalization of their marginality, they have rooted themselves again in spaces that belong to them and to which they belong. They have entrenched themselves in those spaces, *localizing* their initiatives and giving them a new meaning: instead of trying to be incorporated into the promised world, they now claim respect for what they are and have and are dedicated to enriching it; they attempt to reclaim their commons, if they have been wrenched away by developers, in order to regenerate them, or they try to create new ones.

These trends are mainly manifested among those who have resisted developers' subjugation and have avoided being transmogrified into *homines oeconomici* in the *barrios* and villages, and particularly among the Indian peoples. However, they can also be observed among those who have been incorporated into the middle classes. The new operation of the global economy has deprived many of them of what they considered their privileges, throwing them into the informal sector. Some of them crowd themselves, like a mass in panic, into the increasingly narrow access doors to the condition they have lost, while many others are joining forces with those that have never reached their condition. They are thus strengthening their joint efforts to cope with their common political and sociological challenges. Localization or relocalization, taking roots again, rather than globalization, could be the defining trend at the end of the century.

RURALIZATION

Urbanization, as a privileged expression of industrial society, imposed a two-pronged dependency: on goods and services necessary for survival and on mechanisms giving access to them. That is, it imposed dependency on the market and the institutions of the welfare state. The city was reshaped accordingly and fragmented into homogeneous and specialized spaces to accommodate the economic functions defined for people. To get subsistence out of that logic became virtually impossible.

The process has apparently concluded in the industrial societies. Roughly 75 percent of their population is urban, and a good part of nonurban people are assimilated into the same pattern. The invention of the commuter man and the search for a better "quality of life" stopped the growth of big human settlements, but not the logic of their operation, which still defines the daily life of the new *homo transportandus*. But urbanization continues in the South, where the urban population is still increasing at a rate of 4 percent a year. Nine of the ten most populated cities of the world are now in the South. In regions like Latin America the urban population will soon catch up to and surpass the percentage reached in industrial countries. According to the experts, 60 percent of the world's population will be urban in the year 2000.

These phenomena may be misleading. It is possible that the opposite trend has already started. A deceleration of *visible* urbanization has already been observed in many countries, and the nature of urbanization has also been changing. The growth of the city has always occurred at the expense of the *barrio*. The diversity and multifunctionality of the latter, which tends towards self-sufficiency, continually contradicts the economic logic of urbanization. Whole *barrios* have been devastated to establish specialized spaces to sleep, work, or buy goods and services, all of them interconnected by speedways to allow the urbanites to fulfil their functions.

But people have started to react. Because urbanization in the South effectively fulfilled its dissolving and destructive function but was not able to provide employment opportunities and urban goods and services, people have been forced to create subsistence for themselves. They have appealed to their still recent rural traditions, in land takeovers and in the organization of settlements and their defense. With great ingenuity they have endowed themselves, legally or illegally, with basic services, built their own houses, and equipped their spaces in order to use their skills to obtain their own subsistence or to occupy and thrive in the interstices of the society. At the same time, they have maintained an effective interaction with the rural communities they came from to facilitate the flow of people and products in both directions.

The turbulence of recent years activated this social fabric and stimulated a double trend, enriching rural settlements through the reformulation of urban techniques and "ruralizing" the city, that is, reclaiming and regenerating the multifunctional *barrio*, in all its diversity. In the big urban settlements in the South, modern enclaves, widened to accommodate the middle classes, are literally under siege by the so-called urban marginals. They are inextricably linked to them but have, at the same time, great autonomy. They are also linked to the market but do not follow its abstract logic. The "ruralization" of the cities, rather than urbanization, now defines the direction of social change in many regions of the South.

RECLAIMING THE COMMONS

The enclosure of the commons in England separated men and women not only from their land and means of production but also from the social fabric that supported them. Those who were not absorbed by the factories or used as an industrial reserve army were treated as castoffs, and many of them were forced to emigrate.

In the countries of the South the enclosure followed a different pattern. When it did not enslave the people, it subordinated them to the requirements of colonialism, exploiting them without expelling them from their commons. When the expulsion was pushed forward, through methods like the Green Revolution, the capacity to employ the people was always very limited and great numbers were left behind. There were constant resettlements of people, but many of them had no place to emigrate to. Since they could no longer operate as an industrial reserve army, they became disposable human beings.

People reacted, often strictly for reasons of survival. Some of them, those who were able to resist colonialists and developers, concentrated their efforts on the regeneration of their commons. Many others who had lost their commons struggled to reclaim them, or they created new ones, in the city and the countryside. They did not attempt to *come back* to the condition they had before colonization or development; that would have been impossible. They rooted their efforts to improve their differentiated ways of life in their traditions, but they no longer understood their traditions as destiny. They also did not accept the industrial ethos and its arrogant pretension to control the future. They avoided the expectations that root the principle of scarcity, in order to affirm themselves in their hopes after fully recovering their present.

Individualization, in the modern logic, implies the reduction of the person to the minimal unit of abstract categories. In economic society the individual is a passenger in a flight, a client, a student, or a worker – or in the sexist form of the concept, a housewife or a family head; in the nation-state, a citizen or a foreigner. Those individualized in the abstract category of castoffs, the unemployable, were not able to bear this condition. However, in contrast with those constructed as individuals from the day they were born, who, during their lives, lacked the social fabric of community, they still had the condition of concrete men and women, rooted in the reign of gender. They were constructed in, and still bore, commonality. They could thus regenerate and enrich their spaces and construct a convivial society that was no longer a futurist utopia for them. Their actualization of the present has occupied the place of the future, which is alienated by ideologies, and starts to offer them a new quality of life.

Global forces operate today in the name of free trade like a mortal swell that weakens nation-states and compels them to look for political controls in ever larger macrostructures, in order to soften and moderate the blind forces of the market. Rather than following this impulse, people based on their commons who are increasingly incapable of holding back the oceanic force of new economic storms attempt to bring a human scale back to their political bodies and to build, within them, dikes capable of containing those economic forces. In doing so, they have discovered that those global forces can have concrete existence only in their local incarnations. But in that territory David always has the opportunity to win over Goliath.

Every day new documentation appears about the successes of the people in such endeavours, successes they achieve after long, hard struggles.[28] Their failures and new threats are also documented. They confront severe restrictions, and it would be criminal to idealize the misery in which many of them live. They have not yet created an ideal of life, but they are living ideals of the new era that has just begun.

AT THE EDGE

Caught in the middle of extreme social and political polarization, Mexico is now at the brink of a disaster. On the one hand, the rapid rescue plan of President Clinton, which was supported by the World Bank and the IMF but questioned by the American Congress and public opinion, has revealed his determination to prevent the Mexican economy from sinking, thus bringing down the world's financial system. But Clinton does not want to allow changes in Mexico's policy orientation. Inside the country, all the evil forces are free to act: primitive political structures and great economic interests, as well as drug lords and rightist fundamentalists, are occupying the vacuum created by the sudden extinction of hypertrophied presidentialism. They promote policies, as clumsy as they are tough, that reintroduce the worst forms of authoritarianism in the middle of great instability.

On the other hand, an active and alert society, full of vigour and integrity, is winning the streets and the political scene. The immediate purpose of their actions is to stop the atrocities in Chiapas and to create free spaces to promote people's initiatives. But people are also trying to promote alternatives to industrial society.

The Zapatistas brought to Mexico's political agenda the deplorable condition of the Indian peoples. The issue concerns not only the 8 to 15 million acknowledged as Indian by the statistics and the experts. More than 50 million of the 90 million Mexicans are still immersed in the civilization matrix of Middle America. Within that matrix they have taken initiatives that have allowed them to localize again in their own spaces, invert the meaning of urbanization, stop the process of their individualization, and reclaim their commons. Dignity, the main weapon of the Zapatistas, awakened "deep Mexico," and inspired, all over the country, a movement to prevent "fictitious Mexico" (the Mexico of the elites) from prevailing one more time in the name of imported ideals that brought the nation to the current disaster.[29]

It does not seem possible that the recent forms of authoritarianism can stop such a novel impulse. But it will not be easy to advance much in the current climate. The country is already in a severe economic recession, which comes after ten years of "sacrifices" imposed on the people. A different struggle, in which every sector claims everything for itself when there is not much to give, has started, and the controls imposed by the IMF, more rigid than ever, give no room for flexibility. The survival instinct has appeared in different sectors. Some people are inventing our own Jews. In the name of "every man for himself!" they can easily lead us to the horror. Falcons of all sizes are now falling over the country.

I do not know if the powerful interests that, inside and outside Mexico, are trying to prevent the dangerous example of a black sheep escaping from the fold will impose an irreparable break. But I have a firm hope that it will be possible to avoid it and that, even in the worst-case scenario, the movement that has opted for dignity, even in the face of death, will continue and will not sell its primogeniture for a plate of lentil soup.

That movement is now facing several challenges, mainly associated with the need to lucidly articulate new forms for its path. It needs to conceive new legal-political designs that can make *formal democracy* – which is built from the top down through abstract codes that bureaucratize and homogenize social and political life and hide elite corruption – compatible with *radical democracy*, which is articulated from the bottom up through culturally transmitted concrete principles, constituting a power in which, as the Zapatistas say, you command by obeying.

There is also the need to explore new fields of ideas where different cultures overlap. Those ideas be the basis for transforming the nation-state, which was constructed as a structure of domination, into a space of harmonious coexistence. In that space, under a democratic umbrella, fully individualized Mexicans, who have adopted the Western gaze and American ideals of living, will coexist with those who still think and act with other patterns and promote other ideals. But it will not be easy in the midst of the current turbulence to dare to conceive the still vague shapes of radical pluralism expressing the notions of cultural relativity and going beyond both universalism and cultural relativism.

In spite of those challenges and the great magnitude of the forces that try to suffocate the alternative, there is still room for hope. It is possible to poison or destroy a convivial society but not to conquer it, as Iván Illich said twenty years ago.

POSTSCRIPT

In the three years since 1996, when this chapter was first written, many things have happened in Mexico and the world, particularly concerning the events and trends I have been examining here. They seem to confirm my main hypothesis, but they require me to do some updating.

The general situation in Mexico has clearly deteriorated during these years, both economically and politically. In economic terms, the government and the international institutions still celebrate their success in handling the "crisis" of 1994–95. Some macroeconomic indicators seem to support their contention, but nothing like a recovery looms on Mexico's horizon. In the coming years there will be more of the same – or a severe recession – and there is no way to avoid increasing instability.

The end of the political regime that governed Mexico for seventy years is increasingly evident. July 6, 1997, when, for the first time, the political opposition won a majority in the Congress, can be used as the date on the death certificate. The power of the president, the main characteristic of that regime, has been severely curtailed, and President Zedillo has in fact abdicated a great portion of the power he still formally retains. Inside the PRI, the now-weakened party that monopolized political power for six decades, the internal struggle for the presidential race in the year 2000 is more intense than ever and has no clear rules. No political structure yet in place is capable of operating as a substitute for the old one, which is now falling apart.

On 16 February 1996, the Zapatistas and the government signed the Acuerdos de San Andrés, which committed the parties to a fundamental change in the relations between Indian peoples and Mexico's society and state. The National Indian Congress, created on 12 October 1996, adopted the accords as an expression of the struggle of all Indian peoples of Mexico. But the government has not honoured its word and signature. Instead, during 1997 and 1998 it continued a military siege of the Zapatistas and used paramilitary groups against the pro-Zapatista communities around the area of conflict. On 22 December 1997 one of these paramilitary groups massacred forty-five people, mainly women and children, in Acteal, one of the pro-Zapatista communities. Pressure by the government provoked the dissolution of the National Mediation Commission (Comision Nacional de Intermediacion, or CONAI). The commission had been mediating Zapatista-government dialogue, which had effectively ceased after 1996. National and international pressure has prevented a "final solution" through the use of force, but the real situation of the people, particularly in the Indian communities, cannot be worse and has been aggravated by natural calamities.

In spite of all these ominous facts, the vitality, imagination, and strength of the Zapatistas, the Indian peoples, and the "civil society" still give room for hope. The Zapatistas are also winning the battle for public opinion at the international level. They are benefiting from increasing solidarity and, there is increasing support for their claims. At the national level, they still have great power to mobilize opposition and are contributing to a new articulation of the otherwise dispersed efforts of independent organizations and movements, using a new political style. In late 1998 a dialogue occurred between the Zapatistas and both the "civil society" and the multipartisan commission of the Congress dealing with the conflict. They discussed, among other things, how to organize a national consultation on the constitutional reform agreed to in the San Andrés accords. They also discussed the transformation of the Zapatistas into a national political force capable of going to every municipality in Mexico to present their views.

The public debate is still dominated by discussion about the improvement of formal democracy, the reform of the state (to accommodate the Indian peoples and other claims), and the direction of economic and social policies. However, a more radical mobilization to reorganize Mexican society from the bottom up, going beyond the nation-state, is also clearly advancing. Two examples illustrate this point.

First, in Oaxaca, within the frame of the New Agreement mentioned above, a constitutional reform and a new law concerning Indian rights were enacted in June 1998. The new legal framework clearly applies what was agreed to in San Andrés and goes beyond the federal Constitution in many respects, establishing a juridically pluralistic regime. It is one of the more advanced laws in the world, fully recognizing cultural and political pluralism and supporting the autonomy of the Indian peoples and their transition from resistance to liberation.

Second, on 23 October 1998, thirty independent organizations and networks, part of Mexican civil society, launched an initiative designed to construct a common political agenda for the year 2000. The quality and scope of the initiative, its solid social base, and the key political actors associated with it reflect the maturity of current efforts.

I am fully aware that many of the arguments presented here, particularly those about the new political proposals (like radical democracy and radical pluralism), the meaning and impact of the Zapatista movement and the reconsideration of human rights, are highly controversial. Unfortunately, I cannot elabourate on them fully here. The interested reader can find a more complete elabouration of those arguments in my *Grassroots Postmodernism: Remaking the Soil of Cultures* (with Madhu S. Prakash).[30] In this book we examine the epic now evolving at the grassroots through which the world's social majorities are escaping from the monoculture of a single global society and regenerating their own cultural and natural spaces. We challenge the three sacred cows of modernity – the idea, entrenched in globalization, that there is only one, universally valid way of understanding social reality; the exclusive and general validity of Western-defined notions of human rights that have become the pretext for recolonization of the South; and the notion of the self-sufficient individual, as opposed to people-in-community, which has grotesquely transformed how we view the human condition.

PART THREE

The Third Style:
America

9 Indian Policy: Canada and the United States Compared

C.E.S. FRANKS

INTRODUCTION

Policies towards Aboriginal peoples in the United States and Canada embody and express fundamental views about society, the individual, and the recognition of uniformity and diversity. Though contrasts and tensions can be found in many other policy areas, the field of Aboriginal issues is a particularly rich and fertile one to explore because here all policies must, as a first step, deal explicitly or otherwise with the problem of cultural, linguistic, and legal differences between groups in the general population. It cannot be avoided. In both the United States and Canada the end result of the long historical encounter between the native indigenous Indian (or "Aboriginal," as they are now termed in Canada) populations and the European–North American immigration has been domination of the indigenous peoples by the more powerful non-native society. The cultural differences between the two populations – far greater than those between any European societies – have given, and still give, this encounter between native and non-native populations in North America a dimension of difficulty, of confrontation of totally unrelated forms of existence, that fundamentally colours and affects native–non-native relations.

The federal governments in both countries have had dominant roles in government-native relations and are still the most important external agencies affecting native populations. Though the policies of the two federal governments have gone through many changes of direction and intent, the end result is similar: with rare exceptions the native populations are the most disadvantaged groups in each country, with medical and health conditions that would shame most third world countries, levels of poverty and economic conditions that are social disasters, problems of cultural adaptation and loss that create severe stress and alienation in individuals and communities, and an unhealthy economic dependence on governments and government handouts.

Both Canada and the United States have within them many strands of political thought and ideology. One of the most important of these, both in the literature that discusses the differences in the political cultures of the two countries and in policies for dealing with Aboriginal peoples, is the conflict between, on the one hand, a focus on individualistic liberalism, with its emphasis on the single citizen to whom rights and duties belong, and, on the other hand, a more conservative, tory, republican view that embodies an emphasis on the group and community through which and within which an individual's life has meaning and purpose. The extreme individualistic interpretation of liberal-democratic ideals conceives of the citizen as an autonomous actor whose social and cultural context is not an issue and is not relevant. Rather, it is a given within which citizens compete in the economic, political, and social marketplace to win what success and rewards their talents and energy allow. The conservative tradition focuses less on the individual and embodies a more organic view of society in which human beings are interdependent and their well-being is interrelated with that of others. In this view, the cultural, social, economic, and political context in which individuals exist and act is of crucial importance, and groups, collectivities, and communities possess and assert rights and needs over and above those of individuals in order to preserve and strengthen this context of community and culture.

Policies towards indigenous peoples crucially depend upon which of these two opposing viewpoints is chosen. Traditional Indian society possesses vastly different cultures and community contexts from the mainstream non-native population. Policies deriving from individual liberalism would suggest that Indians ought to be treated like any other citizens and, if not totally assimilated, then at least integrated enough so that there is no separate legal or political category of "Indian" and as far as the law and government policies and programs are concerned, they are treated the same as other citizens. Policies derived from a conservative, tory view would lead to assertion of the importance of group, community, and context, which in turn would lead to legal and political recognition of Indians as members of distinct groups and cultures that have their own collective rights and identities. A conservative approach would accept and even promote special legal and political relationships between Indians and non-native society.

Discussions of the differences between American and Canadian political cultures argue that the United States emphasizes individual liberalism and marketplace liberal-democratic ideals. American society has become a "melting pot" in which the cultural differences of various immigrant ethnic groups disappear in a process of homogenization. On the other hand, Canada, it is argued, has evolved as a "mosaic" in which the various groups maintain their identity in a "multicultural" society. Canada asserts more of the conservative, tory acceptance of group and community, puts a stronger emphasis on collective interests and rights, and both legally and politically recognizes cultural and linguistic diversity.[1]

If this argument accurately describes differences between the two countries, then the differences would likely be found in policies towards Indians, for Aboriginal peoples represent the most extreme divergence from mainstream culture of any ethnic group in their language, culture, and traditional way of life. Aboriginal peoples are also vastly different from the mainstream in their needs and problems and in their rights stemming from their legal position, treaties, and Aboriginal title. One would expect that Indian policies in the United States would be directed towards assimilation and the melting pot, while Canada would support their distinct cultures and societies and the collective rights of native communities.

Further, one would not expect to find the contrasts between the two countries to be absolute in policies towards Indians; the differences in political culture between Canada and the United States found by Lipset and others are matters of degree, not absolutes, and one must not fall into the fallacy of black and white reasoning when the differences or more likely to be shades of grey. Rather, one would expect to find both strands of thinking and of approaching Indian policies in each country, but one would also expect that Canada would emphasize the group diversity and the distinct culture of Indian societies, while the United States would emphasize the individual and assimilation into the melting pot. Each country, in establishing and reforming its policies towards Aboriginal peoples, has felt pressures to move in both directions. The resulting policies should be expected to show, over time, shifts in policy emphasis between the assimilation and the distinct-culture poles and in the vision of well-being of Aboriginal people towards which policies have been directed.

A central purpose of this investigation of policies towards Aboriginal peoples in the two countries over the last century will be to see if this hypothesis about differences in political culture and policies holds true. It must be recognized at the outset that policies in areas as complex as government relations with Aboriginal peoples are themselves very complex, and so are the origins of and the reasons for these policies. Other factors and causes must certainly intrude. Of notable importance in Canada has been the inclusion of Aboriginal rights in the constitutional reforms of 1981–82, which has given renewed emphasis to Aboriginal issues and has entrenched recognition of cultural and legal differences in the Constitution. Of course, it can then be argued that these constitutional reforms themselves manifest the differences in political culture between Canada and the United States. If this is true, then it is also reasonable to expect policies to have diverged before the Constitution was amended and the amendments to embody a preexisting and generally accepted policy difference. Another argument could be that Canada is a younger country than the United States, that its political culture and system not yet have congealed into a stable and coherent mass, and that the powerful tensions between Quebec and the rest of Canada encourage adaptation and flexibility of a sort not seen in the more stable political environment of the United States. After examining the evidence, I shall return at the end to reconsider what policies towards Aboriginal peoples can tell us about these sorts of arguments about differences between the United States and Canada.

A work this brief cannot, of course, cover as complex a set of issues as these in an exhaustive manner. This chapter is not a comprehensive survey. Its focus is on the ideas and thinking behind Indian policy. The examples provided are intended to illustrate the general thrust of policies, not to explore every example and exception. Space and time force me to concentrate on the grand lines of the argument and to be selective about the fascinating and complex subject matter; inevitably, a more finely nuanced argument would produce a richer and more varied discussion.

DIMENSIONS OF THE ISSUE

Accurate data on many aspects of native issues – including even such fundamental information as size of population – are not easy to find. According to the 1981 census, Canada had 491,460 native people, who made up roughly 2 percent of the population.[2] These people were divided into four categories: status Indian, with 292,705 members; non-status Indian, with 75,110 members; Métis, with 98,260 members; and Inuit, with 25,390 members. For census purposes individuals choose for themselves which group they belong to. For government purposes the categories of status Indian and Inuit are defined by including persons listed as members of a band or on a general list. To be status Indian or Inuit confers a special legal relationship with the federal government and access to a number of government programs. Métis (or mixed native–non-native) and non-status Indians do not have a special relationship with the federal government, nor is there a list of their members like that of status Indians. Some estimates of the size of the Métis population would make it much larger than the census suggests. A recent act of the federal Parliament (Bill C-31 of 1985) has enabled many Indians who lost their status for one reason or another or who never had it because their parents lost it to regain official status as Indians. By 1997 the number of status Indians in Canada had risen to 627,435. Much of this increase derived from the provisions of Bill C-31.[3]

Natives form 58 percent of the population of the Northwest Territories, 20 percent of the population of the Yukon, over 6 percent of the population of Saskatchewan and Manitoba, and a lesser proportion of the population of other provinces. Nearly 60 percent of the natives live in rural areas, although few are on farms. A high proportion have a native language as their mother tongue, including 47 percent of on-reserve status natives. There is a large variety of native languages, including the major families of Algonkians (Cree, Ojibwa), Athapaskan (Dene), Inuktitut (Inuit), Iroquoian, and others. Less than 60 percent of status Indians live on reserves.

Figures on the size of Indian population in the United States also include elements of guesswork. In its 1970 census, the Bureau of Census counted a total of 792,000 Indians.[4] The majority lived in rural areas, mostly on reservations. The Bureau of Indian Affairs (BIA) largely restricts its attention to on-reservation Indians, and a count of those entitled to its services in 1970 was 478,000. By 1980 the total count for Indians had risen to 1,534,000 according to the U.S. Census,[5] while in 1990 the Indian Health Service, in effect counting on-reserve Indians, measured a total of 1,105,486.[6] The Indian population is over 5 percent of the total in five states, and nine out of ten BIA "client" Indians live in nine states. The largest populations are, in descending order, in Arizona, Oklahoma, New Mexico, and Alaska.

The United States has no generally accepted legal definition of an Indian. The census relies on individual self-definition. Federal agencies charged with administering programs directed towards Indians have made eligibility dependent on being half Indian or a quarter Indian or on being listed on a tribal role. But some departments use other definitions. The Department of Health, Education, and Welfare considers persons to be Indian if they are regarded as Indian by the community in which they live. The Indian Reorganization Act of 1934 allowed tribes to create their own membership lists, and tribal criteria vary. Some accept the opinion of individuals, some require recognition by the community, and some require half or a quarter Indian blood.

There are approximately 255 reservations (Bureau of Indian Affairs publications do not agree on the total number) in the United States, including village agencies in Alaska. Their average population is 1,790 persons. More than 160 reservations have fewer than 500 inhabitants, and 75 have fewer than 100. The largest, the Navajo of Arizona, New Mexico, and Utah, has close to 200,000 inhabitants. Two-thirds of on-reservation Indians live on reservations with an Indian population of 5,000 or more. Canada has more reserves, but they have generally smaller populations. In 1997 the Canadian government recognized 623 bands. The majority of Indians belonged to bands with populations of fewer than 1,000. The average membership was 1,006; 67 Canadian bands had populations greater than 2,000.[7]

Size affects the possibilities for policies such as self-government because large populations make possible economies of scale and increase the capacity to perform many functions, such as to run a school system, tribal courts, and health services. Larger populations also make possible policy and program development in crucial areas like education. The small scale and dispersed nature of Indian populations, especially in Canada, is potentially an obstacle to successful accomplishment of many of the functions native self-government ideally should perform. In both countries the Indian populations are young and fast-growing. Income is low, housing often below minimum standards, and infant mortality high. Alcoholism and violence are serious problems, and incarceration in penal institutions much higher than for non-native populations. Educational achievement is lower, and unemployment higher.

Problems as persistent, pervasive, and intractable as those of North American native populations are not only deep-seated but also must be caused by many varied and mutually reinforcing factors. One important factor is that historically native populations have been treated differently from other minorities. They were here first and were estranged from much of their territory and livelihood through force and treaties, which also ensured that they retained a distinct cultural and legal identity. Many native populations live in remote rural areas, where there has been at least some possibility of retaining a lifestyle closer to their hunting and gathering tradition, and this has contributed to socioeconomic divergence. But more important, and common to the native populations of both countries, has been an unwillingness on their part to assimilate into the dominant non-native society. Many native populations have a high retention of language.

Native cultures are so different from the dominant western European culture that the two come into conflict more often than they harmonize. In these conflicts the smaller native cultures have usually lost out to the more powerful and dominant non-native society. At the same time, native populations have stubbornly resisted assimilation. Where to go from here, how to resolve and reconcile these differences and problems, form the core issues in Indian policies now as in the past.

INDIAN POLICY IN THE UNITED STATES TO 1970

Indian policy in the United States for much of the nineteenth century was one of conquest and subjugation, as the frontier of colonization moved inexorably westwards. An oversimplification, though not much of one, would be to say that the historical difference between American and Canadian handling of native populations was that the United States decimated theirs by war, Canada theirs by starvation and disease. The immense powers of the Bureau of Indian Affairs over Indians in the United States began with the Indian Trade and Intercourse Act of 1834 and its companion act establishing the Bureau. All too often the provisions of treaties between Indians and governments were broken. At best their terms were begrudgingly honoured, with as little as possible actually given to, or done for, the Indians, regardless of what the treaties said. As the nineteenth century drew to a close, the vastly reduced Indian populations in both the United States and Canada were largely confined to reserves, to be treated as wards of the state, and in tutelage. Especially in the American west, treaties had given Indians large reserves of land, where tribes had some measure of autonomy in administration and social and cultural matters. Nevertheless, the forces for assimilation were powerful, and gathering strength.[8]

These forces achieved their most powerful legal statement in the Dawes Act, passed by the United States Congress in 1887. Most government policies and legislation have both real and stated goals. Sometimes these are congruous, sometimes there is a measure of overlap, while sometimes they diverge widely. In the Dawes Act, they diverged widely. The act's stated intention was the cultural transformation of Indians into mainstream Americans, or "assimilation."[9] This was to be done by Christian schools and the breaking up of tribal lands held collectively by allotting them to individual Indians. The less openly stated, but perhaps even more important, motive was acquisition of Indian lands by whites. Poorly conceived, and often unscrupulously administered, the allotment policy proved to be more successful in the second intention than the first. Under the process of "allotment"

Washington broke up much of the tribal land base, withdrawing some property from Indian ownership and distributing other, sometimes marginal, land to individual tribal members. "Surplus" lands, often the richest, were sold to white settlers. By 1934, when the process of allotment ceased, 66 percent of Indian lands – some 86 million acres – had been taken from Indians.

Though in retrospect the process of allotment looks like little more than a pernicious land grab, at the time it was defended in humanitarian and Christian reform terms. By assigning allotments to individual Indians and granting them United States citizenship, the process would allow the Indian to become a part of greater America, able to participate fully and equally with other citizens. One reformer claimed that the Dawes Act was the beginning of a new era in dealing with Indians; its supreme significance "lies in the fact that this law is a mighty pulverizing engine for breaking up the tribal mass. It has nothing to say to the tribe, nothing to do with the tribe. It breaks up the vast 'bulk of things' which the tribal life sought to keep unchanged. It finds its way straight to the family and to the individual."[10] As in earlier movements for assimilation, strong elements of Christian evangelism motivated the allotment policy, as also did a quite compatible, closely related, and equally strong vision of individualistic liberalism and a firm belief in the virtues of private property. The Indian Rights Association, a group of organized reformers of Christian beliefs, had been an important supporter of allotment and assimilation. The association was not, however, uncritical of government policy, and had been both a strong defender of Indian treaty and other rights of Indians and a strong supporter of programs to assist Indians in both survival and their "progress" towards civilization.[11]

Regardless of the success of the allotment policy in its unstated goal of separating Indians from their lands, it failed in its other, stated goal of assimilating Indians into mainstream America. To encourage assimilation, Indian children were placed in English-speaking boarding schools, village settlements dispersed, tribal members moved to individual tracts of land, and native religious ceremonies such as the sundance outlawed. In spite of these drastic impositions by the Bureau of Indian Affairs, supported by various Christian denominations and the Indian Rights Association, the Indians remained firmly Indian. With their economic base sadly depleted by the loss of land, however, they became more, not less, dependent on government for services and support.

The Dawes Act and the policies of allotment and assimilation dominated American Indian policy for many decades. The Indian Rights Association, recognizing the harms caused by the allotment policy, withdrew its support for the program. Nevertheless, with its Christian faith and firm belief in the Western model of human progress and development, it still strongly supported assimilation. In this it had many allies. In 1920 an Indian Bureau investigator and supporter of assimilation, Rev. E.M. Sweet, reporting that the religious dances of the Pueblo Indians were objectionable because of immoral activities associated with the ceremonies, including accounts of public fellatio, simulations of sexual intercourse, exposure by male clowns of their genitals, and children being flogged with yucca leaves as part of clan initiations.[12] Despite the suspect evidence on which this report was based, the Commissioner of Indian Affairs, Charles H. Burke, an ardent assimilationist himself, attempted through a series of BIA edicts to limit and control Indian dances and ceremonies, in effect to suppress native Indian religion and cultural traditions.

Although these measures were strongly opposed by the Indians themselves, they produced little reaction in the general public. On the other hand, the Bursum Bill of 1921, which threatened the land and water rights of New Mexico's Pueblo Indians, did produce a strong countermovement. The bill was defeated in Congress after a difficult struggle. The Indian Rights Association had supported the Bureau's efforts to outlaw Indian ceremonies, but it was part of the opposition to the Bursum Bill. Moreover, the association was joined in this struggle by social reformers, artists, and writers (including D.H. Lawrence) who disagreed with the association on assimilation and the outlawing of Indian religious ceremonies.

Among the most interesting and certainly the most influential of these reformers was John Collier, a left-wing intellectual. Leaving his job as director of the state adult education programme in California because of government surveillance and cuts to his programme, Collier found himself in the winter of 1920, at the behest of Mabel Dodge (whom he had known before in New York), in Taos, New Mexico (rather than Mexico itself, where he had intended to go), with his wife, three children, and six dogs. Mabel Dodge, a wealthy widow who was later to marry Tony Luhan, a Taos Indian, was the financial supporter and centre of the writers' and artists' colony at Taos, which then included, from time to time, D.H. Lawrence and Georgia O'Keefe, among others. Collier stayed in New Mexico for ten years. His experience there changed his life.[13]

He was captivated by Pueblo communal life and its ceremonial expressions, particularly as it was in opposition to the individualistic and market economic materialism of the Western world. He later wrote that his experience with the Pueblo Indians showed him

the truth which our age had lost: that societies are living things, sources of the power and values of their members; that to be and to function in a consciously living, aspiring, striving society is to be a personality fulfilled, is to be an energy delivered into the communal joy, a partner once more in the cosmic life ... To know the spirit of the Indians of the United States is to know another world. It is to pass beyond the Cartesian age, beyond the Christian age, beyond the Aristotelian age, beyond all the dichotomies we know, and into the age of wonder, the age of dawn man. There all dichotomies are melted away: joy requires sorrow, and sorrow, joy; man and society and the world are one; fantasy and the old, hard wisdom of experience join in the rituals, the moralizing tales, the songs, the myths; idealism and ideality are joined with searching and undeviating practicality. And the child is joined with the man.[14]

Collier was a firm believer in the group and the community as the context and shaper of the human spirit, and also a firm believer in the authenticity and value of the traditional culture and religions of the Indians.

Collier, imbued with this belief in, even romanticization of, traditional societies and his long-standing concern for building personality through social institutions, embarked on a career in Indian affairs. He achieved national prominence and succeeded in getting many reforms through Congress, sometimes with the support of the Indian Rights Association, often in opposition to it. In 1934 President Franklin Delano Roosevelt, as part of his New Deal, appointed John Collier as Commissioner of the Bureau of Indian Affairs. Congress, the Bureau itself, and the public at large still contained many supporters of assimilation, but Collier's appointment, with his support of group identity and rights and his fierce opposition to assimilation for the first time gave the contrary policy strand a position of power in the administration. Nor was he reluctant to use his new position to forward his views. Collier reoriented United States Indian policy.

The Indian Reorganization Act of 1934, Collier's achievement, was an abrupt about-face of Indian policy, reversing the policies of assimilation and individualism and replacing them with emphasis on collective rights and community. Collier argued for seven basic principles for the administration of Indian affairs that were, in effect, a succinct recipe for self-government. He argued for regeneration of Indian societies, new status and responsibilities to tribes, preservation of the land base, freedom for Indians to practise their own religion, democratic government for tribes, and further research into Indian matters.[15] This curious blend of community-minded idealism and faith in science was to guide Indian policy for twenty years. The Indian Reorganization Act not only put a stop to allotment but also actually did a little to expand the Indian land base. It helped replace boarding schools with day schools. It provided small amounts of money for economic development on reservations and subsidies for setting up tribal business corporations. But its most important result was that it encouraged Indian tribes to organize for their common welfare and to adopt constitutions and bylaws. The majority of tribes were reorganized under these provisions.

Tribal constitutions under the Indian Reorganization Act included creation of the institutions of representative government and business and cooperative corporations, both of which were largely alien to native culture. The Bureau of Indian Affairs still retained a great deal of control over reservations. Nevertheless, the act gave Indian tribes a measure of self-government, control over their own affairs, and a veto over some federal actions. Collier himself believed that "The change, in principle, was from maximal to minimal authority; from denial of Indian cultural values to their emphasis; from expectation of Indian doom to expectation of Indian triumph; from one-pattern policy to a policy of multiple options; but first and last from denial to intense encouragement of group self-determination and self-government."[16]

In a political system as complicated as that of the United States, with its multitude of actors and conflicting interests and viewpoints, it is not in the nature of things that a reformist vision articulated by a single leader like John Collier would achieve complete success. Arrayed against it were forces like the Indian Rights Association, with its belief in assimilation; western landowners who coveted Indian lands; the majority of the employees of the Bureau of Indian Affairs, who had been trained in and still supported the old way of doing things; and the many members of Congress with whom these forces were allied. Collier himself, who had an abrasive, authoritarian personality, failed to retain the support of many allies and found himself in conflict even with the Indians he most appreciated, the Pueblo and Navajo tribes. Many of the reforms of his "new deal" were watered down or reversed by Congress by the time he left the office of commissioner in 1945. The Indian Reorganization Act itself was a watered-down version of what Collier had wanted and served more interests than Indian self-government. Revisionist historians have argued that, among other pernicious things, the act enabled the BIA to establish puppet governments in tribes that in turn collaborated in the exploitation of tribal resources.[17]

Revisionists have also criticized Collier's achievements.[18] To some Indians the New Deal years marked an era of increased tribal discord and factionalism under the new systems of government. His policies are faulted for neglecting to promote aggressive land acquisition for tribes and for failing to protect the existing Indian land base. While emphasizing Collier's good intentions, revisionists argue that his achievements were undermined by his naive and romantic perceptions of Indians, by his paternalism, and even by his lack of understanding of Native American cultures. Nevertheless, his firm and steady direction over a crucial twelve-year period did help to make permanent change possible. The Indian Reorganization Act created a largely successful administrative reorganization following a century of mismanagement and mistaken and failed policies that had drastically depleted Indian resources and reduced Indian populations to subsistence.

Collier's vision and policies represent an apogee for emphasis on the group, culture, and the community in American Indian policy. Pressures to move in the opposite direction still existed, however, and as one observer has noted, "After the fading of the New Deal, the status of Native Americans as wards of the federal government seemed to go against the American tradition of self-reliance. Senator George Malone (R–New Mexico) complained that Indian reservations represented 'natural socialist environments' – a charge echoed by Interior Secretary James Watt three decades later. Break up the tribal domains, so the argument ran, remove the protective arm of government, and cast the Indian into the melting pot and the marketplace. Everyone would benefit."[19]

These forces ranged against Collier's belief in the collectivity and indigenous cultures never vanished; they simply carried on a rearguard resistance and waited for their time to come again. Powerful members of both houses of Congress disliked Collier's "new deal" approach and favoured both assimilation and policies akin to allotment. Four years after Collier left the Bureau, in 1949, the Hoover Commission on government organization gave semiofficial sanction to these views. It proposed a major policy reversal: the Indian should be integrated into the rest of society. Assimilation was once again to become the dominant goal in government policy. By 1954 "termination" became the name for a series of policies intended to dismantle the reservation system, disband tribal nations, and distribute their assets among tribal members. With or without Indian consent, termination proceeded.[20] Civil and criminal jurisdiction over Indian reservations, which had been under federal and tribal jurisdiction, was transferred to some states. Some tribal lands were broken up and sold, and the federal government turned many functions over to the states, such as education and housing.

Termination did not work. A notorious illustrative failure was the 3,000 Menominees in Wisconsin, who had 200,000 acres of their own lands. The tribe had large cash reserves that provided jobs and income. The Menominees had been a long-standing sore point with some members of Congress, having first won a land rights case in the courts early in the century, and then, in 1951, having won a judgment against the United States for mismanaging their forest resources. Congress passed the Menominee Termination Act in 1954. The reservation became a county, and tribal assets became controlled by a corporation in which individual Menominees held shares. Tribal lands were subject to state and local taxes. The hospital, previously financed by Washington, was shut down. Some Menominees had to sell their shares in the corporation. The corporation, to survive, leased and even sold land to non-Indians.

After ten years, the state and federal governments were spending more to support the Menominees than they had before termination.[21] The tribe began to fight back, and in 1973 Congress passed the Menominee Restoration Act, which formally reestablished them as a recognized federal tribe and reinstated federal services. Some of the losses of land and resources however could not be undone. The Menominee were only one, and the most notorious, out of many ugly stories caused by the policy of termination. In most of its features the termination policy embodied the hidden but real land-grab motives of the earlier allotment policy while, again like allotment, professing the more noble motives of economic advancement and assimilation. On the more noble intents, like its predecessor, termination was a failure.

In July 1970, faced with hostility among the Indian population and with clear evidence that termination not only did not work but was a disaster, President Nixon formally renounced the policy.[22] Termination was to be replaced with "self-determination." Congress followed President Nixon's lead, and repealed termination legislation for the Choctaw, authorizing the "Five Civilized Tribes of Oklahoma" (the Choctaw among them) to choose their own leaders for the first time since the early 1900s, and restoring Indian jurisdiction to the Metlakatla reservation in Alaska. A bill passed in December 1970 restored sacred lands to the Taos Pueblo. The momentum had shifted away from assimilation and individualistic liberalism. Policies were now moving in the other direction, towards cultural pluralism, community, and collectivity.

American Indian policy was far from uniform or unchanging during this period. The two strands of individualistic liberalism and communitarian pluralism jousted with each other, with the assimilationist, individualistic strand dominating most of the time, but never without its critics. John Collier drew on a long tradition of social reform and communitarian thought and action in his work for Indians and on Indian policy. He himself had been active in social reform in New York before moving to California to take over adult education. Much of his legacy, in establishing governments for reservations, in extending the land base, in closing down residential schools, in stopping the government from interfering in religious ceremonies, lasted after him, despite the reversal of policy with the introduction of the disastrous policy of termination. But termination itself did not last long, and once experience showed that it did not work and in fact created more problems than it resolved, it was dropped in less than two decades, to be replaced with self-determination, a more communitarian, cultural, and pluralistic policy.

In looking at American Indian policy one must be conscious of the distinction between real and stated policies. As was found in the policy of allotment, the defensible and, to some, laudable publicly stated objectives can conceal much less acceptable but nonetheless real hidden ones. Also, the inertia of bureaucracy and the political system must be recognized. Collier could announce his intentions, in which both the real and stated goals coincided, but that was no assurance that the Bureau of Indian Affairs would implement them. Even when the Indian Reorganization Act was passed by Congress, resistance within the Bureau slowed, and in some instances prevented, change. Forces within Congress that had resisted and delayed Collier's "new deal" took control at the time of termination. But, again, the public pronouncements on termination were more absolute than the actual practice. The public statement represented a change in intention and direction; changes certainly occurred, but they were incremental, and by no means affected all, or even the majority, of Indians.

INDIAN POLICY IN CANADA TO 1970

In the period up to 1970 Canada's Indian policy did not display the drastic policy shifts found in the United States. Rather, Canada's Indian policies and programs evolved in a steady manner and a uniform direction, continuing for the most part the pre-Confederation policies of treaty-making, relocation of Indians on reserves, opening up of Indian lands for settlers, and modest programs for government support of on-reservation Indians. At Confederation, in 1867, the policy of treaty-making and settlement of Indians on reserves was well-established.[23] Treaty-making continued into the twentieth century and is not yet complete. The bands of many native Canadians in both the West and the North have never signed treaties. To the extent that there was a conscious intention about what to do with the Indians once they were on reserves, government seemed inclined largely to leave them alone, to provide minimal assistance in health, education, economic development, and management of band resources, to assist Indians who wanted to become enfranchised (that is, to gain the right to vote in federal elections, to leave the reservation and abandon Indian status, to become citizens of Canada equal to non-natives in rights and political and legal position). Canada had neither the ardent enthusiasm for assimilation displayed by American Christian reformers nor the American zeal for separation of Indians from their reservation lands.

Nevertheless, Canada did not entirely escape from these forces. During both the nineteenth and early twentieth centuries the generally small reserves in Canada were made even smaller through various efforts by government and citizens to alienate Indians from their lands. But there was no major policy comparable to allotment, and, at least within the last hundred years, the actual reductions to reserves have been minimal. Probably less than 10 percent of the reserve lands of Canadian Indians were alienated. This is not to claim that the Canadian polity was more kindly disposed towards Indians than the American. Pressure to alienate land may have been reduced simply because reserves in Canada are generally small compared with those of the American West.

In place of the Indian wars through which the American West was conquered and the system of large Western reservations put in place, the Canadian government consolidated its power in the West after the herds of buffalo had been destroyed and after the Indian populations had been decimated by starvation and disease. In many instances Indian leaders came to government to ask for help for their starving and ailing people. Canada's version of the American Indian wars were the two Riel rebellions, which pitched the Métis (mixed blood), not the Indians, against the government. To a large extent the Riel rebellions form another chapter in Canada's unhappy history of French-English relations, not of Indian-white relations. Riel himself was only one-eighth Indian, seven-eighths French. For the most part, Canadian Indians on reserves were not subject to enforced estrangement from communal land and tribal identity as were many American Indians. Rather they were left on reserves as wards of the state, whose destiny if they were successful was to leave the reserve and become members of the greater non-native society, or if they were unsuccessful to remain on the reserves in an undeveloped, dependent state. Isolation or assimilation were the pillars of Canadian Indian policy for nearly a century. To a large extent, the government saw itself, in its relationships with Indians, as the custodians of a dying race, best left alone and isolated on reserves, but whose more advanced members should be encouraged to join the greater non-native civilization. This mind-set dominated Canadian Indian policy until well after World War Two, indeed until the 1970s. As Diamond Jenness observed in 1968, Canada "has secluded most of her Indians on out-of-sight reservations and confined her Eskimoes to the Arctic, refusing to invite either race to unite with her in developing the common homeland, but clinging irrationally to the pre-Dominion myth of the white man's supremacy."[24]

Though some conscientious and dedicated public servants and others attempted to improve the lot of the Indian and to reform the administration, Canada had no reformers comparable in influence to John Collier in the United States. To the extent that Canadian Indian policy embodied the two strands of communitarian versus individualistic values, it partook of both streams. On-reserve and northern Indians were left alone and, at least until well into the twentieth century, allowed to practise their own religious and other ceremonies; but the desired and stated goal of active intervention was to assimilate the Indians into mainstream culture. In this, particularly in establishing boarding schools for Indian children, the government was strongly supported by the Christian churches. Nowhere, until towards the end of this long period, can be distinguished any strong voices for the authenticity of Indian culture, language, religion, and ceremonies. Unlike the United States, nowhere and at no time did any Canadian scholars, politicians, or social reformers successfully, or even prominently, defend the Indian community and group existence as important in themselves and deserving protection and encouragement for this reason alone. The communitarian ideological strand did not extend to cultural pluralism. Instead we find a belief in the great civilizing mission of the British Empire and in Canada's role as an integral component of the Empire. This greater British community and its ideology, the raison d'être of English Canada in its origins in the loyalists who supported the British in the American war of independence, was at the centre of Canadian values.

If John Collier can be said to be the most interesting figure in twentieth century American Indian administration and the one whose career and concerns best reflect the issues in policy and administration, then Duncan Campbell Scott must surely be his equivalent for Canada. Scott, the son of a Methodist clergyman, was born in 1862, twenty-two years before John Collier. Unable to pursue his preferred career in medicine because of lack of money, in 1879 at the age of sixteen Scott became a copy clerk in the Department of Indian Affairs. His father's support for Sir John A. Macdonald, the founding and at that time recently reelected prime minister of Canada, enabled Scott to get this post merely by submitting a specimen of his handwriting. For fifty-three years, from 1879 until his retirement in 1932, Scott served in the department, gradually advancing until he became its deputy superintendent general (chief administrative officer) in 1913, and remaining in that position until 1932. For the first half of the twentieth century the administrative and policy history of the Canadian government's

Indian policies was inseparable from the character and work of Duncan Campbell Scott. His policies and attitudes survived him in the department, remaining largely unchanged until after 1970.

Though only one generation separated Scott from Collier, Scott's sensibilities and interests are those of the nineteenth century, while Collier's are those of the twentieth. Scott believed firmly in assimilation and once told Parliament that: "The happiest future for the Indian race is absorption into the general population, and this is the object of the policy of our government. The great forces of intermarriage and education will finally overcome the lingering traces of native customs and tradition."[25] He later expressed his views even more strongly to a parliamentary committee investigating changes to the Indian Act intended to make enfranchisement easier: "I want to get rid of the Indian problem. I do not think as a matter of fact, that this country ought to continuously protect a class of people who are able to stand alone. That is my whole point. Our objective is to continue until there is not a single Indian in Canada that has not been absorbed into the body politic, and there is no Indian question, and no Indian Department."[26]

Under Scott Indians were educated in residential schools, normally run by Christian churches with a large measure of government financial support. Destruction of the children's links to their ancestral culture and their assimilation into the greater non-native society were the stated objectives of the schooling system. Regardless of successive studies that showed that the residential schools failed in their purposes of education and assimilation, while at the same time conditions in them led to epidemic proportions of disease and death amongst native children, particularly from tuberculosis, Scott continued to support the schools. On the eve of his retirement he pointed to the number of children in school, the length of their stay, and the regularity of their attendance as proof of their success. If he had looked at the outcomes of his policies, the actual assimilation of children into non-native society, their success in finding employment, their adjustment to the community in which they lived (for most, the reserve), he would have found a much different and unhappier result. The system was disastrous to native individuals and to native culture and communities. But that is not how bureaucracies normally count.

To encourage assimilation, Scott promoted amendments to the Indian Act designed to make enfranchisement possible by decision of the department even if the Indians in question had not consented, or even opposed it. Despite overwhelming hostility from the Indians, Parliament passed the amendments Scott wanted. Now the department could enfranchise Indians if they joined the armed services, became a member of a profession, received a university degree, or were, in the opinion of the department, generally fit to join the Euro-Canadian society. Already the act provided that Indian women who married non-Indian men lost their legal status as Indians. Hostility by Indians and others to these coercive measures led to their not being used; nevertheless, they do show the attitudes and motivations behind Indian policy and administration.

As in the United States, Canadian Indian policy was inspired by the assumptions of nineteenth century Christianity, by cultural imperialism of the dominant non-native society, and by faith in market-capitalistic economics. There was, as in the United States, a reluctance not only approaching but surpassing obstinacy to recognize the validity and autonomy of Indian culture and society. In so far as assimilation failed, which it did, Canadian Indian policy was one of neglect, which was not always benign, combined with extreme paternalism. Indian bands, though they might be organized with chiefs, had no real power. That lay with the Indian agent, who in effect had control over band funds, band government, and band administration, extending even to details such as who got what house on the reserve. The Canadian government, like the American, attempted to stamp out central elements of native culture, such as the potlatch of the West Coast Indians and the sundance of the Prairies. Indians, generally speaking, were segregated from the rest of society, while the government expected the Indian "problem" to disappear, either through assimilation or through the continuing decrease in numbers of Indians. Assimilation remained the stated goal. Even the most sympathetic of anthropologists, Diamond Jenness, concluded his study of the conditions of Canada's Eskimos in 1964 with the opinion that, with population growing because of improved health services beyond what the local resources could sustain, the only thing that could be done to help them was to move them south where they could assimilate to civilization.[27] The growing numbers of Aboriginal people in Canada's big cities – Toronto, Vancouver, and Winnipeg all have Indian populations larger than the Northwest Territories – suggests that his view was prophetic.

Scott the administrator personifies the efficient bureaucrat, dedicated to his position and the policies of his agency, protecting it from criticism and attack from within and without, loyally and largely anonymously serving his political masters regardless of their political persuasion, doing what he could to improve the effectiveness of the department in achieving its goals of assimilation and elimination of the Indian problem, and, over his stay of more than half a century, never once questioning whether these goals were right or whether there might be other goals more sympathetic to Indians and Indian culture. His career as an administrator makes him appear a rather formidable, severe, and not very complex man.

But Scott had another side: he wrote poetry. Not only did he write poetry, but he was perhaps the best of the Canadian "confederation" poets, and among his poems are many dealing with the North, and natives. Many of his poems portray Indians as a "weird and waning race," as did much of the popular literature of the period (for example, the earlier *Last of the Mohicans*). In a few of them individual Indians appear as real human beings rather than cardboard cutouts, but by and large, despite valiant efforts by critics to defend his Indian poems,[28] they are dated, lightweight, and unsuccessful. Much better are his poems about the North and canoeing, like "Spring on the Mattagami," "Rapids at Night," and "Night Hymns on Lake Nipigon," where he expresses his own feelings and experience as a white man travelling in the strange and, to him, hostile northern wilderness that was home to the Indians. "Night Hymns," especially, depicts the sense of fear, even terror, that travellers often experience in the North – felt in this poem by canoeists in their frail craft on a huge lake with a storm approaching, the whites singing "Adeste Fideles" in "noble Latin" to keep their spirits up, while the Indians sing the same song in "uncouth and mournful" Ojibwa.

Scott, as administrator, had to travel in this northern wilderness to conclude treaties with the Indians. His accounts of his 1905 trip show his distaste at the dirt and squalor of Indian life. Without the companionship of other educated whites, Scott had been alienated, not inspired, by the wilderness: "I spent day after day without seeing a living thing – except the Indians and our own party – the landscape for the most part desolate beyond compare. Loneliness seven times distilled. A country never to be the glad home of any happy people."[29] By contrast, in his expedition of 1906 Scott ensured that he was accompanied by two sympathetic companions, Edgar Pelham and the artist Edmund Morris. While the journey of 1905 had produced no poetry, the journey of 1906 resulted in important poems, including "Spring on the Mattagami." It can be wondered how much Scott's distaste for the northern wilderness, his views after first-hand experience that no civilized people could live there, reinforced his belief that assimilation was the only acceptable Indian policy. John Collier's experience among the Taos Pueblo Indians produced the opposite result. He became enamoured of Indian culture, ceremony, and community. Of course, by the standards of Western civilization, New Mexico, with its benign climate, fertile valleys, and well-established and settled agricultural Indian communities, is a much more hospitable place than the Canadian North, where to survive, bands had to be nomadic, and life in the summer, when Scott travelled, was plagued with black flies and mosquitoes. Mabel Dodge would not have been able to establish her artists and writers colony in Moosonee, nor would John Collier have lived there for ten years.

In "Powassan's Drum," the most puzzling of Scott's Indian poems, the subtle pounding of the Indian medicine man's drum creates a hypnotic effect and disturbing visions in the listener. The poem is difficult to decipher. Dagg dismisses it for gaining critical esteem because it "easily fit[s] our image of the Indian. We want drums and we get them."[30] But more likely it was inspired by a traumatic encounter of Scott with Indian religion and, more particularly, a powerful Indian medicine man. This had occurred during his 1905 treaty-making trip, when the medicine man had conducted a ceremony affirming the power of his religion and culture. After the ceremony Scott was so disturbed that he did not leave his tent for two days. This close encounter with a different culture and religion had no lasting effect on Scott, however, at least insofar as he viewed Indians and administered Indian affairs.

The eminent Canadian critic Desmond Pacey wrote of Scott's poetry that

The final peacefulness of these poems is achieved not by the transcendental leap, but by the stoical acceptance of suffering as the inevitable lot of man. The dominant mood is heroic endurance. Calm and stability is finally attained through an inner spiritual discipline, not through some magical release. We have the sense of a harsh and lonely world, the vicissitudes of which we can and therefore must endure without disgrace. In Toynbee's language, the challenge of a stern environment has elicited the response of courage. Is it too much to suggest that in these quietly powerful poems, seldom brilliant but always competent in style and solid in substance, we catch an authentic glimpse of the Canadian spirit at its finest?[31]

Pacey here presages the descriptions of the Canadian psyche by Northrop Frye[32] and Margaret Atwood,[33] and for that matter, Seymour Martin Lipset.

It can be wondered how a person with the acute sensibility and insight of a good poet like Duncan Campbell Scott can combine these gifts with the obtuseness and narrowness of his vision as an administrator of Indian Affairs. Dagg argues that Scott was far more sensitive to Indians and aware of their problems in adjustment and assimilation than he is often given credit for but that his work as a poet must be viewed separately from his work as an administrator. Titley concludes that though Scott was a capable and efficient administrator, his position in government was merely a source of income rather than an abiding passion. That he reserved for his poetry. If this is true, then Scott would be guilty of one of the worst of bureaucratic sins, indifference. But I find little difference in the sensibility of Scott the poet and Scott the administrator: in both areas he worked within the confines of the nineteenth century Canadian-British Empire ethic. Christianity, progress, and the Empire were inevitable. The wilderness was alien, to be viewed both with a romantic vision of power and truth, but also as something to be feared. Brief incursion into the wilderness inspired poetry, but then it was to be left for civilization. Indians, the inhabitants of this wilderness, had some strengths and admirable characteristics, but like all decent human beings, their lot, if they were lucky, was to leave the wilderness and become civilized. No right-thinking person could behave or believe otherwise. Certainly Scott could not, nor could other Canadians of the time. Scott's inability to get beyond the conventions and rigidities of his times makes him, at best, a very good minor poet. But the imprint he refined as bureaucrat dominated the Department of Indian Affairs for decades after he retired.

There was no Canadian counterpart to John Collier or the American Indian Reorganization Act of 1934. Nor, on the other hand, was there a counterpart to the American policy of termination. Indeed, there was no Canadian counterpart to the Indian Rights Association as an interest group concerned with government policies and programs and pushing for better administration of Indian affairs. Though parliamentary committees examined the administration of Indian Affairs from time to time and often found much wanting both in policies and their application – legislators are, more often than bureaucrats, concerned with outcomes rather than outputs – little was done to change what was for the most part a closed system. The Department of Indian Affairs dealt with its own clientele, the Indians. The churches ran the schools without much intrusion from outside interests, pressure groups, or publicity. The Indians themselves had virtually no resources of funds, rights, access to interest groups, or social reformers. The exceptions to this only serve to prove the bleak state of the majority of Canada's Aboriginal people.

In 1958, Parliament under Prime Minister Diefenbaker gave Indians the right to vote in federal elections. But not much else changed. There were, however, small signs of growing discontent and signs of enough problems and dissatisfaction that public discussion, if not change, was imminent. In the early 1960s the important and influential Royal Commission on Organization of Government pointed out that Canada faced problems in the status and socioeconomic well-being of Indians.[34] Under this and other pressures, the government for the first time appointed a group of outside experts to examine the conditions of Indians. Their report, normally referred to by the name of their chairman, the anthropologist H.B. Hawthorn, documented in detail the severe problems of Canada's Indian populations. The Hawthorn Report of 1966 was an important step towards not only recognizing that a change from self-sufficiency to dependency had occurred in Canada's Indian populations but that this had created unhealthy conditions and substandard existence.[35] The report recommended a communal rather than an individualistic approach to Indian matters. In view of their position and problems Indians should be treated as "citizens plus."

In response, the federal government devoted more resources to improving education and health, extending welfare, and encouraging economic development. These steps had the consequence of increasing the influence of an already dominating federal administrative apparatus on Indian individuals and communities. The end result was a system of neither self-government nor self-administration. Both political power and administrative responsibility remained with the federal government and in the hands of, and controlled by, non-natives.[36] Aboriginal communities in Canada, as in the United States, were serviced as the clientele of the administrative state. Nor was this colonialism in the normal sense of the term. Colonialism implies that the colonial power exploits native peoples as a labour force for economic gain. But in Indian administration in Canada little was to be gained directly from the natives. Quite the contrary, Canada's Indians found it difficult to gain employment and share in meaningful economic activity. The real economic gains from government's dealings with Indians were, as in the United States, the economic rents and other advantages accruing to the dominant society from their takeover of Indian lands and resources, not in the direct employment of a colonized people.

In the late 1960s the federal government began to examine Indian issues in a process that supposedly was one of consultation with Indian groups and leaders. Indians themselves recognized many of the problems with the Indian Act and the existing policies and administration, and were in favour of change. However, when the federal government made public its proposals in a white paper on Indian policy in 1969,[37] they came as a complete surprise.[38] The federal government proposed termination of all special treatment for Indians, including the Indian Act. Its white paper argued that equality, or nondiscrimination, would be the key to the solution of Indian problems and that special rights had been a major cause of these problems. The goals of equality and nondiscrimination were to be achieved by terminating the federal legislation and bureaucracy that had developed over the past century and by transferring to the provinces the responsibility for Indians and the administration of Indian programs. The Department of Indian Affairs itself was expected to be phased out within five years. In effect, at just about the time that the United States was proposing to end the policy of termination, the Canadian government was proposing that Canada should pursue the same disastrous route.

These proposals completely opposed and contradicted the conclusions and recommendations of the Hawthorn study. They also opposed the Indians' own suggestions and repudiated all that the consultative process appeared to have been working towards. The white paper aroused a tremendous and hostile outcry and stimulated Canadian Indians to organize and take political action in a way they never had before.[39]

Canadian policy towards natives before 1969 might at best have been described as moving toward grudging acceptance of cultural differences and the importance of culture and community to natives. The white paper proposed a drastic shift to liberal individualism and a denial of group rights in some ways even more extreme than the failed termination policy in the United States. The white paper's emphasis on individual rights was consistent with Prime Minister Trudeau's own political philosophy and approach to linguistic and cultural diversity in Canada. But it was not an appropriate solution to Indian problems. It was inserted into the Indian policy discussions by the newly strengthened prime minister's office in complete disregard of the consultative processes and participatory democracy. It was also a failure. Resistance to the white paper was so strong that none of its major proposals was ever adopted. What was to emerge as a new policy centred more on the culture and group rights. This was self-government, a policy analogous to the self-determination being articulated in the United States at the same time.

If I were to end my comparison of Indian policy in the United States and Canada in 1970, then both my starting hypotheses would be refuted. The strand of communitarian, cultural, and pluralistic political ideology was much more prevalent and influential in Indian policy in the United States than in Canada. No individual in Canada reflects, either from an outside public-interest perspective or from an inside administrative position, the commitment of John Collier to the value and need to preserve Indian cultures and religions. The American government was far more tolerant of Indian diversity in political organization, the legal system, and religious practices than the Canadian. The Canadian government exercised more control over Indian bands, allowed them less autonomy in administration and religion, maintained residential schools longer, and articulated the policy of assimilation more consistently than did the American. Nor was Canadian Indian policy more flexible and innovative than the American. Quite the opposite: policies in Canada were more stable and scarcely changed from 1890 to 1970. Although versions of assimilation, allotment, and termination remained part of the complex matrix of American government Indian policy at the end of the period, as they had at the beginning, they had been countered, and to some extent defeated, by the opposing and influential Collier-type strand of communitarian pluralism. At no time in Canada was there such a drastic reversal of policy as Collier's own "new deal." For that matter, at no time was there a reversal of Canadian Indian policies; the few changes simply modified, or more often strengthened, the existing polices of assimilation. Unmoderated by this countervailing approach, Canadian Indian policy did not deviate from assimilation and custodianship. Both policies and administration had immense stability. The collectivist and cultural and pluralist strands were stronger in the United States, and the United States was the more innovative and changeable.

Canadian Indian policy throughout the period was tempered by a measure of indifference. With important qualifications like the residential school system and the banning of the potlatch, sundance, and other religious ceremonies, Canadian Indians were left on their reserves to fend for themselves. Policies like allotment did not threaten the majority of Indian lands as it had in the United States. Although Duncan Campbell Scott's articulation of the department's goal of assimilation was as extreme as anything in the United States, the policy was not pushed forward as ruthlessly and relentlessly as were allotment and termination in the United States. With the exception of Scott's views on assimilation and Trudeau's white paper, expressions of policy intentions were both more varied and more extreme in the United States than in Canada. Americans advocating termination, allotment, or a new deal for Indians were engaged in political campaigns; there, articulations of policy partook of rhetoric and were intended to convince, reinforce, inspire, and persuade, as is most political rhetoric. The changes in policy, for the most part, were more moderate than the rhetoric would suggest. Canadians did not generally indulge in such rhetoric, not because they were incapable of it, but because there was no need for it. Indian policy was established. It had remained the same for a century. No influential pressure groups objected to it. There was no need for public argument about it, at least not until Trudeau's white paper – as individualist and liberal as any policy articulation in the United States – aroused such a strong

backlash. Indian policy in the two countries in the post-1970 period
tells a different story.

SELF-DETERMINATION
IN THE UNITED STATES

With the calamitous failure of termination in the United States and
the defeat of Trudeau's white paper policy of assimilation, both countries looked for new policies that would lead Indian administration
out of the morass of a dominating, colonial bureaucracy and would,
at the same time, offer some hope, in the foreseeable future, of
resolving the severe economic and social problems faced by indigenous peoples. In the United States self-determination and the Alaska
Claims Settlement of 1971 are the two main products of this reconsideration. In Canada an even greater variety of approaches has been
attempted in the efforts to achieve self-government. In both countries
success has been mixed.

The Alaska Native Claim Settlement Act (ANCSA) was a result of the
pressure to develop the huge reserves of oil discovered at Prudhoe
Bay on the north shore of Alaska in 1968.[40] Under the act, the natives
of Alaska received title to 40 million acres, or 11 percent of Alaska.
The land was divided among 220 village and 12 regional corporations.
To be eligible to benefit under the act, a person had to be a citizen
of the United States, fall within the category of Indian, Eskimo, or
Aleut, and to have been living on 18 December 1971, the date of
enactment of the act. Alaska natives were also to receive approximately
one billion dollars of financial compensation.

Both villages and regions were to set up corporations to manage and
receive the lands and funds. These corporations are the key to the act
and to the possibilities for self-government. The corporations were created to receive the land and funds under the act. Individual natives
own shares in both types of corporation. These shares could not be
sold or traded until 1991, but after that the field was open. In many
ways the corporate approach in the Alaska settlement echoed the allotment policy of the previous century. It was likely to become a way of
alienating natives from their land. Like allotment, the ideology behind
it was individualistic market capitalism, and again like allotment,
regardless of its stated goals, the Alaska settlement contained in it possibilities for non-natives to profit from native resources and for being
an instrument of assimilation. Congress in fact intended the act "to
integrate the Natives of Alaska into the institutions of Alaska."[41]

The corporations appear to have been intended to serve a series of
multiple and conflicting functions. On the one hand they were the

vehicle through which land, and the resources of the land, were held and preserved for natives and native communities. On the other hand, they were structured like business corporations, with shares and shareholders and the opportunity for shareholders to dispose of these shares – quite possibly to non-natives and other strangers to the community. On the one hand, the creation of the corporations affirmed and recognized the importance of the community and the group rights of natives; on the other hand, it created two distinct classes of natives: those born before 18 December 1971, who were fully participating shareholders; and those born after (half the native population by now), who did not own shares, unless obtained by inheritance, and hence were not able to participate fully in the economic, business, and political life (and other aspects, as well, because they are closely connected) of the community. Not the least of the problems with the corporations was that they were supposed to be profitable, using the forest and other resources as means for generating economic activity. This conflicts with traditional native views on man's relationship to the natural world.

The act and the corporations have received close attention and scrutiny from many sources.[42] Berger, who had previously conducted the very important Mackenzie Valley Pipeline inquiry for the government of Canada,[43] concluded that there were severe problems in the claim settlements in Alaska and that the source of many of these problems lay in the corporate form of organization. This was an unfamiliar form of organization to Alaska natives. Many corporations had not been well run and were likely to become insolvent. There was a strong possibility of control of corporations passing from native hands through the sale of shares after 1991. Berger's main recommendations were that the land held by the corporations be returned to tribal governments so that it would be held as a community rather than a personal resource and that native self-governments ought to be recognized as legitimate political entities. Tribal governments, which would also have jurisdiction over fish and wildlife, would be the vehicles for self-government.

In order for development of native lands, whether in the United States or in Canada, to be compatible with native beliefs and traditional uses of resources, the development must embody principles of stewardship. This the Alaska corporations have failed to do. Much of their exploitation of forest resources does not meet the criteria of sustainable development.[44] The Yakima tribe in Washington State have succeeded in blending forest exploitation with sustainable development in a way that harmonizes with traditions of their culture, but the Alaska native corporations, being private for-profit businesses, have adopted institutional structures and modes of operation that have led to damage to the culture. Corporate decisions were made in isolation from the influence of traditional values and beliefs.

The evolution of self-government for natives in Alaska is still not completed. The choice that was established in 1971 was not the right one, and in 1988 amendments were made to the Alaska Native Claims Settlement Act that went some way towards meeting the concerns of the natives. Shares in a corporation can no longer be transferred to an outsider without the approval of a majority of shareholders. Under-developed land cannot be taxed, and corporation lands cannot be seized in bankruptcy proceedings. This goes further than the original act in recognizing and safeguarding land as a community rather than an individual resource. However it still does not resolve all the problems identified by Berger and others.

In the rest of the United States the policy that replaced termination was "self-determination." The Self-Determination Act of 1975, according to its introductory language, was needed

because the prolonged Federal domination of Indian service programs has served to retard rather than enhance the progress of Indian people and their communities by depriving Indians of the full opportunity to develop leadership skills crucial to the realization of self-government, and has denied to the Indian people an effective voice in the planning and implementation of programs for the benefit of Indians which are responsive to the true needs of Indian communities. [Congress declares its commitment to] the establishment of a meaningful Indian self-determination policy which will permit an orderly transition from Federal domination of programs for and services to Indians to effective and meaningful participation by the Indian people in the planning, conduct, and administration of those programs and service.[45]

The reality of the Self-Determination Act does not, however, live up to this grand prologue. Its real purpose is, in effect, to permit the Secretary of the Interior to contract with Indian tribes to administer Bureau of Indian Affairs programs. The act requires the bureau to convert, at least in part, from a service delivery agency to one supervising the delivery of services by tribes. It has not entirely successfully made this change. Bureau personnel have not been committed to the change, and low morale, among other internal problems, has prevented effective implementation. Costs of programs have increased because the bureau maintains a supervisory function, even when service delivery is contracted to tribes. Tribes need to maintain close relationships with Washington, regardless of how autonomous they become.[46] Some tribes fear that contracting will lead to termination.

There have been proposals for block funding of tribal administration, but so far actual reform has been modest. By 1985 about 25 percent, or $250 million of the budget of the Bureau of Indian Affairs, was contracted out. A critical review of the self-determination strategy in 1994 concluded that it was a "scam," and that it was clear that Congress is not prepared to yield any real power to tribal councils, except in exchange for budgetary relief.

In other words, Congress is willing to allow tribes to make more decisions for themselves as long as they are prepared to pay for them. This makes a good deal of sense inside the Washington beltway as a deficit-reduction measure. It makes no sense at all on the reservations, however, where tribes have no visible means of support – other than gambling and resource liquidation. Hence, the congressional cost-shifting strategy, cleverly cloaked behind warm phrases such as "self-governance" and "New Federalism," is in fact a guarantee of growing social problems and discontent in Indian country.[47]

This concern was justified. As we shall see in more detail below, under President Reagan federal support of native Americans was cut severely. Reductions affected jobs, health care, reservation economies, and schools. In a major statement on Indian policy in 1982, President Reagan declared that responsibilities and resources should be restored to the government closest to the people served. For Indians this meant that the policies of the 1975 Self-Determination Act were a good starting point. But according to the president, "since 1975, there has been more rhetoric than action. Instead of fostering and encouraging self-government, federal policies have by and large inhibited the political and economic development of the tribes. Excessive regulation and self-perpetuating bureaucracy have stifled local decision-making, thwarted Indian control of Indian resources, and promoted dependency rather than self-sufficiency." The administration intended to reverse this trend by removing the obstacles to self-government and by creating a more favourable environment for the development of reservation economies. This sort of double-speak, here promising self-government and economic development while there drastically reducing the resources available to Indians, has been a characteristic of American government pronouncements on Indian policy since at least the time of allotment. Real objectives are unmentioned; the stated ones are laudable but bear little relationship to the actual programs as implemented. Here, without doubt, the real impact of Reagan's pronouncements was to be more cuts in expenditures on Indians.

On the positive side, the Indian Child Welfare Act of 1978 codified judicial decisions on tribal jurisdiction over Indian children.[48] Family law had long been within tribal jurisdiction. The Indian Child Welfare Act gave tribal courts jurisdiction over an Indian child even off-reservation. This was an important effort to improve the system and institutions, both judicial and social, dealing with child welfare.

At this point in time, self-government has a firmer legal foundation in the United States than in Canada. The powers of tribes and their rights of self-government are recognized as Aboriginal, inherent, and preexisting. "They derive from the original sovereignty of the tribe, a sovereignty which has been limited, both geographically and substantively, but never ended."[49] Because of this independent source of sovereignty, courts and Congress have both agreed that parts of the U.S. Bill of Rights do not apply to the actions of tribal governments. Many tribes have their own courts and police forces and exercise full jurisdiction within reservation over civil matters and minor criminal offences. At present there are over one hundred tribal courts in the United States.

But there are also many conflicting pressures and trends in Indian self-government in the United States. Tribal courts have developed and improved during the last decades to the point where they are important forces towards affirming Indian rights and Indian culture. At the same time, decisions of the Supreme Court have severely limited the jurisdiction of tribal courts.[50] The Self-Determination Act and other acts of Congress have expressly recognized Indian problems as group and community issues. On the other hand, the pronounced individualistic market liberalism of recent administrations, combined with recent economic problems, have placed tribes and reservations in a difficult position. By 1993, in what was initially a demonstration project, 28 tribes in 12 states had taken control of funding and decision making previously controlled by the bureau. Nevertheless, self-government is not a reality for most tribes, nor is it likely to become so, though progress continues to be made.[51]

SELF-GOVERNMENT IN CANADA

The bottom-up approach has followed a multipath, twisted, and often confusing route. There are three main streams to this route to Aboriginal self-government. One, the "comprehensive claims policy," is associated with the resolution of outstanding Aboriginal land claims (usually covering large tracts of land) where either treaties never existed or a reserve system was not implemented. In effect, the comprehensive settlements are modern versions of treaties. The second, usually on a smaller scale, involves status Indians who already have reserves established by treaty or other means and involves creating a formal structure for Aboriginal self-government for that band or group of bands. The possibility is also open under this or other policies for self-government for Aboriginals living off-reserve in large cities. Third is the devolution of responsibilities to Indian bands under the present provisions of the Indian Act. Each policy and process has its successes at this point. Some examples will illustrate the variety and complexity of the present situation.

The first of the comprehensive settlements was the James Bay agreement. It involved three parties: the government of the province of Quebec, the Indian and Inuit of Northern Quebec, and the federal government. In the 1960s the huge James Bay region of Quebec was populated mainly by Cree Indians living in a traditional life style, with a smaller Inuit population in the very northern part of the Ungava Peninsula. The federal Parliament had given Northern Quebec to the province of Quebec in 1912, but no settlement of Indian or Inuit claims was made at that time. In the late 1960s the provincial government of Quebec created plans to develop the immense hydroelectric power resources of the rivers flowing westwards from the interior of northern Quebec into James Bay. These plans were developed without consultation with the native population. When they were announced, the reaction of northern natives was to fight the issue in the courts, where their claims were recognized, and politically, where negotiations began among the three parties.

The end result, the James Bay and Northern Quebec Agreement of 1975, in many of its features was based on the Alaska claims settlements. It gave the Quebec provincial government the right to develop the hydro resources. But it also gave the Northern natives rights to land, financial compensation, and to some measure of self-government. Of the 410,000 square miles of Northern Quebec, somewhat under 5,000 square miles is "category I," owned by the natives; 60,000 square miles is "category II," where natives have exclusive use of traditional activities such as hunting, fishing, and trapping; while in the remaining ("category III") land, native uses receive special consideration. In addition, there was financial compensation of $225 million to Northern natives. This is roughly on the same per capita scale as the Alaska settlement. Northern Quebec had at the time about 7,500 Cree Indians and somewhat fewer than 5,000 Inuit. Alaska had more than five times as many native peoples.

The James Bay and Northern Quebec settlement created structures of government with functions similar to those of local government, though they also have responsibilities in education, policing, and land management.[52] Corporations were created to manage the compensation monies. Members of the Cree and Inuit communities are also members of the corporation and benefit from their activities. There is no identification of a special group as shareholders, nor can shares be transferred to outsiders. Similarly, land is held by community institutions rather than by individuals or privately owned corporations. Kativik, the Inuit self-government of the Far North, is a "public government," in which all citizens, regardless of race, participate. Northern Inuit are a clearly dominant majority population. In contrast, the James Bay Cree governments are "ethnic," in which only the Cree participate. There is a larger non-native population in this region.[53]

The James Bay settlements have many problems, particularly in the area of relationships with other governments, where the natives feel, quite legitimately, that the provincial and federal governments have not lived up to their commitments.[54] An excessive amount of the time and energy of the Cree and Inuit leaders goes into negotiating with these other governments rather than into administering and creating policies for their own people and lands. This problem is not, however, unique to the natives of Northern Quebec.

In comparison with the United States, the most interesting feature in the James Bay and Northern Quebec settlements is that though they were obviously based on the Alaska settlement, they went much further in recognizing and ensuring the preservation of the community. The financial corporations, the self-government institutions, the land itself, are expressions of and belong to the community. They are not individually owned.

In 1986, the federal government announced a new comprehensive claims policy. It abandoned its previous requirement that any settlement include complete extinguishment of all other claims and, in so doing, opened the door to the real possibility of action in a field that had seen too much talk and too little action. The new policy stated that comprehensive claims settlements would include full ownership by the Aboriginal people of some land; guaranteed wildlife harvesting rights; participation in land, water, and environmental management throughout the settlement area; financial compensation; resource revenue sharing; measures to stimulate economic growth; and a role for the Aboriginal people in the management of heritage resources and parks in the settlement area. As of July 1997, twelve claims had been settled, including six under an umbrella claim by fourteen First Nations of the Yukon. These involved 48,000 Aboriginal people, full ownership of over a half-million square kilometres of land, a financial package totalling $1.8 billion, and other considerations.

After James Bay and Northern Quebec, the next settlements were in the Northwest Territories. The Northwest Territories were ripe for Aboriginal self-government. The territories cover over a million square miles, but have only about 60,000 inhabitants. They are unique in North America in having a majority population of native descent. Until the 1960s they were administered out of Ottawa, but since then a series of advances have created a political and administrative centre at Yellowknife with a territorial legislative assembly, a cabinet government similar to those of the provinces, and a large territorial administrative structure. Land and resources still remain in the hands of the federal government, however, and the federal government also has a significant control over the activities of the territorial government because it controls the purse strings through its annual funding of the government. The territories themselves raise virtually no revenues locally.

Overall, the Northwest Territories present a medley of successes and failures.[55] Though natives form the majority of the population, they occupy only a small portion, at the lower levels, of the public service. Since employment in government is the most important part of the northern economy, this is no trivial form of discrimination. Self-government has not been translated into self-administration.[56] Nor have policies in fields such as education responded to northern and native needs. The economy of the Northwest Territories, like other northern regions of Canada, divides into three sectors: a modern large-scale resource extraction economy that is predominantly non-native, well-off, and directed and controlled by the south; a traditional small-scale renewable resource extraction economy that is shrinking, not well-off, and largely native; and a welfare economy based on transfer payments that is growing and largely native.

The future of the Northwest Territories, both economically and in terms of self-government, is still uncertain.[57] For the mistakes of the South to be avoided, there must be greater native participation in both the modern economy and in government administration. Participation in the middle and upper levels of these sections, however, requires education and professional competence. The education system of the territories has failed to permit more than a handful of natives to gain these qualifications. Local government can, and should be, an important part of self-government, but so far the local level has been subordinated to the territorial.

The native population of the territories is composed of Indians (Dene), largely of the Western Arctic and Mackenzie basin, and the Inuit of the Eastern Arctic. The Inuvialuit or COPE (Committee for Original People's Entitlement) settlement in the Mackenzie River delta added to the James Bay agreements by giving natives a share in revenues from resource extraction. It did not, however, include provisions for self-government.

The Inuit of the Eastern Arctic had been so dissatisfied with existing arrangements that they wanted out and in 1976 began pushing for a new, Inuit territory. In Nunavut the Inuit will comprise 80 percent of the population. The Nunavut agreement, which was signed in 1993, was ratified by federal statute in December of that same year. The new territory will come into existence in 1999. Like Kativik, but unlike the James Bay Cree, Nunavut will have a "public" government. The Nunavut agreements include provisions for land entitlements, financial compensation, self-government, and significant Inuit participation in management of wildlife and the environment. The twenty thousand Inuit will receive $1.14 billion over a fourteen-year period.

In 1991 the federal government and the Gwich'in (Dene/Métis) of the Northwest Territories reached agreement on a comprehensive settlement. The Gwich'in had signed a treaty with the federal government in 1921, but the land provisions of the treaty had never been implemented. This settlement was confirmed in federal legislation in December 1992. Like the preceding ones, it recognized Aboriginal ownership of a substantial amount of land (8,658 square miles in the Northwest Territories and 600 square miles in the adjoining Yukon) and rights over wildlife and renewable resource management over a wider area. The Gwich'in will share in resource revenues in the Mackenzie River valley. The agreement includes provisions for Aboriginal self-government.

Between 1993 and 1997 agreements were reached with most of the Yukon First Nations. In 1993 the Sahtu Dene and Métis of the Northwest Territories also reached an agreement. In some ways even more of an achievement was the agreement with the Nisga'a of British Columbia in 1997. British Columbia is unusual among the Western provinces in not having treaties with its Aboriginal peoples from previous to European settlement. Further, the provincial government of British Columbia only recently agreed to take some responsibility for enabling a settlement to be achieved. (It must be remembered that in Canada, Crown or "public" lands belong to the province, unlike the federal ownership of public lands in the United States.) This agreement has met with resistance from many British Columbians, including some of the Nisga'a.

The time taken to reach the settlements outside Quebec has ranged from six to twenty-four years, with the majority taking over fourteen years. Settlements with eight other First Nations will have taken more than twenty-four years to be reached, and three other claims from the 1970s are still unresolved.[58] Many comprehensive land claims still remain to be resolved, especially in British Columbia.

Progress has also been made on the stream of smaller claims and negotiations for self-government. For example, in 1986 the Sechelt Indian band of British Columbia was granted self-government by act of Parliament. This prosperous and successful band was thereby enabled to control and administer their own valuable lands and resources. Many other Indian groups, however, do not like the Sechelt model because the self-government it creates is more of a local, municipal government than the sovereign political entity proposed by some native leaders. Nevertheless, the government of Canada and the Department of Indian Affairs have continued a program of negotiation with individual bands and tribes to achieve some form of self-government. Though progress has been slow, there have been some notable achievements.[59] The Manitoba bands have collectively reached an agreement on self-government with DIAND. At this point the bottom-up approach is proving reasonably successful. National native leaders still oppose it, however, for being merely a municipal, not a third-order, type of government and for ignoring the issue of constitutional recognition. The Royal Commission on Aboriginal Peoples also did not think much of this approach. The federal government in 1997 was negotiating with over eighty Aboriginal groups for this sort of self-government.

At the same time, the Department of Indian Affairs has attempted to divest itself of actual responsibility for administering Indian bands. Insofar as the Indian Act permits, the department has delegated responsibility for much of its program administration and service delivery to native bands and band councils. At present over one hundred First Nations have specially designed policies of this sort, and First Nations now control 88 percent of DIAND's budget for delivering programs on reserves. This is far more than has been achieved under self-determination in the United States, where only 25 percent of funds is administered by Indian tribes. With the top-down, constitutional approach to self-government apparently at a dead end, the bottom-up, community- and band-oriented approach is the only currently viable option. It is fraught with problems, however, such as overly detailed and exacting controls by the Department of Indian Affairs, inadequate funding, and the small scale of some bands and reserves. Much progress has, nevertheless, been made from the bottom up, and at present several hundred proposals for self-government are at various stages of consideration.[60]

Both in Canada and the United States it has been found that the devolution of service administration to bands and tribes has not reduced the costs of federal administration. Instead, the focus of bureau-departmental activity has shifted from service delivery to audit, accountability, and control, which require the same amount of manpower.

Perhaps this is not surprising. The capacity of bureaucratic organizations to preserve and expand themselves is at least as pronounced a feature of Indian administration as the intractability of the problems.

Successful self-government in both countries needs an economic base for the self-governing unit and its members. This is not easy to achieve. In Canada unresolved land claims and legal battles stand in the way of effective self-government, as does the split between federal and provincial governments over responsibility for Indians and ownership of land and resources. In the province of British Columbia most of the large Indian populations have not signed treaties, and the land claimed by Indian tribes exceeds the total land mass of the province. In the United States the inertia of the system and the prevailing political ethos of retrenchment have prevented much progress. As we shall see in the next section, rhetoric in favour of self-determination has not prevented the American government from withdrawing much of its financial support for Indians. Self-government is the appropriate policy goal for both countries. However, achieving the stated ideal is often confounded by the real, but hidden, policies and by political forces with very different interests from those of Aboriginal peoples. It will also have an impact on native communities themselves.[61]

The Canadian government has side-stepped the question of constitutional entrenchment of the right to self-government by accepting the idea that the inherent right to self-government already exists in the Constitution. Its negotiating policy leaves the responsibility for initiating discussions with the Aboriginal people. Their shopping list can include, among others, education, language and culture, police services and law enforcement, health care, social services, housing, property rights, and adoption and child welfare. Aboriginal people set the pace of negotiations and shape their own forms of government to suit their particular historical, cultural, political, and economic circumstances. At the same time, the government is firm that self-government will be exercised within the Constitution, which therefore does not mean sovereignty in the international sense. The government states that the Canadian Charter of Rights and Freedoms will apply fully to Aboriginal governments, as it does to all other governments in Canada. When all parties agree, the rights of a self-government may be protected in new treaties under §35 of the 1982 Constitution Act. The Canadian Criminal Code and other such key federal and provincial laws will prevail over those of the self-governing body.

FINANCING SELF-GOVERNMENT

Though the rhetoric of self-determination in the United States and self-government in Canada expresses the same sentiments and objectives,

Table 9.1
Expenditures on Indians, Canada and the United States Compared (× 1,000, current $)

	1975	1990	1990/1975 ratio
INDIAN POPULATION			
Canada (on reserve)	200,693	297,972	1.48
United States (I.H.S.)	587,468	1,105,486	1.88
FEDERAL EXPENDITURES, EXCLUDING HEALTH			
Canada	389,400	2,277,343	5.85
United States	812,270	1,597,150	1.97
FEDERAL EXPENDITURES, HEALTH			
Canada	48,492	495,074	10.21
United States	293,103	1,252,970	4.27
FEDERAL EXPENDITURES, TOTAL			
Canada	437,892	2,772,472	6.33
United States	1,105,373	2,850,120	2.57

Note: The sources for the data for these tables are, for the United States, *Budget Views and Estimates for Fiscal Year 1991: A Report Submitted to the Budget Committee by the Select Committee on Indian Affairs, United States Senate,* especially appendix 2 to that report, by Roger Walke, Analyst in American Indian Policy, Congressional Research Service, the Library of Congress, "Trends in Indian-Related Federal Spending, FY 1975–1991." For Canada the sources are Department of Indian Affairs and Northern Development (DIAND), *Annual Reports,* DIAND; *Basic Departmental Data,* 1990; and for health expenditures, National Health and Welfare, *Annual Reports.*

this does not mean that the real policies are the same. Much of policy-making is in implementation, and in the complex world of competing interests and bureaucracies of modern government, many factors other than stated goals, including unstated conflicting goals and interests and separate questions of financial support, can profoundly affect what stated policies actually do and mean when implemented. Practice can change while philosophy remains constant. We have already seen criticisms of self-determination in the United States for saying one thing while actually meaning another; the Canadian government has been similarly, though less vociferously, condemned. This section will examine the financing of Indian programs to determine whether the real policies differ while the stated policies remain the same and if so, to what extent. Financial support is one of the best indicators of what policies actually mean in practice.

Data comparing the United States and Canada are presented in tables 9.1 and 9.2. Two financial years have been used: 1975–76 and 1990–91. These years capture the periods of major recent changes in funding:

Table 9.2
Expenditures per Indian, Canada and the United States (Current Dollars)

	1975	1990	1990/1975 ratio
FEDERAL EXPENDITURES, EXCLUDING HEALTH			
Canada (on reserve)	1,940	7,642	3.94
United States	1,383	1,445	1.04
FEDERAL EXPENDITURES, HEALTH			
Canada (on reserve)	242	1,661	6.86
United States	499	1,133	2.27
FEDERAL EXPENDITURES, TOTAL			
Canada (on reserve)	2,182	9,303	4.26
United States	1,882	2,578	1.37

the contractions in spending of the Reagan years in the United States and the renewed concern with Indian matters in Canada following the entrenchment of Indian rights in the Constitution in 1982.

Table 9.1 presents the total amounts spent on Indians in the two countries for the two fiscal years and the ratios of change between them, while table 9.2 presents the amount per Indian and their ratios of change. The population figures for the United States are those of the Indian Health Service, while for Canada they are those of the Department of Indian Affairs for on-reserve Indians, these being closely comparable categories. These two populations are similar in terms of their special status as a federal responsibility in both countries, and it is towards them rather than towards off-reserve natives that the bulk of federal expenditures is directed.

In 1975 the amount spent per native by the respective federal governments on native-directed programs was roughly similar. The total in Canada was Can$2,182 per Indian, while in the United States it was U.S.$1,882.[62] These totals include general federal expenditures on native-directed housing, education, and administration; transfer payments; and health expenditures of the specific native health service agencies. These programs are closely comparable, though there are minor differences both in program content between the two countries and in program content over time in each country. Both the populations and the programs included are consequently satisfactorily similar to make a useful comparison. Figures for both tables are given in current dollars of the two countries.

In 1975 Canada's dollar figure per Indian was about 15 percent higher than the U.S. figure, but the margins of error in this measurement are high enough that this difference is not significant. By 1990 there had been a dramatic change. In 1990 total expenditures per Indian in Canada had risen to $9,303, while in the United States they had scarcely changed at $2,578. That is, 1990 expenditures in Canada had increased by a factor of 4.26 over 1975, while in the United States 1990 expenditures were only 1.37 times those of 1975. Health expenditures increased much faster than general program expenditures in both countries. In the United States by 1990 expenditures on health had more than doubled and nearly equalled the remainder of expenditures. Health expenditures in Canada had increased much more, by more than six times, but still equalled only one-fifth of the expanded total. In the United States expenditures per Indian other than health expenditures were virtually the same in 1990 as in 1975 in current dollars. Taking inflation into account, in constant dollars expenditures on Indians in the United States actually declined during this period at an annual rate of 2.11 percent, or over $2 billion of total decrease. In comparison, even allowing for inflation, expenditures in Canada still rose significantly.

Using budget provisions as the measure, Indian policies in Canada and the United States were at approximately the same place in 1975 but have diverged enormously since then. Increases in expenditures in Canada have been more or less steady, with no major shift points indicating a change in policy. The shift point in the United States occurred in 1982, with the cuts to social programs of the Reagan administration. In the United States, until these changes, per capita expenditures on Indians had exceeded non-defence spending per capita for the population as a whole, while by 1990 they were substantially lower. In Canada expenditures per capita on Indians have consistently remained above those on the general population.

The growing differences between the two countries can be explained by two factors. First, general social programs in the United States were reduced during the Reagan years. While there was no specific shift in stated policy towards them, Indians, as one of the least-advantaged groups, suffered disproportionately heavily from these reductions. Second, the increased political visibility and importance of Indians in Canada, particularly since entrenchment of Aboriginal rights in the 1982 Constitution Act, has led to corresponding increases in expenditures.

This analysis of budgets shows a profound and growing difference between the two countries in real policies since the mid-1970s, despite the similarity in stated policies. Aboriginal issues in Canada have grown increasingly important and prominent on the political agenda, while in the United States, along with other disadvantaged people,

Indians have become less important. The marked shift to the right in American politics has taken its toll on Indian programs, as it has on others. Canada, so far, has had no comparable policy shift, though under the Chrétien Liberal government elected in 1993, budget-cutting to reduce the huge deficit is already producing significant reductions in expenditures on social and other programs, with more to follow.

Nevertheless, expenditures on Canada's Aboriginal peoples continue to be high and remain well above those of the United States. In 1997, according to DIAND, except for health, Canada spent far more in gross amounts on Aboriginal peoples than did the u.s.[63] In health Canada spent $1,052.3 (all figures in millions) compared with $3,495.5 for the United States. But in education it was $899.1 compared with $747.3; in post-secondary education $275.4 to $66.5; in housing $176.5 to $27.1; in social development $1,031.1 to $197.3; in economic development $56.6 to $22.3.

THE DIFFERENCES IN POLICIES

As we have seen, Indian polices divide into two distinct periods, especially in Canada. Before 1970 the stated Canadian policy goal was assimilation. Actual outcomes belied this goal, for despite the half-hearted efforts of the Department of Indian Affairs, only a small proportion of Indians became enfranchised, apart from women who were forced to do so because of their marriage to non-Indians. The real, and different, objective of the department appears to have been that of all good bureaucrats in a Westminster-model parliamentary system: to keep their minister and the government out of trouble. This meant keeping the influential interest groups – for Indian policy, the churches – on the department's side and ensuring that causes (and even more so, opportunities) for complaints among their clientele – the status Indians – were few. By the measure of the number of scandals and public controversies during the period (virtually none), the bureaucracy did this quite successfully. Canadian Indian policies did not change significantly in the first hundred years after Confederation.

In comparison, American Indian policies saw dramatic reversals during this same period. The allotment efforts succeeded in alienating Indians from most of their lands, though they failed in their stated intention of assimilation; Collier's "new deal" introduced a complete reversal of previous policy goals to cultural retention, nonassimilation, self-government, and preservation and even extension of tribal lands and resources. After the Second World War, in another complete reversal of stated policy, the policy of termination replaced the "new deal," only in turn to be replaced itself after 1970 with a more pluralistic, communitarian (at least in stated goals) policy of self-determination. Up to 1970 it was in the United States, not Canada, that communitarianism and cultural pluralism were prominent strands in stated policies. Though this strand was weaker than the individualist liberal one for most of the period, it never completely disappeared and, after 1970, was the explicit policy of Congress and government. Indian policy in the United States, unlike Canada, was an important part of politics.

The contrasting nature of the frontier in the United States and Canada help explain the differences in policies. In Canada the Indian population in the West had been subdued, decimated through disease and the virtual extinction of the buffalo and confined to reservations before settlement began. There were no Indian wars, no concessions of large tracts of land as reserves, and few lingering disputes over water and desirable agricultural land. After the Riel rebellions the settlement of the Western agricultural frontier in Canada was, for the most part, peaceful. Settlement was presaged by the advent of the RCMP and by the surveyor who divided the prairies into rigorously square 640-acre sections. In the United States confrontations between the wave of Euro-American settlement and Indians were more frequent and on a much more equal footing. Competition between Indians and whites over land and other resources did not end with the creation of reservations; that was only one episode in a story that has not yet ended. These different situations postulated different roles for government: in Canada a bureaucracy whose main concern was enforcement of the treaties and treaty provisions and some efforts at assimilation; in the United States a bureaucracy pushed one way by their clientele, the Indians, another way by the influential Western members of Congress who responded to non-native land-owning and farming interests, and still another way by reform groups like the Indian Rights Association.

The contrast in frontiers is even more striking in comparing the Canadian North to the American West. In the North, agricultural settlement was generally not possible. What the whites wanted were natural resources – fur, timber, minerals, and, more recently, petroleum. Duncan Campbell Scott's mission in Northern treaty-making was to free up the land for these uses by the dominant society; even more than in the South were the Indians confined to reservations, out of sight or thought for most of the non-native population. The non-native population itself was, and still is, largely confined to small towns and cities centred around mines, timber mills, or other resource-based industries. Reserves often were many miles from these non-native centres. Once the Indians were confined to reserves the department could administer its wards as it saw fit, without external interference.

Whatever the reason, the result was that in Canada the Indians were, until the second half of the twentieth century, largely left alone on their reserves. The intrusion of residential schools and interference with Indian religions and ceremonies had certainly begun earlier, but Canadian policy for Indians remained largely one of laissez faire. The greatest impact of Euro-Canadian society upon most Canadian Indians in this century came with the expansion of government services for Indians in the period beginning in the late 1950s. By the mid-1970s Canadian Indians were not only subjected to a colonial administration, as they had been for the past century and more, but they were also subjected to the delivery of government programs in health, welfare, housing, and education that disrupted their traditional nomadic hunting and gathering lifestyle and threatened their traditional culture. The seeds of the policy turmoil of the 1970s were sown in these decades, when traditional Indian society was being disrupted by government service delivery and a new generation of Indian leaders (mostly trained in the residential schools) no longer accepted this paternalism and interference. In comparison, in the United States the problems and conflicting objectives facing Indians and Indian administration had been defined in the nineteenth century: making the land, water, and other resources available for non-native development; enabling Indians to enjoy a reasonable standard of living, whether through assimilation or other means; protecting Indians from intrusions from the greater society; and, not least, controlling a potentially unruly population. These issues did not change. The policies for dealing with them did.

The post-1980 period tells a much different story. Here, though stated policy goals began to converge in the two countries, the real policies began to diverge widely. Aboriginal issues assumed an importance in Canada that they had never had before. Part of this change came from a very real, if belated, recognition in Canada of the problems faced by Aboriginal peoples and the disadvantages they suffered through government and other causes. Court cases affirming Aboriginal rights and entrenchment of these rights in the Constitution in 1982 gave even more strength to these forces. It is true to say that by the 1990s, in real terms, there was a marked difference between Indian policies in the United States and in Canada and that by then Canada did, indeed, reflect a strong communitarian strand of cultural pluralism while the United States paid lip service to the same values but did not back this up with financial resources.

Part of the reason for this difference can be found in the peculiar problems facing the Canadian polity at this time. Quebec secession has been a real possibility since at least the 1960s. Federal efforts to accommodate Quebec, including the work of the Royal Commission on Bilingualism and Biculturalism in the mid-1960s, also promoted "multiculturalism" as a parallel recognition of the contributions of Canadians of neither English nor French descent.[64] Recognition of the rights of Aboriginal people to their cultural and linguistic identity formed part of this general acceptance of diversity. The values and world vision that had motivated Duncan Campbell Scott and generations of Indian administrators had been lost to the Canadian polity by the 1980s. Cultural pluralism and encouragement of diversity had replaced them. In Indian policy this meant self-government; the exact meaning of self-government was (and still is) to be determined.

The overwhelming facts in Indian policy in the United States since 1980 have been tolerance of diversity, self-determination, and a severe enough limitation of resources to make self-determination difficult. In Canada they have been tolerance of diversity, self-government, and growing resources, but slow progress in actually implementing self-government. The economic development of Aboriginal communities and reserves in both countries remains the key problem in their development and well-being. So far neither country has found a satisfactory answer. But in both countries, at this point in time, the communitarian, pluralistic strand of policy has a prominent position in stated goals and intentions. Insofar as Indian policy is concerned, the argument that Canada is more pluralistic and communitarian while the United States is more individualistic did not hold true for most of the past century, but has become much more true since 1982.

Aboriginal people in Canada have now been given many political and legal resources in their struggles against the larger European society. Court cases, beginning with *Calder* in 1973 and certainly not ending with *Delgamuukw* (another British Columbia case) in 1997, have recognized Aboriginal rights in a way denied previously by governments. Entrenchment of Aboriginal rights in the constitution in 1982 has given the Aboriginal people even more powers. However, from the perspective of 1998 and this analysis of Canadian and u.s. policies towards Aboriginal peoples over the past century, the Canadian constitutional provisions seem more like a statement of what Canada wants to be than what it actually is. This of course is what statements of values, articulations of principles, and the affirmation of myths and symbols are all about. They are more descriptions of where a collectivity (or its leaders) think they want to go, and what they want to become, than they are statements of fact that accurately describe the past (or the present, for that matter).

The principles entrenched in Canada's 1982 Constitution Act have become standards that have established a new direction for Aboriginal policies, unlike any of those in the past. The United States has, historically, enjoyed a much more varied and rich medley of considerations in its Indian policy. Since 1981 these have narrowed to a rhetoric that posits a very limited role for national government and, in turn, a practice that limits real options and developments. But the possibility, even likelihood, exists that the United States at some future date will once again draw on its rich historical tradition and again recognize and encourage diversity and even communitarianism in its Indian policies.

Notes

1 For Canada we have adopted the usage of the Royal Commission on Aboriginal Peoples (RCAP): "The term Aboriginal peoples refers to organic and cultural entities that stem historically from the original peoples of North America, not to collections of individuals united by so-called 'racial' characteristics." *Report of the Royal Commission on Aboriginal Peoples*, vol. 1, *Looking Forward, Looking Back* (Ottawa: Minister of Supply and Services, 1996), xiv. When discussing Mexico, we adopt the term customarily used in that discourse: indigenous.

2 This is a conventional view of Canadian federalism, simplifying what is admittedly a complex and dynamic distribution of governing authority. See Robert J. Jackson and Doreen Jackson, *Politics in Canada*, 3d ed. (Scarborough, ON: Prentice-Hall Canada, 1994), chap. 6. For a contrasting view see Andrée Lajoie, "Le Québec et la Constitution Canadienne ou le procès du Fédéralisme" (University of Montreal, Centre for Research in Public Law, March 1995, unpublished).

3 The Royal Commission on Aboriginal Peoples concluded, according to a population model supplied by Statistics Canada, that the best figure for 1996 was 2.7 percent. *Report*, vol. 1, 15.

4 Various analyses may highlight the history of European-Aboriginal contact according to different historical intervals. Canada's Aboriginal Action Plan of 1998, for example, prefers pre-contact, contact and cooperation, displacement and assimilation (early nineteenth century

to about 1970), and renewal. *Gathering Strength: Canada's Aboriginal Action Plan* (Ottawa: Minister of Public Works and Government Services Canada, January 1998.)

5 6 Peters (31 U.S.) 515.

6 5 Peters (30 U.S.) 1.

7 The phrase is in both cases. Marshall wrote in his earlier decision – *Johnson and Graham's Lessee v. McIntosh* [8 Wheaton (21 U.S.) 543] – that Indians had only a lesser right of occupancy that could be (and in this case was) abolished.

8 RCAP, *Report*, vol. 1, 44–5.

9 Edward J. Hedican, *Applied Anthropology in Canada: Understanding Aboriginal Issues* (Toronto: University of Toronto Press, 1995), 9.

10 Peter H. Russell, *Constitutional Odyssey: Can Canadians Become a Sovereign People?* 2d. ed. (Toronto, University of Toronto Press, 1993), 12.

11 Brian Slattery, "The Hidden Constitution: Aboriginal Rights in Canada," in Menno Boldt and J. Anthony Long, eds., *The Quest for Justice: Aboriginal Peoples and Aboriginal Rights* (Toronto: University of Toronto Press, 1985), 120.

12 Menno Boldt, *Surviving as Indians: The Challenge of Self-Government* (Toronto: University of Toronto Press, 1993), 274–8.

13 The Royal Commission on Aboriginal Peoples calls it "displacement and assimilation." *Report*, vol. 1, 36ff.

14 Paul Tennant, "Aboriginal Rights and Indian Self-Government in the Penner Report," in Boldt and Long, *Quest for Justice*, 323.

15 Olive Patricia Dickason, *Canada's First Nations: A History of the Founding Peoples from Earliest Times* (Toronto: Oxford University Press, 1992), chap. 21.

16 The classic analysis of population in New Spain was undertaken by Borah. See Woodrow Borah, "The Historical Demography of Aboriginal and Colonial America: An Attempt at Perspective," in William M. Denevan, ed., *The Native Population of the Americas in 1492* (Madison, WI: University of Wisconsin Press, 1976), 13–34, and, with Sherburne F. Cook, *Essays in Population History: Mexico and the Caribbean*. 3 vols. (Berkeley, CA: University of California Press, 1972–79).

17 See Bartholome de Las Casas, *Apologetica historia de las Indias*, Edmundo O'Gorman, ed. 2 vols. (Mexico, D.F.: Universidad Nacional Autonoma de México, 1967.) Another example of his writing is *Tratados*. 2 vols. (Mexico, D.F.: Fondo de Cultura Economica, 1965).

18 A number of scholars have analyzed this subject. A few examples include Nancy M. Farriss, *Maya Society under Colonial Rule* (Princeton, NJ: Princeton University Press, 1984); Charles Gibson, *The Aztecs under Spanish Rule: A History of the Indians of the Valley of Mexico, 1519–1810*

(Stanford, CA: Stanford University Press, 1964); Clarence H. Haring, *The Spanish Empire in America*, 2d ed. (New York: Harcourt, Brace and World, 1963); and Jose Llaguno, *La personalidad juridica del indio y el III Concilio Provincial Mexicano (1585)* (Mexico, D.F.: Editorial Porrua, 1963).

19 The best study of this ideological schism and of Mexican liberalism during the period is Charles Hale, *Mexican Liberalism in the Age of Mora, 1821–1853* (New Haven, CT: Yale University Press, 1968).

20 See, for example, Robert J. Knowlton, *Church Property and the Mexican Reform, 1856–1910* (DeKalb, IL: Northern Illinois University Press, 1976); Charles Berry, *The Reform in Oaxaca, 1856–1876* (Lincoln, NE: University of Nebraska Press, 1981); Daniel Cosio Villegas, ed., *Historia Moderna de México*. 10 vols (Mexico, D.F.: Editorial Hermes, 1955–72); Luis Gonzalez y Gonzalez, "El agrarismo liberal," *Historia Mexicana 7*, 469–96; and John Tutino, *From Insurrection to Revolution in Mexico* (Princeton, NJ: Princeton University Press, 1986).

21 Boldt and Long, *The Quest for Justice*, 8–12.

22 Russell, *Constitutional Odyssey*. The first round of megaconstitutional politics began with the Fulton-Favreau amending formula announced in 1964, the second with election of the Parti Québécois government in Quebec in 1976, and so forth.

23 Patriation reference case: "In the matter of an act for expediting the decision of constitutional and other provincial questions, being R.S.M. 1970, c. C-180," Supreme Court of Canada, decision of 28 September 1981. See Edward McWhinney, *Canada and the Constitution 1979–1982* (Toronto: University of Toronto Press, 1982), 80–9 and appendix.

24 Article 4 of "Consensus Report on the Constitution," Charlottetown, 28 August 1992, final text.

25 Royal Commission on Aboriginal Peoples, *Integrated Research Plan* (Ottawa: RCAP, July 1993.)

26 "Gathering Strength: Canada's Aboriginal Action Plan."

27 *Delgamuukw v. R.*, File No. 23799, 11 December 1977; 23 S.C.R. 799.

28 Restated, that is, from *R. v. Adams*, (1996) 3 S.C.R. 101 at 103.

29 *R. v. Sparrow* (1990) 1 S.C.R. 1075.

30 A good study of the limits of the land reform is John Gledhill, *Casi Nada: A Study of Land Reform in the Homeland of Cardenismo* (Albany, NY: Institute for Mesoamerican Studies, State University of New York, 1991).

31 Royal Commission on Aboriginal Peoples, *Partners in Confederation: Aboriginal Peoples, Self-Government, and the Constitution* (Ottawa: Minister of Supply and Services, 1993), chap. 2.

32 RCAP, *Partners*, chap. 2.

33 Canada suffered the embarrassment of being found by the United Nations Human Rights Commission, on application by Sandra

Lovelace, a Maliseet Indian, to have violated article 27 of the International Covenant on Civil and Political Rights. Upon marrying a non-Aboriginal person, Lovelace had been ascertained no longer to be Aboriginal (as provided by the Indian Act) and denied the benefits of the act. Consequent to the commission finding, Parliament enacted Bill C-31 striking that part of the Indian Act and adding reinstatement provisions. (Bill C-31 created further problems. For example, some bands do not wish to reinstate because of the strain additional members would put on already scarce resources, or for other reasons.) *Royal Commission on Aboriginal Peoples*, vol. 1, 229; *Lovelace v. Canada* (1981), 2 *Human Rights Law Journal* 158; 68 I.L.R. 17.

34 RCAP, *Partners*, chap. 2.
35 Indian treaties have constitutional standing (in Canada) but are not treaties as understood in international law, nor do they have standing in international law. Peter W. Hogg, *Constitutional Law of Canada*, 3d. ed. (Toronto: Carswell, 1992), 682–6.
36 James Bay and Northern Quebec Agreement, 11 November 1975, subsequently enacted into legislation by Parliament and the Quebec Legislative Assembly. See Billy Diamond, "Aboriginal Rights: The James Bay Experience," in Boldt and Long, *The Quest for Justice*, 265–85.
37 RCAP, vol. 2, pt. 2, 540ff.
38 *R. v. Drybones*; *Partners*, chap. 2.
39 See Stavenhagen's chapter 2 in this collection for a description and discussion of these proposals.

CHAPTER TWO

1 For the concept of internal colonialism, see Michael Hector, *Internal Colonialism: The Celtic Fringe in British National Development, 1536–1966* (Berkeley, CA: University of California Press, 1975). It was apparently first applied to the Aboriginal peoples of America by the Cherokee anthropologist Robert K. Thomas in "Colonialism: Classic and Internal," *New University Thought* 4(4) (winter 1966–67), 44–55. More recently, see Ward Churchill, *Struggle for the Land: Indigenous Resistance to Genocide, Ecocide and Expropriation in Contemporary North America* (Toronto: Between the Lines, 1992), 23–4.
2 For the concept of an agonic struggle and the research method appropriate to it, see Michel Foucault, "The Subject and Power," in Hubert L. Dreyfus, ed. (Fabienne Durand-Bogaert, tr.), *Michel Foucault: Beyond Structuralism and Hermeneutics* (Chicago: The University of Chicago Press, 1982), 208–26.
3 I often use the term "Canadian" to stand for "non-Aboriginal Canadian" for reasons of brevity. This is not to suggest that Aboriginal

people are not Canadian. In the section on mutual recognition I explain in what sense Aboriginal peoples are members of Aboriginal nations and "Canadians," in the broad sense of members of a confederation of Aboriginal nations with the federal-provincial confederation.

4 The sketch I present is based on two articles written for the Canadian Royal Commission on Aboriginal Peoples. These articles are based on extensive discussion at the Royal Commission and on the research carried out under its auspices. One of the articles was drawn upon by the commissioners in writing the chapter on a new relationship in the final report of the Royal Commission. Although this sketch is similar in many respects to that chapter, it is not the same, nor is it a presentation of the commission's views. I wish to thank the co-directors of research, Marlene Brant Castellano and David Hawkes, and Dr Fred Wien for permission to use material from my two submissions to the commission. In addition, the research presented in the final report gives further support to my arguments on history, treaties, the colonial relationship, and the five principles. Moreover, some arguments presented here are defended in more detail in my book *Strange Multiplicity: Constitutionalism in an Age of Diversity* (Cambridge: Cambridge University Press, 1995). For the concept of an intermediate description, see *Strange Multiplicity*, 99–116.

5 See Olive Patricia Dickason, *Canada's First Nations: A History of the Founding Peoples from Earliest Times* (Toronto: Oxford University Press, 1992).

6 For an introduction to the Indian Act, see Donna Lea Hawley, *The Annotated 1990 Indian Act, Including Related Treaties, Statutes and Regulations* (Toronto: Carswell, 1990).

7 For the stages view and its refutation, see Tully, *Strange Multiplicity*, 7–17, 58–98.

8 For a good example of the backlash, see Melvin H. Smith, *Our Home or Native Land? What Governments' Aboriginal Policy Is Doing to Canada* (Altona, MB: Friesen Printers, 1995). For a discussion and criticism of the court decision on which Smith's argument is based (and which is under appeal), see Frank Cassidy, ed., *Aboriginal Title in British Columbia: Delgamuukw v. The Queen* (Montreal: The Institute for Research on Public Policy, 1992).

9 One of the best-known competing research projects on the demands of justice in postcolonial and culturally diverse societies is the discourse ethics of Jürgen Habermas. Setting aside the differences in our two research projects, the five principles presented here relate to his project in the following way. The first three principles are the discursive application of the conditions of his two procedural principles, D and U, to this case of reaching agreement on action coordination

between Aboriginal and non-Aboriginal peoples. The last two substantive principles are norms that already enjoy widespread agreement among Aboriginal and non-Aboriginal people and now require further testing in dialogue under the conditions of the first three principles. See Jürgen Habermas, "Discourse Ethics: Notes on a Program of Philosophical Justification," in *Moral Consciousness and Communicative Action*, tr. Christian Lenhardt and Shierry Weber Nicholsen, introduction by Thomas McCarthy (Cambridge, MA: MIT Press, 1995), 43–115. For a promising application of discourse ethics to Aboriginal–non-Aboriginal relations, see Kenneth L. Avio, "Discourse Ethics, Constitutional Contract and the Problem of Implementation: Application to Aboriginal Rights," unpublished paper, Department of Economics, University of Victoria, Victoria, BC, 1995.

10 For the two concepts of equality that warrant these demands for recognition, see Charles Taylor, "The Politics of Recognition," in Amy Gutman, ed., *Multiculturalism* (Princeton, NJ: Princeton University Press, 1994), 25–74.

11 For the arguments against extinguishment, see Mary Ellen Turpel et al., "Treaty Extinguishment of Aboriginal Title: The Legal and Historical Context," Royal Commission on Aboriginal Peoples, unpublished paper, 18 October 1993.

12 For the various arguments for the inherent right of self-government summarised here, see Royal Commission on Aboriginal Peoples, *Aboriginal Self-Government: Legal and Constitutional Issues* (Ottawa: Minister of Supply and Services Canada, 1995), and Grand Council of the Crees, *Sovereign Injustice: Forcible Inclusion of the James Bay Crees and Cree Territory into a Sovereign Québec* (Grand Council of the Crees, Nemeska, Eeyou Astchee (Quebec), Canada: 1995).

13 This is Chief Justice Marshall's formulation. For a discussion, see Tully, *Strange Multiplicity*, 117–24.

14 See Darlene Johnston, *The Taking of Indian Lands in Canada: Consent or Coercion?* (Saskatoon, SK: University of Saskatchewan Native Law Centre, 1989).

15 I use the phrase "confederation (or federation)" because, as is well known, the relations of both the federal-provincial confederation and the Aboriginal nations–federal government confederation are partly federal relations and partly confederal. For the sake of brevity, I use "confederation" to stand for both types of relation.

16 For the views of the then Grand Chief of the Assembly of First Nations, see Ovide Mercredi and Mary Ellen Turpel, *In The Rapids: Navigating the Future of First Nations* (New York: Viking, 1993).

17 See Minister of Indian Affairs and Northern Development, *Aboriginal Self-Government: The Government of Canada's Approach to Implementation of*

the Inherent Right and the Negotiation of Aboriginal Self-Government (Ottawa: Minister of Public Works and Government Services, 1995).

18 For the distinction between a modus vivendi, or balance of power, agreement and a just agreement, see Habermas, "Discourse Ethics," 70–6.

19 For discussions of sharing, see Royal Commission on Aboriginal Peoples, *Sharing the Harvest: The Road to Self-Reliance* (Ottawa: Minister of Supply and Services Canada, 1993); *Aboriginal Peoples in Urban Centres* (Ottawa: Minister of Supply and Services Canada, 1993); and *The Path to Healing* (Ottawa: Minister of Supply and Services, 1993).

20 Chief Justice John Marshall, *Worcester v. the State of Georgia*, January term, 1832, reprinted in *The Writings of Chief Justice Marshall on the Federal Constitution* (Boston: James Monroe and Company, 1839), 446. See Tully, *Strange Multiplicity*, 126.

21 For an example of this concern, see Menno Boldt, *Surviving as Indians: The Challenge of Self-Government* (Toronto: University of Toronto Press, 1993).

22 For a discussion of this concern and various responses, see Royal Commission on Aboriginal Peoples, *Aboriginal Peoples and the Justice System* (Ottawa: Minister of Supply and Services Canada, 1993).

23 For an introduction to the characteristics of Aboriginal governments, see J. Anthony Long, "Political Revitalization in Canadian Native Indian Societies," *Canadian Journal of Political Science* 23(4) (1990): 751–74, and Boldt, *Surviving as Indians*, 132–61.

24 I am thinking specifically of the excellent work by Will Kymlicka on liberalism and minorities. See Will Kymlicka, *Multicultural Citizenship: A Liberal Theory of Minority Rights* (Oxford: Clarendon Press, 1995), and Will Kymlicka, ed., *The Rights of Minority Cultures* (Oxford: Oxford University Press, 1995).

25 For a reconstruction of Aboriginal emancipatory narratives of harmony, see Mark S. Dockstator, "Towards an Understanding of Aboriginal Self-Government: A Proposed Theoretical Model and Illustrative Factual Analysis," DJ thesis, Osgoode Hall Law School, York University, June 1993.

26 See Robert Bringhurst, *The Black Canoe: Bill Reid and the Spirit of Haida Gwaii* (Vancouver: Douglas & McIntyre, 1991).

CHAPTER THREE

1 George Psacharopoulos and Harry Anthony Patrinos, eds., *Indigenous People and Poverty in Latin America. An Empirical Analysis* (Washington, DC: The World Bank, 1994).

2 Luz María Valdés, *Los indios en los censos de población* (Mexico: Universidad Nacional Autónoma de México, 1995).

3 Estimates of the total indigenous population vary considerably, as different criteria for definition and classification are used. Usually census and government figures tend towards lower estimates, while anthropologists and other scholars tend to provide higher figures. See Alexia Peyser and Juan Chackiel, "La población indígena en los censos de América Latina," in *Estudios sociodemográficos de pueblos indígenas* (CELADE [Centro Latinoamericano de Demografía], Santiago, Chile, 1994), and Mary Lisbeth Gonzalez, "How Many Indigenous People?" in Psacharopoulos and Patrinos, eds., *Indigenous People and Poverty.*

4 Rodolfo Stavenhagen, *Derecho indígena y derechos humanos en América Latina* (Mexico: El Colegio de México and Instituto Interamericano de Derechos Humanos, 1988). Also Bartolomé Clavero, *Derecho indígena y cultura constitucional en América* (Mexico: Siglo XXI Editores, 1994).

5 Alfonso Caso, *La comunidad indígena* (Mexico: Secretaría de Educación Pública, 1971). Also, Gonzalo Aguirre Beltrán, *El proceso de aculturación* (Mexico: UNAM, 1957).

6 Ley de Derechos de los Pueblos y Comunidades Indígenas del Estado de Oaxaca.

7 For a good introduction, see Alison Brysk, "Acting Globally: Indian Rights and International Politics in Latin America," in Donna Lee Van Cott, ed., *Indigenous Peoples and Democracy in Latin America* (New York: St Martin's Press, 1994).

8 Alicia Ibarra Illanez, *Los indígenas y el estado en el Ecuador* (Quito: Abya-Yala, 1987). Also, Melina H. Selverston, "The Politics of Culture: Indigenous Peoples and the State in Ecuador," in Van Cott, ed., *Indigenous Peoples and Democracy.*

9 María Consuelo Mejía Piñeros and Sergio Sarmiento Silva, *La lucha indígena: Un reto a la ortodoxia* (Mexico: Siglo XXI Editores, 1987).

10 This has been described as "thinking locally and acting globally," in contrast to environmental organizations that are said to think globally and act locally. See Brysk, "Acting Globally," in Van Cott, ed., *Indigenous Peoples and Democracy.*

11 Guillermo Bonfil, *Utopía y revolución: El pensamiento político de los indios en América Latina* (Mexico: Nueva Imagen, 1981).

12 Eric Hobsbawm and Terence Ranger, eds., *The Invention of Tradition* (Cambridge: Cambridge University Press, 1983). Also, Benedict Anderson, *Imagined Communities* (London: Verso, 1983).

13 There may be special circumstances that stimulate the rise of an indigenous intelligentsia. In Mexico during the 1970s, a training course for "indigenous ethno-linguists" was organized briefly by a group of anthropologists in public office. In the early 1980s, the privately organized Mexican Academy for Human Rights offered seminars on human rights

to representatives of indigenous organizations. Some of the indigenous leaders and intellectuals of later years took part in these activities.

14 Arturo Arias, "Changing Indian Identity: Guatemala's Violent Transition to Modernity," in Carol A. Smith, ed., *Guatemalan Indians and the State, 1540 to 1988* (Austin, TX: University of Texas Press, 1990). Also, Yvon Le Bot, *La guerra en tierras mayas: Comunidad, violencia y modernidad en Guatemala (1970–1992)* (Mexico: Fondo de Cultura Económica, 1995).

15 Yvon Le Bot, *Subcommandante Marcos, El sueño zapatista* (Mexico: Plaza & Janés, 1997), has a report on lengthy interviews with Marcos in the summer of 1996. For a collection of Zapatista documents, see Ejercito Zapatista de Liberación Nacional, *La palabra de los armados de verdad y fuego* (Mexico, D.F.: Editorial Fuenteovejuna, 1994 [3 vols.]). An excellent background analysis of the rebellion is in George A. Collier, *Basta! Land and the Zapatista Rebellion in Chiapas* (Oakland, CA: The Institute for Food and Development Policy, 1994). A good account of the earlier organizational efforts that led to the emergence of the EZLN and rival organizations is provided by Ma. del Carmen Legorreta Díaz, *Religión, política y guerrilla en Las Cañadas de la Selva Lacandona* (Mexico: Cal y Arena, 1998).

16 The National Indian Congress (Congreso Nacional Indígena) held its third working session in Mexico City in October 1998.

17 For an early formulation of "internal colonialism" as applied to the relations between Indian peoples and the wider society, see Rodolfo Stavenhagen, "Clases, colonialismo y aculturación," *Revista América Latina* (Rio de Janeiro, Centro Latinoamericano de Investigaciones en Ciencias Sociales) 6(4) (1963): 63–104). (Published in English as "Classes, Colonialism and Acculturation," *Studies in Comparative International Development* 1(6) [1965].)

18 On Nicaragua, see Carlos Vilas, *State, Class, and Ethnicity in Nicaragua* (Boulder, CO: Lynne Rienner Publishers, 1989); for Guatemala, see Le Bot, *La guerra en tierras mayas.*

19 Mejía and Sarmiento, *La lucha indígena*; Xavier Albó, "And from Kataristas to MNRistas? The Surprising and Bold Alliance between Aymaras and Neoliberals in Bolivia," in Van Cott, ed., *Indigenous Peoples and Democracy.*

20 While the mestizos came to power in countries like Mexico, the traditional racial-cultural hierarchies, with the descendants of the Spanish colonizers or other European settlers at the top, prevailed well into the twentieth century in other countries.

21 Bonfil, *Utopía y revolución.* For a good view of indigenous thinking in a wider context, see Roger Moody, ed., *The Indigenous Voice: Visions and*

Realities (London: Zed Books [2 vols.], 1988), and Franke Wilmer, *The Indigenous Voice in World Politics* (Newbury Park, CA: Sage Publications, 1993).

22 Bolivia's Aymara vice-president, Victor Hugo Cárdenas, frequently states publicly that Indians are not opposed to modernization but have their own concept of it, which does not necessarily coincide with Western notions.

23 Le Bot, *Subcommandante Marcos*, 338–46.

24 Rodolfo Stavenhagen, "La situación y los derechos de los pueblos indígenas de América," in *America Indigena* 52 (1–2) (1992): 63–118.

25 Collier, *Basta! Land and the Zapatista Rebellion.*

26 For a discussion of these issues in the Amazonian context, see Martin von Hildebrand et al., *Reconocimiento y demarcación de territorios indígenas en la Amazonia* (Bogotá: CEREC, 1993).

27 Rodolfo Stavenhagen and Diego Iturralde, eds., *Entre la ley y la costumbre: El derecho consuetudinario indígena en América Latina* (Mexico: Instituto Indigenista Interamericano & Instituto Interamericano de Derechos Humanos, 1990).

28 Article 1 of both international rights covenants adopted by the UN General Assembly in 1966 asserts that "All peoples have the right to self-determination." Indigenous organizations have long argued that they should be treated as "peoples" according to international law. This is resisted by most governments.

29 Lydia Van de Fliert, ed., *Indigenous Peoples and International Organisations* (Nottingham, England: Spokesman, 1994).

CHAPTER FOUR

1 The research on which this paper is based has been supported by the Donner Canadian Foundation. Monique Jileson served as research assistant for the production of this paper. I am grateful to Michael Asch, Alan Cairns, Hans Mohr, and John Tait for their comments on an earlier draft.

2 Department of Indian Affairs and Northern Development, *Indian Population Register by Sex and Residence, 1991*, March, 1992. The 1991 census counted 189,365 on-reserve Indians (Statistics Canada, *Profile of Canada's Aboriginal Population*, February 1995). Another useful summary of statistics and interpretations of Aboriginal populations can be found in Royal Commission on Aboriginal Peoples (RCAP), *Report of the Royal Commission on Aboriginal Peoples*, vol. 1, *Looking Forward, Looking Back*, chap. 2, "From Time Immemorial: A Demographic Profile" (Ottawa: Minister of Supply and Services, 1996), 11–27.

3 A useful review of some of these conditions can be found in RCAP, *Report*, vol. 3, *Gathering Strength.*

4 Statistics Canada, *Aboriginal Peoples Survey, 1991*, 1, "Disability," 2, "Housing" (March 1994); and *Language, Tradition, Health, Lifestyle and Social Issues,* June 1993. Also, N. Janet Hagey, Gilles Laroque, and Catherine McBride, *Highlights of Aboriginal Conditions, 1981–2001* (Ottawa: Department of Indian and Northern Affairs, December 1989), pt. 2, "Social Conditions."

5 Mary Jane Norris, "The Demography of Aboriginal People in Canada," in Shiva S. Halli et al., eds., *Ethnic Demography: Canadian Immigrant, Racial and Cultural Variations* (Ottawa: Carleton University Press, 1990).

6 I am grateful to Stephanie Taylor for her excellent unpublished research paper, "The Charter and Aboriginal Self-Government in Canada: An Analysis of the Applicability of the American Model," for contributing to my understanding of these issues. Useful sources include Felix S. Cohen, *Handbook of Federal Indian Law* (Albuquerque, NM: University of New Mexico Press, 1982); Edward M. Morgan, "Self-Government and the Constitution: A Comparative Look at Native Canadians and American Indians," *American Indian Law Review,* 12 (1) (1984): 39–56; and Vine Deloria Jr and Clifford M. Lytle, *American Indians, American Justice* (Austin, TX: University of Texas Press, 1983).

7 *Worcester v. Georgia,* 6 Peters (31 U.S.) 515 (1832).

8 *Cherokee Nation v. Georgia,* 5 Peters (30 U.S.) 1 (1831).

9 *Johnson and Graham's Lessee v. McIntosh,* 8 Wheaton (21 U.S.) 543 (1823).

10 *U.S. v. Kagama,* 118 U.S. 375 (1886).

11 Ward Churchill, "American Indian Self-Governance: Fact, Fantasy, and Prospects for the Future," in Lyman H. Letgers and Fremont J. Lyden, eds., *American Indian Policy: Self-Governance and Economic Development* (Westport, CT: Greenwood Press, 1994); Vine Deloria Jr, ed., *American Indian Policy in the Twentieth Century* (Norman, OK: University of Oklahoma Press, 1985), especially chap. 8, Robert A. Nelson and Joseph F. Sheley, "Bureau of Indian Affairs Influence on Indian Self-Determination," 177–96.

12 RCAP, *Report,* vol. 2, *Restructuring the Relationship,* pt. 1, 115.

13 A useful summary of these court decisions up to 1996 can be found in RCAP, *Report,* vol. 1, "The Role of the Courts," 216–29.

14 Kathy Brock, "Taking Control: Dismantling Indian Affairs and Recognizing First Nations Government in Manitoba," in Douglas M. Brown, ed., *The State of the Federation 1996* (Kingston, ON: Institute of Intergovernmental Relations, Queen's University, 1996).

15 *RCAP, Report,* vol. 2, pt. 1, 116.

16 Ibid., 215.

17 Ibid., 219.

18 These various models are discussed in RCAP, *Report,* vol. 2, pt. 1, chap. 3.1, "Models of Aboriginal Government: An Overview," 245–79.

Among other useful studies of self-government are Menno Boldt, *Surviving as Indians: The Challenge of Self-Government* (Toronto: University of Toronto Press, 1993); Frank Cassidy and Robert L. Bish, *Indian Government: Its Meaning and Practice* (Halifax: Institute for Research on Public Policy, 1989); Grand Chief Edward John, "Getting out of the Way: On the Road to Aboriginal Self-Government," *Canadian Public Administration* 37(3) (fall 1994): 445–52; John H. Hylton, ed., *Aboriginal Self-Government in Canada: Current Trends and Issues* (Saskatoon, SK: Purich, 1994).

19 RCAP, *Report*, vol. 2, 181.

20 Ibid., 165–72.

21 Ibid., 272–8.

22 The Royal Commission on Aboriginal Peoples considered some of the issues of financing Aboriginal self-governments in its *Report*, vol. 2, pt. 1, chap. 3.2, "Financing Aboriginal Self-Government." See also Donald Purich, "The Future of Native Rights," in J.R. Miller, ed., *Sweet Promises: A Reader on Indian-White Relations in Canada* (Toronto: University of Toronto Press, 1991), 421–37.

23 RCAP, *Report*, vol. 2, pt. 1, chap. 3.2 "Financing Aboriginal Government," 280–310. The quotations are taken from 281–4.

24 This and the following quotations are taken from RCAP, *Report*, vol. 5, *Renewal: A Twenty-Year Commitment*, 55–8.

25 RCAP, *Report*, vol. 2, pt. 1, 202.

26 RCAP, *Report*, vol. 5, 120.

27 Ibid., 125.

28 Ibid., 126.

29 Ibid., 127–30.

30 I discuss this problem in more detail in C.E.S. Franks, "Representation and Policy-Making in a Federal and Parliamentary System," in C.E.S. Franks et al., eds., *Canada's Century: Governance in a Maturing Society. Essays in Honour of John Meisel* (Montreal and Kingston: McGill-Queen's University Press, 1995).

31 Examples of Aboriginal leaders considering entrenchment essential can be found in Ovide Mercredi's comments quoted in Kathy Brock, "Taking Control," and in Georges Erasmus's comments in Larry Krotz, *Indian Country: Inside Another Canada* (Toronto: McClelland and Stewart, 1990), 208–14. The Royal Commission on Aboriginal Peoples, in *Partners in Confederation: Aboriginal Peoples, Self-Government and the Constitution* (Ottawa: Minister of Supply and Services, 1993), emphasizes reform of statutes, while the Assembly of First Nations, in its *First Nations and the Constitution: Discussion Paper* (Ottawa: First Nations Circle on the Constitution, 21 November 1991), 9, emphasizes the need for constitutional amendment.

32 See, for example, Menno Boldt and J. Anthony Long, "Tribal Philosophies and the Canadian Charter of Rights and Freedoms," in Menno
Boldt and J. Anthony Long, eds., *The Quest for Justice: Aboriginal Peoples
and Aboriginal Rights* (Toronto: University of Toronto Press, 1985), 167–
9; Marie Smallface Marule, "Traditional Indian Government: Of the
People, by the People, for the People," in Leroy Little Bear, Menno
Boldt, and J. Anthony Long, eds., *Pathways to Self-Determination: Cana-
dian Indians and the Canadian State* (Toronto: University of Toronto
Press, 1984), 36, 44; Assembly of First Nations, "'Sharing Canada's
Future' An Analysis," in *First Nations and the Constitution: Discussion
Paper*; Ira Barkin, "Aboriginal Rights: A Shell without the Filling,"
Queen's Law Journal, 15 (1990): 311; Mary Ellen Turpel, "Aboriginal
People and the Charter: Interpretive Monopolies, Cultural Differences," *Canadian Human Rights Yearbook* (1989–90), 3–45; and Ovide
Mercredi and Mary Ellen Turpel, "Individual Rights and Collective
Responsibilities," in their *In the Rapids: Navigating the Future of First
Nations* (Toronto: Viking, 1993), 96–106.
33 RCAP, *Report*, vol. 5, 231.
34 RCAP, *Report*, vol. 2, pt. 1, 227.
35 Ibid., 228.
36 Ibid., 230.
37 Ibid., 231.
38 Ibid., 233.
39 Good discussions of these issues can be found in many places. The
main sources I have used in this discussion include Joel Feinberg, *Social
Philosophy* (Englewood Cliffs, NJ: Prentice Hall, 1973); also H.L.A. Hart,
"Are There Any Natural Rights?" and Margaret MacDonald, "Natural
Rights," reprinted in A.I. Melden, ed., *Human Rights* (Belmont, CA:
Wadsworth, 1970). A valuable source on issues of minority and group
rights is Will Kymlicka, *Liberalism, Community, and Culture* (Oxford:
Oxford University Press, 1989).
40 A useful introduction to problems of procedural justice can be found
in Martin P. Golding, *Philosophy of the Law* (Englewood Cliffs, NJ: Pren-
tice Hall, 1975), chap. 6, "Dispute Settling and Justice," 106–25.
41 RCAP, *Report*, vol. 2, pt. 1, 121.
42 For example, Boldt and Long, "Tribal Philosophies," 169; Marule,
"Traditional Indian Government," 44; and Mercredi and Turpel, *In the
Rapids*.
43 For example, Colin H. Scott, "Custom, Tradition and the Politics of
Culture: Aboriginal Self-Government in Canada," in Noel Dyck and
James B. Waldram, eds., *Anthropology, Public Policy and Native Peoples in
Canada* (Montreal and Kingston: McGill-Queen's University Press,
1993), chap. 13, 311–33; and Daniel Salee, "Identities in Conflict: The

Aboriginal Question and the Politics of Recognition in Quebec," *Ethnic and Racial Studies* 18(2) (April 1995): 277–314.

44 Brian E. Titley, *A Narrow Vision: Duncan Campbell Scott and the Administration of Indian Affairs in Canada* (Vancouver, BC: University of British Columbia Press, 1986).

45 Donald G. Lenihan, Gordon Robertson, and Roger Tass, *Reclaiming the Middle Ground* (Ottawa: The Institute for Research on Public Policy, 1994), chap. 7, "Liberalism and the Inherent Right to Self-Government"; and J. Anthony Long, "Traditional Political Values and Political Development: The Case of Native Indian Self-Government," paper presented at the annual meeting of the Canadian Political Science Association, June 1989.

46 RCAP, *Partners in Confederation*, 39: "individual members of Aboriginal groups enjoy the protection of Charter provisions in their relations with Aboriginal governments."

47 See Ontario, Royal Commission Inquiry into Civil Rights (the McRuer Commission), *Report* 2, vol. 4, "A Bill of Rights for Ontario," 1475–1607. This is an excellent discussion of the relationships between legislatures and courts in defining and affirming rights. Also, see Donald V. Smiley, "Courts, Legislatures, and the Protection of Human Rights," in M.L. Friedland, ed., *Courts and Trials* (Toronto: University of Toronto Press, 1975). More recent studies of the area include Michael Mandel, *The Charter of Rights and the Legalization of Politics in Canada* (Toronto: Wall and Thompson, 1989); Christopher P. Manfredi, *Judicial Power and the Charter: Canada and the Paradox of Liberal Constitutionalism* (Toronto: McClelland and Stewart, 1993); and C.E.S. Franks, "Representation and Policy-Making, 68–86.

48 McRuer Commission Report. See also my "Representation and Policy-Making."

49 I am grateful to Michael Asch for emphasizing this point to me.

50 C.E.S. Franks, "Native Canadians: The Question of Their Participation in Northern Public Services," *Population Research and Policy Review*, 8 (1989): 79–95.

51 Useful studies of the economic conditions of Aboriginal peoples include Frank Cassidy and Shirley B. Seward, eds., *Alternatives to Social Assistance in Indian Communities* (Halifax: Institute for Research on Public Policy, 1991), especially Hugh Shewell's contribution, "The Use of Social Assistance for Employment Creation on Indian Reserves: An Appraisal"; Statistics Canada, 1993, *Schooling, Work and Related Activities, Income, Expenses and Mobility*; and Hagey et al., *Highlights of Aboriginal Conditions 1981–2001*.

52 See, for example, Boldt, *Surviving as Indians*, 209–16; Martin Dunn, *Access to Survival: A Perspective on Aboriginal Self-Government for the*

Constituency of the Native Council of Canada (Kingston, ON: Institute of Intergovernmental Relations, 1986); Lenihan et al., *Canada: Reclaiming the Middle Ground*, 5–24; Cassidy and Bish, *Indian Government*, 66–8.

53 See C.B. Macpherson, *The Life and Times of Liberal Democracy* (Oxford: Oxford University Press, 1977).

54 Peter Cheney, "The Money Pit: An Indian Band's Story," *Globe and Mail*, 24 October 1998, A1, 12–13; "How the Sawridge Millions Tore Apart a Native Community," *Globe and Mail*, 31 October 1998, A1, 6–7.

55 RCAP, *Report*, vol. 2, pt. 2, "Problems of Legitimacy," et seq., 842–3.

56 A third article in the same *Globe and Mail* series (n54, above) describes one Cree community in northern Quebec as a "model village." John Gray, "From a Scattered Community, a Model Village," *Globe and Mail*, 7 November 1998, A7.

57 This discussion is drawn from Alan Kary, "Ideology, Identity and the *Charter*: Being Native in the 90s," paper prepared for the New England Political Science Association Annual General Meeting, Portland, Maine, 5–6 May 1995. Also, see the discussion papers prepared by the Native Women's Association of Canada, "Native Women and Aboriginal Treaty Rights"; "Native Women and the Charter"; "Native Women and Self-Government"; and "Native Women and the Canada Package."

58 Quoted in Kary, "Ideology," 7.

59 A useful discussion of some of these issues in criminal justice can be found in P.A. Monture-Okanee and M.E. Turpel, "Aboriginal Peoples and Canadian Criminal Law: Rethinking Justice," *University of British Columbia Law Review*, (1992), special edition: 239–77. A general discussion of the problems cultural variety poses to the law can be found in Adda B. Bozeman, *The Future of Law in a Multicultural World* (Princeton, NJ: Princeton University Press, 1971).

60 J.A. Corry and J.E. Hodgetts, *Democratic Government and Politics*, 3d ed. (Toronto: University of Toronto Press, 1959), chap. 2, "Ideals of Government," especially 25–6.

CHAPTER FIVE

1 The two relevant sections I am referring to in the Constitution Act, *1982* are §15 and §35. Section 15(1) reads, "Every individual is equal before and under the law and has the right to the equal protection and equal benefit of the law without discrimination based on race, national or ethnic origin, colour, religion, sex, age or mental or physical disability." However, in §15(2) a provision is made for affirmative action programs that can, in a sense, trump the rights laid out in §15(1). Section 35 pertains specifically to Aboriginal peoples; §35(1) reads, "The existing aboriginal and treaty rights of the aboriginal

peoples of Canada are hereby recognized and affirmed." The exact meaning and content of Aboriginal rights that are "hereby recognized and affirmed" remains controversial, which has the consequence of confusing the relationship between the basic rights of equality spelled out in §15 and the Aboriginal rights protected by §35.

2 I am using the concept of Aboriginal sovereignty in this chapter to capture, albeit crudely, the special relationship that Aboriginal peoples have to their territories. While I would argue that this special relationship also means "ownership" in the Western legal tradition, here I simply want Aboriginal sovereignty to be understood as it is articulated in the languages and traditions of Aboriginal peoples themselves. For example, the Gitksan and Wet'suwet'en hereditary chiefs characterize their sovereignty by stating that "the ownership of territory is a marriage of the Chief and the land. Each Chief has an ancestor who encountered and acknowledged the life of the land. From such encounters come power. The land, the plants, the animals and the people all have spirit – they all must be shown respect. That is the basis of our law." Gisday Wa and Delgam Uukw, *The Spirit in the Land: Statements of the Gitksan and Wet'suwet'en Hereditary Chiefs in the Supreme Court of British Columbia 1987–1990* (Gabriola, BC: Reflections, 1992), 7.

3 For accounts of Aboriginal conceptions of sovereignty see Gerald Alfred, *Heeding the Voices of Our Ancestors: Kahnawake Mohawk Politics and the Rise of Native Nationalism in Canada* (Oxford: Oxford University Press, 1995); Russel Barsh and James Youngblood Henderson, *The Road: Indian Tribes and Political Liberty* (Berkeley, CA: University of California Press, 1980); Harold Cardinal, *The Unjust Society: The Tragedy of Canada's Indians* (Edmonton, AB: M.G. Hurtig, 1969); Mark Dockstator, "Towards an Understanding of Aboriginal Self-government: A Proposed Theoretical Model and Illustrative Factual Analysis," Faculty of Law, York University, 1993; Grand Council of the Crees of Quebec, *Sovereign Injustice: Forcible Inclusion of the James Bay Cree and Cree Territory into a Sovereign Quebec* (Nemaska, Eeyou Astchee: Grand Council of the Crees, 1995); Oren Lyons et al., eds., *Exiled in the Land of the Free: Democracy, Indian Nations, and the U.S. Constitution* (Santa Fe, NM: Clear Light Publishing, 1992); Antonia Mills, *Eagle Down Is Our Law: Witsuwit'en Law, Feasts, and Land Claims* (Vancouver, BC: University of British Columbia Press, 1994); Six Nations, *The Redman's Appeal for Justice: The Position of the Six Nations That They Constitute an Independent State* (Brantford, ON: Six Nations, 1924); James Tully, *Strange Multiplicity: Constitutionalism in an Age of Diversity* (Cambridge: Cambridge University Press, 1995); Mary Ellen Turpel, "Indigenous Peoples' Rights of Political Participation and Self-Determination: Recent International Legal Developments and the Continuing Struggle for Recognition," *Cornell*

International Law Journal 25(3) (1992):579–602; Mary Ellen Turpel and Ovide Mercredi, *In the Rapids: Navigating the Future of First Nations* (Toronto: Viking Press, 1993); Wa and Uukw, *The Spirit in the Land*; Robert Warrior, *Tribal Secrets: Recovering Indian Intellectual Traditions* (Minneapolis, MN: University of Minnesota Press, 1995); Wub-E-Ke-Niew, *We Have the Right to Exist* (New York: Black Thistle Press, 1995). For accounts of Aboriginal rights in the liberal tradition, see Will Kymlicka, *Liberalism, Community, and Culture* (Oxford: Oxford University Press, 1989); Will Kymlicka, *Multicultural Citizenship: A Liberal Theory of Minority Rights* (Oxford: Oxford University Press, 1995); Patrick Macklem, "Distributing Sovereignty: Indian Nations and the Equality of Peoples," *Stanford Law Review* 45(5) (1993):1312–67; Bradford Morse, ed., *Aboriginal Peoples and the Law: Indian, Métis and Inuit Rights in Canada* (Ottawa: Carleton University Press, 1991); Royal Commission on Aboriginal Peoples, *Partners in Confederation: Aboriginal Peoples, Self-government, and the Constitution* (Ottawa: Minister of Supply and Services, 1993); Brian Slattery, "The Land Rights of Indigenous Canadian Peoples," Department of Philosophy, University of Saskatchewan Native Law Centre, Saskatoon, 1979; John R. Wunder, *A History of American Indians and the Bill of Rights* (New York: Oxford University Press, 1994).

4 Kymlicka, *Liberalism, Community, and Culture*, 154.

5 I shall draw mainly from two sources: Kymlicka, *Liberalism, Community and Culture* and Kymlicka, *Multicultural Citizenship*. See also Kymlicka, "Liberal Individualism and Liberal Neutrality," *Ethics* 99(4) (1989):883–905; Kymlicka, *Contemporary Political Philosophy: An Introduction* (Oxford: Oxford University Press, 1990); Kymlicka, "Liberalism and the Politicization of Ethnicity," *Canadian Journal of Law and Jurisprudence* 4(2) (1991):239–56; Kymlicka, "The Rights of Minority Cultures: Reply to Kukathas," *Political Theory* 20(1) (1992): 140–6; Kymlicka, "Two Models of Pluralism and Tolerance," *Analyse und Kritik* 14(1) (1992):33–56; Kymlicka, "Group Representation in Canadian Politics," in L. Seidle, ed., *Equity and Community: The Charter, Interest Advocacy, and Representation* (Montreal: Institute for Research on Public Policy, 1993); Kymlicka, "Reply to Modood," *Analyse und Kritik* 15(1) (1993):92–6; Kymlicka, "Concepts of Community and Social Justice," in F. Hampson and J. Reppy, eds., *Global Environmental Change and Social Justice*, forthcoming; Kymlicka, "Dworkin on Freedom and Culture," in J. Burley, ed., *Reading Dworkin* (Oxford: Oxford University Press, 1995); Kymlicka, "Misunderstanding Nationalism," *Dissent* 42 (winter 1995): 130–7; Kymlicka and W.J. Norman, "Return of the Citizen," *Ethics* 104(2) (1994):352–81.

6 Kymlicka mainly draws from the following texts: Ronald Dworkin, *Taking Rights Seriously* (London: Duckworth, 1977); Dworkin, *A Matter of*

Principle (London: Harvard University Press, 1985); John Rawls, *A Theory of Justice* (Cambridge, MA: Harvard University Press, 1971); Rawls, *Political Liberalism* (New York: Columbia University Press, 1993).

7 For a few of the "standard" communitarian critiques of liberalism see Alisdair MacIntyre, *After Virtue* (London: Duckworth, 1981); Joseph Raz, *The Morality of Freedom* (Oxford: Oxford University Press, 1981); Michael Sandel, *Liberalism and the Limits of Justice* (Cambridge: Cambridge University Press, 1982); Charles Taylor, *Sources of the Self* (Cambridge: Cambridge University Press, 1990); Michael Walzer, *Spheres of Justice* (New York: Basic Books, 1983). For a good summary of the liberal-communitarian debate see Stephen Mulhall and Adam Swift, *Liberals and Communitarians* (Oxford: Blackwell, 1992); also Catharine Mackinnon, *Toward a Feminist Theory of the State* (Cambridge: Harvard University Press, 1991); Iris Marion Young, *Justice and the Politics of Difference* (Princeton, NJ: Princeton University Press, 1990). For a discussion about "thick" and "thin" conceptions of culture see Michael Carrithers, *Why Humans Have Cultures* (Oxford: Oxford University Press, 1992); Clifford Geertz, *The Interpretation of Cultures* (New York: Basic Books, 1973), especially chap. 1, "Thick Description: Toward an Interpretive Theory of Culture"; James Clifford, *The Predicament of Culture: Twentieth-Century Ethnography, Literature, and Art* (Cambridge, MA: Harvard University Press, 1988), especially chap. 12, "Identity in Mashpee."

8 Kymlicka, *Liberalism, Community and Culture*, 12; also his *Multicultural Citizenship*, chap. 5.

9 Kymlicka, *Liberalism, Community and Culture*, 13, and *Multicultural Citizenship*, 81.

10 Kymlicka, *Liberalism, Community and Culture*, 13 (emphasis added).

11 Ibid., 13.

12 Kymlicka, *Multicultural Citizenship*, 76 (emphasis added).

13 Ibid., 76–7.

14 Ibid., 84.

15 Kymlicka, *Liberalism, Community and Culture*, chap. 8. On 166, Kymlicka quotes: "Rawls's own argument for the importance of liberty as a primary good is also an argument for the importance of cultural membership as a good."

16 Kymlicka, *Multicultural Citizenship*, 10 (emphasis added).

17 Ibid., 11.

18 Strictly speaking, at least in the Canadian legal and political context, Aboriginal peoples were never conquered. I take conquered to be the most destructive form of the "overrun" practice of colonization. For example, the Beothuk of Newfoundland can be said to have been conquered, but only to the extent that they no longer exist. From an

Aboriginal perspective, as long as an Aboriginal community is occupying a homeland, they remain unconquered.

19 Kymlicka, *Multicultural Citizenship*, 108.

20 His difference of philosophical opinion lies at the centre of contemporary debates in political liberalism. For views of the "benign neglect" approach, see Nathan Glazer, *Affirmative Discrimination: Ethnic Inequality and Public Policy* (New York: Basic Books, 1975); Glazer, *Ethnic Dilemmas: 1964–1982* (Cambridge: Harvard University Press, 1983). In the Aboriginal context see Melvin H. Smith, *Our Home or Native Land?: What Governments' Aboriginal Policy is Doing to Canada* (Victoria, BC: Crown Western Press, 1995). For example, at 264 Smith says, "a new native policy must be built on the twin principles of jurisdictional integration for natives within the mainstream of Canadian society, thus enhancing a sense of self reliance and personal achievement, and on the principle of equality under the law consistent with the rule of law and the Constitution. Moreover, such a policy must be formulated and implemented absent any sense of collective guilt over what may have happened in times past. Until now, this sense of guilt has been allowed to hang like a pall over all efforts at native policy reform."

21 Kymlicka includes the English and the French as holding prior occupancy because they were self-governing entities at the time of the formation of the Canadian state; however, Aboriginal peoples think of prior occupancy in the context of the time before the arrival of the Europeans. The difference between the two interpretations is that in Kymlicka's view we don't question the legitimacy of French and English sovereignty at the time of Confederation.

22 The distinction between Aboriginal peoples and immigrants is important for Kymlicka, as it lays out the differences of political powers each holds within the Canadian state; in Kymlicka's theory, immigrant groups are not entitled to rights of self-governance.

23 Smith, *Our Home Or Native Land*; Jeremy Waldron, "Superseding Historic Injustice," *Ethics* 103 (1992):4–28.

24 Kymlicka, *Multicultural Citizenship*, 110.

25 See Olive Patricia Dickason, *The Native Imprint: The Contribution of First Peoples to Canada's Character.* vol. 1, *To 1815.* (Athabasca, AB: Athabasca University Educational Enterprises, 1995); Royal Commission on Aboriginal Peoples (RCAP), *Partners in Confederation: Aboriginal Peoples, Self-Government and the Constitution* (Ottawa: Minister of Supply and Services, 1993); Royal Commission on Aboriginal Peoples, *Treaty Making in the Spirit of Co-Existence: An Alternative to Extinguishment* (Ottawa: Canada Communication Group, 1995); Royal Commission on Aboriginal Peoples, *Report*, vol. 1, *Looking Forward, Looking Back* (Ottawa: Minister of Supply and Services, 1996); James Tully, *Strange Multiplicity:*

Constitutionalism in an Age of Diversity (Cambridge: Cambridge University Press, 1995).

26 For example, see Gerald Alfred, *Heeding the Voices of Our Ancestors*; Treaty 7 Elders and Tribal Council, Walter Hidebrandt, Dorothy First Rider, and Sarah Carter, *The True Spirit and Original Intent of Treaty 7* (Montreal: McGill-Queen's University Press, 1996); Don Monet and Skanu'u (Ardythe Wilson), *Colonialism on Trial: Indigenous Land Rights and the Gitksan and Wet'suwet'en Sovereignty Case* (Gabriola Island, BC: New Society Publishers, 1992); Grand Council of the Crees of Quebec, *Sovereign Injustice*; Daniel Raunet, *Without Surrender, without Consent: A History of the Nisga'a Land Claims* (Vancouver, BC: Douglas and McIntyre, 1996); Boyce Richardson, ed., *Drum Beat. Anger and Renewal in Indian Country* (Ottawa: Assembly of First Nations, 1989); Wa and Uukw, *The Spirit in the Land.*

27 For the purposes of my argument, I assume that a legitimate entity can represent the citizenship of a First Nation in negotiations with the provincial and federal governments. I am aware that I have simplified the process in which a "legitimate" voice arises from within a First Nation; however, for the most part, First Nations peoples can and do have legitimate forms of political representation.

28 For example, Aboriginal leaders are used as "consultants" in first ministers conferences; that is, they do not speak for themselves about the content of their "special" rights, just as they are excluded from the discussions concerning Aboriginal policy and legislative processes.

29 RCAP, *Partners in Confederation*; RCAP, *Treaty Making in the Spirit of Co-Existence*; James Tully, "Aboriginal Property and Western Theory: Recovering a Middle Ground," in E.F. Paul, F.D. Miller, and J. Paul, eds., *Property Rights* (Cambridge: Cambridge University Press, 1994); Tully, *Strange Multiplicity.*

30 Tully, *Multicultural Citizenship*, 116.

31 I mean this in the way Western political theorists construe the meaning of "citizen." For example, *Black's Law Dictionary* defines citizens as "members of community inspired to common goal, who, in associated relations, submit themselves to rules of conduct for the promotion of general welfare and conservation of individual as well as collective rights." Henry John Campbell. (St Paul, MN: West Publishing Company, 1968).

32 I say that Aboriginal peoples *may* have relinquished their sovereignty, because Kymlicka leaves as an open issue whether the possibility exists for some communities to remain sovereign, for example the Gitksan Wet'suwet'en of British Columbia.

33 Waldron's argument basically states that although the taking of lands from Aboriginal peoples may have been unjust at some time in the

distant past, it does not follow that Aboriginal peoples have just claims to these lands at the present time. He argues that the rights of Aboriginal peoples and their moral claims of ownership to their lands have somehow been superseded by time itself. Now that many generations of European settlers have settled on Aboriginal lands, it is the Europeans who have legitimate moral claims of ownership and, in a sense, are the innocent victims in the recent surge of Aboriginal land claims. Waldron's view ignores the significance of the political relationship between Aboriginal peoples and the European newcomers: his argument amounts to a philosophical sleight of hand designed, not just to condone the stealing of Aboriginal lands but to absolve contemporary colonial governments of responsibility for acting to resolve outstanding Aboriginal lands claims. Waldron, "Superseding Historic Injustice."

34 Of course, this is not to say that compensation ought not play a role in renewing the relationship.

CHAPTER SIX

1 Frelinghuysen was speaking in the American Senate debate on the removal of the Cherokee Indians from North Carolina. Thomas Frelinghuysen, "Speech Delivered in the Senate of the United States, April 7, 1830," in Anon., *Speeches on the Passage of the Bill for the Removal of the Indians* (Millwood, NY: Kraus Reprint Co., 1977), 6.

2 *Webster's Third New International Dictionary*, s.v. "colony."

3 As can be seen above, "sovereignty" and "underlying title" are key terms. These terms are highly contested, and it is not my intent to attempt to clarify their meaning through extensive discussion. What I mean by the term "sovereignty" is that a recognized nation-state possesses something we call "sovereignty" that, at minimum, includes "supreme power especially over a body politic" and "freedom from external control" (*Webster's* s.v. "sovereignty"). I use the term "underlying title" to refer to the aspect of sovereignty that is expressed in relation to the territorial base of a recognized nation-state. As can be seen by the reference to Webster's dictionary, I am using what I understand to be "common" usage definitions, and hence, I hope, when taken at this level, my usage of the terms is clear enough to the reader so as not to require further exposition.

4 Brian Slattery, "The Land Rights of Indigenous Canadian Peoples, as Affected by the Crown's Acquisition of the Territory" (PHD diss., University of Oxford, 1979).

5 Michael Asch and Patrick Macklem, "Aboriginal Rights and Canadian Sovereignty: An Essay on *R. v. Sparrow*," *Alberta Law Review* 29(2): 498–517; Asch, "Aboriginal Self-Government and the Construction of

Canadian Constitutional Identity," *Alberta Law Review* (Constitution Series) 30(2): 465–91; Asch, "Errors in the *Delgamuukw* Decision: An Anthropological Perspective," in Frank Cassidy, ed., *Aboriginal Title in British Columbia: Delgamuukw v. The Queen* (Vancouver and Montreal: Oolichan Books and the Institute for Research on Public Policy, 1992); Asch and Catherine Bell, "Definition and Interpretation of Fact in Canadian Aboriginal Title Litigation: An Analysis of *Delgamuukw*," *Queen's Law Journal* 19 (2): 503–50.

6 *Calvin's Case* (1608), 7 Co Rep 1a, 2 State Tr 559.

7 To indicate this point, here is the full quote from the senator, a portion of which was cited at the beginning of the chapter (above, n1): "Mr President: In light of natural law, can a reason for a distinction exist from the mode of enjoying that which is my own? If I use land for hunting, may another take it because he needs it for agriculture? I am aware that some writers have, by a system of artificial reasoning, endeavoured to justify, or rather excuse, the encroachments made upon Indian territory and to denominate these abstractions the law of nations, and, in this ready way, the question is dispatched. Sir, as we read the sources of this law, we find its authority to depend upon either the conventions or common consent of nations. And when, permit me to inquire, were the Indian tribes ever consulted on the establishment of such a law? Whoever represented them or their interests in any congress of nations, to confer upon the public rules of intercourse and the proper foundation of dominion and property? The plain matter of fact is, that all these partial doctrines have resulted from the selfish plans and pursuits of more enlightened nations; and it is not matter for any great wonder, that they should so largely partake of a mercenary and encroaching spirit in regard to the claims of the Indians."

8 In *Re: Southern Rhodesia* (1919) AC 210 (PC), p. 233.

9 Asch, "Errors in the *Delgamuukw* Decision."

10 See, in particular, J. Edward Chamberlin, "Culture and Anarchy in the Canadian Northwest," and Sharon Venne, "Understanding Treaty 6: Indigenous Perspective," in Michael Asch, ed., *Law, Equality and Respect for Difference: Essays on Aboriginal and Treaty Rights in Canada* (Vancouver, BC: University of British Columbia Press, 1997).

11 Department of Indian Affairs and Northern Development, *Statement of the Government of Canada on Indian Policy 1969* (Ottawa: The Queen's Printer, 1969).

12 *Calder et al. v. Attorney General of British Columbia* (1970), 74 WWR 481 (B.C.C.A.).

13 I realize that, technically, in law these are two questions: What were the rights prior to colonization? and What rights survived colonization?

Nonetheless, for clarity in this summary I will define them as two aspects of the same question.

14 *Hamlet of Baker Lake v. Minister of Indian Affairs* (1979), 107 D.L.R. (3d) 513 (F.C.A.). This decision was at the trial division of the Federal Court. It has never been appealed.

15 Ibid., 557.

16 Ibid., 43.

17 *Apsassin et al. v. Canada* (1988), 1 C.N.L.R. 73, 89.

18 *Delgamuukw v. British Columbia* (1991), 79 D.L.R. (4th) (B.C.S.C.) 185, 441; affirmed (1993) 104 D.L.R. 470 (B.C.C.A.).

19 *R. v. Sioui* (1990) S.C.R. 1025.

20 *Jones v. Meehan* (1899), 175 U.S. 1, cited in *Sioui*, 10–11.

21 *R. v. Sioui.*

22 *R. v. Sparrow* (1990), 1 S.C.R. 1075, 12–13.

23 Asch and Macklem, "Aboriginal Rights and Canadian Sovereignty."

24 *Milirrpum et al. v. Nabalco Pty. Ltd. and the Commonwealth of Australia* (1971), FLR 141 (SCNT).

25 *Mabo v. Queensland* (1992), 107 A.L.R. 1 (Aust. H.C.), 27, cited in Richard Spaulding, "Are Aboriginal Rights Discriminatory?" (Master of Laws thesis, Queen's University, Kingston, 1995), 16.

26 Ibid.

27 *Mabo*, 82, cited ibid., 221.

28 United Nations, General Assembly, *Declaration on the Granting of Independence to Colonial Countries and Peoples* (New York: United Nations, 1961), cited in Michael Asch, *Home and Native Land: Aboriginal Rights and the Canadian Constitution* (Toronto: Methuen Publishers, 1984), 130.

29 *Western Sahara (Request for Advisory Opinion)* (1975), International Court of Justice: 6, 14.

30 Ibid., 39.

31 Ibid., 31.

32 Asch, *Home and Native Land.*

33 Venne, "Understanding Treaty 6"; Wendy Aasen, "Report on Treaty 8 in British Columbia," prepared for the Royal Commission on Aboriginal Peoples by the BC Treaty 8 Tribal Council (unpublished, 1993); Rene Lamothe, "'It Was Only a Treaty': Treaty 11 according to the Dene of the Mackenzie Valley," prepared for the Deh Cho Tribal Council, the Dene Nation and the Royal Commission on Aboriginal Peoples (unpublished, 1993); Shirleen Smith, "The Treaty Relationship: Dene and Treaty 11," prepared for the Royal Commission on Aboriginal Peoples by the Deh Cho Tribal Council (unpublished, 1993); Paul Williams, "Kayanerenh Teskenonhweronne: Relations between the Haudenosaunee and the Crown, 1664–1993," prepared for the Royal Commission on Aboriginal Peoples (unpublished, 1993); and Bill

Wicken, "An Overview of the 18th Century Treaties Signed between the Mi'kmaq and Wuastuwiuk Peoples and the English Crown, 1725–1928," report submitted to the Royal Commission on Aboriginal Peoples (unpublished, 1993). Also, see Asch's fieldnotes (n49, below) of an interview on Treaty 11.

34 At this point, the provinces of British Columbia and Newfoundland represent the major areas where there are still not treaties. In recent years there has been the development of a process to negotiate such treaties in British Columbia. However, Newfoundland insists that the true indigenous people of that place were exterminated and therefore that the land can be considered a de facto *terra nullius* with respect to sovereignty and underlying title of contemporary Indigenous peoples.

35 Catherine Bell and Michael Asch, "Challenging Assumptions: The Impact of Precedent on Aboriginal Rights Litigation," in Asch, ed., *Law, Equality and Respect.*

36 *Re: Southern Rhodesia.*

37 *Calder,* 169–70, cited in Asch, *Home and Native Land,* 50.

38 Brian Slattery, "Aboriginal Sovereignty and Imperial Claims," *Osgoode Hall Law Journal* 29(4), 697. Slattery develops an argument analogous to the culture argument that he bases on the presumption of a "principle of territoriality," which suggests that "every human society whose members draw the essentials of life from territories in their possession ... has a right to these territories as against other societies and individuals." He later (ibid., 701) uses this principle to assert that the lands in Canada and the United States could not have been "legally vacant territories" prior to colonization and hence that a *terra nullius* thesis is inapplicable. While I accept that the principle of territoriality may be useful in certain circumstances, I believe that the principle that human culture itself always contains institutions and values reconcilable to the concepts of sovereignty and underlying title, as constituent elements of its nature, provides a firmer basis upon which to rest the rights discussed here.

39 Another approach is to assert that the issue of sovereignty and underlying title rests solely on their recognition by other recognized states.

40 Michael Asch and Sally Merry, untitled manuscript prepared for the Law Program of the Canadian Institute for Advanced Research (unpublished, 1995).

41 Asch, *Home and Native Land.*

42 Asch, "Aboriginal Self-Government."

43 Slattery, "Aboriginal Sovereignty."

44 Ibid., 699n18.

45 Royal Commission on Aboriginal Peoples, *Partners in Confederation* (Ottawa: Minister of Supply and Services, 1993).

46 There is a question as to the strength of the powers of the Aboriginal vis-à-vis those of the provincial and federal levels that are explicitly recognized in the Constitution. While the specifics have, of course, yet to be resolved, the approach taken does seem to point to an American-style resolution to the issue whereby the Aboriginal sovereign exists but is, in an ultimate sense, subordinate to the Congress – or in the Canadian case the Parliament and, perhaps, the legislatures. The difference would be that, because Aboriginal rights are constitutionalized in Canada, passage of laws that interfered with them would undergo a specific process not required by normal legislation.

47 Leroy Little Bear, "Aboriginal Rights and the Canadian 'Grundnorm,'" in J.R. Ponting, ed., *Arduous Journey: Canadian Indians and Decolonization* (Toronto: McClelland and Stewart, 1986), 246.

48 Cited in Asch, *Home and Native Land,* 116.

49 In a 1970 interview with an individual present at the treaty negotiations between the Crown and the Dene at Wrigley in the summer of 1921, I had occasion to ask about terms relating to land cession. What follows is an excerpt from the transcript of that tape. In it, "the old man" is the elder upon whom the Dene at Wrigley were relying for advice on negotiations, and "Julian" is the Chief who is reported to have signed the agreement. The numbers refer to the position on the tape recorder where the information may be found. I begin the tape by asking "Ed," the translator, to ask the individual being interviewed if he had ever heard of some of the places mentioned in the written treaty document as being "ceded" to the Crown through these negotiations.

326 This is a part of treaty where it says what Indians will give away. Ask him if he's ever heard any of this. Remember, Julian said there were names that no one knew. Were these the names? (Ed cannot read or understand the treaties in their original forms).

369 He was there from the start of the meeting and not a thing was mentioned about land. If there had been, the Indians wouldn't have signed it.

373 Now they make explicit it will be ceded. Did he hear that? Has he ever seen the Coppermine River (no); again each place he has never seen. (Long statement on land by me from treaty).

444 *Nothing about land was said at the treaty. That's what the old man was trying to make sure* (emphasis mine).

50 To make an "agreement" requires a "meeting of the minds" between the parties. It has been argued that such a meeting of the minds did not take place because cultural differences did not enable Aboriginal peoples to comprehend Western concepts such as cession. I believe

that this view does not reflect what I know of the evidence. As in the Dene case cited above and others such as those cited in n33 above, Indigenous peoples were able to understand the concept well enough. Therefore, the lack of agreement stems not from a lack of understanding of "cession" but rather from their *refusal* to agree to it as a term in the negotiations.

51 I am referring here, for example, to Canada's continued insistence on clauses related to "extinguishment" or "cession" found in modern "land claims" agreements.

52 It is possible that the development of "prescription" as an alternative to *terra nullius* may also be a considered a "temporary" solution.

53 Royal Commission on Aboriginal Peoples, Transcripts of the Public Meetings of the Royal Commission on Aboriginal Peoples, The Pas, Manitoba, 20 May 1992, 252.

54 Royal Commission on Aboriginal Peoples, Transcripts of the Public Meetings of the Royal Commission on Aboriginal Peoples, Eskasoni, Nova Scotia, 6 May 1992, 162.

55 Union of British Columbia Indian Chiefs, "Treaty-Making and Title: A Non-Extinguishment Alternative for Settling the Land Question in British Columbia, discussion paper no. 1" (1989), 23.

56 Michael Asch and Norman Zlotkin, "Affirming Aboriginal Title: A New Basis for Comprehensive Claims Negotiations," in Asch, ed., *Law, Equality and Respect.*

57 I.e., ordinary Canadians.

58 As stated above, the issue with "prescription" is that, while it is historically contextualized, this thesis provides no convincing argument to explain how Aboriginal peoples became incorporated into Canada without their consent, particularly given that many Aboriginal peoples in Canada overtly do not accept the proposition.

59 For example, United Nations' Resolution 1514 (XV) on colonial populations asserts that a colony exists in the prima facie sense only when it is determined that the people are ethnically and/or culturally distinct and geographically separated from the administering power (cited in Asch, *Home and Native Land*, 39). However, it never suggests that Indigenous peoples in places like Canada are different in the sense that, should the same principles apply, they have nonetheless already lost their right to self-determination vis-à-vis the Canadian state without their consent.

60 The conquest thesis is particularly suspect within contemporary values. As Bill Wilson of the Native Council of Canada stated (cited in Asch, *Home and Native Land*, 29), "When the German forces occupied France, did the French people believe they didn't own the country? I sincerely doubt that there was one French person in France during the war that

ever had the belief that France belonged to Germany, which is why, of course, they struggled with our assistance to liberate their country and once again take it back for themselves." Similarly, one would not seriously suggest that the former Soviet Union retained the right to govern Ukraine even after Ukraine voted for independence.

61 As this policy is now developing, Canada is attempting to negotiate agreements that include cession with those indigenous peoples, like the Inuit, who seem willing to do so. At the same time, they are isolating and strongly disadvantaging those indigenous peoples, like the Dene of Deh Cho and the Treaty 8 region as well as the Lubicon, who refuse to accede to it.

62 Should this thesis ultimately prove untenable in the short term, it seems clear that the courts would subsequently rely on the proposition that, as domestic courts, they are not competent to hear cases that challenge Canadian sovereignty. At the same time, it might be unlikely that an indigenous people would be in a position to challenge Canadian sovereignty in an international court.

63 Personal communication.

64 Indeed, they will likely be at least as difficult as those now being undertaken between Israel and the Palestinians. It is interesting to note that this is the only case where both sides believe that they hold the true underlying title and where negotiations are now based upon some at least tacit acceptance of the validity of each other's claim to it.

CHAPTER SEVEN

1 The political actors did not simply entrust judges with interpreting Aboriginal rights from the beginning. Only after several constitutional conferences failed to reach mutual agreement on the meaning of these rights was their definition entrusted to the judiciary.

2 This method is adapted by Régine Robin from the works of S. Z. Harris, more particularly, *Discourse Analysis Reprints* (Paris: Mouton, 1963). This is an adaptation of Harris's technique in a context where his syntactical postulates are not endorsed; the expressions under scrutiny are simply put, when necessary, in the position of the subject of the verb in order to make the predicates evident, so as to facilitate content analysis. See also A. Lajoie, M.-C. Boivin, and S. Perrault, "L'efficacité spécifique respective des méthodes juridiques et linguistiques pour l'interprétation des concepts flous en droit constitutionnel," in Danièle Bourcier, ed., *L'Écriture du droit* (Paris: Diderot, 1966), 597.

3 *Royal Proclamation 1763* (U.K.), R.S.C. 1985, Appendix II, no. 1; *St Catherine's Milling and Lumber Co. v. R.* (1888), 14 A.C. 46 (P.C.); *Calder v. British Columbia* (A.G.) (1973), S.C.R. 313; *Constitution Act, 1982,*

being Schedule B to the *Canada Act, 1982* (U.K.), 1982, C. 11; *R. v. Van der Peet* (1996), 2 S.C.R. 507; *R. v. NTC Smokehouse Ltd.* (1996), 2 S.C.R. 672; *R. v. Gladstone* (1996), 2 S.C.R. 723; *R. v. Pamajewon* (1996), 2 S.C.R. 82; *R. v. Adams* (1996), 3 S.C.R. 101; *R. v. Côté* (1996), 3 S.C.R. 139; *Delgamuukw v. British Columbia (A.G.)* (11 December 1997), 23 S.C.R. 799.

4 Andrée Lajoie, Jean-Maurice Brisson, Sylvio Normand, and Alain Bissonnette, *Le statut juridique des peuples autochtones au Québec et le pluralisme* (Cowansville, QC: Éditions Yvon Blais, 1996).

5 *Nianentsiasa v. Akwirente* (1859), 3 L.C.J. 316 (Q.B.). ˙

6 *Bastien v. Hoffman* (1867), 16 R.J.R.Q. 264 (Q.B.); *Consolidated Statutes of Lower Canada*, C. 14.

7 *Connolly v. Woolrich* (1867), 17 R.J.R.Q. 75 (Sup. Ct.); affirmed (*sub. nom. Johnstone v. Connolly* [1869], 17 R.J.R.Q. 266 [Q.B.]).

8 *Picard v. Groslouis* (1888), 7 Q.L.R. 131 (C.S.P.); *Commissaire aux terres indiennes v. Paiement dit St-Onge* (1856), 8 R.J.R.Q. 29 (Q.B.).

9 However, lately even common law judges have started to distinguish somewhat between land ownership and political jurisdiction, as reflected in *Van der Peet* and *Delgamuukw*.

10 *Connolly v. Woolrich*.

11 *Johnstone v. Connolly*. "Even recognizing the aboriginal custom of marriage as a foreign legal rule, a Christian Lower Canada court could not admit it, because it collides with the principles of our law and does not meet the essential characteristics of marriage in Canadian law" (translation ours).

12 *R. v. Groslouis* (1944), 81 C.C.C. 167 (C.S.P.).

13 *Corinthe v. The Ecclesiastics of the Seminary of St Sulpice* (1910), 38 C.S. 268; affirmed (*sub. nom.: Corinthe c. Séminaire de St-Sulpice* [1911], 21 Q.B. 316); affirmed ([1912] 5 D.L.R. 263 [P.C.]); *R. v. Bonhomme* (1917), 16 Ex. 437; affirmed ([1918] 56 S.C.R. 679); *Gouin & Star Chrome Mining v. Thompson & Doherty* (1917), 24 R.L. 271; reversed on other grounds (*sub. nom.: Quebec [A.G.] v. Canada [A.G.]* [1920], 56 D.L.R. 373 [P.C.]); *Lazare v. St Lawrence Seaway Authority* (1957), C.S. 5.

14 *Royal Proclamation*, 1763; *St Catherine's Milling and Lumber Co. v. R.*

15 Lajoie, et al., *Le statut juridique*.

16 *R. v. Bonhomme*; *Gouin & Star Chrome Mining v. Thompson & Doherty*; *Lazare v. St Lawrence Seaway Authority*; *Doherty v. Giroux* (1915), 24 Q.B. 433; affirmed (1916), 30 D.L.R. 123 (S.C.C.).

17 *Lazare v. St Lawrence Seaway Authority*.

18 Ibid.

19 *Corinthe v. The Ecclesiastics of the Seminary of St Sulpice*.

20 *Corinthe v. Séminaire de St-Sulpice*.

21 *Corinthe v. The Ecclesiastics of the Seminary of St Sulpice*.

22 Ibid.; *Corinthe v. Séminaire de St-Sulpice.*
23 *Jacobs v. United Power Co.* (1927), 65 C.S. 133.
24 *An Act Respecting Indians*, R.S.C. 1886, ch. 43, amended by 61 Vict.,
   ch. 34, as it read at the time of the cases. This act and its subsequent
   amendments are known today as the *Indian Act*, R.S.C. 1985, ch. 1-5.
25 *Boucher v. Montour* (1901), 20 C.S. 291.
26 *Brossard v. D'Aillebout* (1914), 15 R.P. 412 (Sup. Ct.).
27 *Calder v. British Columbia (A.G.).* Note that the only Quebec judge who
   took part in the decision was Pigeon J., who did not express an opinion on the subject of Aboriginal rights or title. His opinion however
   forms the *ratio decidendi* of the majority decision to dismiss the appel-
   lants' claim on a point of procedure.
28 *Max "One-Onti" Groslouis v. La Société de développement de la Baie James*
   (1974), R.P. 38 (Sup. Ct.); *An Act to Extend the Boundaries of the Province
   of Quebec*, 2 Geo. V 1912, ch. 45, S.2(C).
29 *Société de développement de la Baie James v. Kanatewat* (1975), C.A. 166.
30 *Québec (A.G.) v. Paul* (1977), C.S.P. 1054; *Québec (A.G.) v. Dumont* (11
   November 1977), C.S. Hauterive, no. 655-05-0003330-76 (Sup. Ct.).
31 *Naskapis de Schefferville v. Québec (A.G.)* (1982), 4 C.N.L.R. 82 (Sup. Ct.);
   Québec (A.G.) v. Duchesneau, J.E. 81-681 (C.S.P.); *Pinette v. Québec (A.G.)*
   (1980), C.P. 226.
32 *Deer v. Okpik*, J.E. 80-1004 (Sup. Ct.).
33 *Kanatewat*, 171.
34 *Re: Stacey and Montour and The Queen* (1981), 63 C.C.C. (2d) 61 (C.A.).
35 *Constitution Act, 1982*, §35(1): "The existing aboriginal and treaty rights of
   the aboriginal peoples of Canada are hereby recognized and affirmed."
36 *Constitution Act, 1982*, §25: "The guarantee in this Charter of certain
   rights and freedoms shall not be construed as to abrogate or derogate
   from any aboriginal, treaty or other rights or freedoms that pertain to
   the aboriginal peoples of Canada, including (a) any rights or freedoms
   that have been recognized by the Royal Proclamation of October 7,
   1763; and (b) any rights or freedoms that now exist by way of land
   claims agreements or may be so acquired."
37 *R. v. Sparrow* (1990), 1 S.C.R. 1075.
38 *Van der Peet; NTC Smokehouse; Gladstone; Pamajewon; Adams; Côté;
   Delgamuukw.*
39 *Québec (A.G.) v. Adams* (1985), C.S.P. 1001; affirmed (1985), 4 C.N.L.R.
   39 (Sup. Ct.); affirmed (1993), R.J.Q. 1011 (C.A.). *R. v. Coté* (1988),
   R.J.Q. 1969 (C.P.); affirmed (*sub. nom.: Decontie v. R.*[1989], R.J.Q.
   1893 [Sup. Ct.]; affirmed (*sub. nom.: Côté v. R.* [1993], R.J.Q. 1350
   [C.A.]). *R. v. Ross* (1989), 1 C.N.L.R. 140 (Sup. Ct.).
40 *Québec (A.G.) v. Adams* (1993), R.J.Q. 1011 (C.A.); *Côté v. R.* (1993),
   R.J.Q. 1350 (C.A.).

41 *R.* v. *Côté* (1996), 174 (Lamer CJ); *R.* v. *Adams* (1996), 3 S.C.R. 101, 120–2.

42 The Sparrow test has been revisited in two recent cases. In *Gladstone*, it was modified to take into account rights that were not intrinsically restricted (commercial fishing rights), while in *Delgamuukw*, it was specifically adapted to Aboriginal title.

43 *Delgamuukw*, 111.

44 *Sioui* v. *Québec (A.G.)*, J.E. 85–947 (Sup. Ct.); *R.* v. *Ross; Côté* v. *R.; Québec (A.G.)* v. *Adams* (Beauregard and Proulx JJ).

45 *Québec (A.G.)* v. *Adams* (Barrette J.C.S., and Rothman J.C.A.); *R.* v. *Adams* (1996), 116–19 (Lamer CJ); *R.* v. *Côté* (1996), 3 S.C.R. 139.

46 *R.* v. *Oakes* (1986), 1 S.C.R. 103. At issue was the presumption of innocence as it might be qualified under §1 of the Charter, which guarantees rights and freedoms "subject only to such reasonable limits ... as can be demonstrably justified in a free and democratic society." The Supreme Court ruled that §1 empowers legislatures to limit a Charter right if "(a) the legislature's objective is of sufficient importance and (b) the limitation is rationally connected to the objective, as little restrictive as possible of the right in achieving the objective, and the benefit resulting from the limitation is greater than the burden or cost of the limitation."

47 For a recent narrowing of the *Sparrow* test, see *Gladstone* at 762–80.

48 *R.* v. *Côté; R.* v. *Adams.*

49 *La bande d'Eastmain* v. *Gilpin (no.1)* (1987), R.J.Q. 1637 (C.P.). In that case a provincial court judge expressed the view that the regulatory powers conferred to a Cree Band Council by the James Bay Convention were a form of residuary Aboriginal sovereignty. *Québec (A.G.)* v. *Adams* (Rothman, J.C.A., dissenting).

50 *Pamajewon.*

51 *Protection de la jeunesse – 623*, J.E. 93–1018 (C.Q.).

52 *R.* v. *Kokkinerk*, J.E. 93–1379 (C.A.); *R.* v. *Neeposh*, J.E. 94–562 (C.Q.).

53 *R.* v. *Cross* (1992), R.J.Q. 1001 (Sup. Ct.) at 1008: "The accused here and their compatriots were no doubt motivated by a sincere and honest belief in the legitimacy of the natives' land claims and the frustration, bitterness and intense anger which are the legacy of centuries of neglect, unfairness, hostility, contempt, discrimination and racism. Some will say that there is no place for such comments in a sentence pronounced by a court. I do not agree with such views. The criminal acts committed during the Oka Crisis, try as one might, cannot be entirely dissociated from the historical and political origins and background of that crisis."

54 *R.* v. *Naapaluk* (1993), 25 C.R. (4th) 220; *R.* v. *Alaku* (1993), 112 D.L.R. (4th) 732.

55 On the reception of certain forms of community justice mechanisms and Aboriginal criminal customs in Canadian criminal law, see Hugues Melançon, *La reconnaissance des systèmes juridiques autochtones en droit criminel Canadien,* (LLM diss., Faculty of Law, University of Montreal, 1995, unpublished).

56 *Indian Act,* §88.

57 *An Act Respecting Health Services and Social Services,* S.Q. 1991, C. 42.

58 Groupe-Conseil sur la Politique Culturelle du Québec, *Une politique de la culture et des arts* (Roland Arpin, chairman), presented to Liza Frulla-Hébert, Minister of Culture, Quebec.

59 Above, n2.

60 Rémillard MNA, Quebec National Assembly, *Journal des débats,* 31 (21 June 1990): 3973–4 (pre-crisis).

61 Rémillard MNA (Minister for Justice), Quebec National Assembly, *Journal des débats* 31 (30 April 1991): 1444–8 (post-crisis).

62 Ryan MNA (Minister for Public Security), Quebec National Assembly, *Journal des débats* 31 (18 October 1990): 4513–64 (post-crisis).

63 Rémillard MNA, Quebec National Assembly, *Journal des débats* 31 (11 April 1991): 1277–81 (post-crisis).

64 Ibid.

65 Blackburn MNA (Minister for Recreation, Fish and Game), Quebec National Assembly, *Journal des débats* 31 (9 December 1991): 11331–2 (post-crisis).

66 Sirros MNA (Minister for Aboriginal Affairs), Quebec National Assembly, Commissions Parlementaires, Commission des Institutions, *Journal des débats* (12 June 1991), CI-9141–4 (post-crisis).

67 Perron MNA, Quebec National Assembly, *Journal des débats* 31 (21 June 1990): 3977–80 (pre-crisis); Lazure MNA, Quebec National Assembly, *Journal des débats* 31 (18 October 1990): 4513–64 (post-crisis). Motion of the Quebec Cabinet (9 February 1983). Premier René Lévesque: "Their belonging to Indian and Inuit nations, which were the first nations to inhabit this country and to develop it for the benefit of man, places before Quebec's society unquestionable demands, occasionally to recognition of particular rights, always to a strict right to benefit from the totality of the services offered to the general population" (our translation). Quebec National Assembly, *Journal des débats* 28 (19 March 1985): 2493.

68 Ciaccia MNA (Minister for Aboriginal Affairs), Quebec National Assembly, *Journal des débats* 31 (21 June 1990): 3977–80 (pre-crisis).

69 Our research shows that during the 1989–92 period, a total of 19 MNAs discussed Aboriginal rights (see table 7.1). Of those 19 members, 9 were from the PQ, 7 from the PLQ, and 3 from the PE. Even if the number of PQ MNAs who affirmed the existence of Aboriginal

rights was small in absolute terms (5), it was in fact larger than for PLQ and PE members. Thus, the number of PQ MNAs who actually spoke on the issue of Aboriginal rights is somewhat misleading, since the PQ had adopted a more comprehensive party position on Aboriginal rights in 1983 and 1985, while in power.

70 Claveau MNA, Quebec National Assembly, *Journal des débats*, 31 (6 November 1991): 10391–3 (post-crisis).

71 Harel MNA, Quebec National Assembly, Commissions parlementaires, Commission des institutions, *Journal des débats* 31 (28 May 1991): CI-1574 (post-crisis); Perron MNA, intervening in the debate about a National Day for Aboriginal Peoples, *Journal des débats* 31 (21 June 1990): 3973–4 (pre-crisis).

72 Perron MNA, *Journal des débats* 31: 3973–4; Lazure MNA, *Journal des débats* 31: 4538–40.

73 Ibid.

74 Harel MNA, *Journal des débats* 31 (21 January 1991): CI-877–87 (post-crisis).

75 Perron MNA, *Journal des débats* 31 (21 June 1990): 3973–4 (pre-crisis); Lazure MNA, *Journal des débats* 31 (18 October 1990): 4538–40 (post-crisis).

76 Ibid.

77 Ibid.

78 Perron MNA, *Journal des débats* 31 (21 June 1990): 3973–4 (pre-crisis).

79 Perron MNA, *Journal des débats* 31 (21 June 1990): 3973–4 (pre-crisis); Lazure MNA, *Journal des débats* 31 (18 October 1990), 4538–40 (post-crisis).

80 Ibid.

81 Ibid.

82 Perron MNA, *Journal des débats* 31 (21 June 1990): 3973–4 (pre-crisis).

83 Harel MNA, *Journal des débats* 31 (28 May 1991): CI-1574 (post-crisis); Perron MNA, *Journal des débats* 31 (21 June 1990): 3973–4 (pre-crisis).

84 Trudel MNA,Quebec National Assembly, *Journal des débats*, 31 (18 October 1990): 4538–40 (post-crisis).

85 Harel MNA, *Journal des débats* 31 (28 May 1991): CI-1574 (post-crisis).

86 Chevrette MNA, Quebec National Assembly, Commissions Parlementaires, Commission des Institutions, *Journal des débats* 31 (24 April 1991): CI-1361 (post-crisis).

87 Rémillard MNA, *Journal des débats* 31 (21 June 1990): 3973–4 (pre-crisis); Ciaccia MNA (Minister for Aboriginal Affairs), *Journal des débats* 31 (21 June 1990), 3977–80 (pre-crisis).

88 Sirros MNA (Minister for Aboriginal Affairs), Quebec National Assembly, Commissions Parlementaires, Commission des institutions, *Journal des débats* 31 (30 April 1991), CI-1444–8 (post-crisis).

89 Ibid.

90 Belisle MNA, Quebec National Assembly, *Journal des débats* 31 (31 October 1990): 4786–816 (post-crisis). The context of this affirmation should however be taken into account: it is used as an argument to exclude Aboriginal representation on the commission on the political and constitutional future of Quebec.

91 Savoie MNA (Minister for Revenue), Quebec National Assembly, *Journal des débats* 31 (12 November 1991): 10491–2 (post-crisis).

92 Ciaccia MNA (Minister for Aboriginal Affairs), *Journal des débats* (21 June 1990): 3977–80 (pre-crisis); Sirros MNA (Minister for Aboriginal Affairs), *Journal des débats* 31 (10 April 1991): CI-1234–5 (post-crisis).

93 Ryan MNA (Minister for Public Security), *Journal des débats* 31 (18 October 1990): 4513–64 (post-crisis).

94 Ibid.

95 Sirros MNA, (Minister for Aboriginal Affairs) *Journal des débats* 31 (10 April 1991): CI-1235, 1241, 1243 (post-crisis).

96 Rémillard MNA (Minister of Intergovernmental Affairs), *Journal des débats* 31 (30 April 1991): CI-1444–8 (post-crisis).

97 Ryan MNA, Quebec National Assembly, Commissions Parlementaires, Commission des Institutions, *Journal des débats* 31 (24 April 1991): CI-1361–64 (post-crisis).

98 It follows from the very nature of implicit discourse and the consequent requirements of the method used for its analysis (described above) that it is not possible to connect the content we have ascribed to it with specific excerpts of the reports of the debates; it is inferred from the whole subtext. Hence we will simply "narrate" the implicit conceptions as they emerge from our work, without notes.

99 *Monologism* is characterized by techniques of application and interpretation of the law according to the single set of majority values in a given society (or state, if it is also statocentric); its alternative, *dialogism*, allows a choice among several integrating principles for the application/interpretation of the law. See Gérard Timsit, "Sur l'engendrement du droit," (1988) R.D.P. 39–75, and *Les noms de la loi* (Paris: P.U.F., 1991).

100 It is entirely possible that Ryan would have shared their opinion, except that he was confined, more often than not, by his capacity as Minister of Public Security, to answering questions about police intervention; the pragmatic tone of his discourse made him an implicit member of this subgroup.

101 Ciaccia was federal deputy minister for Indian Affairs in the 1970s and then a key negotiator of the James Bay agreement.

102 Lajoie, et al., *Le statut juridique.*

103 As developed, among others, by Weber. See M. Reinstein, ed., *Max Weber on Law in Economy and Society* (Cambridge: Harvard University Press, 1955); J.-G. Belley, "l'État et la régulation juridique des sociétés globales:

pour une problématique du pluralisme juridique," *Sociologie et sociétés* 18, (1): 11–32; J. Griffiths, "What is Legal Pluralism?" *Journal of Legal Pluralism* 24 (1986): 1; J. Carbonnier, *Sociologie juridique* (Paris: P.U.F., 1978); A.-J. Arnaud, *Critique de la raison juridique* (Paris, L.G.D.J., 1981).

104 Preferring the dialogical approach, successive provincial governments have, since Oka, largely refrained from criminal law enforcement in Mohawk communities. In 1994 an agreement between the provincial government and the Band Council of Kahnawake provided for the official recognition of Mohawk peacekeepers as the local police force. In 1996, the same type of arrangement was arrived at for the community of Kanesatake (Oka).

CHAPTER EIGHT

1 *Ambitos de comunidad* and commons are not equivalents, but they correspond to analogous traditions. *Ambitos de comunidad* are the social and cultural spaces, linked in various ways to physical spaces, where the Indian peoples or a group of them express their way of being. For reasons of brevity, I am using "commons" here to allude to *ámbitos de comunidad*.

For many years, the word *ejido* alluded to the *ámbitos de comunidad* of the Indian peoples. *Ejido* comes from *exitus* (exit). It designated the land "at the exit" of the villages, used in common by the Spanish peasants in the sixteenth century. It had some resemblance to the Anglo-Saxon commons. When the Spaniards came to the American continent, they found a variety of social institutions and land tenure systems. They had no other word but *ejido* to refer to them, and they used it to designate them generically. The Indian peoples were forced to use that word to deal with the Spanish Crown in trying to reclaim their own physical and cultural spaces. In time they adopted the term with a variety of denotations and connotations. In this century, the slogan unifying the Indian and peasant struggle to start a revolution was *la reconstitución de los ejidos*, reclaiming the old Indian territories. After the Revolution, the word became associated with the new land tenure system. The original *ejidos* became "Indian communities," and *ejido* began to designate a new form of land tenure, which now is the denotation of the word, although it also keeps some of its old connotations.

2 Paper presented by the Consejo Ejecutivo of the Consejo General de las Regiones Autónomas Pluriétnicas de Chiapas, in the Asamblea Nacional Indígena Plural por la Autonomía, held in the federal Congress, 9–11 April 1995 (quoted in *Proceso*, 17 April 1995, 23). The debate about political reform includes frequent references to the "re-foundation" of the republic.

3 Raimundo Panikkar, "The Myth of Pluralism: The Tower of Babel –
   A Meditation on Non-Violence," in *Cross-Currents* (New York) 29 (2)
   (1979): 197–230; Panikkar, "The Dialogical Dialogue," in F. Whal-
   ing, ed., *The World's Religious Traditions* (Edinburg: T.& T. Clark,
   1984).

4 *Comunalidad*, a neologism recently constructed by the Indian peoples,
   which they use to provoke in others a reflection about what they are,
   can be translated as "commonality," if we mix "commons" and "polity,"
   two words without equivalent in Spanish. *Comunalidad* alludes not only
   to the "communal condition," which is the precise meaning of the
   word, but to a contemporary and concrete expression of that mode of
   social existence. Jaime Martínez Luna, "¿Es la comunalidad nuestra
   identidad?," *Opciones* 1 (1992), and "Autonomía y autodeterminación
   de los pueblos indios," unpublished manuscript, 1994.

5 The municipality was a juridic-political transplant from Spain, that
   operated during the colonial period as a tool of domination. Independent Mexico inherited that structure. It took from the Cádiz Constitution the ideal of municipal freedom but did almost nothing to
   implement it. The revolutionaries in the second decade of this century
   also attempted to realize that ideal but were forced to a compromise in
   the Constitution: they created the "free municipality," but imposed
   many formal restraints on it. The municipality thus became another
   link in the vertical system of control of an openly centralized regime.
   See Gustavo Esteva, "Recuperar el piso," in Raúl Olmedo, ed., *El Municipio y la participación cuidadana* (Mexico: UNAM, 1996). See also
   Manuel Carrera Stampa, *Archivalia Mexicana* (Mexico: Instituto de Historia de la UNAM, 1952); J.E. Casariego, *El Municipio y las Cortes en el
   Imperio Español de Indias* (Madrid: Talleres Gráficos Marsiega, 1946);
   François Chevalier, "Les municipalités indiennes en Nouvelle Espagne,
   1520–1620," in *Anuario de Historia del Derecho Español*, 15 (Madrid,
   1944), 16–106; Luis Weckman, *La herencia medieval de México*, vol. 2
   (Mexico: El Colegio de México, 1984).

6 Among the Indian peoples, municipal *cargoes* are not jobs to which
   someone may aspire in search of political privilege or as part of a political career but responsibilities that are accepted and give prestige in
   exchange for service. The system is analogous to the original regime of
   the Roman *municipium*, in which the *municeps* is the citizen of the
   municipality who can have public duties, or *cargoes*, coming from *munus*
   (duty, cargo, task, which must be done for the community; also "gift,"
   from the Indo-European *moi-n*, or "exchange of services") and *-ceps* (he
   who can grip, take hold of, as in "capable," whose root is *capere*, to
   take). See Guido Gómez Silva, *Breve diccionario etimológico de la lengua
   española* (Mexico: FCE, 1993). In the Roman tradition, however, the

municipium is the city in which all citizens may enjoy the same privileges as the Roman citizens.

7 Gobierno de Oaxaca, *Nuevo Acuerdo con los Pueblos de Oaxaca* (Mexico: Gobierno de Oaxaca, 1994).

8 On the recent debate about human rights, see "La polémica de los derechos humanos," *Eslabones* 8 (1994): 1–176; Gustavo Esteva, "Derechos humanos como abuso de poder," *Kwira* 44 (1996): 24–36; Just World Trust, "Rethinking Human Rights," Proceedings of International Conference, Kuala Lumpur, Malaysia, 1994; C. Lafer, *La reconstrucción de los derechos humanos: Un diálogo con el pensamiento de Hannah Arendt* (Mexico: Fondo de Cultura Económica, 1994); Pat Lauderdale, "Indigenous North American Alternatives to Modern Law and Punishment: Lessons of Nature" (unpublished manuscript, University of Innsbruck, 1991); Raimundo Panikkar, "The Dialogical Dialogue," 202–21; Panikkar, "Is the Notion of Human Rights a Western Concept?" *Interculture* 82–3 (1984): 2–78; Panikkar, "The Religion of the Future," *Interculture* 23 (107, 108) (1990): 1–24, 25–78; Panikkar, "The Pluralism of Truth," *World Faiths Insight*, n.s. 26 (1990): 7–16; Panikkar, "La diversidad como presupuesto para la armonía entre los pueblos," *Wisay Marka* (Barcelona) 20 (1993): 15–20; Rodolfo Stavenhagen, *Derecho indígena y derechos humanos en América Latina* (Mexico: El Colegio de México-Instituto Interamericano de Derechos Humanos, 1988); Robert Vachon, "L'étude du pluralism juridique – une approche diatopique et dialogale," *Journal of Legal Pluralism and Unofficial Law* 29 (1990): 163–73; Vachon, *Human Rights and Dharma* (Montreal: Intercultural Institute of Montreal, 1991), 1–10.

9 Carlos Moreno, "Estructura agraria en Oaxaca: Notas para el diagnóstico de la marginalidad campesina," manuscript.

10 The municipality of San Pedro Molinos, in Oaxaca, has two communities: the "main town," San Pedro Molinos, and its subordinate town, Asunción Vistahermosa. The latter, at present, has a larger population than the main town, but has been denied real participation in the government of the municipality and appropriate access to its public funds. The two communities are in continual struggle for those funds, and on other matters. The case is typical in Oaxaca. To control an excessively independent municipality, the authorities have in many cases reduced it to the rank of a subordinate town.

11 Gustavo Esteva, "Recuperar el piso," in Raúl Olmedo, ed., *El municipio y la participación ciudadana* (Mexico: UNAM, 1996).

12 The conventional bibliography on "autonomy" and "autonomous regions" does not give an appropriate account of recent initiatives and struggles. See the proceedings of a series of workshops organized by El Colegio de México, beginning in October 1994, "Autonomy and self-

determination of the Indian Peoples." Unpublished manuscript. See also the proceedings of the Foro Nacional Indígena de San Cristóbal and the dialogues of San Andrés, published in *Ce Ácatl*, issues 73–80, and Gustavo Esteva, *Táctica, estrategia y sentido en la lucha por la autonomía de los pueblos indígenas* (Oaxaca: Cultura para el Tercer Milenio, 1996).

13 There is increasing debate on federalism in Mexico that opposes the current centralism. The dominant discussion is concentrated on the redistribution of powers and resources, in order to strengthen the municipalities and state governments. But there is also a vigorous view that can be located within the tradition of opposition to the nation-state as a political design. See Esteva, "Recuperar el piso"; Lucio Levi, "Federalismo," in Norberto Bobbio and Nicola Matteuci, eds., *Diccionario de Política A-J* (Mexico: Siglo XXI, 1982).

14 When President Truman coined the term "underdevelopment," he substantially transformed both the denotations and the connotations of the notion of "development" and trapped the world in the illusion of catching up to the American way of life. For a general critique of development, see W. Sachs, ed., *The Development Dictionary* (London: Zed Books, 1991).

15 Following instructions of President Luis Echeverría (1970–76), the Confederación Nacional Campesina – the official, corporative peasant organization – organized 58 regional congresses of Indian peoples from 7 March to 15 August 1975, which ended in the First National Congress of Indian Peoples in Pátzcuaro, Michoacán, on 7–10 October 1975. On 8 October, at this congress, the representatives of the *Consejos Supremos* (Supreme Councils) of all Indian peoples decided to create the National Council of Indian Peoples.

During the congress, some voices were heard denouncing the lack of legitimacy of many *Consejos Supremos*, which had been organized from the top down and with the intervention of local *caciques*. Their weaknesses were later in evidence when the National Council lost presidential support during the following administrations. However, in spite of the fact that the effort was implemented in the corporative context of a presidential instruction, the vitality and strength of Indian peoples was also in evidence in what constituted the first serious attempt to create a national organization of all Indian peoples of Mexico. For an insider account of the experience, see Vicente Paulino López Velasco, *Y surgió la unión ... Génesis y desarrollo del Consejo Nacional de Pueblos Indígenas* (Mexico: Centro de Estudios Históricos del Agrarismo en México, 1989).

16 Fausto Sandoval, "La casa que recoge nuestro camino," *Opciones*, 4 (1992): 8–10.

17 Marcos Sandoval, "Discurso pronunciado ante los reyes de España," *Medio milenio* 1 (1992): 8–9.

18 The people of San Andrés have many magnificent stories. They love to tell of the time when a terrible plague of enormous grasshoppers devastated whole areas of Oaxaca and came to San Andrés. When the plague came to San Andrés, the Triquis ate them all, and it ended there. They now have a prayer begging for the plague to come back. They eat grasshoppers in a thousand forms and are experts in capturing them. The children, particularly, know how to skillfully manipulate a hat in the grass to capture them. The grasshoppers are rich in protein and very tasty.

In mentioning the tasty grasshoppers of San Andrés, I am not trying to compare them with an American steak, reducing them, like an expert, to the amount of protein in them, nor am I suggesting trying them as an exotic delicacy. I remember how much we laughed when a man from the Sonora desert came to town, after a long walk, and was offered chicken soup with a sauce that we had rejected before because it was very thick. "Disgusting," he said; "too wet." His reaction belongs, in fact, to the same category of events that compel many Americans to go to McDonalds in Moscow, Beijing, or Mexico City: they are eating their food, what they know, what their palates recognize. They do the same, by the way, when eating "cultural" or "ethnic" food, Chinese food, Thai food, Mexican food, whatever food of the world ... in America. They usually reject that same food in the corresponding countries, for very legitimate reasons. But for Americans and other "industrial eaters," the abundance, richness, and diversity of ethnic and other foods hide the simple fact that they are eating only American food, the same standard food – frozen, industrialized, "chemicalized" food. In fact, they are "eating miles": the American table is, on average, two thousand miles from the place of production. A German researcher recently estimated that ten thousand miles of travel is involved in the production of a yoghurt container, after accounting for the distance travelled by all the ingredients and packaging. The name of the item on the menu or the restaurant or the cook's nationality do not change this fact.

The illusion of both abundance and diversity produced by the "food" designed by the experts and distributed by corporations prevents any possibility of perceiving or feeling the lack of *comida* (for this term, refer to the article by Esteva at the end of this note). How can one recover the very notion that *comida* cannot be displaced? How can we see that you cannot reproduce or imitate the fire of Doña Refugio? "Food" may travel two thousand or twenty thousand miles, but *comida* never moves out of the very place where it was born. The context giving meaning to *comida* cannot be defined by the "local colour" of the restaurant, the quality of the food itself, or the genius of the cook. The context is necessarily social, all the human world embedded in *comida*, its soul, its heart.

On the differences between food and *comida*, see Gustavo Esteva, "Re-embedding Food in Agriculture," *Culture and Agriculture* (Bulletin of the Culture and Agriculture Group) 48 (1994).

19 See Gustavo Esteva, *Crónica del fin de una era* (Mexico: Posada, 1994).

20 Iván Illich, *Tools for Conviviality* (Berkeley, CA: Heyday Books, 1973).

21 Michel Foucault, *Power/Knowledge* (New York: Pantheon Books, 1977).

22 Gianfranco Pasquino, "Revolución," in Norberto Bobbio and Nicola Matteucci, eds., *Diccionario de Política* (Mexico: Siglo XXI, 1981).

23 Among the traits of such coalitions are the following: they give expression to generalized motives of social discontent, articulating a radical critique of the regime causing the discontent; they are open and inclusive, allowing the participation of all ideologies and social classes; they have flexible organizational structures without centralized political direction that are used to coordinate actions rather than administer claims, but they can have an "activating nucleus," disciplined and coherent, with more rigid structures; they are self-limited in their transitory campaigns (to stop a dam, a road, a nuclear plant, specific human rights violations) or their campaigns concerning specific issues (against pollution, garbage, traffic, and so on, or for effective suffrage, respect for human rights, freedom of expression), explicitly delinking themselves from abstract and totalizing ideologies or an aspiration to power; they generally use democratic means and legal procedures, including civil resistance, as well as emblems articulating the collective action, but they can go beyond the framework of the law; and they actively resist the creation of personalized leadership and ideological or party affiliations. See Gustavo Esteva, *Crónica del fin de una era* (Mexico: Posada, 1994).

24 As Gunder Frank has shown, these movements are in fact very old, although they are adopting new forms. The "new" movements are those now considered "classic": workers movements, modern parties, and so on, which have, in fact, appeared only recently. See A.G. Frank and Marta Fuentes, *Nine Theses on Social Movements* (Amsterdam: ISMOG, 1987).

25 Gustavo Esteva, with Teodor Shanin, "Pensar todo de nuevo," "Inventar la alternativa," and "Las perspectivas alucinantes," *Opciones* 3–5 (1992): 2–4, 6–8, 11–12.

26 In Mexico the political debate seems concentrated on the improvement of formal democracy. There are, however, many voices revealing its limitations and deficiencies and exploring political alternatives. See Archipiélago, "La ilusión democrática," *Opciones* 31 (1993): 2–3; Jordan

Bishop, "El mito contemporáneo de la democracia," *Opciones* 35 (1993): 6–8; Esteva, with Shanin, "Pensar todo de nuevo," "Inventar la alternativa," and "Las perspectivas alucinantes"; Foucault, *Power/Knowledge*, Tomás Ibáñez, "La increíble levedad del ser democrático," *Opciones* 31 (1993): 3–5; Martín Miguel Rubio Esteban, "O partidos o democracia," *Opciones* 31 (1993): 5.

27 The term "majority," like Nixon's "silent majority," alludes *only* to numbers. By referring to social majorities in the plural, one accepts the diversity of groups representing an arithmetical majority.

28 The Ecologist, *Whose Common Future? Reclaiming the Commons* (London: Earthscan, 1993).

29 Guillermo Bonfil, *México profundo* (Mexico: SEP, 1990).

30 Gustavo Esteva and Madhu S. Prakash, *Grassroots Postmodernism: Remaking the Soil of Cultures* (London and New York: Zed Books, 1998).

CHAPTER NINE

1 Seymour Martin Lipset, *Continental Divide: The Values and Institutions of the United States and Canada* (New York: Routledge, 1990).

2 Statistics Canada, *Canada's Native People*, (Ottawa: Minister of Supply and Services, 1984).

3 Indian Affairs and Northern Development, *Indian Population Register by Sex and Residence, 1997* (Ottawa, 1998), xv.

4 Sar A. Levitan and Barbara Hetrick, *Big Brother's Indian Programs – With Reservations* (New York: McGraw-Hill, 1971), 7–10.

5 U.S. Bureau of Census, *1980 Census of Population* (Pittsburgh, PA: Superintendent of Documents, USGPO, n.d.), vol. 1, chap. C (PC80-1-C); vol. 2, chap. 1E (PC80-2-1E).

6 U.S. Senate, Select Committee on Indian Affairs, *Budget Views and Estimate for Fiscal Year 1991* (Washington, DC: Superintendent of Documents, USGPO, 1991), appendix 2: Congressional Research Service, *Trends in Indian-Related Federal Spending, Fiscal Years 1975–91*.

7 Indian Affairs and Northern Development, *Indian Population Register*, xviii.

8 Henry E. Fritz, *The Movement for Indian Assimilation, 1860–1890* (Philadelphia, PA: University of Pennsylvania Press, 1963).

9 Stephen Cornell, "The New Indian Politics," *The Wilson Quarterly* 10(1) (New Year's, 1986): 113–31; Vine Deloria Jr, *Custer Died for Your Sins: An Indian Manifesto* (Norman, OK: Oklahoma University Press, 1968), 46–53; Fritz, *Indian Assimilation*, 206–21.

10 Quoted in Francis Paul Prucha, *Indian Policy in the United States: An Historical Essay* (Lincoln, NE: University of Nebraska Press, 1981), 28.

11 Vine Deloria Jr, "The Indian Rights Association: An Appraisal," in Sandra L. Cadwallader and Vine Deloria Jr, eds., *The Aggressions of*

Civilization: Federal Indian Policy since the 1880s (Philadelphia, PA: Temple University Press, 1984), 3–18.

12 David M. Strausfield, "Reformers in Conflict: The Pueblo Dance Controversy," in Cadwallader and Deloria, eds., *The Aggressions of Civilization*, 24.

13 Kenneth R. Philip, *John Collier's Crusade for Indian Reform, 1920–1954* (Tucson, AZ: University of Arizona Press, 1977).

14 John Collier, *The Indians of the Americas* (New York: Norton, 1947), 28, 196.

15 Prucha, *Indian Policy in the United States*, 33–4.

16 Quoted ibid., 44.

17 Jay B. Nash, Oliver LaFarge, and W. Carson Ryan, *New Day for the Indians: A Survey of the Workings of the Indian Reorganization Act* (New York: Academy Press, 1938); Ward Churchill, "American Indian Self-Governance: Fact, Fantasy and Prospects for the Future," in Lyman H. Letgers and Fremont J. Lyden, eds., *American Indian Policy: Self-Governance and Economic Development* (Westport, CT: Greenwood Press, 1994), 37–53; Wilcomb E. Washburn, "A Fifty-Year Perspective on the Indian Reorganization Act," *American Anthropologist* 86(2) (June 1984): 279–89.

18 Lawrence M. Hauptman, "The Indian Reorganization Act," in Cadwallader and Deloria, eds., *The Aggressions of Civilization*, 132–3.

19 Cornell, "The New Indian Politics," 120.

20 Deloria Jr, *Custer Died for Your Sins*, chap. 3.

21 Ibid., 65–72.

22 James E. Officer, "The Indian Service and Its Evolution," in Cadwallader and Deloria, eds., *The Aggressions of Civilization*, 87–90.

23 J.E. Hodgetts, *Pioneer Public Service: An Administrative History of the United Canadas, 1841–67* (Toronto: University of Toronto Press, 1955).

24 Diamond Jenness, *Eskimo Administration*, vol. 5, *Analysis and Reflection* (Montreal: Arctic Institute of Canada, 1968 [Technical Paper no. 21]), 28.

25 Quoted in E. Brian Titley, *A Narrow Vision: Duncan Campbell Scott and the Administration of Indian Affairs in Canada* (Vancouver, BC: University of British Columbia Press, 1896), 34.

26 Quoted ibid., 50.

27 Jenness, *Eskimo Administration*, 40–58.

28 Melvin H. Dagg, "Scott and the Indians," in S.L. Dragland, ed., *Duncan Campbell Scott: A Book of Criticism* (Ottawa: The Tecumseh Press, 1974).

29 Quoted in Sandra Campbell, "A Fortunate Friendship: Duncan Campbell Scott and Edgar Pelham," in K.P. Stich, ed., *The Duncan Campbell Scott Symposium* (Ottawa: University of Ottawa, 1980), 119–20.

30 Dagg, "Scott and the Indians," 190.

31 Desmond Pacey, "The Poetry of Duncan Campbell Scott," in Dragland, ed., *Duncan Campbell Scott,* 102. (Originally published in *The Canadian Forum,* 28 [1948–49], 107–9.)

32 Northrup Frye, *The Bush Garden: Essays on the Canadian Imagination* (Toronto: Anansi, 1971); Northrup Frye, "National Consciousness in Canadian Culture," in James Polk, ed., *Northrup Frye, Divisions on a Ground: Essays in Canadian Culture* (Toronto: Anansi, 1982).

33 Margaret Atwood, *Survival: A Thematic Guide to Canadian Literature* (Toronto: Anansi, 1972).

34 Royal Commission on the Organization of Government, *Special Areas of Administration,* chap. 22 "Northern Affairs," 147–80. Report, vol. 5, 1963 (The Glassco Commission Report).

35 H.B. Hawthorn, ed., *A Survey of the Contemporary Indians of Canada: A Report on Economic, Political, and Educational Needs and Policies* (Ottawa: Queen's Printer, 1966).

36 J. Rick Ponting and Roger Gibbins, *Out of Irrelevance: A Socio-Political Introduction to Indian Affairs in Canada* (Toronto: Butterworth, 1980), chap. 5, "Peopling the Bureaucracy"; Howard Adams, *Prisons of Grass: Canada from the Native Point of View* (Toronto: General Publishing, 1975).

37 Department of Indian and Northern Affairs, *Statement of the Government of Canada on Indian Policy,* 1969 (the "White Paper").

38 Sally Weaver, "A New Paradigm in Canadian Indian Policy for the 1990s," *Canadian Ethnic Studies* 22(3) (1990): 8–18.

39 Sally Weaver, *Making Canadian Indian Policy: The Hidden Agenda, 1968–70* (Toronto: University of Toronto Press, 1981).

40 Gary C. Anders, "A Critical Analysis of the Alaska Native Land Claims and Native Corporate Development," *The Journal of Ethnic Studies* 13(1) (spring 1985): 1–12; J.S. Frideres, "Native Settlements and Native Rights: A Comparison of the Alaska Native Settlement, the James Bay Indian/Inuit Settlement, and the Western Canadian Inuit Settlement," *The Canadian Journal of Native Studies* 1(1) (1981): 59–88.

41 Thomas Berger, *Village Journey: The Report of the Alaska Native Review Commission* (New York: Hill and Wang, 1985), 15.

42 Ibid.; see also Anders, "A Critical Analysis"; Steven McNabb and Lynn A. Robbins, "Native Institutional Responses to the Alaska Claims Settlement Act: Room for Optimism," *Journal of Ethnic Studies* 13(1) (spring 1985): 13–28.

43 Mackenzie Valley Pipeline Inquiry, *Northern Frontier, Northern Homeland: The Report of the Mackenzie Valley Pipeline Inquiry* (Ottawa: 1977) (the "Berger Report").

44 Linda Kruger and Graciela Etchart, "Forest-Based Economic Development in Native American Lands: Two Case Studies," in Letgers and Lyden, eds., *American Indian Policy,* 210.

45 Quoted in Douglas Sanders, *Aboriginal Self-Government in the United States* (Kingston, ON: Queen's University Institute of Local Government, 1987), 42.

46 Robert L. Bee, *The Politics of American Indian Policy* (Cambridge, MA: Schenkman, 1982).

47 Russel Lawrence Barsh, "Indian Policy at the Beginning of the 1990s: The Trivialization of Struggle," in Letgers and Lyden, eds., *American Indian Policy*, 58–9.

48 Joanne Louise Carriere, "Representing the Native American: Culture, Jurisdiction and the Indian Child Welfare Act," *Iowa Law Review* 79 (March 1994): 585–652.

49 Quoted in Sanders, *Aboriginal Self-Government*, 48.

50 Vine Deloria Jr, and Clifford M. Lytle, *American Indians, American Justice* (Austin, TX: University of Texas Press, 1983).

51 U.S. House of Representatives, Subcommittee on Native American Affairs, Committee on National Resources, "Tribal Self-Governance Act of 1993: Hearing," 25 February 1994 (103d Congress, 2d Session, Serial 103–20).

52 Frideres, "Native Settlements and Native Rights."

53 Richard F. Salisbury *A Homeland for the Cree* (Montreal and Kingston: McGill-Queen's University Press, 1986).

54 Boyce Richardson, *Strangers Devour the Land* (New York: Knopf, 1975).

55 Gurston Dacks, *A Choice of Futures: Politics in Northern Canada* (Toronto: Methuen, 1981).

56 C.E.S. Franks, "The Public Service in the North," *Canadian Public Administration* 27(2) (summer 1984): 210–26.

57 Graham White and Kirk Cameron, *Northern Government in Transition: Political and Constitutional Development in the Yukon, Nunavut and the Western Northwest Territories* (Ottawa: Institute for Research in Public Policy, 1995).

58 Auditor General of Canada, "Indian and Northern Affairs Canada – Comprehensive Land Claims," in *Report to the House of Commons*, September 1998, chap. 14.

59 John H. Hylton, ed., *Aboriginal Self-Government in Canada: Current Trends and Issues* (Saskatoon, SK: Purich, 1994).

60 Ibid.

61 Roger Gibbins and J. Rick Ponting, "An Assessment of the Probable Impact of Aboriginal Self-Government in Canada," in Alan Cairns and Cynthia Williams, eds., *The Politics of Gender, Ethnicity and Language in Canada* (Toronto: University of Toronto Press, 1986), 171–245.

62 In the interests of simplicity I have not taken inflation or exchange rates into account. The differences between the two countries are so pronounced that including these variables makes no difference whatsoever to the conclusions.

63 See DIAND website, "Indians in Canada and the United States," http://www.inac.gc.ca

64 Raymond Breton, "Multiculturalism and Nation-Building," in Cairns and Williams, eds., *The Politics of Gender*; Will Kymlicka, *Multicultural Citizenship: A Liberal Theory of Minority Rights* (Toronto: Oxford University Press, 1995); Les Pal, *Interests of State: The Politics of Language, Multiculturalism and Feminism in Canada* (Montreal and Kingston: McGill-Queen's University Press, 1993); V. Seymour Wilson, "Canada's Evolving Multicultural Policy," in C.E.S. Franks, J.E. Hodgetts, O.P. Dwivedi, Doug Williams, and V. Seymour Wilson, eds., *Canada's Century: Governance in a Maturing Society. Essays In Honour Of John Meisel* (Montreal and Kingston: McGill-Queen's University Press, 1995).

Contributors

MICHAEL ASCH, who recently retired from his post as Professor of Anthropology at the University of Alberta, is author of the influential *Home and Native Land*, 1984. He writes on many issues of Aboriginal rights and practices and continues his long-standing work with the Dene of the Deh Cho region.

CURTIS COOK, Professor of Political Science at Colorado College, is editor of *Constitutional Predicament: Canada after the Referendum of 1992* (1994).

GUSTAVO ESTEVA, columnist for the newspaper *Reforma*, calls himself a "grassroots activist and deprofessionalized intellectual." His books include *The Struggle for Rural Mexico*, 1983; *Food Policy in Mexico: The Search for Self-Sufficiency* (ed., with James Austin), 1987; and *A New Source of Hope*, 1993.

C.E.S. (NED) FRANKS is Professor of Political Science at Queen's University and Fellow of the Royal Geographical Society of Canada. His interests include parliamentary government and public administration. His recent books are *Public Administration Questions Relating to Aboriginal Self-Government* (1987) and *The Myths and Symbols of the Confederation Debates* (1993).

RICHARD JANDA is Professor in the Faculty of Law at McGill University.

ANDRÉE LAJOIE is Professor of Law at the University of Montreal and Director of its Centre for Research in Public Law. She has given special attention to Quebec and its Aboriginal peoples.

JUAN LINDAU, Professor of Political Science at Colorado College, is author of *La elite gobernante mexicana* (1993) and several articles on Mexico and U.S.-Mexico relations.

HUGUES MELANÇON is a doctoral candidate in the Faculty of Law at the University of Montreal.

GUY ROCHER is a member of the Faculty of Law at the University of Montreal and of the Centre for Research in Public Law.

RODOLFO STAVENHAGEN is at the Center for Sociological Studies at Colegio de Mexico, having held faculty positions in the United States and Mexico and having written several books on Mexico and Latin America. He has also been Undersecretary of UNESCO and was founder of the Mexican Academy of Human Rights.

JAMES TULLY is Professor of Political Science at the University of Victoria and Fellow of Christ's College, University of Cambridge. His masterful effort to devise a political philosophy that can do justice to the variety of claims for political recognition in a multicultural society is *Strange Multiplicity: Constitutionalism in an Age of Diversity,* 1995.

DALE TURNER is on the faculty at Dartmouth College. He has also written for the Royal Commission on Aboriginal Peoples.

Index